The do-it-yourself approach to learning...

3ds max® 4

Workshop

201 West 103rd Street,
Indianapolis, Indiana 46290

Duane Loose

3ds max 4

3ds max® 4 Workshop

Copyright © 2001 by Que® Corporation

International Standard Book Number: 0-7897-2546-0

Library of Congress Catalog Card Number: 2001086862

Printed in the United States of America

First Printing: June 2001

04   03   02   01   4   3   2   1

Trademarks

Warning and Disclaimer

Publisher
Robb Linsky

Acquisitions Editor
Laura Norman

Development Editor
Laura Norman

Managing Editor
Thomas F. Hayes

Project Editor
Tonya Simpson

Copy Editor
Julie McNamee

Indexer
Cheryl Landes

Proofreader
Jeanne Clark

Technical Editor
David Campbell

Team Coordinator
Julie Otto

Interior Designers
Karen Ruggles
Michael Nolan

Interior Artwork
Duane Loose

Cover Designers
Karen Ruggles
Duane Loose

Page Layout
Lizbeth Patterson

Contents at a Glance

Table of Contents

xi

About the Author

Duane Loose is an industrial designer who spent his formative years up in the prairie regions of southern Alberta. At the age of six, he saw a burning satellite reenter the earth's atmosphere over Winston Bohne's frozen duck pond. That singular experience began a lifelong obsession with science fiction, which was tolerated by his dad, who worked in the real space-exploration efforts of the '60s and '70s at Vandenberg Air Force Base in California.

After he completed his college studies, Duane spent 16 years as an award-winning industrial designer and design consultant to several Fortune 100 companies. In his spare time, he drew spaceships and robots and taught undergraduate and graduate design courses at M.I.T., Rhode Island School of Design, and California State University at Long Beach. These days he keeps his hand in education as a member of the faculty advisory committee of the Industrial Design Department at Brigham Young University. They actually ask him to give his opinions about the future of computer animation and storytelling in Industrial Design.

In 1994, to everyone's surprise, Duane's lifelong devotion to outer space, UFOs, extraterrestrials, and conspiracy theories was vindicated when he was hired as the Supervising Art Director for CGI/Development at Creative Capers Entertainment, Inc., a computer animation and original content development studio in Glendale, California. Duane's duties there include digital content creation, art direction, concept development and visual design, story development, and treatments for Creative Capers feature film, TV, and video game projects. It's a tough job—someone has to do it.

In addition to several films currently in development, Capers's current projects in production include

- Michael Bedards's "Sitting Ducks"—An episodic computer-animated series coming to TV in Fall 2001.
- Intergalactic Bounty Hunter—A three-episode classic Sci-Fi action/adventure PC and console game for Infinite Loop, a division of Pan Interactive. First episode release is scheduled for Summer 2001.

Duane is the sufficiently sane father of 12 children and stepchildren and resides with his beautiful wife, Susanne, and their family in beautiful Lake Elsinore, California, which is not close enough to Area 51.

Dedication

This book is dedicated to the following people who deserve credit for how I've turned out.

My wife, Susanne, always gives her selfless support in everything I do. She is the greatest mom a kid could have and the best wife and partner I could ever imagine. I'm a lucky man.

My mom and dad, Gordon and Wilma, not only taught me how to work hard, but also gave me the courage and the discipline to find my talents and follow my heart. I was and still am a lucky boy.

My 12 children and stepchildren: McKenzie, Jessica, Dante, Tim, Aubrey, Casey, Joseph, Hyrum, Lorraine, Martin, Allegra, and Savanah. They have taught me how to be a father—a task that I have sometimes been too small to do well.

From my siblings I have learned perseverance and dedication to right, intense, and uncomfortable honesty; how to laugh at life and at myself; and how to do a decent clutch job! Thank you, Laura, Kile, Tim, and Patti.

The men of the ManKind Project—Los Angeles Center, especially my friends Larry Nissen, Les Sinclair, John Smith, John Bisnar, Joff Pollon, and Derek Sherman, who have taught me what it means to be a man of integrity, passion, and purpose. Thank you!

And finally to my teachers and friends Lou Periello, Sensei, 5th Dan Aikido; and Dr. Ron Winfield, Sempai, 3rd Dan Aikido.

Acknowledgments

I am very grateful to my acquisitions and development editor, Laura Norman, for her encouragement, ideas, unflinching and sometimes brutal honesty, and dedication to excellence! This book is as much a product of her creativity as it is mine. My thanks to Robb Linsky, Publisher of Que Publishing, for listening to our case for the kind of book we wanted to write.

I also want to thank all the other members of the production team at Que books: Tonya Simpson, Julie McNamee, Jeanne Clark, and Cheryl Landes, who have worked long and hard to edit, format, design, and produce the book you hold in your hands. How they do it is still a sophisticated mystery. May it always be so!

I am very lucky to have had Dave Campbell of Discreet, as my technical editor for this book. His intense and long-term dedication to max and max artists has helped to forge this workshop into a tool that empowers the reader to a higher level of proficiency. Thank you, Dave, for your enthusiasm and creativity!

Jason Priest, fellow max artist, has been an ever-present source of feedback for the content of this book. I am also grateful to Mat Kaustinen of Boomer Labs, boy genius and creator of Foley Studio Max, for his help and shameless boosterism of my *max Workshop* books. Joe Linzer is a devoted max user and has provided some great insights to this book. Thank you Joe, Jason, and Mat.

Finally, I want to thank Shawn Steiner, our discreet representative, for his friendship and his constant support of all the artists at Creative Capers Entertainment.

3ds max 4

Tell Us What You Think!

As the reader of this book, *you* are our most important critic and commentator. We value your opinion and want to know what we're doing right, what we could do better, what areas you'd like to see us publish in, and any other words of wisdom you're willing to pass our way.

As Publisher for Que, I welcome your comments. You can fax, email, or write me directly to let me know what you did or didn't like about this book—as well as what we can do to make our books stronger.

Please note that I cannot help you with technical problems related to the topic of this book, and that due to the high volume of mail I receive, I might not be able to reply to every message.

When you write, please be sure to include this book's title and author as well as your name and phone or fax number. I will carefully review your comments and share them with the author and editors who worked on the book.

Fax:	317-581-4666
Email:	feedback@quepublishing.com
Mail:	Robb Linsky
	Que
	201 West 103rd Street
	Indianapolis, IN 46290 USA

Introduction

"The power is in the basics" - Yoshimitsu Yamada Sensei, 8th Dan, Shihan, Aikido

3ds max 4 Workshop is the sequel to *3D Studio MAX 3.0 Workshop* published in May 2000 by Hayden Books (see Figure Intro.1).

Figure Intro.1 3ds max 4 Workshop is a new Workshop for new users of max 4 and builds on the previous Workshop: 3D Studio MAX 3.0 Workshop.

Both books have been written with the intention to empower you as a new or intermediate max artist in your quest to master the great tools found in the 3ds max 4 toolbox. The goal of this book is to introduce you to the basics of max 4 in the shortest time possible.

Even though this book builds on the work started in *3D Studio MAX 3.0 Workshop*, it is not simply an updated version of the previous book. *3ds max 4 Workshop* is a new book with new projects written specifically for new software. Like its prequel, this book is built on a foundation of the basic principles you will need to know to be a successful max artist.

To that end, the projects in *3ds max 4 Workshop* are complex, challenging, and fun! Think of this as a "Boot Camp" for max 4—basic training designed to stretch and strengthen your capabilities as a max artist.

I know what it's like to be frustrated with a new tool, not knowing how to start and finish the process needed to bring an idea to life. Beginning with that end in mind, I have attempted to create the books I wish I had when I started using max. The power to unlock the secrets of max is in the basics—and the basics are what this book is all about.

Who This Book Is For

If you are a *new* user of max looking for a complete and integrated tutorial in the use of max 4's many basic techniques and tools, this book is for you. At the completion of this book, you will have a full understanding of the basic principles and practices for the specific use of 3ds max 4 to create your digital content.

If you are an artist taking your first step into the world of digital content creation (DCC) and animation, and you have no other experience using tools of this kind, this book is definitely for you! All of what you already know about art, design, and animation will be used to full advantage in max 4. At all levels of artistic expertise, max makes it simple and easy to learn the tools and fundamental techniques found in this book.

If you are an experienced user of previous versions of MAX or other digital content creation (DCC) software, this book and the projects in it were developed to reinforce the lessons of *3D Studio MAX 3.0 Workshop* and give you a completely new project to extend your mastery of the power of the basic tools, techniques, and principles of the software.

If you want to learn an A-to-Z process of how to make a short movie titled *Area 51*—including pre-production design, animation basics, special effects, lighting, modeling techniques, material development and compositing, UFOs, and aliens—this book is for you.

3ds Max 4 Sets the Standard

Published by discreet, a division of Autodesk, Inc., and now in its fourth major revision, 3ds max 4 continues discreet's commitment to advanced animation and image-creation features and world-class rendering technology.

In the beginning, max was mainly known for its price/performance, giving users an image- and animation-creation tool comparable to software costing $30,000 or more for less than $3,000. As the user base for max has grown, it continues its reputation as the only viable PC-based professional animation system of its kind, giving artists a full suite of modeling, material, lighting, and character animation tools.

A major feature of max software is its open architecture, which enables artists with the technical knowledge to create plug-ins. Plug-ins are specialized software that help create unique geometry, materials, and effects within the max environment. This open-code aspect of max has been one of the most revolutionary features of the software, resulting in hundreds of free and commercial plug-ins for your use as a max artist.

Because of max's power, price, and plug-in development, it has become the software of choice of many major television, motion picture, and multimedia/game development studios. The list of entertainment productions using max for content creation reads like a list of Who's Who in entertainment: *South Park*; *City of Angels*; *Godzilla*; *Lost in Space*; *Anaconda*; *Contact*; *The Ghost and the Darkness*; *James and the Giant Peach*; *Deep Rising*; *The Craft*; *The Sweet Hereafter*; *King of the Hill*; *The Simpsons*; *Ally McBeal*; *Storm of the Century*; *Pandora's Clock*; *The Visitor*; *The Outer Limits*; *The Real Adventures of Johnny Quest*; Tomb Raider I, II, and III;

The New Superman Adventures; Madden NFL; Need for Speed; Jet Moto III; NCAA Final Four 99; Ray Man; and Metal Gear Solid.

This impressive list of credits continues to grow. With more than 132,000 users worldwide, the expanding max community continues to be the most open, cooperative, and innovative group of artists in the world of digital content creation.

3ds Max 4—New and Mega-Improved

Max 4 contains many incremental improvements and several sweeping changes. In some cases, entire sections of the tool set were thrown away and rewritten from scratch by the best programmers in development today. Don't be concerned that some of this might seem like a foreign language; you'll learn more in later chapters of this book.

Throughout the book, new features of max 4 are tagged with this icon: 👁. The same icon is used in max's User Reference to lead you easily to the new features in max 4. Here's a brief overview of some of the key new areas of max 4 you'll want to know about:

- **IK**—A new Inverse Kinematics (IK) architecture has been created for max 4.
- **Bones**—Bones in max 4 have been completely redesigned with much improved visual design and representation of bone attributes. They are editable like any mesh object, and any max object can be used as a bone for animation.
- **Manipulators**—A new class of helper object designed to control the movements and animation of any max object or feature.
- **Controllers**—Controllers have been split into two categories: Controllers and Constraints. Controllers maintain the same function as before, whereas Constraints restrict an object's movement based on other objects in the scene.
- **Skin**—Max's Skin modifier has improved features for envelope shapes, envelope and lattice controls, and a new gizmo rollout. Model mesh can be morphed based on key poses, creating more realistic muscle flex and skin stretch and movement.
- **User Interface**—Every aspect of the UI—including keyboard shortcuts, toolbars, icons, color schemes, and the new right-click Quad Menus—can be customized to fit your needs.
- **Viewports**—Viewports, the Command Panel, and virtually every other part of the max 4 interface can be resized and repositioned within the interface.
- **Transform Coordinate Display**—The existing XYZ status display now has three edit/spinners with which you can manually input transform values for position, rotation, and scale.
- **Web Content**—All Web-based text and imagery is now fully integrated into your workflow. You can have a Web browser open in one of the viewports and use Web images for viewport backgrounds or drag-and-drop textures.
- **Visible Materials**—Composite and multiple material maps with full alpha blend and opacity are now visible in the viewport.
- **Quad Menus**—A new system of fully customizable right-click menus called Quad Menus creates a powerful productivity tool.

3ds max 4

- **Modifier Stack**—This has been completely redesigned for more useful and productive access to the stack hierarchy.
- **Track Bar**—The Track Bar has been redesigned to allow viewing of four types of animation key frame information, including the sound track.
- **ActiveShade**—An amazing new interactive rendering mode that allows you to add and adjust lights and materials in real time.
- **Rendering**—Multi-layered single pass rendering is now possible.
- **Software Lock**—A new software lock replaces the infamous hardware lock (dongle). At last!
- **Modeling**—New objects include a Hose Primitive and an Editable Poly Object, a revamped surface subdivision modifier, Hierarchal Subdivision Surfaces (HSDS), and a new MeshSmooth.

How to Get the Most from This Book

Each chapter in *3ds max 4 Workshop* is divided into two parts: a discussion of creative principles and a Workshop/tutorial to put those principles into practice. The intent is to show you both the *why* and *how* of digital content creation.

3ds Max 4: The Art of Fishing

Learning a new tool such as max 4 can be related to an old saying about self-sufficiency and fishing. "Give a man a fish and you feed him for a day. Teach a man to fish and you feed him for a lifetime." The intent of this book is to teach you the how and the why of what you will be creating in the Workshop so you can be self-sufficient in your use of this great software.

Rather than lead you through several unrelated tutorials, each chapter builds on the foundation of the previous chapter. In fact, you will be creating all six scenes needed to produce your own version of a short movie titled Area51.avi. While you are building the movie step by step and layer by layer, you'll be learning the basics of pre-production design, shot structure, camera setup and animation, composition, modeling, animation, special effects, lighting, sound, and post-production compositing that max artists use in their daily work.

Throughout the book, you will find tips, warnings, and notes that contain important information to help you master the concepts in the Workshop and develop a productive creative process.

As you learn the max 4 toolset, you'll soon discover that your only limitation is your own imagination. As you follow the project instructions, experiment with the shot elements. Be creative, curious, and take some risks. The best asset you have for mastering max is your own amazing brain and insatiable curiosity.

Under the Hood—What's in 3ds max 4 Workshop

"It ain't the paintjob that counts, it's what you got under the hood!" - Hank Studman, greatest mechanic on Earth.

3ds max 4 Workshop explores the fundamentals of all major areas of DCC (digital content creation) production within the context of creating the elements needed to complete a short movie with titles and sound. The book is structured to show you the professional processes used to visualize, model, texture, light, and animate your scene, including its special effects and titles.

Chapter 1, "Navigating the Max 4 Interface," introduces you to the concepts of creating in the three-dimensional world, shows you how the new structure and features of max interface can be customized, describes how to navigate in the max workspace, and provides an overview of the project you'll be creating.

Chapter 2, "Virtual Viz: The Art of Pre-Production for Digital Content Creation," will introduce you to the basic principles, elements, and techniques of the pre-visualization, DCC production process, storyboards, and scene composition principles and design. This chapter will result in the creation of the animatic for Area51.avi.

In Chapter 3, "Giving Form to Feeling: The Art of Modeling," you'll be introduced to the design principles that will bring amazing reality to your models, and you'll learn the basic techniques you can use to create anything you can imagine. The work in this chapter will enable you to finish the set models for the first scene for Area51.avi: SC-01.

Chapter 4, "Visual Touch: The Art of Material and Texture Development," shows you how to develop and apply the most realistic and convincing textures possible.

In Chapter 5, "Photon Paint: The Art of Lighting," you learn the basic principles of lighting, how to organize and control the parameters of your scene lights, and the use of a special lighting effect: Projector Maps.

Chapter 6, "Machines in Motion: Modeling and Kinematics," introduces you to Forward Kinematics, dynamic systems, and how to use expressions to control animation. The Workshop in this chapter completes the second scene for Area51.avi: SC-02.

In Chapter 7, "Character Design and Animation Principles and Process Overview," you learn the basic principles and techniques of designing, creating, and animating characters in max.

Chapter 8, "Trompe L'oeil: The Art of Visual Effects," introduces you to the principles of special effects illusion and pyrotechnics.

Chapter 9, "The Creative Sword: The Art of Post-Production in 3ds Max 4," shows you how to use max's built-in compositing tool, Video Post, to put together all the scenes needed for the final movie—Area51.avi.

Appendix A, "3ds Max 4 Installation and Setup," covers how to install and set up max 4 and includes information regarding minimum and recommended system requirements.

Appendix B, "Dr. D's Essential Guide to Standard Material Component Maps," contains an in-depth look at the effect procedural and image maps can have when they're added to the components of the materials you'll create in max 4.

Appendix C, "What's on the CD-ROM," outlines how the contents on the CD are structured and how to use that content to help you complete this Workshop.

Appendix D, "How to Make the Cooling Tower Interior"; Appendix E, "How MeshSmooth Works"; Appendix F, "Animation Principles in Practice"; Appendix G, "Adding Rendering Effects to Your Max 4 Imagery"; Appendix H, "Completing Sc-02"; and Appendix I, "Animating the Fireflies," are additional help files that walk you through the creation of some of the components of this workshop from scratch or are just additional resource material for adding your own unique touch to the project.

Always One More Thing

Depending on the time and freedom you have to focus on the tutorials and the information in the chapters, it might take a few weeks to complete the book. However, whether you can spend an hour each day or 10 hours each day in learning the software is not the important thing. What is important is that you set aside the time, consistently every day, to practice, learn, and master this wonderful tool. Your investment will show in your work.

3DS MAX 4 INTERFACE

WORKSHOP OVERVIEW

0 - 7 8 5 7 - 2 5 4 6 - 0

Navigating the Max 4 Interface

"The loftier the building, the deeper must the foundation be laid."
- Thomas Kempis

The first stone in the foundation of using 3ds max 4 is to understand its user interface. If you are a new user of max, you should go through the entire chapter because the basic structure of the user interface will be explained. If you are more experienced with previous versions of max, there are some new features in the interface that you'll want to know about. Those features are tagged with an eyeball icon ●. You'll see this icon again in max's User Reference, where it is used to indicate the features and functions new to max 4.

Max 4 contains the deepest and most powerful toolset for digital content creation available, and its interface was designed with considerable input from experienced max users. The interface components can be easily arranged to accommodate your personal workflow and can be configured to emulate other 3D software such as MAYA, Lightwave, and even previous versions of 3D Studio MAX. This is especially useful if you are upgrading from one of these other programs to max 4.

The concepts and techniques needed to effectively use the 3ds max 4 interface are simple to learn and will take some practice to master. Learning the basic UI structure is the first step in that process.

3ds Max 4 Interface Overview

Start 3ds max 4 by clicking its shortcut icon 🔲 on your desktop. When it opens you'll see the user interface, as shown in Figure 1.1. On the tear card included with this book, there is a more comprehensive diagram of the UI, which outlines all the major parts of the max interface.

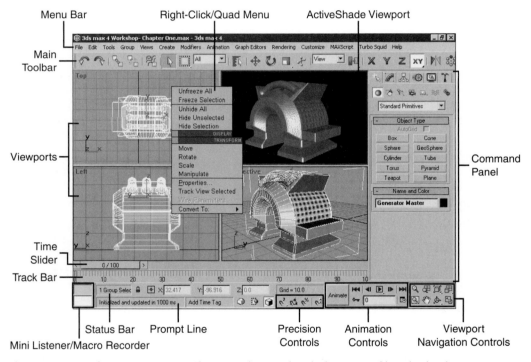

Figure 1.1   The max 4 user interface was designed with the input of hundreds of max users. It's an artist's tool designed to be easy to use and to give you fast access to frequently used tools.

The tools in max are grouped according to functionality. It might help to think of the interface as an organized toolbox, with separate drawers for hammers, screwdrivers, and so forth. The tools that you'll use most often can be accessed through a system of keyboard shortcuts and the new right-click Quad Menus. The toolset features that you will access less often are organized into convenient drop-down menus and rollouts just a few mouse clicks away. You'll find a listing of the basic keyboard shortcuts on the inside front and back covers of this book.

Understanding the functional groupings of the UI is the first step to navigating the interface successfully. The max user interface is divided into four basic groups, each with new features for max 4. The Menu Bar is examined first, in the next section.

Max 4 Menu Bar

The Menu Bar is a standard Windows drop-down menu group, which follows standard Windows protocol. The max 4 Menu Bar contains 13 menus—more than any of the previous versions of max.

The following outline of the menus in the Menu Bar will give you a foundation for understanding the rest of the interface. Take note of the new additions to the Menu Bar and the new options in the menus indicated by the eyeball icon 👁. Don't worry about understanding all the menu commands now. Just familiarize yourself with what the menu headings generally refer to and their location in the interface. Click each menu item to open it as you read the following list:

- **File**—Includes all the standard commands for saving and opening your max project files; setting up and using XRef objects and scenes; merging, importing and exporting geometry from other max files and 3D software; 👁 Pop-up Notes, special file management, and information items; and the View Image command used to view still images and movies.

- **Edit**—Includes commands to undo and redo any max command or action; a specialized version of saving and loading files called Hold and Fetch; deleting and cloning (copying) objects; broad selection commands (including a tool to redefine Selection Sets), and the Object Properties panel.

- **Tools**—Commands under the Tools menu relate to displaying, selecting, isolating, and repositioning objects in relation to other objects within the max workspace. The menu also includes specialized cloning functions, such as Array, Mirror, and Snapshot. The Light Lister is used to display and control the basic features of the lights you'll create in your scenes.

- **Group**—An organizational tool that contains commands for creating, opening, editing, and removing groups.

- **Views**—Contains the commands that relate to undoing and redoing viewport-specific operations and display options such as Ghosting, Showing Dependencies, and Shading Selected Faces; and displaying non-3D elements such as background images, grids, and the Transform Gizmo.

- 👁 **Create**—Divided into five submenus, which contain all the basic objects, shapes, lights, and particle effects available for creating your scenes. These tools are also found in the Tab Panels, Command Panels, and Quad Menus.

- ⊚ **Modifiers**—Divided into multiple submenus, which contain all the major commands and tools for modifying (changing) the shape of the objects you create in max. These tools are also found in the Tab Panels, Command Panels, and Quad Menus.

- ⊚ **Animation**—Gives you access to all the newly developed Inverse Kinematics, Constraints, Bones, and other animation helpers in max 4.

- ⊚ **Graph Editors**—Consolidates the Track View and Schematic View windows under one heading. Both of these editors are specialized animation and organizational tools that allow you to control all aspects of your animation hierarchies, trajectories, and scene component structure in a powerful graphical, diagrammatic way.

- **Rendering**—Includes the commands that control the major visual elements affecting rendering process; image compositing; ⊚ the new ActiveShade commands; material and texture development; environmental effects such as fog, lens flares, and so forth; making, viewing, and saving previews of your animation; and the Ram player: a powerful tool for playback of sequential images and movies.

- **Customize**—Contains all tools for customizing the look and feel of the max 4 user interface. Using the commands in this menu, you can customize the Menu Bar, Tab Panels, Floating Toolbars, Quad Menus, Keyboard Shortcuts, and the Color Scheme—all of which can be saved and reloaded. This menu also contains tools for adjusting environment variables such as file paths, units of scale, grid and snap settings, plug-in management, and the general preferences that specify how max is set up for day-to-day use.

- **MAXScript**—For those max users who have a little software engineer lurking in their psyche, this menu contains the controls used to create scripts, which are mini software programs that you write to tell max to do something.

- **Help**—Gives you access to a library of reference material comprised of the complete contents of the manuals that came with your software, and tutorials to help you learn the software. The menu also contains a command to connect you with discreet's support Web site.

Note

Keep in mind that the Menu Bar items are fully customizable and their commands can be found in several other places inside the max interface. As you progress through this Workshop, you will find that you prefer certain menu access modes for certain processes. The interface was designed in this way to allow users of other 3D software to easily migrate to max 4 and to create more flexibility for you in your production process.

The Menu Bar continues to be a powerful functional tool, especially when max is used in Expert mode, which is accessed by pressing Alt+X on your keyboard. When you activate Expert mode, you'll see that all the interface controls except the Menu Bar disappear. This mode is indeed for experts and won't be used in this Workshop. You can experiment with it on your own, as you like. Press Alt+X again to restore the UI to Nonexpert mode.

The next major functional group of max commands is found in the Main Toolbar, just below the Menu Bar.

Understanding the Main Toolbar

The Main Toolbar is one of 11 similar toolbars also known as Tab Panels in the max interface. The other 10 are hidden by default—you'll learn how to access them later in this chapter. The Main Toolbar contains the basic function controls and commands in max for selecting, moving, and organizing objects and rendering your scene. It duplicates some of the most frequently used commands found in the Menu Bar.

You will use this toolbar often, and it's important to understand how it's configured. This is also a good time to show you how a toolbar can be detached to float in the interface.

On the extreme left side of the Main Toolbar are two vertical parallel lines. Right-click those lines and select Float, as shown in Figure 1.2. This detaches the toolbar from the top of the interface and allows it to float over the viewports.

Right-click or drag here

Figure 1.2   If you have used other programs, such as Adobe Photoshop or Adobe Illustrator, you will be familiar with the concept and utility of floating menus. The Command Panels can also be detached and resized using the same process shown here.

Another way to float the Main Toolbar is to click the parallel lines and drag the toolbar down into the viewport area. After you float the toolbar, place your cursor over its bottom edge and resize it until it looks like Figure 1.3.

Tip   If your display is set to less than 1,280×1,024, you will not be able to see the entire length of the Main Toolbar. To access the part of the interface that can't be seen, you can either detach and resize the Main Toolbar/Tab Panel or move your cursor over a blank section of the toolbar, which causes the cursor to change to the helping hand icon [hand icon]. Use the helping hand to drag the toolbar sideways to see the rest of the toolbar icons.

3ds max 4

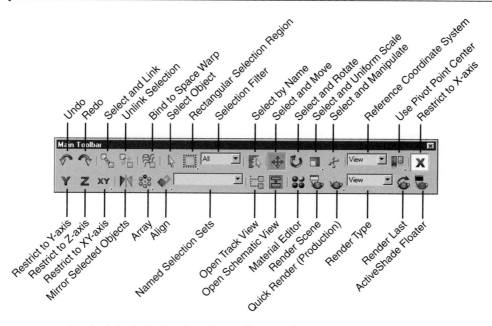

Figure 1.3 The tools included in the Main Toolbar are the foundation for everything you will do in max 4. Notice that some of the tools have small triangles in the lower-right corners of their icons. This is a max convention indicating that the command or tool has a drop-down menu containing additional selections.

You'll learn more about the specific functionality of these commands as you complete the work in each chapter. Until then, a brief explanation of what the commands do will be helpful. To access the optional selections for icons with triangles in their lower-right corners, click and hold the icon and select the tool mode you want from the drop-down menu:

- **Undo**—When you create or do anything in the max viewport, the program keeps track of that action in a history list. You can specify how many actions are recorded in that history, referred to as undo levels, by changing the number of undo levels in your preferences. The Undo command steps you back in time, one level for each time you click the icon. This effectively reverses any single or multiple action or command that you might have just completed. Right-click the icon to see the history list.

- **Redo**—The opposite of Undo reverses the effect of the Undo command. This allows you to be experimental in your work and try different tools to achieve the result you are looking for without fear of making a permanent mistake. Some actions in max cannot be undone or redone. When that is the case, max will give you a warning regarding the action you are about to take.

- **Select and Link**—Max allows you to link objects together in a parent-child hierarchy used for Inverse and Forward Kinematics animation. After objects are linked, any transformation applied to the parent object in the hierarchy is also applied to the children.

- **Unlink Selection**—Used to unlink objects that were previously linked together.
- **Bind to Space Warp**—A specialized link command used to bind objects to Space Warps. *Space Warps* are simulations of physical effects such as gravity, wind, and bombs. Binding an object or particle system to a Space Warp causes it to animate as it would if the object were under the influence of gravity, wind, and so on.
- **Select Object**—Objects in max must be selected before they can be transformed, manipulated, modified, or animated. Select Object is used to select single or multiple objects for transformation or modification.
- **Rectangular Selection Region**—This is the default selection region mode in 3ds max 4. When it's selected, dragging your mouse in the viewport creates a rectangular selection region around the object(s) you want to select.
- **Circular Selection Region**—When Circular Selection Region is active, dragging your mouse in the viewport will create a circular selection region around the object(s) you want to select.
- **Fence Selection Region**—Allows you to drag to draw line segments enclosing a selection region.
- **Selection Filter**—Lets you choose which objects can be selected in your viewport. When you click this item, a drop-down menu containing the different filter selections will open, as shown in Figure 1.4.

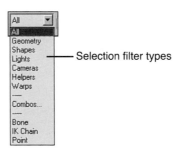

Selection filter types

Figure 1.4   If you choose Lights from the selection filter list, max will limit your object selection to lights only. The other elements can't be selected until you change the selection filter to All or to their specific element type. You can customize and combine object types to create your own selection filters.

- **Select by Name**—Opens a list of all objects currently visible in your viewports.
- **Select and Move**—The first of the transform commands. Using this tool you can select and move objects in the X, Y, and Z directions within the max workspace.
- **Select and Rotate**—Allows you to select and rotate your objects around its X-, Y-, or Z-axis.
- **Select and Uniform Scale**—Scales an object, making it bigger or smaller uniformly in all three axes.

3ds max 4

- ⬚ **Select and Non-Uniform Scale**—Scales an object by stretching it or shrinking it along one of its three coordinate axes.

- ⬚ **Select and Squash**—Causes an object to scale up along one axis while concurrently scaling down on the other two axes (or vice versa).

- 👁 ⚹ **Select and Manipulate**—Controls the function of the new manipulator helper objects in max 4. *Manipulators* are a new class of helper objects that simplify the transformation and animation of the objects to which they are linked.

- View ▾ **Reference Coordinate System**—Allows you to specify the coordinate system used for an object's transformation. When you click this item, a drop-down menu containing seven different reference systems will open, as shown in Figure 1.5.

Figure 1.5   The coordinate system that you choose from this list tells max how to transform the selected object relative to the X-, Y-, and Z-axes of the chosen system.

- ⬚ **Use Pivot Point Center**—Click and hold on this icon to see the other two choices in this flyout menu. These selections determine the geometric center used for Rotation and Scale transformations. Use Pivot Point Center uses an object's own pivot point or its own geometric center for rotation and scaling.

- ⬚ **Use Selection Center**—Allows you to rotate or scale multiple objects around the average geometric center of the selected elements.

- ⬚ **Use Transform Coordinate Center**—Lets you rotate or scale an object relative to the current active Reference Coordinate System.

- **X** **Restrict to X**—When this is selected, the current transform (move, rotate, or scale) is restricted to the X-axis. This allows you to ensure that you don't mistakenly transform the object in the other directions.

- **Y** **Restrict to Y**—Restricts the current transform to the Y-axis of the object.

- **Z** **Restrict to Z**—Limits the current transform to the Z-axis.

- **XY** **Restrict to XY-axis**—The default selection for dual axis restriction. This is useful when you want to restrict the transformation of an object to a two-dimensional plane defined by two axes. The other choices in this drop-down menu are **YZ** Restrict to YZ and **ZX** Restrict to ZX.

- ⬚ **Mirror Selected Objects**—Creates a mirror image of the objects or elements selected.

- ⬚ **Array**—The first of three powerful tools that can be used to create a numerically defined matrix of elements.

- **Snapshot**—The second Array tool, Snapshot creates clones (copies) of an animated object. It's similar to the still pictures taken in stop-motion photography; the snapshot pictures are still frames of a moving object taken at specific intervals. Snapshot is different from copying an object because it re-orders the vertex table and rebuilds the entire object vertex by vertex.

- **Spacing**—The third Array tool, Spacing allows you to distribute clones of an object along a path.

- **Align**—The default selection in a set of five tools designed to help you quickly align your objects, lights, camera targets, and viewports with other elements and geometry in your scene. The other options in the drop-down menu, which you'll learn about as you use them, are ☒ Normal Align, ☐ Place Highlight, ☐ Align Camera, and ☐ Align to View.

- **Named Selection Sets**—An organizational tool similar to Groups, which allows you to select a set of objects in your viewport and give that set a unique name. You can have multiple sets named in this list, and objects can belong to different Selection Sets. After being named this way, a Selection Set can be chosen from this list, which will automatically select all the set objects. This is a powerful tool, especially in scenes with a lot of elements that need to be repeatedly selected for transformation or animation.

- **Open Track View**—Opens the Track View Editor, a modeless dialog box that is used to modify and control the animation you create during Animate mode. *Modeless dialog box* refers to the dialog windows within max 4 that can remain open during all other max functions.

- **Open Schematic View**—Opens the Schematic View Editor, which provides a graphic display of the linked hierarchies in your max scenes. Using the tools in this modeless dialog box, you can select objects for animation and modification and create and modify their animation hierarchies.

- **Material Editor**—The tool you'll use to create the textures for your scene elements.

- **Render Scene**—Sets the parameters controlling every aspect of rendering your max imagery. Everything from image format and size, effects processing, antialiasing filters, and so forth are controlled from this powerful dialog box.

- **Quick Render (Production)**—Click this icon to render an image of your current active viewport without having to go into the Render Scene dialog box. The quick render process uses the settings in the production render parameters of the Render Scene dialog box. The other two options in the drop-down menu of this command are ☐ Quick Render Draft and ☐ ☐ Quick Render ActiveShade.

- **Render Type**—Allows you to specify how much and which parts of a scene are to be rendered. You'll select one of eight options from the menu, changing it as needed to support your process.

- **Render Last**—Renders the viewport that was last rendered, regardless of which viewport is currently active.

- 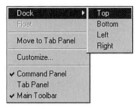 **ActiveShade Floater**—One of the most exciting rendering tools in the history of 3ds max. This tool allows you to interactively adjust texture and lighting in a scene and evaluate the results in near real time. Art directors and animators at all levels have been waiting for this tool.

By the time you have finished this Workshop, the tools in the Main Toolbar will be very familiar. Before you move on to the next tool grouping in the max interface, return the Main Toolbar to its home at the top of the screen by right-clicking it and selecting Dock, Top from the right-click menu, as shown in Figure 1.6.

Figure 1.6   When in doubt, right-click any max object or element to access preferences and parameters that you'll need in your work process. In this case, the dialog box controlling the placement of the Main Toolbar is revealed with a right-click.

Using the Max 4 Command Panel

Located on the right side of the screen, the max Command Panel is divided into six sections. This panel is designed to provide the deeper layers of control and functionality used to edit and animate every minute aspect of the objects you create in max. Figure 1.7 shows this important section of the interface and the names of each Command Panel.

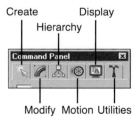

Figure 1.7   The Command Panel's creative and modification tools are also duplicated in the menu items available in the Menu Bar and the Tab Panels. You can also float the Command Panel by right-clicking on the thin border above the Command Panel tabs and selecting Float from the dialog box.

The individual Command Panels provide you with different sets of tools to help you create, modify, organize, and animate the objects in your max scenes. For this section of the Workshop, you'll explore the Create command panel. The other panels will be discussed as you use them to create `Area51.avi`.

The Create command panel contains all the basic tools you'll need to create parametric objects, shapes, lights, cameras, helper objects, Space Warps, and systems. When you read through the description of the various components, please pay attention to how they are organized.

First, click Box in the Create command panel. This will open the full set of basic tools for this panel, as shown in Figure 1.8.

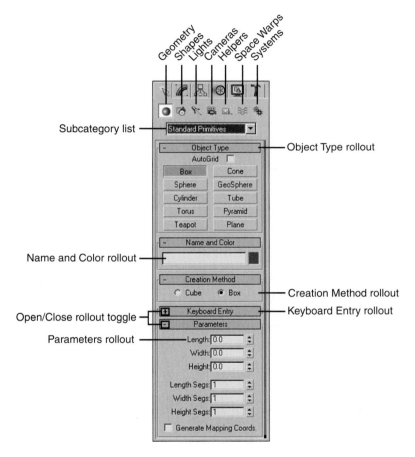

Figure 1.8 Although each Command Panel is designed according to its own specific functional requirements, they all use a similar structural layout. Learning the deep layers of control available in these tools will open up the full power of max 4.

As you read the definitions of the components in the Create command panel, click the icon indicated and get familiar with the basic contents of each section:

- **Geometry**—Provides you with the tools to create 3D parametric objects. There are seven subcategories in Geometry: Standard Primitives, Extended Primitives, Compound Objects, Particle Systems, Patch Grids, NURBS Surfaces, and Dynamics Objects.

- **Shapes**—2D shapes such as rectangles, circles, and so on. You can use NURBS curves or splines (lines) to create 2D shapes in max.

- **Lights**—The five standard lights available for you to use include Target Spot, Free Spot, Omni, Directional, and Target Directional. Lights in max can cast shadows, project images known as GOBOs, and create volumetric effects simulating dust or mist in the light beams.

- **Cameras**—Max provides two standard types of camera objects for your use: Target Camera and Free Camera. Cameras in max simulate the same controls, movements, and functions of their real-world counterparts and can also be used to add special effects to the final rendered images you will be creating.

- **Helpers**—Elements designed to aid in the creation and animation of other objects in your scene. These objects, although visible in the viewports, do not appear in rendered images. Max helper elements are Dummy, Point, Protractor, Grid, Tape Measure, and Compass, as well as Box Gizmos, Cylinder Gizmos, Sphere Gizmos, Camera Matching elements, and a new class of helper named Manipulators.

- **Space Warps**—Divided into four subcategories: Forces, which simulate real-world physical effects such as wind and gravity; Deflectors, which are used to simulate realistic object collision effects; Geometric/Deformable, which are used to create animating motion effects such as waves and ripples; and Modifier-Based Space Warps, which deform object geometry.

- **Systems**—Max provides three standard systems: Bones is used for Inverse Kinematics (IK) animation, Ring Array is a specialized procedural object, and Sunlight creates a realistic sunlight source that can simulate any time of day or night at any latitude and longitude on Earth.

- **Subcategory List**—A list of other types of objects available in each of the tool categories contained within the related command panel. Click Geometry [ic057] in the Create command panel. Open the Geometry subcategory list by clicking Standard Primitives, as shown in Figure 1.9.

Figure 1.9   Many of the toolsets in the Create and Modify command panels have subcategories of tools and commands that can be reached through the subcategory list.

- **Object Type Rollout**—Shows the types of objects available for your use in the subcategory you have selected.

- **Name and Color Rollout**—Allows you to organize your objects and elements by giving them unique names and colors. Object color refers to the default color of the object before a texture or material is applied to its surface. Use this feature to categorize objects in a complex scene.

- **Creation Method Rollout**—Slightly different for each object type. Click each of the object types in turn and watch the creation method change to correspond with the creation structure of the different objects. A pyramid, for example, can be created from its base/apex or from its center.

- **Keyboard Entry Rollout**—Allows you to enter precise dimensions for your geometry before you create it in your scene.

- **Open/Close Rollout Toggle**—Click the plus sign (+) next to Keyboard Entry. This toggle, indicated by a + or – sign, opens and closes the Command Panel rollouts, allowing you to access just the rollouts you want to use.

- **Parameters Rollout**—Controls the dimensional aspects of your max objects. The width, length, and height segments control the complexity of the surface geometry.

The next major feature of the max interface to explore is the viewport structure of the workspace. To know how viewports work in max, you will need to understand the concepts behind creating and moving objects in three-dimensional space.

3D Thinking

Thinking three-dimensionally might seem simple because you and I live in a 3D world, and we often take our perception of that 3D world for granted. To effectively create imaginary worlds in max, you must begin to think of those worlds in terms of the X-, Y-, and Z-coordinates that define them. This requires you to make a shift in how you look at the world around you and learn some new vocabulary to describe that world.

Max uses a 3D mathematical structure to keep track of all the objects in the workspace and their spatial relationship to one another. The key components of this spatial relationship are the max origin, XYZ coordinate system, and units of measurement.

Max Origin

All objects created in the max workspace are referenced to a world origin by the use of X-, Y-, and Z-coordinates. The coordinates of the max origin are 0,0,0, which represent the numeric values of the X, Y, and Z dimensions at the center of the max workspace. The 3D workspace in max is set up to create, modify, and animate your scene elements and objects in reference to this world space origin.

3ds max 4

Distance and location in the world around you is measured in reference to a known location relative to your position. For example, if you live in Boston, from my point of reference (my relative origin) you are 3,000 miles away from my home in Lake Elsinore, California. If you live in San Diego, you would be 80 miles away. Both measurements of distance are accurate based on the point of reference or relative origin used to calculate the measurement. Everything you create in 3D space is measured in relation to the single *world origin* that max uses as its point of reference for measuring distance and defining location.

XYZ Coordinate System

Three basic dimensions define the world you live in: height, width, and depth. These dimensions also relate to the concepts of up and down; left and right; and toward and away, as those directions relate to your own point of view. In max, these directions are defined by the X-, Y-, and Z-*axes*.

An axis is used to symbolize a specific coordinate direction in 3D space. This icon is the universal symbol used for coordinate axes—red, green, and blue lines at right angles to one another, with a common origin and letters specifying the respective X-, Y-, or Z-axis. It is helpful to relate the concept of axes to familiar directions you are already familiar with. Think of the X-axis as horizontal, or left and right, the Y-axis as toward you or away from you, and the Z-axis as vertical, or up and down. Figure 1.10 illustrates this concept.

Figure 1.10   Max uses X-, Y-, and Z-coordinates and axes to describe 3D space and the dimensional relationship of objects in that space.

X-, Y-, and Z-coordinates are used to describe the numerical world position of the objects in your scene. The convention for giving these coordinate numbers is to list them like this: 12,85,–200. The first number is the X-coordinate numeric value, the second is the Y-coordinate numeric value, and the third is the Z-coordinate numeric value. These values can be positive or negative, depending on their location as it relates to the origin. In Figure 1.11, you'll see how the positive and negative coordinate axes relate to their origin.

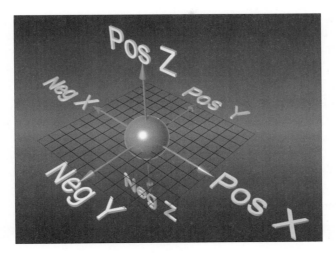

Figure 1.11   Positive X is to the right of the origin, negative X to the left; positive Y is above the origin; negative Y is below it. Positive Z is above the plane defined by the XY axes. Negative Z is below that plane.

Max keeps track of every object's precise location in the world space of the max environment, including changes in the relative location of an object. Understanding this is an important part of animating objects in 3D space.

Units of Measurement

The relative value of the coordinate numbers, or *units*, in max can be specified according to all standard measurement systems. Precision engineering projects might require units configured in decimal inches or the metric system. Architecture and building projects might use standard feet and inches. These measurement conventions are a means to put some numerical value to the height, width, and depth of objects and their X-, Y-, and Z-locations in space.

The grid in each of the viewport windows is set up to follow max's units of measurement. You won't be changing how the units are set up in this Workshop. However, if you want to experiment with this, use the max User Reference outlined at the end of this chapter. Using the keyword *units* will access all you'll need to know to set up your measurement units in max.

3ds max 4

Note

The default units set up in max are called *generic units*, which don't have an intrinsic scalar relationship with any of the standard measurement systems. In other words, generic units are not inches, feet, or centimeters. They are just numerical units, which you can define as you want. You can decide that 1 generic unit equals 1 inch, 1 foot, or 10 feet, and so forth. The scalar relationship is up to your definition. This works well if you work alone and aren't required to create your scene objects using a real measurement system. If you are working in a team, creating assets that other animators will be sharing, it is absolutely necessary that the team use the same units and measurement conventions.

Views and Viewports

A *view* in max is defined by what you are seeing on the screen at any given time. The default configuration in max contains four viewports labeled with their specific view names in the upper-left corner of the viewport. These names appear as white text: Top, Front, Left, and Perspective. (see Figure 1.12).

View name

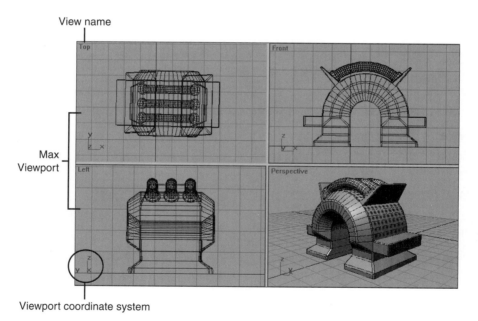

Max
Viewport

Viewport coordinate system

Figure 1.12   Viewports are the windows into the 3D world of the max workspace and are named for the view they are currently displaying, such as Top, Front, Perspective, and so on.

Max views are divided into four basic types—Orthographic, Perspective, Camera, and user-defined Isometric views. With an understanding of how 3D space is defined within the max workspace, the different types of views and their corresponding coordinate systems are the next important thing to learn about 3D thinking.

Orthographic Views

Orthographic views are named for the side of an object that you are looking at: Front, Right, Top, Left, and so forth. Each Orthographic view has a unique XYZ coordinate orientation.

Understanding Orthographic Views

Imagine that you are standing outside a square building surrounded by a parking lot. Following the max origin convention, the building is located at 0,0,0 in space representing its X-, Y-, and Z-coordinates. If you face the front entrance of the building it means that you are looking at the front view of the building. Using this same idea, walking around and facing the right side of the building, you will see the right view. The same goes for the back, left, top, and bottom views. The building is not moving—it is still sitting in its relationship to the world origin. You, your point of view, and your position in world space have moved. These basic views are called Orthographic or *Orthogonal* views.

In the bottom-left corner of each viewport, you will see the coordinate system icon . This icon shows how the view relates to the world coordinate system. You can see that the orientation of the colored lines and X, Y, and Z are different for each view. In the Orthogonal views seen in Figure 1.13, all three axis letters appear but only two lines can be seen.

Perspective and User-Defined Isometric Views

Outside programs such as max, people rarely see anything in orthogonal views. People see the world around them in perspective, which helps to gauge depth, distance, and relative size and location of objects in their field of vision. The ability to see in perspective is created by the curvature of the lens in the eyes. In the Perspective view shown in Figure 1.14, you see all three axes and a flat XY plane with a grid overlay. Think of this XY grid as the *ground plane*.

Isometric views are similar to Perspective views in that you can see all three dimensions of the object at the same time in the viewport. Object edges in an Isometric view are parallel, whereas the edges of an object in a Perspective view look as if they are converging to a vanishing point, thus creating the illusion of depth. Figure 1.15 illustrates how objects seen in Perspective and user-defined Isometric views are different.

World Axis Coordinate Display

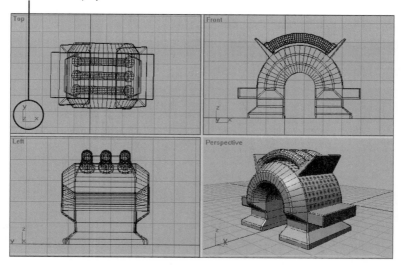

Figure 1.13   The max World Axis Coordinate Display shows how each view relates to the 3D workspace. This will help you orient yourself when you create and modify the elements of your scene. Remember, every view has its own unique coordinate axis orientation.

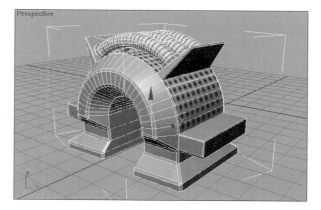

Figure 1.14   When you use Perspective and user-defined Isometric views, all three coordinate axes will be displayed in the viewport.

Camera Views

Camera views are specialized viewports that simulate the optical characteristics mechanics, and controls of cinematic cameras. To use a Camera view, you must have created a camera in your scene. Cameras can also be animated, and max allows the use of multiple cameras.

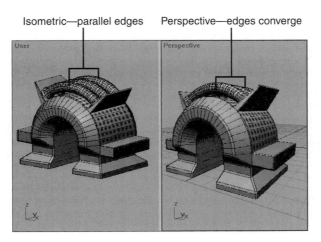

Isometric—parallel edges   Perspective—edges converge

Figure 1.15   Isometric views are referred to as user-defined views because, as the user, you are completely free to define the view using the Viewport Navigation Tools.

Viewport Modification and Navigation Tools

The next major group of tools, located along the bottom of the interface, includes precision input, snap options, animation controls, the Track Bar, and the max listener and prompt line windows. These tools and creative aids will be explained when you begin using them later in the Workshop. Right now, it's important to focus on the viewport modification and navigation tools you'll use to move around the max workspace.

Creating in 3D space can sometimes be difficult if you are not able to see what you need to see in the way you need to see it. Max answers this need by giving you many options for viewing and moving around in your scene. As you explore the remaining tool groups in max 4, create a box in the workspace. The following steps show you how:

1. Click the Create tab in the Command Panel and click Box. The rectangle around the Box button will turn yellow and look like it's pushed in. This means that this tool is active and ready to use.

2. Move your cursor into the center of the lower-right Perspective viewport and drag to define the rectangular base of the box on the XY ground plane. When you have a length and width you like, release the mouse button.

3. Now move the cursor up in the viewport to define the height of the box and click to set the height.

4. After you have created the box, press Esc to exit from Create mode; you will notice that the Box command is no longer active in the Create command panel. Now, look at the box you just created. You'll notice that four white corners of a bounding box surround the box in the Perspective viewport. This indicates that this piece of geometry is selected.

5. Move your cursor over the box and note that the cursor changes from an arrow to a plus-sign shape. This is max letting you know that your cursor has located some valid or selectable geometry.

6. Click in the viewport outside the box to deselect it. The bounding box disappears and the box is no longer highlighted in white. Click the box to reselect it.

7. Move your cursor over the viewport name in the upper-left corner of one of the other viewports. You will see the cursor change into the active viewport change icon ▣. This cursor change is informing you that if you click in this window, it will become the active viewport.

8. Click in the Top viewport. You will see the viewport outlined in yellow, indicating that the Top view is now active. This means that you can create geometry in that viewport and all geometry will be created using the current coordinate axes of the active window.

> **Tip**
>
> Max defines the spatial orientation of most objects in relation to the Top and Perspective views. Using the Top view or Perspective view to model the objects in your scenes ensures that the object's length, width, and height dimensions are oriented correctly in the 3D workspace. Length in max corresponds to the Y-axis, width to the X-axis, and height to the Z-axis.

The steps you used to create the box are the fundamental steps you will use each time you model in max.

Changing Your Viewport Display Mode

Max has several ways to display geometry. These *display modes* are designed to help when you are creating and modifying objects in a scene.

As you look at the viewports, you'll notice that the Perspective view is in what is called Smooth+Highlights mode. It appears solid and is lit to emphasize its 3D appearance. The other views—Top, Front, and Left—are in Wireframe mode. *Wireframe* refers to a transparent display mode, which shows the polygonal structure of the object. *Polygons* are the basic 2D planes from which all surfaces are created.

Figure 1.16 shows the two most common modes of viewing geometry in max.

Learning how to change display modes as you go is an important facet of navigating the max 4 workspace. Click in your Perspective viewport to make it active. Right-click the word Perspective in the upper-left corner of the viewport window. A right-click menu (see Figure 1.17) appears. Select Wireframe from the menu—the right-click menu disappears and the viewport display mode has changed.

You can use the right-click menu to switch between the different viewing modes of the max viewports. Right-click each of the four windows in turn and select Smooth+Highlights mode for each viewport. Then, change the Orthographic viewports back to Wireframe mode. Leave the Perspective viewport set to Smooth+Highlights.

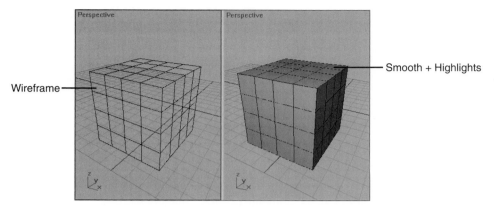

Wireframe

Smooth + Highlights

Figure 1.16 Each display mode has advantages and disadvantages when you are developing your work. Switching between Wireframe and Smooth+Highlights modes gives you a way to more effectively evaluate your modeling work.

Figure 1.17 Right-click the viewport name to change the display mode.

Viewport Navigation Controls

The Viewport Navigation Controls are used to help you change your point of view in relation to the geometry you create. These controls all have combination keyboard-mouse shortcuts, which you'll learn while you learn to use the navigation buttons.

Click the box in the Right view to select it. In the bottom-right corner of the max workspace, you will see the eight Viewport Navigation Controls. See Figure 1.18 for the names of each icon.

These tools are best understood in the context of using them. Follow these steps to learn how each one works. You'll notice that some of them have a small triangle in the lower-right corner of their icons. Following the same convention you learned earlier in this chapter, you can access more control options for these tools by holding your left mouse button down while clicking the icon.

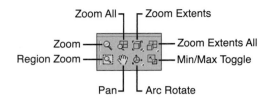

Zoom All ⌐ ┌ Zoom Extents

Zoom ──── ┌─ Zoom Extents All
Region Zoom ──── ─ Min/Max Toggle

Pan ┘ └ Arc Rotate

Figure 1.18   The max Viewport Navigation Controls used with Orthographic viewports are slightly different than the ones used in Camera and Perspective views. Check out the tear card for information on all the Viewport Navigation Controls.

1. Click Zoom Extents All 🔲 . The box in all four viewports expands to fill the available viewing area. This tool is used to zoom in or out far enough so that all the geometry in the scene will fit in the viewport. This feature is handy when some part of the object you want to work with is outside your viewing area.

2. Click Zoom 🔍 , and then drag your cursor up and down in the Top view. You'll see the box zoom in and out in the viewport.

3. Change to the Perspective viewport and then click Min/Max toggle 🔲 . The Perspective viewport fills the entire screen. Click the toggle again to view all four viewports.

4. While you are in the Perspective view, click the Pan tool ✋ and drag in the viewport. The Pan tool pans your point of view (POV) vertically and horizontally in relation to the viewport.

5. Click and hold on the Arc Rotate button. Without releasing the mouse button, move the cursor up to the middle selection, select Arc Rotate Selected 🔲 , and then release the mouse button. Arc Rotate Selected is the icon filled with white, as shown in Figure 1.19.

Figure 1.19   All the Viewport Navigation Controls with alternative modes are accessed in a similar manner. Each one of the alternative modes helps you navigate within the workspace in a slightly different way, supporting your needs as you work in max.

What you have done in this exercise is set your View Rotation tool to rotate around a selected object. After you have picked Arc Rotate Selected from the flyout, its button turns yellow and a yellow circle appears in your Perspective viewport around the box, as shown in Figure 1.20.

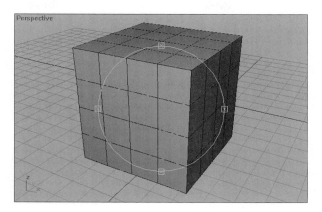

Figure 1.20 When you use Arc Rotate Selected, you can rotate your point of view around the selected object you are creating or modifying.

Move your cursor inside the yellow circle and drag to rotate the box. Notice how the cursor changes to different Arc Rotate cursors when you move it in and out of the circle and onto the little boxes with the Xs in them around the perimeter of the yellow Arc Rotate circle (see Figure 1.21).

Learning and using the Viewport Navigation Tools will speed your creative process. An even quicker way to use these tools is to learn how to use the keyboard and the mouse together.

Keyboard and Mouse Navigation Shortcuts

Max is set up with many shortcuts to make using the program easier and faster. By using the mouse and the keyboard together, you can move around by accessing shortcuts for the Viewport Navigation Controls. The inside front and back covers of this book contain all the most frequently used keyboard and mouse shortcuts in max. Here's a quick exercise to show you the basic process to access these shortcuts:

1. Click in the Perspective viewport and press W on your keyboard. The Perspective viewport expands to fill the entire screen. This is referred to as *maximizing* your view. Press W again and the four viewports reappear, which is *minimizing* your Perspective viewport. The W key is the Min/Max display toggle.

2. Press W to make the Perspective view expand to fill the viewport. Hold down Ctrl+Alt on your keyboard while using the center mouse button to click-drag in the viewport. Your image zooms in when you move the mouse up and zooms out when you move it back.

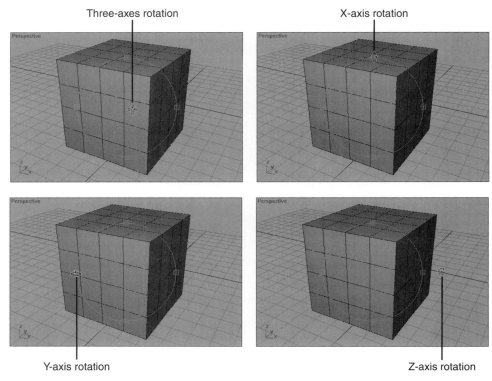

Three-axes rotation   X-axis rotation

Y-axis rotation   Z-axis rotation

Figure 1.21   Max uses different cursor icons to help you choose the correct view rotation axis. The X-, Y-, and Z-Rotation axes for the Arc Rotate Selection tool use the corresponding axes of the screen coordinate system.

 Tip

If your mouse has a wheel instead of a center button, you can use the wheel to zoom in and out without using the keyboard shortcut.

If you have any problems zooming or panning with the middle mouse button or wheel, be sure that your mouse preferences for Windows (in the Control Panel for Windows) designate the middle button to operate as "Middle Button."

Viewport navigation in 3ds max 4 is designed to take advantage of a three-button mouse. If you don't have a three-button mouse, you should get one. Those manufactured by Logitech are recommended—especially the Cordless Wheel Mouse model!

3. Zoom out from the object until it becomes very small. If max stops zooming, release the mouse button momentarily and rezoom.

4. Press Ctrl+Alt+Z on your keyboard and the view zooms in on the box again. This is the keyboard shortcut for the Zoom Extents All navigation control.

5. Hold down the Alt key and, using the middle mouse button, click-drag in the viewport. The box rotates using three axes for Arc Rotation.

6. Using just the middle mouse button, click-drag in the window. The cursor changes into the Pan icon and your point of view pans relative to the direction of your mouse movement.

7. Press T on your keyboard and the viewport changes to the Top view. If you can't see the box, press Ctrl+Alt+Z to bring it into the window. By pressing F, R, L, and P, you can use keyboard shortcuts to access the Front, Right, Left, and Perspective views of your geometry.

Other shortcuts will be presented as you work your way through the rest of the chapters. After you get used to them, the max shortcuts should become an integral part of your daily work process. They are worth learning and will help your productivity. The last important feature of the max UI to discuss is also a new feature to max 4—Quad Menus.

Quad Menus

In previous versions of max, even with the introduction of floating toolbars, experienced users would still find themselves jumping around the various sections of the interface searching for the next tool. Max 4 provides a new way to access any and all the available tools in max through the use of the Quad Menus.

Accessing the Quad Menu is simple—just right-click the box you've created to open the basic Quad Menu as shown in Figure 1.22.

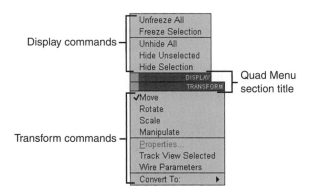

Figure 1.22   The basic Quad Menu is contextual and is different for different object types and processes. This basic menu uses two of the Quads available.

There are several layers of Quad Menus for each individual max object, which are accessed by using the Ctrl, Alt, or Ctrl+Alt keys in conjunction with a right-click on the selected object. Try this by holding down the Ctrl key as you right-click the box object. A different Quad Menu will open, as shown in Figure 1.23.

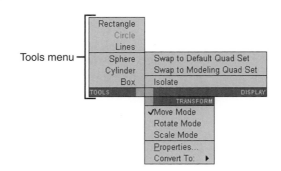

Figure 1.23 Max 4 comes configured with several layers of default Quad Menus, which are accessed through different keyboard and right-click combinations.

You'll learn more about the Quad Menu system, including how to customize them, when you create Area51.avi.

You have learned a lot about the max 4 interface, and there will be many reviews of all these tools and commands as you move forward. The next section of this chapter will cover how max helps you customize your user interface, view the work you are creating, and access max's User Reference and Help Library.

Workflow and Productivity in Max 4

How an artist's mind works is often chaotic as his imagination jumps from idea to idea. If an artist were to approach his day-to-day work in the same nonlinear fashion, nothing would ever get done. The challenge is how to structure a productive process without stifling imagination and creativity.

The flexibility in the max toolset and how it's configured is a huge factor in how productive you will be in your work process. With that in mind, it's important for you to know some of the available ways to customize max's user interface to meet your individual needs and wants.

Customizing the Max Interface

Earlier in this chapter, you learned how to float the Main Toolbar and the Command Panel by right-clicking them and selecting Float from the right-click menu. Figure 1.24 shows the other options available.

Figure 1.24 All these basic features can also be accessed in the Menu Bar under the Customize heading. Use this right-click menu to configure your basic UI layout.

The options for managing the location and basic appearance of the UI components are as follows:

- **Dock**—The Main Toolbar is docked at the top of the UI by default. Accessing the Dock options allows you to put any selected toolbar at the top, bottom, left, or right of the screen. Command Panels can be docked on the left or right side only.

- **Float**—Allows you to detach and float the Command Panels and toolbars. This allows you to change their size and location to support your work process.

- **Move to Tab Panel**—Available as an option for Tab Panels, your own toolbars, and the Main Toolbar only. Using this command moves the selected component onto the Tab Panel.

> **Caution**
>
> Don't get the *Dock* command confused with the *Move to Tab Panel* command. For example, if you move the Main Toolbar to the Tab Panels when the Tab Panels are not currently being displayed, the Main Toolbar disappears from the UI. If you make this mistake, press 2 or Y to display the Tab Panels, select the Main Toolbar, right-click it, and select Convert to Toolbar. This floats the Main Toolbar and allows you to use its right-click menu to dock it in the UI at a place of your choosing.

- **Customize**—Opens the Customize menu, which opens the Customize User Interface dialog box.

- **Command Panel, Tab Panel, Main Toolbar**—The selections in this part of the dialog box are toggles that hide and show the Command Panels, Tab Panels, or Main Toolbar. Select the name of the UI component that you want to hide; select it again to show it.

Accessing and Configuring the Max 4 Tab Panel and Toolbars

If you are an experienced max 3 user you might want to continue your use of the Tab Panels in max 4. As a new user of max, the Tab Panels provide a more graphic depiction of the commands found in both the main Menu Bar and the Command Panels. To view and use the Tab Panels, press 2 or Y. The Tab Panels will appear in the UI just below the Main Toolbar (see Figure 1.25).

Tab Panels

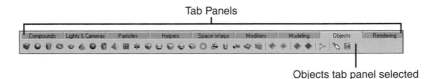

Objects tab panel selected

Figure 1.25   All the elements shown in the Tab Panels are also accessible in the Create command panel and the main Menu Bar. The Tab Panels and customizable Toolbars were a new feature in 3D Studio MAX 3 that were initially developed in response to the numerous requests received from max users for a more graphical user interface. They have proved to be helpful but not necessarily all that useful.

3ds max 4

When you right-click one of the tabs within the Tab Panels, you'll see the *Convert to Toolbar* option in the menu. This command converts the selected Tab Panel into a floating toolbar. This can also be accomplished by dragging the tab onto the viewport area.

To dock the new toolbar or return it to the Tab Panel, right-click the toolbar and select Dock or Return to Tab Panel from the menu. Figure 1.26 shows several Tab Panels converted to toolbars and docked in the UI: the Objects tab panel docked on the left, the Modifiers tab panel on the bottom, the Main Toolbar on the right side with the Command Panels hidden, and the Shapes and Rendering tab panels on the top of the interface. All other Tab Panels are hidden.

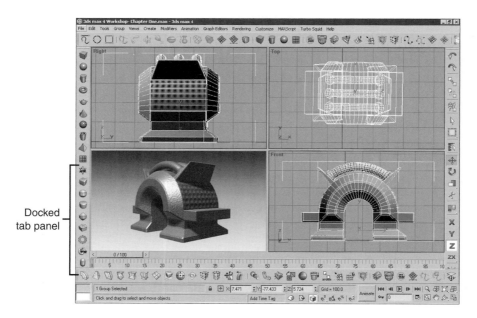

Docked
tab panel

Figure 1.26   The flexibility to have the toolbars you want in the location you desire in the interface is a powerful convenience. Experiment with configurations of your own and save your user interface settings in the main Menu Bar by clicking Customize, Save Custom UI Scheme.

Note

What's the difference between a Tab Panel and a toolbar? Tab Panels and toolbars are differentiated by where they sit in the user interface. Tab Panels that have been detached and are either floating or docked around the perimeter of the UI are called toolbars. Toolbars, including the Main Toolbar, become Tab Panels when they are returned to the Tab Panel interface by using the right-click menu. I call them all toolbars and just think of the Tab Panel as a location that toolbars can be placed in and not as a functional differentiation.

There is a lot more that you can do with toolbars, such as adding your own buttons and commands for specialized functions or scripts you might create. Consult your User Reference for more information on how to create custom menu items for your toolbars.

Using the Customize Menu

The Customize selection in the toolbars' right-click menu is part of a much larger set of commands accessed through the Customize section of the Menu Bar. This is an important menu used to customize your preferences for everything about how max looks and works. Click Customize in the Menu Bar to open the menu shown in Figure 1.27.

Figure 1.27   Using the Customize menu you can create, save, and load customized UI schemes and specify the other preferences that modify how max works.

This menu gives you access to a lot of important max UI configuration components. For now, it's important to understand what each one does so that you know where to go to get what you need.

The Customize menu is divided up into seven parts. The first selection is Customize User Interface. Click it to access the menu shown in Figure 1.28.

> **Caution**
>
> Experts following sound design principles designed the max user interface. The default settings they established should be good enough for you at this point in your learning process. Don't change these settings unless you have read and understand the process outlined in the 3ds max 4 User Reference.

By modifying the settings in the various sections of this menu, you can change everything about the max UI to suit your individual needs. The inside of the front and back covers of this book show some of the keyboard shortcuts taken from the comprehensive lists in this menu. If you want to create new shortcuts, this is where you'll do it. In the later chapters of this book, you will be shown how to modify some of these settings as a part of the creative process to complete Area51.avi.

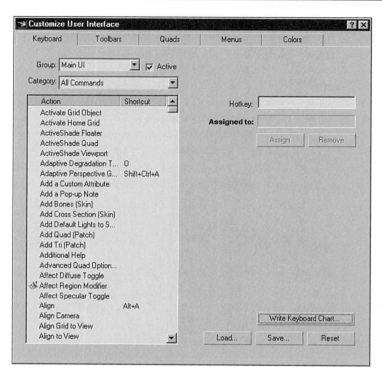

Figure 1.28 Customize User Interface allows changes to the appearance and configuration of every user interface component in the max UI.

The second section of the Customize menu contains the commands to load and save your custom UI schemes and a command to Revert to Startup Layout. As long as you don't save over the default user interface file—DefaultUI.cui—this command restores you to the max default UI settings.

The third section, shown in Figure 1.29, allows you to show or hide toolbars, the Tab Panels, the Command Panels, and the Track Bar. You can also customize the keyboard shortcuts for each toggle.

The command in the fourth section, Lock UI Layout, prevents any changes or reconfiguration of the interface.

The fifth section of the Customize menu contains the following four menus:

- **Configure Paths**—Tells max where you want it to look for the files it uses to load and save scenes, images, texture maps, and plug-ins.

- **Units Setup**—This is the dialog box controlling how the units of measurement in max are set up.

- **Grid and Snap Settings**—Configures the size and layout of the grid seen in your viewports. Snap settings control a set of tools allowing you to more precisely control how geometry is created during the modeling process.

- **Viewport Configuration**—Controls how your viewports are set up. You'll access these commands when you need to change the factors controlling how objects appear in your viewports, the layout of the viewports and the use of Safe Frames, Adaptive Degradation, and Regions.

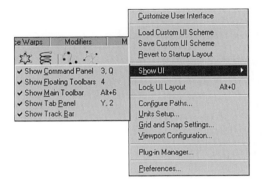

Figure 1.29   The commands in Show UI duplicate those found in the toolbar, Tab Panel, and Command Panel right-click menus.

The final two sections of the Customize menu are Plug-in Manager and Preferences. Plug-in Manager helps you organize and configure how max loads and uses the mini-software components called plug-ins that create the power of what you see in this tool. Click the last menu item, Preferences, to open the dialog box shown in Figure 1.30.

The Preferences dialog box is divided up into eight tabbed sections controlling important settings for your max work. You'll adjust a couple of settings now and more later on in the Workshop:

1. First, change the Scene Undo Levels in the General tab from 20 to 100.

2. Click the Files tab to open it. Change the Recent Files in File Menu to 5.

3. Be sure the Auto Backup is enabled and change the Number of Autobak Files to 6, as shown in Figure 1.31. Click OK to close the Preferences dialog box.

Next is the final section of this chapter, which contains an overview of what you will be creating in *3ds max 4 Workshop* and some information on how to view your work and access the max User Reference Help libraries.

If you have previously worked through *3D Studio MAX 3.0 Workshop*, you'll recognize that some of the techniques presented in that book have been adapted and augmented in this Workshop. You can build on what you learned there by working on some of the optional pieces of this project.

If you haven't read *3D Studio MAX 3.0 Workshop*, you should. All the principles found there relate to everything you'll be learning here and will provide a powerful knowledge base for your development as a max artist. You can easily adapt the project in *3D Studio MAX 3 Workshop* to your work in max 4.

Change Scene
Undo Levels

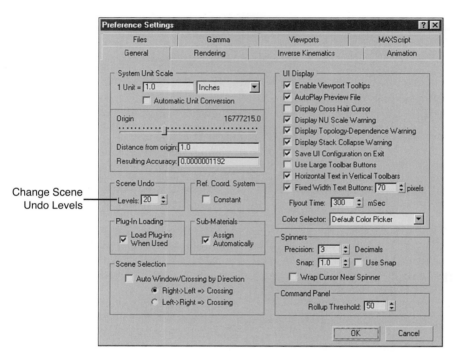

Figure 1.30   The settings in the Preferences dialog box determine the basic settings for much of your work in max.

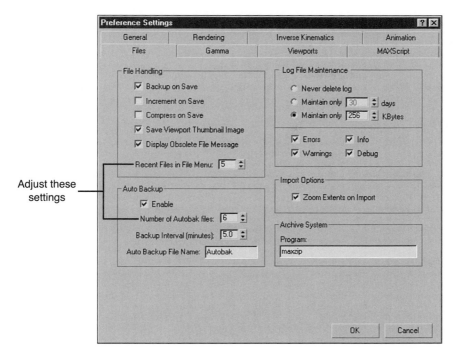

Adjust these
settings

Figure 1.31   When you change the Preference settings, they become the ones max uses every time it's started until you change them again.

Workshop: Area 51: Project Overview

The projects in this book will lead you through the process of creating the storyboards, animatic, titles, and digital content and effects for a short movie titled *Area 51*. Your goal as you do this work should be to use max 4 to create something that improves on the basic imagery and ideas presented here.

The purpose of this Workshop is to empower your progress as a max artist. Adopting the processes that create the elements for Area51.avi and then adapting them to your own vision through experimentation can accomplish this goal. To that end, the intent of this book is to challenge you to work on your own, with guidance and support, to create this scene and raise your proficiency level as a new max user to a higher plane.

Project Structure

The process to create *Area 51* is made up of seven separate major components, some of which you will duplicate during your work in the Workshop sections of this book:

- **Storyboards**—The storyboards for this project were created with the intent of providing you with two things: an example of the visual shorthand needed to effectively communicate ideas concerning shot content and composition, and a basis to show you how the animatic is created. Chapter 2, "Virtual Viz: The Art of Pre-Production for Digital Content Creation," covers the entire pre-production process, including storyboards (see Figure CP.6 in the color section).

- **Animatic**—A rough animated sketch version of a production shot or sequence that is used as a tool to evaluate timing and the flow of action. You will learn how to make a simple animatic using components you'll create and some premade parts provided on the CD.

- **Title and Credit Sequences**—You'll learn how to make two onscreen graphic sequences using the tools and techniques described in this Workshop. The opening title will be a simple text animation; the end credits are known as a *credit crawl* and include an animated logo and customized format, including your own personalized information (see Figure CP.18).

- **Scene Layers**—Scenes are divided into layers to provide you with more artistic freedom while you create the visual components of your project. To be an effective max artist, you must learn to use the layer process presented in this Workshop.

- **Special Effects Layers**—These layers are created separately as well—also to provide you with complete control over the imagery effects (see Figure CP.12 in the color section).

- **Machine and Character Layers**—Separating animated character and machine layers allows you to more freely experiment with their animation, lighting, and special effects (see Figure CP.16).

- **Sound and Sound Effects Layer**—Sound is an extremely important part of your project design and the overall sensory impact of your finished product. It is essential that you be able to include rough and finished sound layers into your work.

The layering process used to create Area51.avi is powerful and effective. After you understand the concepts, you might find, as I have, that it simplifies the creation process as well. This is because layering allows you to adjust each independent layer element to work within the holistic scene.

The flexible way the tools in max are configured recognizes that visual experimentation comprises 70–80% of an artist's work time on any given project. The other 20–30% is spent in applying what is learned in the experiments to the actual creation of the scene elements and in producing the final images.

While you are creating Area51.avi, you will need to see your work as it develops. This will help you evaluate the work you've completed, make necessary adjustments, and move on toward your end goal of completing this Workshop.

Previewing and Viewing Max Image Assets

Max provides several ways to view still image files and animation segments in a variety of formats. This section will show you two ways. You'll learn two additional ways as you work through the Workshop, including how to make animation previews and how to use the RAM player.

These tools are designed to make you more productive by making it easy to view and evaluate your work. The first way to view existing images or movies in max is to use the View File command. Here's how:

1. Click File, View Image File in the main Menu Bar to open the View File browser window. Use the browser controls under the Look In drop-down list to find the files installed on your computer from this book's companion CD. Select All Formats from the Files of Type drop-down list (see Figure 1.32).

Figure 1.32   The View File browser window allows you to view files in 18 different formats.

2. Browse to the drive containing the installed files and double-click the folder titled Avis. The contents of that folder will appear in the large text window. Select Area51.avi to load it into the browser. You'll see a preview image appear in the lower-right corner of the screen, as shown in Figure 1.33.

3. Double-click the filename to play it. Max will use your Windows Media Player for playback. Close the window when you're done. You can use this same process to view the other images on the companion CD.

Using the Asset Browser is another way to view image files in max. It is also a powerful tool for organizing and accessing the many complex elements you might use in your scenes, including any kind of document created within the programs on your computer. The following steps introduce you to this tool:

1. Click the Utilities ![icon] command panel on the right side of the max interface, and then click the Asset Browser button.

2. When the Asset Browser window opens, use the browser on the left side of the window to locate the folder containing the file Area51.avi. You will see a preview image of the file appear on the right side of the Asset Manager. If you double-click the image, the Windows Media Player will open and play the AVI (see Figure 1.34).

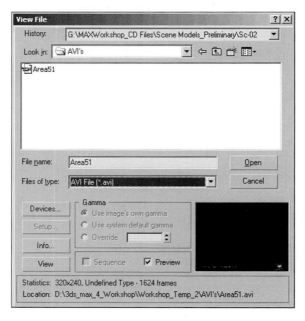

Figure 1.33   Area 51 is the Avi-format movie you will be creating in this Workshop.

Although both ways of viewing files are useful, you might find yourself using View File when you just want to look up a single image and Asset Manager to organize and use multiple images interactively in your scene.

Before moving on to Chapter 2, there is one final piece of the interface you need to know how to access: the User Reference files.

3ds Max 4 Help Functions

The Help functions that are located under Help on the main Menu Bar are good examples of how max's features are designed to help you start creating right away. Click Help in the Menu Bar or press Alt+H to access the menu.

User Reference

The max User Reference is a powerful tool that uses Microsoft Internet Explorer as its functional engine. The User Reference and other help files were installed on your system when you installed max. Accessing the User Reference is a simple process. Press F1 or click Help in the main Menu Bar and select User Reference to open the window shown in Figure 1.35.

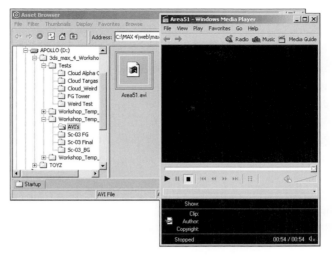

Figure 1.34   Like View File, the Asset Browser utility uses a preview window to display the contents of folders containing images and movies. You can also use Asset Manager to open word-processing files, HTML documents, and so on.

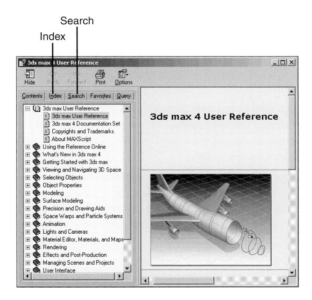

Figure 1.35   Max User Reference files duplicate the entire contents of the max manuals that came with your software. This is an indispensable tool for your study of max 4.

You can use the Index and the Search sections of the User Reference to type in keywords for topics you want to know about. When you're finished exploring the User Reference, close the window and look at the rest of the Help menu selections.

As you can see, there are several additional forms of help available:

- **MAXScript Reference**—Provides information about the built-in scripting language for 3ds max. MAXScript provides 3ds max users with the ability to program and use script control for the functions and tools found in max.

- **Tutorials**—Provides you with some valuable tutorials to speed up your learning process.

- **Additional Help**—Allows you to access the help files that might have come with the commercial plug-ins installed on your system.

- **Connect to Support and Information**—If you're online, clicking this menu selection connects you directly to the discreet 3ds max 4 technical support Web site. This is a powerful way to stay up-to-date on all things relating to 3ds max 4 and its companion products.

- **Plug-in Information**—Clicking this menu selection when you're online connects you directly to www.maxusers.com, presented by Digimation, which is the premiere producer of amazing plug-ins for all max products.

Next Steps

In the subsequent chapters of this book, this section will contain some ideas for those of you wanting to try additional work above and beyond that shown in the chapter. The format for the "Next Steps" section will be to show you imagery that embodies the natural next step of the processes you just completed and to provide you with some ready-made files when appropriate.

The intention of this is to spark your imagination and encourage you to experiment. References to online resources containing related tutorials and to other books and publications that will further your development will also be presented. My hope is that you will be inspired and empowered into your own creative process.

The next step for you regarding this chapter is to begin reading your max 4 reference manuals. *3ds max 4 Workshop* is a great book to help you learn the basics of max in the context of a holistic project. But it isn't a substitute for the minute detail to be found in the reference manuals and the tutorials that came with the max 4 software.

In addition to reading your manuals, now is the time to read Appendix C, "What's on the CD-ROM." This appendix contains important information about how to set up the file structure for this Workshop and shows you where to find all the premade files you'll need along the way.

Coming up is Chapter 2, "Virtual Viz: The Art of Pre-Production for Digital Content Creation." The abbreviation "Viz" is short for visualization. *Viz* is an industrial design term that refers to the process of creating images or artifacts that give form and substance to ideas. If you've ever wondered how to get what you see in your head out into the fresh air, Chapter 2 will help. Move on and sharpen your pencils.

PRE-PRODUCTION

PROCESS / STORY

0-7857-2546-0

Virtual Viz: The Art of Pre-Production for Digital Content Creation

"No great discovery was ever made without a bold guess."
- Sir Isaac Newton (1643-1727)

"Once upon a time..." are powerful words, shared in our collective consciousness, that prepare us for a journey into the realm of imagination. Traditional storytellers use words to invoke the images you see in your mind when you hear or read their stories. If you want to be an artist creating digital content, you must also be a storyteller. The images in your imagination will become the visual vocabulary you'll use to tell the stories you have inside you.

This chapter is a story about *visual language* and the pre-production process. Part of learning this process is to understand the concepts behind how stories, myths, and legends are created and communicated. In many ways, telling effective visual stories is the purpose of everything you will create as a max artist.

Introduction to the DCC Pre-Production Process

Digital content creation (DCC) begins in the collective imagination of the creative team. The process ends in the imaginations of your intended audience. The principle goal of the production process is communication: Did the audience get the story you were trying to tell? The answer to this question isn't dependent on your creative abilities alone. It also depends on how effectively your pre-production process is used to guide the creation of the elements needed to tell your story.

Figure 2.1 outlines the simplified production process followed by most studios. Every studio is different, however, and this process will vary in some degree based on the studio's particular expertise and the unique requirements of its work.

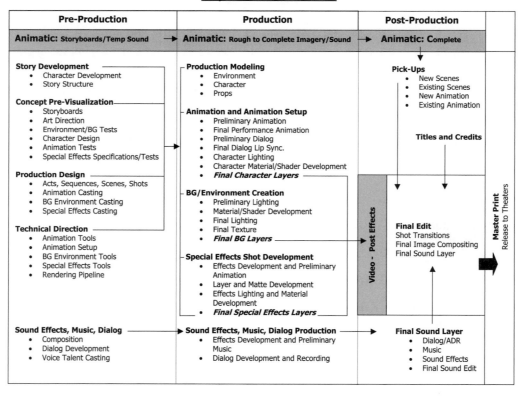

Figure 2.1   The basic DCC production process is divided into three sets of interrelated tasks. The tasks in each set are designed to establish a foundation for the next tasks in the process.

Production Structure

Production is the process of turning all pre-production story development and art direction into real, usable visual assets. The structure of a feature film is usually organized into four distinct content groups: acts, sequences, scenes, and shots. Movies have three acts comprised of 15–25 sequences per act with 10–50 scenes in each sequence. Those scenes might be further divided into hundreds of individual shots.

Using this structure, individual shots in the organizational structure of an entire production would be referred to like this: Act 3_Seq020, SC045_SHOT101_End Titles. This organizational convention and variations of it are the standard in most studios. Without this, it would be impossible to stay organized and keep track of all that has to be done.

Your work in this chapter will focus on the pre-production process, the first part of which is to develop the story you'll tell to your audience.

Myths and Legends

There are only a few prototypical stories or great universal legends that are continually retold in each new age. Considering this idea, you might be able to see how *Titanic* relates to *Romeo and Juliet*; or the similarities between the epic story *Ulysses* and the film *Gladiator*.

One of the greatest storytellers of our time is filmmaker George Lucas. Author Joseph Campbell, considered to be the authority on the power of archetypal myth in our time, was a mentor to George Lucas. Lucas created the stories told in the *Star Wars* double trilogy using the structure of the Hero's Journey, a legend that reveals the struggle and triumph of the human experience.

In an article titled "Of Myth and Men," in the April 29, 1999, issue of *Time* magazine, author Bill Moyers interviewed George Lucas about his approach to storytelling in movies. Here are some excerpts taken from that article, with some comments added:

> *Moyers:* "Joseph Campbell once said all the great myths, the ancient stories have to be regenerated in every generation. He said that's what you are doing with *Star Wars*. You are taking these old stories and putting them into the most modern of idioms, the cinema. Are you conscious of doing that? Or are you just setting out to make a good action-movie adventure?"

> *Lucas:* "With *Star Wars* I consciously set about to re-create myths and classic mythological motifs. I wanted to use those motifs to deal with issues today. The more research I did, the more I realized that the issues are the same ones that existed 3,000 years ago. That we haven't come very far emotionally."

The first step in developing your storytelling ability is to research and understand the great stories that already exist. George Lucas refers to the research that he made to gather information for his work. This research, his own life path, and keen observation of the human condition, brought him to an understanding of the human experience, which is the core component of communication with your audience. In the next excerpt from the interview, Lucas uses the words *motif* and *localization*, two important concepts in storytelling:

Moyers: "You're creating a new myth?"

Lucas: "I'm telling an old myth in a new way. Each society takes that myth and retells it in a different way, which relates to the particular environment they live in. The motif is the same. It's just that it gets localized. As it turns out, I'm localizing it for the planet. I guess I'm localizing it for the end of the millennium more than I am for any particular place."

Motif, in this context, refers to the universal experiences commonly shared by all people in a society. Motifs are also called *themes*, which include fundamental experiences such as death, betrayal, love, good, evil, and so forth. We all have experienced our own versions of those motifs personally, nationally, and sometimes globally. England's survival during World War II is a classic localized example of the global motifs of conflict and triumph.

Stories must contain motifs that your audience can relate to in a personal or localized way. They must be able to see themselves in the story and characters you create. In the next excerpt, Bill Moyers remarks how the *Star Wars* motif has demanded his attention. This is the power of a mythical story to worm its way into the lives of generations of individuals and the consciousness of an entire world:

Moyers: "It's certainly true that *Star Wars* was seen by a lot of adults, yours truly included. Even if I hadn't wanted to pay attention, I realized that I had to take it seriously because my kids were taking it seriously. And now my grandkids take it seriously."

Lucas: "Well, it's because I try to make it believable in its own fantastic way. And I'm dealing with core issues that were valid 3,000 years ago and are still valid today, even though they're not in fashion."

Making a story *"believable in its own fantastic way"* is your core task as a visual artist and storyteller. You must create imagery that has the power to tap into the hearts and minds of your audience. The next excerpt from the interview deals with the power of film and the many different artistic components that go into the film production process:

Moyers: "How do you explain the power of film to move us?"

Lucas: "It takes all aspects of other art forms—painting, music, literature, theater—and puts them into one art form. It's a combination of all these, and it works on all the senses. For that reason it's very alluring, kind of a dreamlike experience. You sit in a dark room and have this other world come at you in a very realistic way."

When all the components of a production—the sound, music, special effects, editing, visual content, and so on—are created in support of the story to be told, the audience becomes so enraptured that they leave the ordinary world behind them. This is the power of the work you will do as a max artist.

Suspension of Disbelief

Your ability to create believable reality will result in a psychological phenomenon called *suspension of disbelief*. When an audience is totally captivated by the film-maker's magic, they willingly choose to believe that what they are seeing is real—they suspend their disbelief. To achieve the suspension of disbelief in your audience, you must not only understand the visual reality of what they will be looking at, you must draw them into the story as if they were living it themselves.

The Structure of a Great Story: The Hero's Journey

The great universal legend that George Lucas has used in his work is referred to as "The Hero's Journey." When you read the structure outlined below, think about Luke Skywalker's adventures in the first three *Star Wars* movies. The heroes' journey and variations of it can be found in *Star Wars* and many other movies you have seen and admired:

- **The Ordinary World**—The hero is an ordinary person, living in the midst of his ordinary world.

- **The Call to Adventure**—The hero receives the call to go on the adventure.

- **The Hero Refuses to Go**—At first the hero refuses to go, or is reluctant to heed the call; held back by fear or external forces.

- **A Mentor Appears**—The hero is aided by a mentor who gives him or her a token of power and helps the hero to respond to the call.

- **The Hero Responds to the Call**—The hero, with the mentor's help, takes the first step, passes beyond the point of no return, and enters the adventure.

- **The Hero Descends into the Non-Ordinary World**—The hero and the mentor move deeper into the adventure, leaving the ordinary world behind. This is also called the *Descent*, in which they are tested and find themselves in the midst of enemies and allies.

- **The Ordeal**—The hero is taken deeper into the darkest recesses of the adventure to face alone the thing he most fears. The hero endures an ordeal of life-threatening proportions. Part of the hero is killed so that another part can live.

- **Transformation**—The hero is transformed by the ordeal, takes possession of the reward, and begins the return out of the darkness. The hero is pursued by his enemies back to the ordinary world.

- **The Gift**—The hero returns to ordinary life, endowed with a boon or a gift of power to benefit the Ordinary World.

Note

The structure outlined in the Hero's Journey can be seen in the plots of most adventure stories. If you are interested in reading more about this classic story structure and how it can empower your work as an artist and storyteller, read the following books: *Hero with a Thousand Faces* by Joseph Campbell and *The Writer's Journey: Mythic Structure for Writers* by Christopher Vogler.

Every culture and time in history produces its own versions of the Hero's Journey. *Star Wars* is the latest of a long line of myths that continue to affect the three distinct generations that will grow up knowing the legends of Luke Skywalker. When Obi-Wan Kenobi taught Luke to "Listen to your Feelings" and "Use the Force" he brought the ancient wisdom of the Jedi into our cultural consciousness. There is a Jedi Knight, or perhaps even a Darth Vader, in every one of us that have enjoyed the movie and its sequels.

The question is, how do myths, like *Star Wars* or the Hero's Journey, become universal? The answer can be found in some current thinking about how ideas and concepts are shared locally and globally.

Memes: Mental Viruses

"*Meme* is a contagious information pattern that replicates by parasitically infecting human minds and altering their behavior, causing them to propagate the pattern. (Term coined by Richard Dawkins, by analogy with "gene".) Individual slogans, catchphrases, melodies, icons, inventions, and fashions are typical memes. An idea or information pattern is not a meme until it causes someone to replicate it, to repeat it to someone else. All transmitted knowledge is memetic. (Wheelis, quoted in Hofstadter.) (See meme-complex)." from the Principia Cybernetica Web.

The motifs described in the previous section are related to a concept called *memes* (pronounced "meem"). The term memes was created by Richard Dawkins, who defines them as intellectual or mental viruses that infect humanity with ideas, mental models, perceptions, experiences, principles, stories, cultural myths, and shared truths. Transmitted through books, films, music, art, and education, memes act much like biological viruses in how they are propagated.

It is through memes that children learn the concepts of danger, hot, ball, red, and the fundamentals of language such as the alphabet and so on. Quotations, such as the ones at the head of this chapter, are memes; if you share that quote with someone, you are spreading an intellectual virus courtesy of Sir Isaac Newton.

When you use your skills to create stories and images that tap into the minds of your intended audience, you are accessing the power of memes. As a max artist, the memes you employ are visual or iconic in nature and have the power to access the embedded imagery that exists in the subconscious mind. In a final excerpt from the Moyers/Lucas interview, the power of visual memes (or motifs as they call it) is discussed:

Moyers: "The mesmerizing figure in the *Phantom Menace* to me is Darth Maul. When I saw him I thought of Lucifer in *Paradise Lost* or the devil in *Dante's Inferno*. He's the Evil Other—but with powerful human traits."

Lucas: "Yes, I was trying to find somebody who could compete with Darth Vader, who is now one of the most famous evil characters. So we went back into representations of evil. Not only the Christian, but also Hindu and other religious icons, as well as the monsters in Greek mythology."

Moyers: "What did you find in all these representations?"

Lucas: "A lot of evil characters have horns." [Laughs]

Moyers: "And does your use of red suggest the flames of hell?"

Lucas: "Yes. It's a motif that I've been using with the Emperor and the Emperor's Minions. I mean, red is an aggressive color. Evil is aggressive."

Moyers: "Is Darth Maul just a composite of what you found in your research, or are we seeing something from your own imagination and experience?"

Lucas: "If you're trying to build an icon of evil, you have to go down into the subconscious of the human race over a period of time and pull out the images that equate to the emotion you are trying to project."

The same concept holds true if you are trying to *"build an icon"* of good, tragedy, comedy, and so forth. Whether you are telling an epic story of adventure, a love story, or a comedic tale of bumbling stooges, you must use the power of memes to tap into the subconscious and evoke emotion.

This short exposé of one kind of story structure will not make you a master storyteller. It's meant to raise your awareness about some fundamental factors you'll want to consider in your work as a max artist.

Your storytelling education will be a lifelong pursuit if you choose to follow that hero's journey. You might never have guessed that creating digital imagery and storytelling was such a psychological endeavor. It is! And to quote a famous meme: "A picture is worth a thousand words."

Introduction to Pre-Visualization

Pre-visualization (Pre-Viz) is the process of making the story you see in your imagination into a preliminary form. In this section, you'll learn about two fundamental ways to quickly visualize the end vision you want to achieve. The first way is by creating concept sketches and storyboards. The second way is by creating a rough version of your film called an animatic.

Before storyboarding begins, conceptual designs of the imagery in the scenes of your movie must be created.

Concept Sketches

During the pre-viz process, the artists responsible for creating the overall visual language of a production are hard at work. They create the *look* or *style* of a production, which is derived from a variety of sources. Elements of visual language come from the artist's imagination and through inspiration from nature, music, novels, the work of other artists, architecture, the classic productions of stage and screen, and so on.

The intention of all pre-production art is to establish a visual language that will support the story being told. Figure 2.2 shows an example of preliminary sketches created to explore the visual language of Tesla machines and VandeGraaff generators.

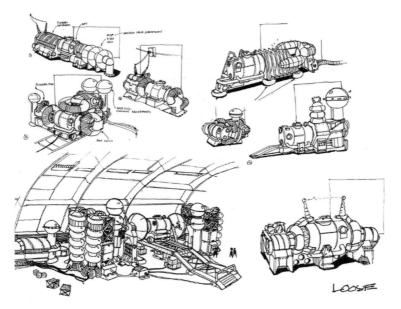

Figure 2.2   Preliminary sketches are created to establish the design and detail of the sets and props in your production.

Drawing and Digital Content Creation

You must be able to draw to be a max artist. Drawing trains you to be aware of proportion, positive and negative space, surface development, value contrast, and so on. The reality is that if you can't draw, an artist who can will be feeding you imagery to create.

The ability to pre-visualize design and animation ideas via diagrams, scribbles, clay sculpture, renderings, and so forth is absolutely essential. Without it, an artist will wander in search of a place to start. Pre-Viz also creates a common language that unites you as the artist with your art director, producer, and client. For this reason alone, these important people want to work with max artists who can produce sketches. To improve your sketching skills, get a sketchbook and draw every day.

The visual language for Area51.avi is meant to be reminiscent of an older, classical style of science fiction. Some of the visual memes are meant to evoke images of a mad scientist's lab, nuclear power plants, and UFOs. The stylistic forms used to create the imagery have been seen before in the spheres of VandeGraaff generators, the torus shapes of Tesla coils, the arcs of electricity from Frankenstein's laboratory, reactor cooling towers, and so forth.

Figure 2.3 shows a concept sketch, which includes story notes. This is an invaluable part of developing the visual language of the story. When you create this kind of sketch, you are creating elements of the *back-story*.

Virtual Viz: The Art of Pre-Production for
Digital Content Creation

Figure 2.3   When you create your concept sketches, include your written thoughts about
how the story and the sketch relate to each other. This is a valuable tool used to
communicate your ideas to the other members of your production team.
Concept Sketch by Duane Loose © 2001, Creative Capers Entertainment, Inc.

3ds max 4

Back-Story: Creating an Alternate Universe

The *back-story* is a fictional and sometimes factual history of the alternate universe you are creating in your story. It's used to develop the rules and logic of the world you're revealing to the audience. The back-story establishes the environment and physical nature of the world and its inhabitants and reveals the nature of their relationships and interactions. Even though the audience might never read the back-story, it will exist in everything they see on the screen. Sometimes the back-story, the inspirational art, storyboards, and pre-production art are called the Story Bible or Character Bible. It's the book that contains the entire world you are trying to create.

In Figure 2.4, you'll see a sketch produced as a guide to create the digital image seen next to it. This is a good example of how a detailed drawing can be translated into an image created in max.

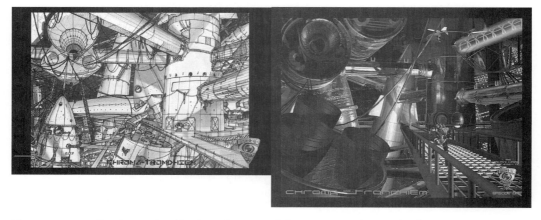

Figure 2.4   Good pre-visualization of your work in max saves time and enhances your creative process. Image from Intergalactic Bounty Hunter, © 2001, Creative Capers Entertainment, Inc.

Storyboards

Storyboards are created to map out every scene sequence and shot in a production. In many studios there are storyboard artists who specialize in pre-production visualization. They are excellent at producing concept sketches and other art to guide you as you create your shots.

Storyboard Terms and Definitions

In Figure 2.5, you can see one of the storyboards created for Area51.avi. You'll notice some interesting hieroglyphics in the storyboard. These diagrams, symbols, and words—which outline camera moves, point of view, and shot transitions—are used by production artists to create the scene.

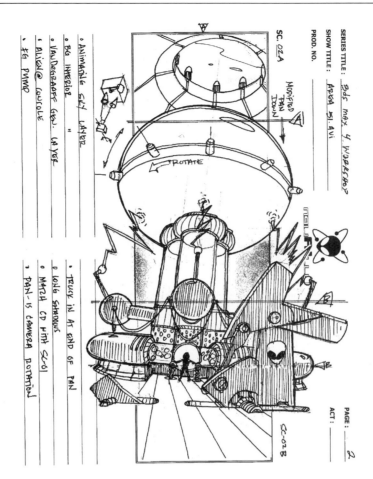

Figure 2.5 Studios will use storyboards of every scene, sequence, and shot to organize their production work. Effective and complete storyboards have been proven to be a necessary aid to keep your work on time and on budget.

The elements in each shot that an animator needs to include must be clearly communicated. These can include atmosphere and lighting notes, camera move instructions, special effects and sound effects direction, animation notes, dialog and voice-over narration, and storyline notes.

After you understand all the conventions, developing a storyboard format that includes these elements is easier than it looks. Figure 2.6 shows the anatomy of a storyboard, including the hieroglyphics you'll need to learn to read and understand it.

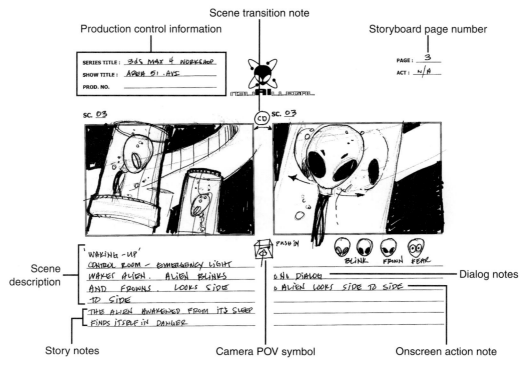

Figure 2.6 The storyboard terminology for feature animation, feature films, and television productions differ in some minor ways.

Even though the storyboard terms used by different studios for TV and film production can differ slightly, their definitions are pretty much the same:

- **Production Control Information**—Tells you which act, sequence, scene, and shot the storyboard is referring to. Television storyboards will also include the episode number and title.

- **Storyboard Page Number**—Helps you keep your storyboards in order, which is very important.

- **Onscreen Action Note**—Provides information about character action and movement in and out of the shot.

- **Scene Description**—Usually describes the scene's most important action, sound effects, and so on.

- **Scene Transition Note**—Indicates the type of transition between scenes, such as cuts, cross dissolves, fade to black, fade in and out, and so forth.

- **Camera POV Instructions**—Control changes in the camera's POV (point of view) from scene to scene.

- **Camera Move Instructions**—Include the basics: Zoom In, Zoom Out, and Pan Left/Right. Zoom In/Out is also referred to as Push (in) and Pull (out), or Dolly In/Out. Panning is a lateral movement and is also referred to as Truck Left or Right.

- **Dialog Notes**—Used to highlight the dialog of the scene. These notes can also include narration, which might be called Voice Over Narration or VO.

- **Story Notes**—Highlights the plot point of the scene.

Using these conventions in your storyboards creates a kind of visual shorthand. Storyboards are not meant to show each and every minute detail of a shot; they are used to communicate the most important details that must be included in the sets and character animation you'll create in max.

Camera POV

Most of the storyboard elements described previously will be readily understood. But the camera POV diagram and the Camera Move instructions might need a more detailed explanation.

Moving or rotating the camera POV can provide a more interesting alternative to simple cuts or cross dissolve transitions between scenes. Figure 2.7 will help you understand how the different elements in the camera POV diagram communicate the intended camera POV movement.

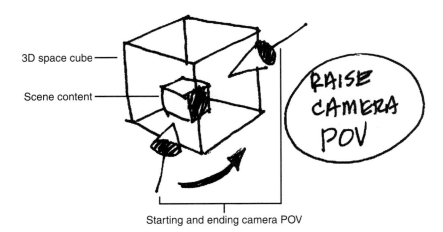

Figure 2.7 Using the camera POV information in the storyboard as a guide for your camera movement and animation in max will help you create effective and seamless shot transitions.

Note

Camera movement created by experienced professionals is a powerful storytelling tool. When you begin to animate your camera movements in max, study the work of professional animators and cinematographers and use their techniques to guide your work. The best examples of a flying camera animation I've seen are in the opening sequences of *Men In Black* and *Fight Club*.

The camera movement in the opening of *Men In Black* is created to show the POV of a bug flying in the desert at night. This is an appropriate use of an active animated camera POV. The opening sequence in *Fight Club* is an amazing journey from the microscopic cellular level of the human body. In both movies, there is an underlying reason for the use of a flying camera. The animators didn't create the animation just because they could; it was done because that is what was required to entertain and tell the story.

Camera POV diagram elements include the following:

- **3d Space Cube**—A visual reference of the volume of the content of the shot seen by the camera.
- **Scene Content**—Shows you what is in each camera view at the beginning and end of the camera move.
- **Starting and Ending Camera POV**—Indicated by the little cone icons and the direction of the arrow describing the camera rotation.
- **Transition Note**—Shows the direction of the camera POV move.

After you begin to use storyboard shorthand in your work, it will become second nature to you. I've included a blank storyboard format on the CD for you to use as you develop your storyboard skills. It's titled `Storyboard.doc` and can be found in `MAXWorkshop\Help_Files\Chapter_2`. This document also includes the diagrams for the visual shorthand discussed in this part of the chapter.

Camera Movement

The way you move your camera in your scenes can either confuse the audience or focus their attention on the story point of the scene. Hyperactive camera movement or fast jump cuts between scenes creates a roller coaster ride for your audience. *Mission Impossible 2*, directed by John Wu, is a great example of how camera movement can be used to pull an audience into the intense action on the screen, thrilling them in the process. This kind of fast, active camerawork is a trademark of Wu's cinematic style and he is a master of it.

Camera movements are built on a foundation of two basic moves: zoom and pan. Figure 2.8 shows how zoom in and out are indicated in a storyboard.

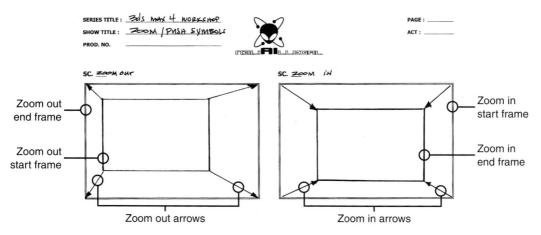

Zoom out end frame

Zoom out start frame

Zoom out arrows

Zoom in start frame

Zoom in end frame

Zoom in arrows

Figure 2.8   The arrows in the zoom in/out diagrams indicate the direction of the camera movement in or out of the scene, and they always connect the start and end frame of the zoom. Also notice that the height and width of the start and end frames are always the same format proportion.

Figure 2.9 shows how pan or lateral camera movement from one shot to another is diagrammed in a storyboard. The diagram for panning left or right begins with a vertical line in the first scene, indicating the center of the starting POV. An arrow above the scene shows the direction of movement. The pan ends at the vertical line in the second scene, also indicating the center of the POV at the end of the pan.

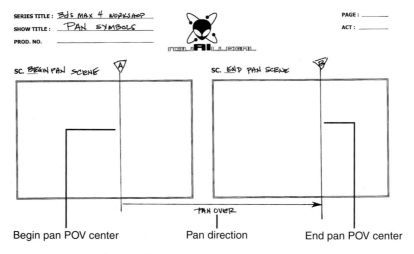

Begin pan POV center

Pan direction

End pan POV center

Figure 2.9   Panning in a shot establishes the dimensions of a more believable world; it shows that there is something beyond the borders of the screen.

Where Do Camera Movement Terms Come From?

Zoom in/out is also referred to as push in and pull out. These are traditional cinematography terms that refer to the actual act of a cameraman pushing a camera in closer to a scene subject or pulling the camera out or back away from a tight shot to reveal more of the scene. Other cinematography terms for the other camera movements used in max are truck, dolly, roll, and orbit.

There are other types of camera moves that you will learn about as you continue your camera-work in max. Beyond the basics are compound moves that combine zooms and pans with other vertical or flying shots. There is also a camera move called a *crane* shot, created by a daring cinematographer who got the bright idea to put the camera on a crane and shoot the scene as the crane either raised or lowered the POV. The crane shot is kind of a vertical pan.

Becoming a successful max artist requires that you learn and incorporate the fundamental principles of cinematography into your work. Max gives you the tools to create great imagery but cannot teach you how to use them effectively. To learn this, you must make the effort to study the works of the masters and understand some basics about scene composition.

Master and Apprentice

There is no substitute for learning from the work of others. Learning from the masters requires analytical research and a deliberate desire to copy and emulate their work. In times past, an apprentice painter would spend countless hours copying the works of the masters, learning the secrets of their techniques by endlessly doing what they did.

To learn the secrets of the masters, you must study the results of their efforts. A library of their work consisting of their books, magazine articles, movies, and so on creates an awareness of visual language and opens up the possibility of experimenting with your own personal visual style. Create a library of your artistic heroes and fill your office walls with their work. Become a virtual apprentice.

Introduction to Scene Composition—Elements and Principles

Scene composition is the invisible structure that organizes your shot elements into the imagery needed to tell your story. Composition can be judged by how it serves that end goal and if it creates the suspension of disbelief. Your audience might not be able to articulate the flaws of a composition in artistic or design terms; they just know they didn't enjoy the show or couldn't follow the story.

> **Composition**
>
> A max artist's work is to give form to feeling, and it is the scene composition that provides the skeleton of the form. If this basic structure is flawed, your imagery— no matter how beautiful—will not have the impact it could have had in a well-designed composition.
>
> The goal of the composition is to create the illusion of 3D space to draw your audience into the magical universe you have created.

The scenes in the short movie Area51.avi are divided into *shot elements* that are combined to create the whole scene. If you were to create all these elements in one single max file, it would create a huge unwieldy file. Eventually it would be impossible to work in the scene and the rendering of each individual frame would take too long.

To remedy this, you will divide the shot elements into individual layers. This will give you more artistic freedom and control over your final imagery than creating your images from one single max file that includes all the effects and animation.

Layer Division and Structure

All the elements of an individual shot are grouped by where they sit in the depth planes or *layers* of the image. In a basic composition, there are three depth-plane layers: foreground, middleground, and background. You'll be creating these layers one by one as you work through the Workshops in this book.

With minor variations, the digital content of the scenes produced in most studios will be divided in a similar fashion. These depth planes are divided further into individual images. When those images are combined, or *composited*, the result is a complete scene such as the ones in our Workshop.

The titles, credits, establishing shot, and interior of the *Area 51* labs in Area51.avi will be created from individually rendered sets of still images. Those images will be composited to form the complete movie. Using discrete layers creates two notable advantages:

- The layer structure gives you the freedom to isolate and modify individual elements of a scene without impacting the animation or lighting of the surrounding elements.

- The layer structure allows cooperative team workflow and reduces the risk of producing mistakes in the final imagery. This means that if something is wrong with an image, individual layers can be revised and re-rendered in a fraction of the time it would take to do the same with nonlayered imagery.

The first step in understanding how to divide a composition into layers is to understand how the background, middleground, and foreground image layers work together to support the visual story you are trying to tell.

To create believable imagery, you must create the illusion that the scene is actually a smaller visible part of a far larger world. The first step in doing this is to divide the composition into three layers or image planes. The following images are from a short test movie created using the concepts and techniques from *3D Studio MAX 3.0 Workshop* and the shot elements created in this book. The movie can be found on the CD in `MAXWorkshop\Help_Files\Chapter_2\` `Area51_Test.avi` (see Figure 2.10).

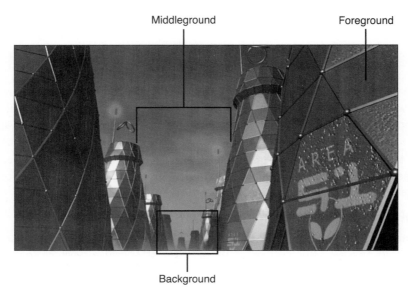

Figure 2.10   Each image layer has its own overlapping structure. Depth and interest are created in the composition by carefully placing each element in the shot.

The image plane closest to your point of view is the *foreground*, or *FG*. In the foreground of this shot are the cooling towers closest to the camera POV. These towers have been rendered separately from the all the other elements in the shot (see Figure 2.11).

The plane that is farthest away from you is the *background*, or *BG*. The BG in this shot is the sky and the animating cloud plane (see Figure 2.12).

The elements between the FG and BG are in the *middleground*, or *MG*, which include the remaining cooling towers, the lights and doodads on top of the towers, and the smoke layer. The two remaining planes, the ground and mist planes, are elements that appear in all three depth image planes and they are composited separately as well.

Organizing your shot elements into an effective composition is accomplished by applying basic artistic principles to your work. These principles might seem simple but they are powerful when used effectively and the quality of your imagery will suffer if they are not employed. Lesson 4 in *3D Studio MAX 3.0 Workshop* is devoted to composition. Here's a brief review of the main points from that lesson.

Figure 2.11   The foreground elements were rendered separately using a specialized material developed for that purpose. This material is called the Matte/Shadow material, which you'll learn how to use in Chapter 9.

Animating cloud layer

Gradient BG Sky Map

Figure 2.12   The animating cloud layer is created by applying an animated texture to the surface of a flat plane, which you'll learn how to do in Chapter 4.

Basic Composition Concepts

There are four basic concepts that should be considered in every composition:

- **Point of View (POV)**—Determines the viewing position of the audience.
- **Focal Point**—Used to direct the viewers' eyes to the important storytelling parts of the composition. Focal points are created by the application of the other basic compositional principles.

Virtual Viz: The Art of Pre-Production for Digital Content Creation

- **Paths of Motion**—Shot elements in your scene create paths of motion in and through the shot. These paths are used to attract and hold the attention of the viewer.

- **The Illusion of Depth**—Must be created if you want to draw your audience into the world of the story you are creating.

POV

The first thing you need to consider in creating your composition is the audience's point of view in the scene. The placement of the camera establishes the point of view. Where you place the audience's POV is an important decision because it affects their perception of the world they are viewing.

A low-angle POV (as from a child's perspective) can be used to exaggerate size, such as that of an approaching monster, thus creating tension and dread. A bird's-eye POV can be used to create the illusion of height and vertigo (see Figure 2.13).

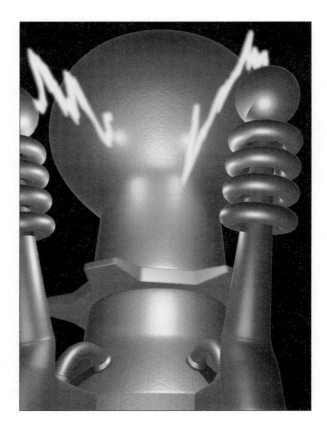

Worm's-Eye POV

Figure 2.13 Using an extreme POV can be very effective when you want to create drama and emphasize relative size and height.

Focal Point

When the layers of a composition are well organized, the eyes of the viewers will be directed to the storytelling parts of the scene called *focal points*. The purpose of a focal point is to tell the point of the story by inviting the viewers to visually enter into the world and stay long enough for the point to be made.

The creative challenge in the visual imagery for any individual act, scene, sequence, or shot is to overcome the attention deficiency of your audience. You have about three seconds to convince the viewers' subconscious to watch what you have put before them. After that you've got another 7 to 10 seconds to tell the core of the story visually. If you get past those first two perceptive thresholds, you will have the attention of the audience. Figure 2.14 shows how the composition of a scene uses contrast and the placement of shot elements to lead the eye to a focal point.

Figure 2.14   Contrast between the light and dark areas of this image draw the eye into the forest and focus it on the figure in the clearing.

Paths of Motion

In the shot you will be creating in the Workshop sections of this book, there will be animated objects and effects. The path of that animation creates a movement vector or a line that defines the direction and energy of an object's motion in space. Paths of motion created when a shot element moves within the scene direct the audience's attention to specific places in the scene (see Figure 2.15).

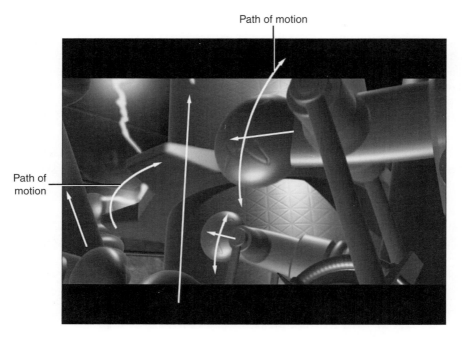

Path of motion

Path of motion

Figure 2.15   Paths of motion are created by the placement, shape, and animation of an object within the composition of a scene.

"It Looks Like It's Going 150mph Sitting Still!"

A car's design or styling will create the visual or implied image of speed. Shot elements have similar vectors that can also create visual or implied motion. The balance between these competing motion vectors is not easy to achieve and might result in visual confusion or noise.

The Illusion of Depth

The illusion of depth doesn't happen just because max is a 3D program. It is created by the deliberate use of overlap, value and color contrast, and atmospheric perspective. The color plates in the color section of this book are good examples of the illusion of depth. As you read the following descriptions, look at the images and observe how these important concepts were put into practice.

Overlap

Overlap is created when an element is placed in the composition so that it obscures parts of the elements behind it. There are two types of overlap that can be used in your scenes to create the illusion of depth in your composition:

- **Physical Overlap**—Used to give the viewer some visual cues to help them understand the relative depth position of the objects within a scene. An obvious place of overlap in *Area 51* is in Sc-01. The dark mass of the foreground tower is silhouetted against the sky.

- **Screen Boundary Overlap**—Created when an individual element (such as the foreground tower) intersects with the borders of the viewport (part of the tower is *off screen*). Psychologically, the viewers know that the rest of the tower that is off screen is still there even though they can't see it. The audience's subconscious completes a picture that includes more of the same things it has already seen.

> **Tip**
>
> Designing your composition so that elements go off screen in the depth layers of the shot creates the visual height, width, and depth you are looking for. This visual depth cue invites the audience to mentally accept that there is more of the off-screen world to explore.

> **Caution**
>
> Overlap is a powerful tool. However, when objects in a scene come close enough to touch each other without overlapping, a tangency in the image is formed. *Tangency* in a composition negates the illusion of depth, and the viewer becomes confused trying to resolve the relative visual depth of each object. If the camera is moving in the shot, tangency is less of a problem. In shots using a fixed camera or slow camera movements, visual tangency is something to watch out for and is easily fixed either by overlapping the adjacent elements or moving the tangent elements farther apart.

Contrast

Contrast—the light and dark values seen in a composition—is used by your eyes to determine an object's position and movement in 3D space. *Color temperature*—the relative warmth or coolness of a color—will also reinforce the illusion of depth. As a general rule of thumb, dark objects and cool colors appear to recede (move back) from the viewer, whereas light objects and warm colors appear to advance (come forward) toward the viewer.

Virtual Viz: The Art of Pre-Production for Digital Content Creation

There are two basic types of contrast used to reinforce the illusion of depth in a scene:

- **Value Contrast**—Created by the deliberate overlap of dark and light values in the shot. When using physical overlap to create depth, it is also important to consider the contrasting value of the elements. *Value* is a term used to describe the relative lightness or darkness of the color or lighting of an element. As you look at the scenes in Area51.avi, you can see the effort made to place dark against light in every depth plane from foreground to background. This iterative placement creates interest and allows the shot elements to be silhouetted against each other.

- **Color Temperature**—Describes whether an element's color is warm or cool in its relationship to the other objects around it. The interior lab scene in Area51.avi is lit up by the hot glow of the plasma generators. The objects in the shadows are lit with blue and textured in cool blue tones, as are the upper parts of the interior of the cooling tower. This helps to create visual depth. It also makes the composition more interesting to look at.

Atmospheric Perspective

Atmospheric perspective provides visual clues about how close or far an object is in relation to your point of view. The world is smothered in an ocean of air full of invisible particles of dirt, smoke, and water vapor. Light passing through the mass of air between mountains or buildings far away from my POV makes them appear hazy. The closer I am to them, the less distance the light has to travel to reach my eyes, so they appear sharper and less hazy. This visual cue tells my brain they are closer.

This is the idea behind atmospheric perspective. Fog or atmospheric haze gives the viewer information about depth in the environment around him (see Figure 2.16).

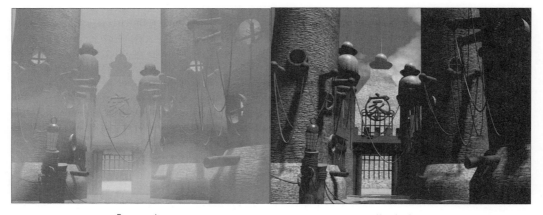

Foggy morning   Noontime haze

Figure 2.16   Both images show how atmospheric perspective can be used to create image depth. Fog creates it by causing your scene to disappear into the mist. Haze, as seen on a sunny day, makes objects far from your POV appear softer and less defined and reduces their color saturation.

It's important to remember that the ideas discussed are just a few of the concepts and ideas I've found to be valuable. There are many other approaches to creating digital content that are just as valid. I encourage you to search them out and study them. Put the ideas and principles that work for you into practice and synthesize your own personal approach to digital content creation in max.

Max Workshop: Creating the Animatic

An important part of the pre-visualization process is to create an animatic, also known as a Leica reel (pronounced *like-uh* as in "*like a* rolling stone"). To create the animatic, scanned images of the storyboards for Area51.avi were created. You'll use max's built-in compositing tool, Video Post, to combine the storyboards, timing each image to approximate the timing desired for the production short.

This process is a smaller example of the same process used in feature film pre-production. By adding temporary sound and dialog tracks to the animatic, directors and producers can see an entire production in rough form. This enables them to make inexpensive adjustments to point of view, scene length, and so on.

The coolest thing about an animatic is that it lives through the entire production process, constantly being updated with pre-production and production imagery and sound as it becomes available.

For example, an animatic seen in the middle of a production might still have storyboard images mixed in with rough wireframe animation and finished rendered shots. This creates an indispensable tool that enables the directors and producers to see the progress of an entire production from beginning to end. Before you get started, there are some important format issues to discuss.

Area 51 Animatic Format

An important decision to make at the beginning of your work concerns the format of the finished work you'll produce. The intended use of your imagery, whether it's for TV, feature film, or video, will dictate the format you'll use. Format parameters include the size and resolution of the imagery produced and the number of frames-per-second (FPS).

Area51.avi will use a 640×346 letterbox format, 1.85 image aspect ratio. Standard video format is 640×480. Using a letterbox format gives Area51.avi a filmic (or cinematic) look and also gives us room at the top and bottom of the screen to add in some finishing touches to your movie.

The standard frame rate for feature films is 24 frames per second. That means that every second of the movie is made up of 24 separate images. A 10-second shot has 240 frames/images, a 1-minute short has 1,440 frames, and so on. The total length of the *Area 51* animatic will be 48 seconds or 1,152 frames long and consists of the 7 scenes and the scene transitions described in the storyboard.

Making an Animatic Using Video Post

The first step to making the animatic is to open max. When it opens, select File, Save from the Menu Bar and save this new file as Area51_Animatic.max.

You'll be learning how to use Video Post as you work with it to complete this chapter's Workshop. Click Rendering, Video Post in the Menu Bar. This will open the Video Post dialog box shown in Figure 2.17. Then follow the steps in the next section to begin creating the *Area 51* animatic.

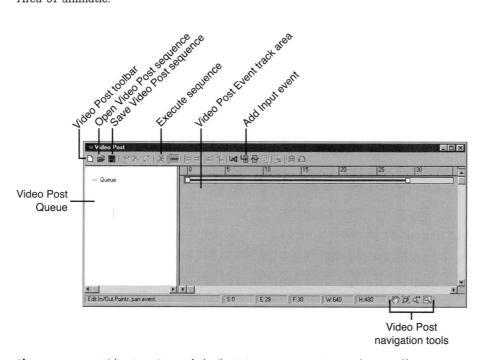

Figure 2.17 Video Post is max's built-in image compositor and post-effect creation tool. Post effect refers to any image special effects that are added to an image after rendering.

A general rule in animation is that frame 0 should be reserved for other purposes and not used in the frame count of your scenes. This will help you keep the start and end times of your animation and compositing consistent. For example, a 10-second scene at 24 FPS (frames per second) uses 240 frames. The first frame is frame 1; the final frame of the scene will be frame 240. If you used frame 0 as the first frame, the final frame of the 240 frame sequences would be frame 239. To avoid number confusion, use frame 1 as your starting frame number.

Adding Image Input Events

Image Input Events are the image files used by Video Post in its effect and composition processes. You'll create seven input events; one for each scene in the storyboard. Later on in this section, you'll make some adjustments to the format parameters of these images, which will create the letterbox format desired for this project:

1. Click Add Image Input Event 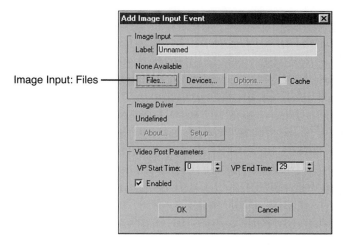 to open the dialog box shown in Figure 2.18, and click Files.

Image Input: Files ——

Figure 2.18 This is the main image input control dialog box, which Video Post uses to select and adjust the images and effects seen in the composited and post-effects imagery.

2. Use the Select Image File for Video Post Input dialog box to browse to and select the first storyboard image: MAXWorkshop\Help_Files\Chapter_2\ Sc-00.tif.

3. After you have selected the image, click Open to exit the browser and return to the Add Image Input Event dialog box, which now shows the path to the first storyboard image for the animatic. Change the VP Start Time to 1 and the VP End Time to 240 (10 seconds), as shown in Figure 2.19.

4. Click OK to exit this dialog box and add the image to the Video Post Queue, as shown in Figure 2.20.

5. Click Add Image Input Event again and select and open Workshop\Help_Files\Chapter_2\ Sc-01.tif. Don't change the VP Start Time or End Time at this point; you'll do that later.

6. From the same directory, select and open the rest of the storyboard file images, Sc-02–06.tif in turn. Don't change their VP length. When all seven of the storyboard images are loaded, your VP Queue should look like the one shown in Figure 2.21.

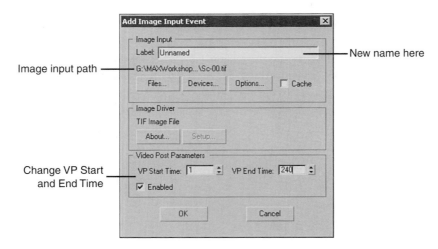

Figure 2.19   You can give your image input files different names by typing a new name in the Label text box if you want. If you don't, Video Post will use the saved name of the image file as the label for the image in the Video Post Queue.

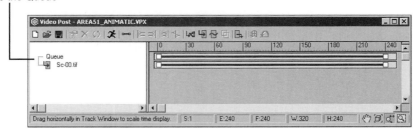

Figure 2.20   You'll use this process seven more times to add the rest of the storyboard scenes to the VP Queue.

7. Click the Zoom Extents icon to bring all the tracks into view (see Figure 2.22).

With all the storyboard images loaded, the next task is to put them into their proper sequence within the length of the movie.

Adjusting Image Input Event Tracks

The event tracks for the storyboard images in this queue are lined up beginning at frame 0 except for Sc-00, which is the only image set to its proper length. This is not correct and needs to be changed.

Seven storyboard
files in the Queue

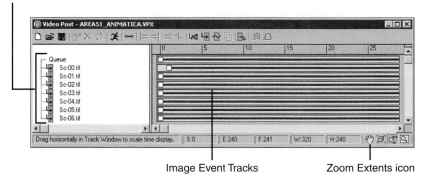

Image Event Tracks   Zoom Extents icon

Figure 2.21   Just like the compositing you'll do later in this book, the storyboard files have
to be in sequential order for this process to work.

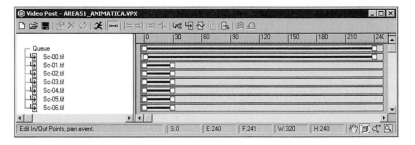

Figure 2.22   Using Zoom Extents will enable you to see the entire VP Queue length. This will
become even more useful when you begin moving these images into their
proper sequence.

Sc-00 is in the right place; it's the first image that will appear in the movie. Sc-06 needs to
appear at the end of the movie, ending at frame 1,152 (48 seconds). The length of the other six
event tracks must be adjusted and they will also need to be moved into their proper sequential
place in the movie.

Each scene must be long enough to accommodate the time needed to create a transition to the
next scene. This means that if you want a scene to be 4 seconds or 96 frames long, and you
want a 2-second or 48-frame transition into the next scene, the overall length of the scene must
be 6 seconds. The scene will overlap the next scene it's transitioning into by 48 frames.

Tip

If you make a mistake selecting or adding any image event or image filter event
into the Video Post Queue, just select the offending item and click the Delete
Current Event icon and begin again.

The following steps will show you how to put the scene events into their correct start and end positions within the VP Queue and prepare for the intra-scene transitions:

1. First, click Zoom Time 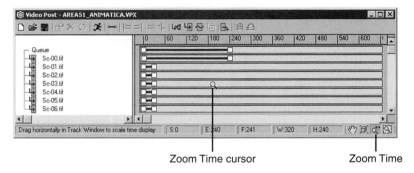 in the navigation tools. Drag in the window until you can see frame 600, as shown in Figure 2.23. When you're done zooming, right-click anywhere inside the VP dialog box to exit Zoom Time mode.

Zoom Time cursor   Zoom Time

Figure 2.23   You'll use this tool a lot as you move the event tracks for your animatic into their proper locations.

Because of the 2-second transition between Sc-00 and Sc-01, they must overlap for 48 frames in the track window. This means that Sc-01 starts at frame 192, 48 frames before Sc-00 ends at frame 240. The math looks like this: 240-48=192. Sc-01 starts at frame 192.

Sc-01 is an 8-second shot with a 2-second transition on its front end and a 2-second transition on its back end, for a total transition time of 4 seconds. This gives it a total length of 12 seconds or 288 frames. Sc-01's end frame is frame number 479.

2. Double-click Sc-01 in the VP Queue. When the Edit Input Image Event dialog box opens, change the VP Start Time to 192 and the VP End Time to 479. Click OK to close the dialog box. Your VP Queue and Track Area now show Sc-01 in its correct location (see Figure 2.24).

Tip

Use the frame information in the S, E, and F sections of the status bar at the bottom of the VP window to move your image tracks to precise frame locations. The number shown in the S box is the current *start* frame number of the selected image event. The E shows the *end* frame number and F is the total number of *frames* in the track.

3. Here's another way to move your image input file tracks using the numbers in the status bar display. Double-click Sc-02.tif and change its VP Start Time to 1 and its VP End Time to 336. This gives it a scene length of 336 frames (10 seconds)—240 frames plus 4 seconds (96 frames) of overlapping transition time split between Sc-01 at the beginning of the scene and Sc-03 at the end of the scene.

Sc-01 selected

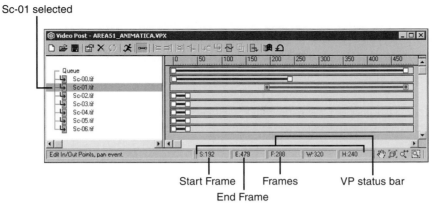

Start Frame | Frames | VP status bar
End Frame

Figure 2.24 Moving tracks around to precise locations can be difficult. Use Video Post's status window to help you know exactly where your selected image event track is in time.

4. Select Sc-02, click the middle of its track, and drag it to the right. Watch the number in the S box in the status bar and stop when it reaches 431 (see Figure 2.25).

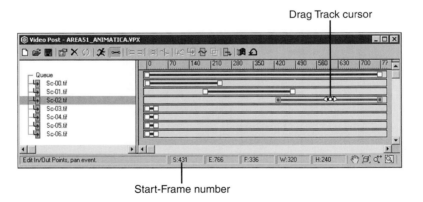

Drag Track cursor

Start-Frame number

Figure 2.25 Image event tracks can be dragged to precise locations within the Track Area using the VP status display.

Sometimes the Track Area is zoomed too far out for you to drag accurately to a specific number. When that happens, use the Zoom Region tool 🔍 to zoom in on the track you are adjusting. Then drag it again while watching the status bar to find the precise frame location you want. When you're finished, click Zoom Extents to bring the entire queue length back into view.

Tip

Virtual Viz: The Art of Pre-Production for Digital Content Creation

5. In this final step, you'll set the scene lengths and start frames for the remaining four image files. First, using the values in Table 2.1, change each scene VP End Time to the value shown. Then drag the images to their correct start frame location. Use the status display to help you move the track. The VP settings for Sc-00, Sc-01, and Sc-02 are also shown.

Table 2.1   Storyboard Images VP End Time and Start Frame

Image Input Filename	VP Start/End Time	Frame Count
Sc-00	1/240	240
Sc-01	193/480	288
Sc-02	433/768	336
Sc-03	721/912	192
Sc-04	913/960	48 (Abut w/Sc-03)
Sc-05	961/1056	96 (Abut w/Sc-04)
Sc-06	1057/1152	96 (Abut w/Sc-05)

Your VP dialog box should now have all the storyboard images in place and look like Figure 2.26.

Seven tracks in
correct sequential order

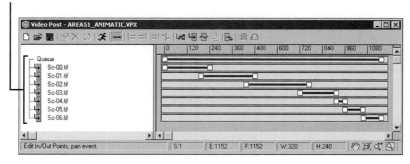

Figure 2.26   By now you might be seeing the value of keeping your work well organized. It's an anal-retentive imperative, especially when using track-based tools such as Video Post or Track view.

Where Did These Scene Length Numbers Come From?

There are a lot of ways to calculate how long a particular scene needs to be. In principle, the scene length is determined by the dialog, action, story that needs to be told, and energy needed in the scene. The scene lengths used for this animatic were calculated by counting one-one thousand, two-one thousand, and so on, while looking at the storyboards. It was a wild guess based on some experience and some experimentation. Remember that this is a rough approximation of the final movie, and the scene lengths and transitions will change as you complete the Workshop.

In the end, a mistake in this part of the process isn't a big deal because it's very easy to change. The place to experiment and take risks with timing is in the animatic. That's the sole reason for its existence. So, in answer to the question, "Where did the frame length numbers come from?" I refer you to the theme meme of this chapter: "No great discovery was ever made without a bold guess."

Adding the Cross Fade Transition Layer Event

There are three cross dissolve transitions in the *Area 51* animatic. They are between Sc-00 and Sc-01; Sc-01 and Sc-02; and Sc-02 and Sc-03. To create these transitions, you'll add Cross Fade Transition Image Layer events to the Video Post Queue. The reason you placed the storyboard images for these four scenes where you did was to create enough overlap of the image sequences to allow a smooth transitional fade between them. Here's how it's done:

1. Hold down the Shift key, select both Sc-00 and Sc-01 in the VP Queue, and click Add Image Layer Event ▣ . Select Cross Fade Transition from the list, name this transition `Sc-00 to Sc-01 XFade` and click OK to add it to the Queue, as shown in Figure 2.27.

2. Double-click Sc-00 to Sc-01 XFade in the VP Queue. Change its VP Start Time to `193`, and its VP End Time to `240`. This will align the transition with the beginning of Sc-01 and the end of Sc-00 (see Figure 2.28).

3. Hold down the Alt key and select Sc-00 to Sc-01 XFade Sc-02, as shown in Figure 2.29.

4. Click Add Image Layer Event ▣ and once again select Cross Fade Transition from the list, name this event `Sc-01 to Sc-02 XFade`, and add it to the Queue. Select this new transition and change its VP Start Time to `433` and its End Time to `480`, as shown in Figure 2.30. The transition is aligned correctly between Sc-01 and Sc-02.

Cross Fade Transition added to Queue   Select Cross Fade Transition here

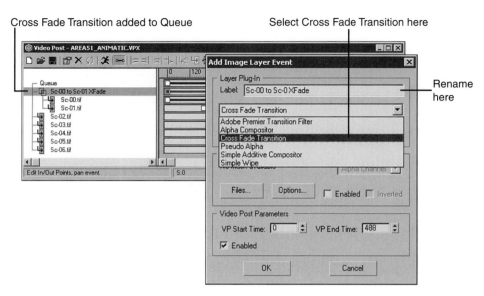

Rename
here

Figure 2.27   The transition is added to the Queue but its length and location are incorrect.
Adjusting both is the next step.

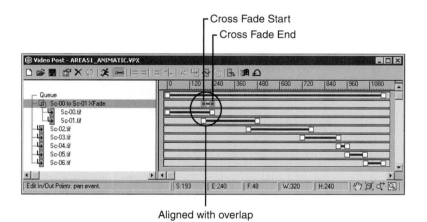

Aligned with overlap

Figure 2.28   Adding a Cross Fade Transition tells Video Post to fade one set of images out
while another fades in. The Start Time and End Time of the cross fade must correspond with the corresponding Start Times and End Times of the images you
are transitioning between.

Cross Fade and Sc-02 selected

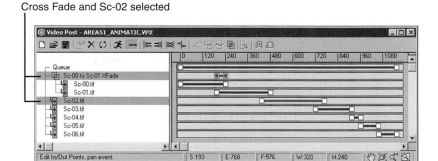

Figure 2.29   The way the Cross Fade Transition is added to the image events might seem strange until you get used to the logic of Video Post and see how the structure is organized. Sc-01 can't be combined directly with Sc-02 because it's part of an existing transition.

Two Cross Fade events

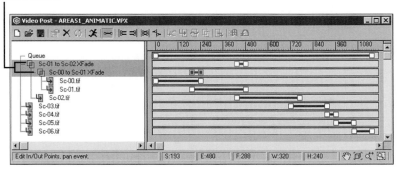

Figure 2.30   One of the great things about Video Post is that it allows you to use image layer event filters from other programs. If you have Adobe Premiere or PhotoShop, you can use many of their transition and image modification effects in Video Post. It's like having a mini version of After Effects.

5. Select Sc-03 and the Sc-01 to Sc-02 XFade event and add the third and last Cross Fade Transition. Name this transition Sc-02 to Sc-03 XFade and change its VP Start and End Times to 721 and 768 (see Figure 2.31).

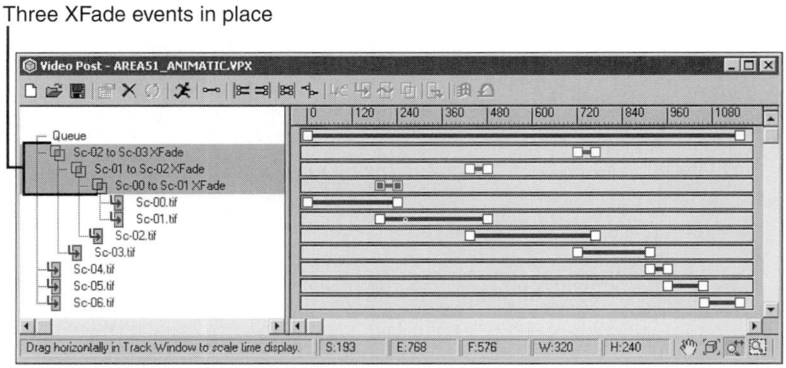

Three XFade events in place

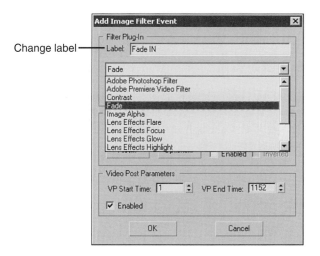

Figure 2.31 The Cross Fade Transitions between the image sequences are complete. The next step is to add the fade in and out at the beginning and end of the Leica reel.

Add a Fade Image Filter Event

Image Filter events are a little different from the layer events you have been using because they can be added to the entire queue and not be associated with a specific sequence. In this case, you'll add a Fade event to the VP Queue at the beginning and the end of the shot. Be sure that no layer or event is selected before you proceed:

1. Click Add Image Filter Event ![icon] and select Fade from the list, as shown in Figure 2.32. Name this event Fade IN. Click OK to add Fade IN to the VP Queue.

Figure 2.32 Renaming the Fade events will help you keep track of multiple events that do the same thing in different places in the VP Queue.

2. Add a second Fade event to the VP Queue by following the same procedure in step 1, and name it Fade OUT. Your VP Queue should look like Figure 2.33.

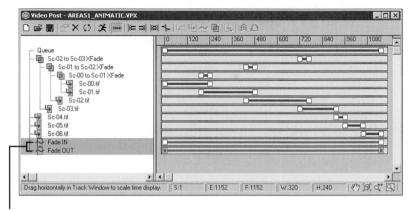

Two Fade events
added to VP Queue

Figure 2.33   Image Filter events include Lens Effects, which will be used in this book to add special effects to the lights and materials in your scenes.

3. Double-click the Fade OUT event. This is the Fade event used at the end of the animatic. Change its VP Start Time to 1104. Don't change the VP End Time. Then click Setup to open the Fade Image Control dialog box shown in Figure 2.34.

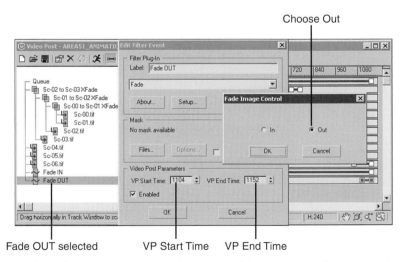

Choose Out

Fade OUT selected   VP Start Time   VP End Time

Figure 2.34   The Fade event is a very simple version of the more complex Cross Fade Transition used in the previous section. It's also very easy to use.

4. Select Out from the Fade Image Control dialog box and click OK. Double-click the Fade IN event and change its VP End Time to 48. Click Setup and select In from the Fade Image Control dialog box. Your VP Queue is almost complete (see Figure 2.35).

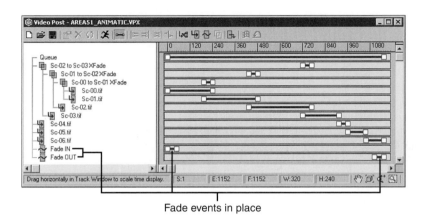

Fade events in place

Figure 2.35   Both Fade events are 48 frames (2 seconds) in duration. The Fade IN event will fade from black into Sc-00; and the Fade OUT event will fade the last 48 frames of Sc-06 into black.

Adding the Image Output Event

The final component of this VP Queue is an image output event to create the AVI format movie. Once again, be sure that none of the existing layers or events are selected when you add the output event to the Queue.

Click Add Image Output Event [icon]. When the Add Image Output Event dialog box opens, click Files. Browse to MAXWorkshop\Avi's and name this file Area51_Animatic.avi. Then click Save, which will open up the Video Compression dialog box shown in Figure 2.36.

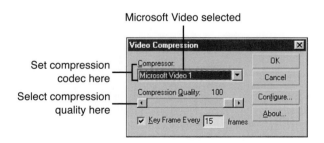

Figure 2.36   Use Microsoft Video 1 if you're unsure about the other compression algorithms available in the list shown in Figure 2.37.

Click the Compressor drop-down menu to see all the video compressor options currently available on your system. There is a huge difference in the size and quality of the files produced by these different algorithms. When rendering an 8-second shot such as TheEnd.avi from *3D Studio MAX 3.0 Workshop*, Microsoft Video produced a 500MB (megabyte) file of very high quality. In most cases, I have found the Indeo video codecs to be superior to the other options, but the Indeo codecs won't create the letterbox format; they are limited to an image aspect ratio of 1.33, such as 640×480 or 320×240. You can get around this limitation.

Note   Indeo video compression creates a very small, very high-quality AVI even when set at 75% quality. If you don't have Indeo, you can download it at the Ligos Web site: http://www.ligos.com/indeo/downloads/.

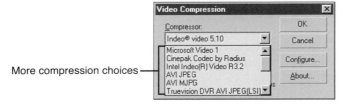

More compression choices

Figure 2.37   Indeo Video 5.1 produced excellent quality comparable to the Microsoft codec, using only 5MB of space. I choose Indeo whenever formatting permits.

If you want to try out some of the different compression codecs for rendering your AVI, you can change the setup of your image output event by double-clicking it in the VP Queue and selecting Setup from the dialog box, as shown in Figure 2.38.

Caution   If you choose a compression codec that doesn't support the output rendering size or format that you have specified in the Execute Scene dialog box, you'll get an error message and your imagery won't render. If this happens, double-click your output event, click Setup in the Edit Output Event dialog box, and change the Compressor selection.

Saving the Video Post Queue Sequence

Your Video Post window is complete for now and should look like Figure 2.39.

Before you render the animatic, save this Video Post sequence by clicking the Save Sequence icon 💾 . Browse to MAXWorkshop\Effects and save this sequence as Area51_Animatic. Max will add a .vpx suffix to the file indicating that it's a Video Post sequence. Now save your max file by using the keyboard shortcut Ctrl+S.

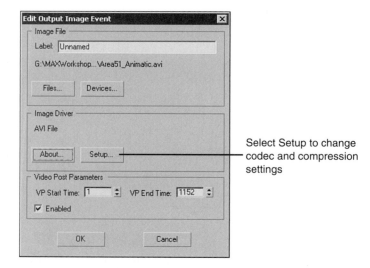

Select Setup to change codec and compression settings

Figure 2.38   Choosing Setup in this dialog box takes you back to the Video Compression dialog box shown in Figures 2.36 and 2.37.

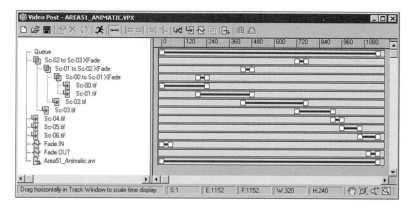

Figure 2.39   In the coming chapters, you will use this Video Post file many times to continue to build toward the full rendered version of Area51.avi.

Saving Your Work Is Important!

Experienced digital artists follow this fundamental rule: Save your file and save it often. You know from reading Chapter 1, "Navigating the Max 4 Interface," that max has an automatic file backup feature that is enabled automatically when you install max. Although this is a powerful tool, it is basically a band-aid for those who forget to save their work. Do not rely on this feature to save your work for you.

Making the Modified Letterbox Format

There is one final necessary tweak to the image event settings for the animatic before you render it. You are going to create the AVI using a letterbox proportion. The storyboard images were created specifically to allow you to use this cinematic format. The aspect ratio of the letterbox format is 1:85, which yields a 640×346 image area. If you render the animatic in 640×480 format and center the images, a border is created above and below the letterbox area, which will be used to add some personalized information to your AVI in Chapter 9, "The Creative Sword: The Art of Post-Production in 3ds max 4." This is also how you can get Indeo to work as a compressor for a letterbox format. Follow these steps to make the necessary adjustments to all storyboard files in the VP Queue:

1. Click the Sc-00 image input event in the Video Post Queue. When the Edit Image Input Event dialog box opens, click Options to access the Image Input Options dialog box shown in Figure 2.40.

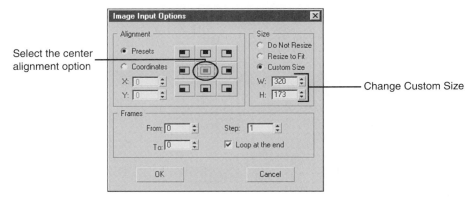

Figure 2.40   The changes you are making will create a letterbox format with black bars above and below the image. Those bars will be used later to customize `Area51.avi`.

2. Click the Custom Size button and change the Width (W) to 320 and the Height (H) to 173. This will preserve the letterbox format of the storyboards.

3. In the Alignment section of the dialog box, click the center format. It turns red and a dotted line appears in its box. This centers the 1:85 letterbox format storyboard images in the standard 1:33 aspect ratio rendered output. Click OK when you are done and OK again to return to the VP Queue.

4. Complete this process by choosing the remaining storyboard image input files—Sc-01 through Sc-06—and changing their image input settings to match Sc-00. Save your Video Post sequence and your max file when you are finished.

Execute Scene

The final step in this process is to click the Execute Scene icon ⚒. If you get the File Overwrite Warning (see Figure 2.41), click Yes.

Figure 2.41   The File Overwrite Warning will appear whenever there is an active Image Output Event in your Video Post Queue and you have previously executed the scene and written image data to the output file. In this case it's Area51_Animatic.avi. You can safely ignore this warning by clicking Yes. No files will be overwritten until you use the Execute Scene dialog box Render command.

After you get past the File Overwrite Warning, the Execute Video Post dialog box shown in Figure 2.42 opens.

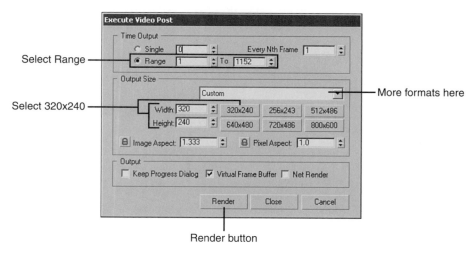

Figure 2.42   A more complex version of this dialog box can be found in the Render Scene dialog box in the Main Toolbar. Make the adjustments indicated and render your animatic.

The Execute Video Post dialog box allows you to select the frames you want to render and the output size format. By choosing the 320×240 format, you are staying in the 1:33 aspect ratio that the Indeo compressor uses for its output. Click Custom to view the available output formats (see Figure 2.43).

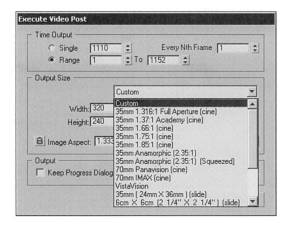

Figure 2.43   The Output Size options list contains just about every standard format used in DCC today. If you can't find what you want, you can specify your own.

To create the modified letterbox format you want for the animatic, set the output size to 320×240. This will allow the storyboard images to sit centered in a taller format, creating black borders at the top and bottom of the AVI. Be sure that Range is active and set to 0/1152. Every Nth Frame should be set to 1. When you're ready, click Render and read a book for about 20 minutes.

Using the smaller 320×240 format will help render the animatic a bit faster. When the rendering is finished, click File, View File, and browse to MAXWorkshop\AVI's\Area51_Animatic.avi and open it. You'll be using the animatic often and will be making adjustments to the timing of your scenes as you create them in the remaining chapters of this Workshop.

This completes the process of creating an animatic for Area51.avi. And if you think about it, it's also the first step in creating your own show reel—the record of your best work.

This chapter has taken you through the basics of storytelling, pre-visualization, storyboards composition, and creating an animatic using Video Post. Video Post is a simple tool that I really enjoy using. It's like an old beat-up truck that starts every morning, runs great, gets me where I want to go, and is impossible to break. It's also an underused tool, especially with all the fancy and expensive alternative compositing software available. You'll learn a lot more about Video Post by the end of this book.

Next Steps

A possible next step for this chapter would be to add a temporary soundtrack to the Leica reel. For those of you who have read *3D Studio max 3.0 Workshop*, Lesson 10 will point you in the right direction.

Any soundwave file loaded into the Track View Editor will automatically be combined with an AVI rendered in Video Post. You'll learn more about this in Chapter 9.

Another next step would be to develop a storyboard of your own or create more scenes for `Area51.avi`. You can add them into the existing Leica reel Video Post Queue or create an entirely new one, which will be easy now that you know how.

A third next step would be to explore the other kinds of transitions available in Video Post, such as the Simple Wipe Image filter event, or if you have Adobe Premiere, try using some of its transition effects.

My computer just finished rendering the `Area51_Animatic.avi`—total rendering time 14 minutes (on a Dell Precision 420 dual P3 933MHz with 512MB RAM). The animatic looks pretty good. It will look even better after the real digital content you will be creating in this book takes the place of these placeholder images. This is the real power of the animatic process. It's all set up and all you have to do is swap out the still images for sequential image files of the same format and duration.

Ahead of you in Chapter 3, "Giving Form to Feeling: The Art of Modeling," are concepts that will be of great benefit in your work as a max artist. You'll be learning some of the design principles and techniques used by industrial designers to create more sophisticated and aesthetically pleasing products, transportation, and architecture.

Applying industrial design concepts to digital content creation is not new. Many of the great visual artists involved in creating feature films, television, and interactive entertainment today have studied and use ID concepts extensively in their work: Joe Johnston, Doug Chiang, John Dykstra, Syd Mead, and Ridley Scott among the many. Then there's you and me, the bold guessers, still struggling to get our ideas out of our heads.

So that's what is ahead. Get ready for "Giving Form to Feeling—the Art of Modeling."

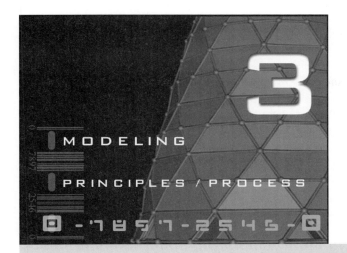

Chapter **3**

Giving Form to Feeling:
The Art of Modeling

"Curiosity about life in all of its aspects, I think, is still the secret of great creative people." - Raymond Lowey, industrial designer

Dozens of books and hundreds of tutorials are available that show you how to model everything from cars to superheroes. Unfortunately, few attempt to help you discover the principles behind the techniques, or tell you why you are doing what you are doing when you are doing it. Step-by-step instructions are often essential to create a recipe that yields the desired result; however, when it comes to visually creating the authentic emotional context of a story, you can't always rely on a recipe to help you. You must have a deep abiding devotion to, and understanding of, basic design principles.

One of the founding fathers of modern architectural and industrial design, Le Corbusier, said, "Where principle is put to work, not as a recipe or as a formula, there will always be style." Personal style is important, but what a successful DCC artist needs is the curiosity to explore and create beyond the limitations of the recipes and formulas found in most tutorials.

The purpose of modeling, and your task as a max artist, is to create believable reality and to give a physical form to the feeling and atmosphere of your story. The audience for your work is extremely sophisticated and hard to impress. They are so used to seeing a hyper-reality in the visual content of their entertainment that it is increasingly difficult to facilitate the suspension of their disbelief. The remedy for this is a return to the basic principles of storytelling and design and the application of those principles to your modeling work.

This chapter introduces you to some of the fundamental modeling principles and tools you'll use to design and create the kinds of objects and environments that your audience expects.

Modeling Basics: Principles and Practice

"Every curve and line has to have real meaning; it cannot be arbitrary." - Frank Lloyd Wright

The word arbitrary is defined as *determined by chance, whim, or impulse, and not by necessity, reason, or principle*. The architecture, machines, characters, and props in Area51.avi exist because they are needed to tell the story. The same reasoning can be applied to the component parts of each individual object as well. Every line and curve in your modeling work must have a reason for existing, and that reason will be discovered in an understanding of the function of the object—its story, if you will.

Many max artists, when they first begin to learn modeling, are content to copy and modify the things they see in real life. However, a time will come in your work when you are called on to create something that has never been seen before. When this happens, you must know the answers to two important questions. "What are the most important principles that I need to use to design and build the visual story?" and "Which tools and techniques should I use to build the models that will tell the story?"

Basic Design Principles

As a visual storyteller, the models you create must appear believable regardless of their context. The basic principle many professional industrial designers use to guide their work is "Form Follows Function." This meme is the fundamental principle of industrial design. It means that the design and appearance of the objects, buildings, and machines you'll build in max are derived from functional criteria, including how the model is used in the scene, the model's location, and the model's animation.

Form and detail combine to tell a story that enables the audience to immediately understand the purpose and function of the model you've created. This means that the form and function of your models must look as if they could actually exist and function in a believable manner.

Master Modeling Principle: Form Follows Function

The basic principles of industrial design were first articulated and put into practice by a group of architects, artists, designers, engineers, and craftsmen working at the Bauhaus School in Germany, which existed from 1919 to 1933. The names of the Bauhaus masters and their students, such as Josef Albers, Walter Gropius, Paul Klee, Marcel Bruer, and Mies van der Rohe might not be familiar, but they are responsible for articulating the design concepts behind the buildings, consumer products, furniture, and so on that we enjoy today.

Streamlining, Human Factors, and Airport Seating

Raymond Lowey, Henry Dreyfus, and Charles and Ray Eames are considered to be among the most influential industrial designers of the 20th century. Raymond Lowey, known as one of the founding fathers of ID, created the concept of streamlining and applied it to everything from pencil sharpeners to locomotives. Dreyfus illuminated the concept of Human Factors, also know as Ergonomics, in his landmark work: "The Measure of Man." And chances are that you have sat in the airport seating created in 1961 by Charles and Ray Eames, which has been universally used in airports for 40 years.

"Form Follows Function" means that the appearance of an object, building, or machine is derived from how the object is manufactured or built, its functional engineering criteria, human factors, and the material from which the object is made. Figure 3.1 shows two versions of the pump you'll build in Chapter 6, "Machines in Motion: Modeling and Kinematics." On the left is a test model used to experiment with the animation of the pump. On the right is a model that incorporates the visual language needed to integrate the form with the function of the Alien machine (also see Figure CP.16 in the color section).

Tip

Creating functional test models before you create final aesthetic forms is an important practice that will speed up your modeling process. So before you create any model or animation, take some time and make a test model to experiment with the size and interrelationship of the model components and to test out the animation.

Alien pump functional test model   Final alien pump: form and function

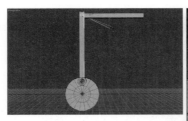 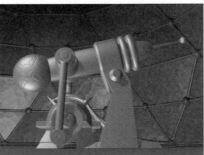

Figure 3.1   The components of the pump were first designed to fulfill the functional and animation requirements of the pump. Then, component forms were developed that fit the function and the Alien visual language.

Context: Beginning with the End in Mind

Another important factor to consider in the modeling process is *context*. Context refers to a model's placement and use within the scene and helps determine the level of detail and surface development required for its appearance.

Knowing where and how an object will be used in a scene determines the level of detail required to meet the needs of the scene. An object's *level of detail*, or *LOD*, is important in two ways: It communicates spatial information about the object in the composition of the scene, and it is a factor in determining the complexity of individual objects.

The LOD of an object should vary depending on its position relative to the viewer. Figure 3.2 shows two versions of the VandeGraaff generator. The one on the right is intended to be used in the foreground and needs to have a higher LOD to bring it forward to the viewer—to make it more complete and believable. The model on the left is designed for use in the background. It has a lower level of detail because it's farther away from your point of view (POV) and doesn't require a lot of detail to serve its purpose in the scene. A simple rule to remember is that background objects can be more of a visual shorthand version of their more complex foreground counterparts.

Consider the Context

Before you begin modeling your object, you must consider its place within the context of the shot, the duration of time the object is on the screen, whether it is animating or sitting still, and so on. Sometimes the impact of a beautiful modeling job is lost on the audience because it isn't in the shot long enough for it to register in the viewers' perception. When this is the case, create your models using the dominant memes that will best communicate its visual reality in the shortest time possible.

Low level of detail   High level of detail

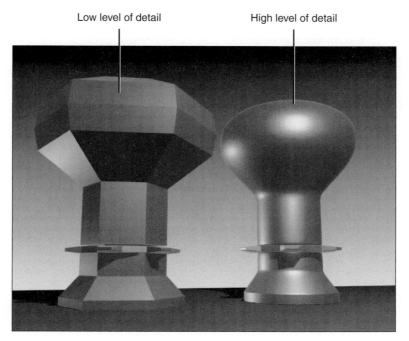

Figure 3.2   When you model in max, think about where the object will be seen in the depth layers of the shot, and then adjust the level of detail, texture, and surface geometry accordingly.

Visual Memes: Relating to What the Audience Knows

Your audience members come equipped with memes already planted in their brains. Everything they have seen, read, and experienced is available for you to access and use in your imagery. If you create models that use memes, you will create images that relate to what the viewers already know. If you do your meme homework, you don't have to work very hard to tap into the images and emotions that already exist in their minds.

When you create the Alien for this Workshop, you are accessing a meme that has been seen in hundreds of forms. The image of the "Grey" Alien is almost universal in its symbolism and has been seen in movies, television shows, and comic books for the past 50 years. Where did the image of a bulbous head with large oval eyes come from? Research reveals that it has been with us for a lot longer than 50 years and can find its roots in images of the dwarves and elves from ancient European legends. Regardless of the origin, the Grey Alien head has indeed become an example of one of the memes in our current culture (see Figure 3.3).

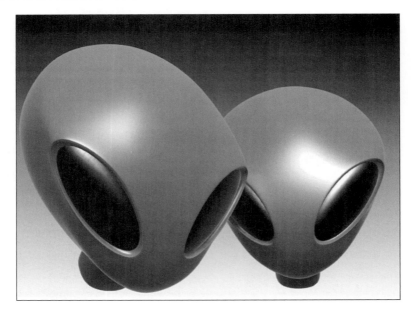

Figure 3.3   The classic image of the Grey Alien is a good example of how a meme can become a universally recognized icon. And it's an example of how an overused icon can become a cliché.

Area51.avi is full of visual memes—the name conjures the entire myth of Roswell, captured alien spaceships, alien autopsy, and abduction. Visual memes are powerful components of your storytelling toolbox. However, it's easy to fall into the trap of superficial use of the meme concept, and overuse of visual memes can create visual clichés. When you use meme imagery, add your own unique twist and don't just copy what you've already seen. If you've seen the cliché, chances are your audience has also and they might dismiss your imagery as immature or unprofessional.

Tip

The Basic Modeling Process

After the functional and contextual aspects of an object are determined, it's time to develop its form and detail. The first step in this process is to create some form of pre-visualization as discussed in Chapter 2, "Virtual Viz: The Art of Pre-Production for Digital Content Creation."

Sketching before you model is absolutely necessary because it provides you with a visual guide for your digital process. Pre-viz will also help you avoid the common beginner mistake of using max to design your models. This is called *designing in the computer* and you must not be tempted to waste your time in this wild goose chase.

Max is first and foremost a creation tool! If you try to use it to work out all the details of a design, you'll waste a lot of time and find yourself back at the beginning of the process: starting over with pencil and paper.

Figure 3.4 shows the sketch created for the cooling tower you'll build in this chapter.

Figure 3.4   Basic form, proportion, and details are worked out on paper first before you begin the modeling process in max.

When you design your models, you will begin by finding the basic forms that define its shape. In this case, the basic form of the cooling tower is a tapered cylinder. After the form is established, you'll divide it into proportional parts and pieces, which are then detailed with texture, color, and so on. This is the sequence you'll follow as you create the models for Area51.avi—creation of form, division of form, and application of detail.

Form

Forming an object means giving it volume, mass, shape, style, and dimension and embodying those visible attributes in a 3D shape. Not all forms for the objects you create in max are simple.

Some of the objects you'll be creating in this Workshop are complex, such as the Alien head you'll create later in this Workshop.

When you begin modeling in max, it might be hard to know where to start. Begin by looking for the most basic subshapes or primitive forms used to create the whole object. This low-level evaluation of the form of an object will help you discover the different combinations of shapes that produce the form you are trying to create.

Figure 3.5 shows how basic shapes were used to create the form of the Tesla Coil towers that you'll use for Sc-02.

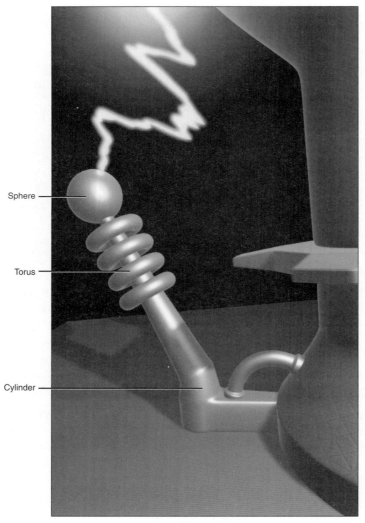

Figure 3.5   All natural and manufactured forms can be created by combinations of basic geometric shapes. Learn to perceive the basic forms and shapes that make up the objects you create in max.

Now consider the Alien equipment shown in Figure 3.6. It started as two cylinders that were modified using the techniques described in this chapter.

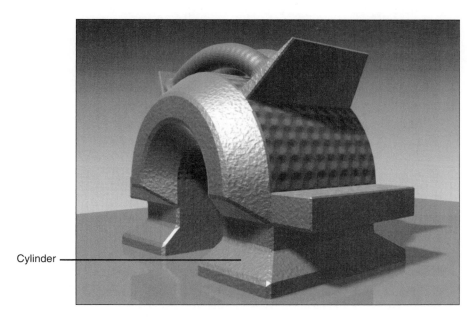

Cylinder

Figure 3.6   Modifying basic shapes using the tools in the Modify command panel created the sophisticated details in the form of the Alien equipment.

Division of Form

The second part of the process of modeling is to decide how an object's form is divided. This is actually a concurrent part of developing the form and must be considered in the up-front design of the object. Although these three parts of the modeling process are discussed separately, they are not discrete, independent pieces. How you develop one part will affect the process of developing the others.

Division of a form refers to how an object is split into its parts or subforms. The proportional relationship of the subforms will influence your viewer's perception of an object's size, scale, weight, and so on.

Figure 3.7 shows two cooling towers whose forms are divided using two different proportions. Notice how the proportional division of the form influences your perception of the relative mass of the towers, even though they are the same height and the base is the same diameter.

Division of form creates a structure for the third part of the modeling process—enhancing the appearance of the form through the application of detail.

Figure 3.7   Proportional division of form reinforces the perception of size, mass, and weight in your max models and communicates important pieces of information to the viewer, including an object's intended purpose.

Detail

The texture and detail of an object are the final components of its visual form. Although detailing a form is the last 5% of the process of modeling, getting it done properly sometimes takes the most time and effort.

When a model is successfully detailed, it allows the audience to believe that what you are presenting to them is real. Figure 3.8 shows the Area 51 cooling tower with its surface detail in place. The form has been divided into a system of triangular and trapezoid plates, a lattice superstructure has been added, doors have been created, a pitted texture has been applied to the surface, and a painted sign can be seen on the lower surface next to the door. All these final details bring the model to life.

Details, Shmetails!

A poorly detailed form can negate the impact of your modeling efforts. Too much detail and the object will appear over-designed; not enough detail and it might appear unfinished.

Achieving the right balance among texture, surface geometry, and detail is difficult. Like all design processes, the balance relies on the intangible factors of your individual sense of style and taste.

Lattice superstructure

Trapezoid plate

Triangular plates

Pitted texture

Exterior signage

Doors

Figure 3.8   Detail is added to make your models beautiful, ugly, old, worn out, brand new, damaged, and so forth. This can be accomplished by a combination of changes in the actual geometry of an object and in the detail applied to its surface.

Create the form of your object (its division and detail) by applying the simplest, most appropriate modeling process possible. The next sections of this chapter continue to explain the basic principles and processes of modeling as you create the cooling tower model for Sc-01.

Introduction to Polygon Modeling

Using the different modeling tools in max will help you discover which tools and techniques you should use to build the models that tell the story. In the next section of this chapter, you'll learn about the basic modeling techniques used by professionals every day.

> If you need help, the completed scene with all the models for Sc-01 can be found on the companion CD in the following directory: `MAXWorkshop\Help_Files\ Chapter_3\EXSC_01.max`

Tip

Before you proceed, click File, Reset in the Menu Bar. When the query dialog box appears, click Yes. This will reset max, giving you a fresh workspace to create Sc-01.

After you reset, click File, Save and save this file as `MAXWorkshop\Scene Models\Sc-01\ Sc-01_Tower.max`.

In the previous section, the cooling tower was used to illustrate a basic design and modeling process. In this section, you'll learn the basics of polygon modeling by creating this model. The first step in this process is to learn how surfaces in max are created and the basic building blocks used in polygon modeling.

Polygons, Surfaces, and Parametric Primitives

A polygon is one of the four main building blocks used to create surfaces. The other three are vertex, edge, and face. These four subobjects are the most basic elements used to define surfaces and they can be moved, scaled, rotated, and modified individually and collectively.

Building every model from scratch—vertex by vertex, polygon by polygon—would not be very productive, so max includes ready-made objects that can be used as a starting place for your modeling work. Some of these ready-made objects are called *primitives*, which are max's versions of the basic geometric forms discussed previously in this chapter.

Open max and look at the Create command panel . The default list of Standard Primitives is open in the Geometry category (see Figure 3.9).

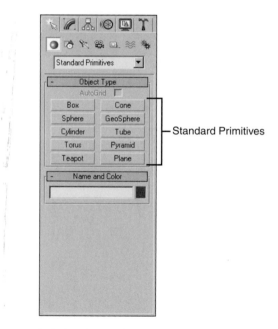

Figure 3.9   Standard primitives include familiar 3D forms that can be modified and combined.

Primitives are defined by a set of parameters controlling their height, width, depth, radius, circumference, and so on. These parameters are defined at the time you create the primitive 2D shapes and 3D objects in max. These objects and shapes are referred to as *parametric* because they are defined by adjustable parameters.

Choosing a primitive that is similar to the shape of your intended model is the first step. In this case, the cooling tower in Sc-01 is made from a Cylinder primitive, although you could also use a Cone or a Tube primitive to achieve the same result.

> **Tip**
>
> When you create parametric primitives, don't be concerned with creating them with exact dimensional parameters at first; the parameters are easy to modify using the Modify command panel after you have created the object.

The storyboard for Sc-01 shows that the cooling tower has a faceted exterior surface. After you create the cylinder, you'll modify its surface mesh to re-create the faceted design seen in the storyboard and concept sketches. Follow these steps to begin making the cooling tower for Sc-01:

1. Click Cylinder and drag in the Perspective viewport to create its base radius. When you have defined the base, let go of the mouse button, move your cursor up in the viewport, and click to establish the cylinder's height.

2. With your cylinder selected, click the Modify command panel , where you'll see the cylinder's parameters, as shown in Figure 3.10.

Figure 3.10   The parameters of all basic 2D and 3D primitives in max—which control the dimensional aspects of their topology—can be adjusted in the Modify command panel. (Your cylinder's parameters might be different from those shown.)

> **Note**
>
> When a primitive object is created in max, the dimensional parameters shown in the Modify panel define its topology as a parametric object. *Topology* is defined as the properties of geometric forms that remain invariant under certain transformations, such as bending or stretching. This means that no matter how you push, bend, twist, or mush this form around, its basic parameters will remain unchanged from the settings shown in the Modify panel, until you modify those parametric values or collapse the box into one of three base geometry types.

3. Change the cylinder's parameters to these values: Radius: 40, Height: 120, Height Segments 14, Cap Segments: 2, Sides: 22. Remove the check mark from Smooth and change the name of this object to Cooling_Tower_Master. Your perspective view and Parameters rollout should look like Figure 3.11.

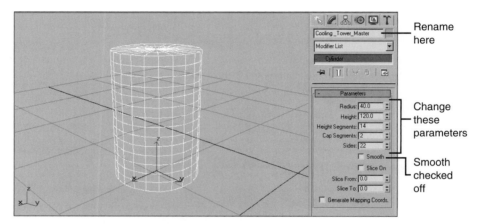

Figure 3.11   This is the basic shape for the cooling tower model. Its parameters include enough segments to create the faceted surface seen in the Sc-01 storyboard.

Changing the number of segments of an object's topology changes the number of polygons used to define its surface. The more segments used, the higher the polygon count.

Polygon count can increase dramatically with minor changes in an object's topology—so be careful when you increase the number of polygons used, and use just what you need to achieve the form you are trying to create. High polygon count in a single object is not a problem, but in a complex scene involving many high-polygon models, it can slow you and your system down.

Surfaces, Meshes, and Subobjects

It's important to realize that 3D objects in max are hollow shapes defined by a surface, which has no mathematical thickness. This means that the cylinder you just made is not solid like a piece of wood dowel; its surface is just an enclosure that defines its shape.

A surface is also referred to as a *mesh*, and the editable mesh, which defines an object, is made from a structure of vertices, edges, faces, and polygons that are common to all polygon surfaces. The four basic subobjects that are used to create surface meshes are vertex, edge, face, and polygon:

- **Vertex**—A vertex is a point in space and is the most fundamental subobject in max. Vertices are used to define the faces in the structure of max surfaces.

- **Edge**—An edge is a line that connects two vertices, forming the side of a face.

- **Face**—A face is a triangle formed by three vertices and three edges. These faces create the surface of an object and provide max with the mathematical data needed to create visible, renderable surfaces.

- **Polygon**—Polygons are created by two coplanar faces. Usually, a polygon is the area you see within the lines of a surface shown in Wireframe display mode.

Converting to Editable Mesh: Accessing Subobjects

Before you can access and modify the subobjects in your models, you must either convert the parametric primitive into an editable mesh or apply an Edit Mesh modifier. Both ways are valid, but only one will preserve the parametric nature of your model.

The conversion of a parametric primitive into an editable mesh removes all parametric controls, including the creation parameters used when you created the object. This means that when you convert the cylinder you just created into an editable mesh, you'll no longer be able change its dimensions or the number of segments that define the surface using the original parameter controls. You'll be able to modify its size and so forth as an editable mesh, but not as you did with the simple parametric input of the primitive shape.

Right-click Cooling_Tower_Master to access its Quad Menu and select Convert To, Convert to Editable Mesh, as shown in Figure 3.12.

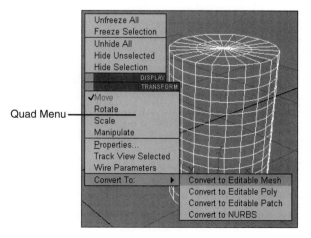

Figure 3.12   Using the Quad Menu to access the tools and commands in max is an important part of your productivity. Over the course of this Workshop, you will learn how to use this tool and how to create your own customized toolbars and keyboard shortcuts.

Converting an object to an editable mesh is the simplest way to get access to the subobjects that define its mesh surface. Although conversion removes the object's parametric controls, you can use other tools to modify the overall size and complexity of the mesh. After you convert the cylinder to a mesh, the Modify command panel changes from the parametric rollout to the editable mesh rollout, as shown in Figure 3.13.

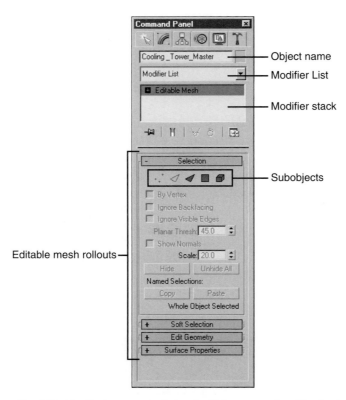

Figure 3.13 The Editable Mesh command panel will become a familiar tool—you will spend a lot of time selecting and modifying geometry subobjects to create the exact look you want for your max models.

Under the Selection rollout, you'll see the icons for the four major subobjects and a fifth icon that selects the Element level. The Element level is another name for the base geometry you are editing—in this case, the cylindrical mesh: Cooling_Tower_Master.

Basic Vertex Editing

The next step is to create the faceted surface of the cooling tower. Because of the way you will modify the cylinder in the subsequent process, it's important to complete this step first.

The mesh surface of your cylinder is made up of rectangular polygons. To create the trapezoidal polygons needed for the cooling tower, you will modify the vertices that define those polygons.

Follow these steps to change rectangular faces into triangles and trapezoids:

1. Click Vertex in the Selection rollout—little blue dots appear at each corner of the rectangles that define the surface mesh. These are the vertices that define the corners of the rectangular polygons (see Figure 3.14).

All vertices visible

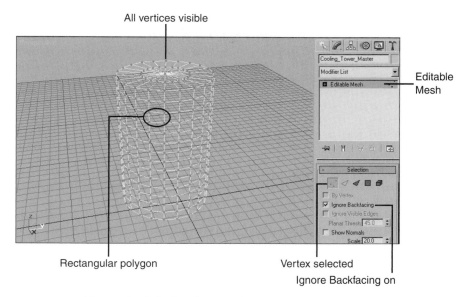

Editable Mesh

Rectangular polygon

Vertex selected

Ignore Backfacing on

Figure 3.14   Max uses blue as the default color to indicate when a vertex subobject selection is active. When any subobject in the surface mesh is selected, it turns red.

2. Click Ignore Backfacing in the Selection rollout. This will keep you from inadvertently selecting the wrong vertices during this process.

3. Click Select Object, hold down the Ctrl key, and select two adjacent vertices in the first row above the bottom of the Cylinder mesh, as shown in Figure 3.15. If you need to zoom in or rotate your viewport to get a better view for this, use the Viewport Navigation Controls.

Tip

If you need help using the Viewport Navigation Controls, refer to the tearcard, where you'll find a complete diagram of all the commands and their keyboard shortcuts.

4. To create the surface polygons needed for the cooling tower, you'll use the Collapse command in the Edit Geometry rollout. Drag your cursor in the rollout window to scroll down to the Collapse command, as shown in Figure 3.16. The Helping Hand cursor appears when your cursor is over an area of the rollout that can be used to drag and scroll it.

Giving Form to Feeling: The Art of Modeling

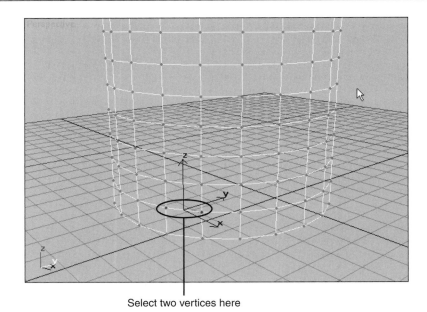

Select two vertices here

Figure 3.15   When you select the vertices, they turn red to let you know that these are your active selections and ready for modification.

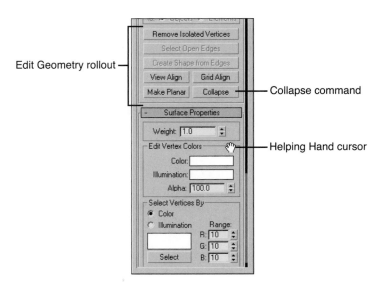

Edit Geometry rollout —

— Collapse command

— Helping Hand cursor

Figure 3.16   The Collapse command is similar to two other vertex-editing commands: Weld and Fuse. These three commands modify selected vertices in slightly different ways and are tools used frequently in mesh modification. Check them out in your max User Reference.

5. Click Collapse to join the two selected vertices at a point exactly between their former positions in space. This also creates the first two triangular and trapezoidal polygons needed for the surface detail of the cooling tower (see Figure 3.17).

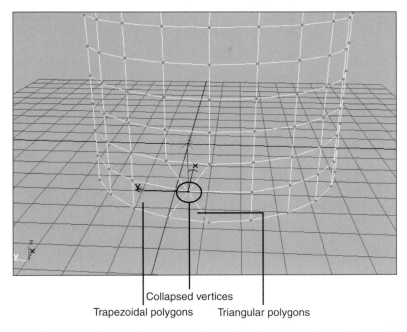

Collapsed vertices

Trapezoidal polygons   Triangular polygons

Figure 3.17   Collapse can be used on any number of vertices you select—it's not limited to just two.

6. The next step is tedious repetition of the same process. Select the next two adjacent vertices in this first row and repeat the collapse process. Continue selecting and collapsing pairs of vertices until the base of your cooling tower looks like Figure 3.18.

The next part of the process is to work your way up the surface of the mesh, repeating the collapse technique you just used on the base of the cooling tower. However, before you do that, here's a way to make this process a little less tedious.

Sharpen the Saw: Creating a Keyboard Shortcut

During the course of completing the Workshops in this book, there will be frequent opportunities to stop, take a step back, and explore some of the productivity features in the max interface. It's good to do this in the middle of a process, so you'll see how the concept can be put into immediate practice. These productivity sections are titled "Sharpen the Saw" after a concept taught by Steven Covey in his landmark book *The Seven Habits of Highly Effective People*.

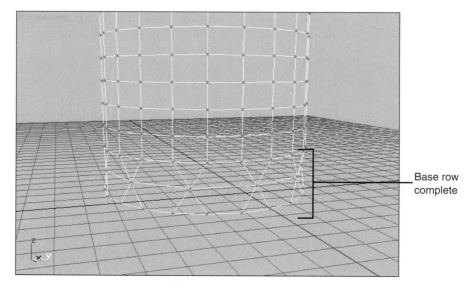

Base row
complete

Figure 3.18   You can speed up the task of collapsing vertices to create the faceted surface of the cooling tower by creating a shortcut command (as described in the next section).

Sharpen the Saw

Steven Covey gives the following example about principles of balanced self-renewal and personal productivity.

Suppose you were to come upon someone in the woods working feverishly to saw down a tree.

"What are you doing?" you ask.

"Can't you see?" comes the impatient reply. "I'm sawing down this tree."

"You look exhausted!" you exclaim. "How long have you been at it?"

"Over five hours," he returns, "and I'm beat! This is hard work."

"Well, why don't you take a break for a few minutes and sharpen the saw?" you inquire. "I'm sure it would go a lot faster."

"I don't have time to sharpen the saw," the man says emphatically. "I'm too busy sawing!"

From The Seven Habits of Highly Effective People by Steven R. Covey, A Fireside Book published by Simon and Schuster.

Instead of continuing to select and collapse each pair of vertices in exactly the same manner as outlined in the previous steps, you can create a keyboard shortcut for the Collapse command that will save you some mouse clicks:

1. Click Customize, Customize User Interface in the Menu Bar. This opens the Customize User Interface dialog box shown in Figure 3.19.

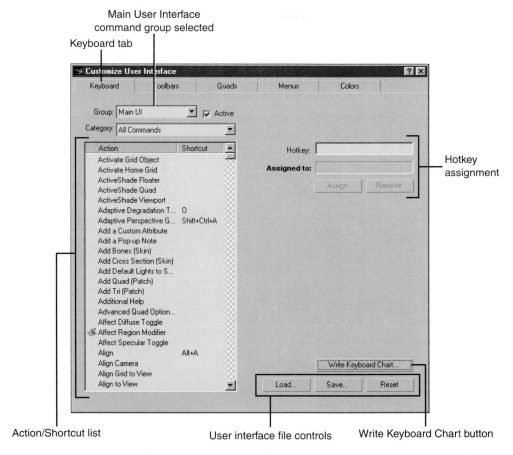

Figure 3.19   Most experienced max users customize their interfaces to create shortcuts, tool-bars, and Quad Menus that fit the way they work.

2. Select Edit/Editable Mesh from the Group drop-down list (see Figure 3.20).

3. Select Collapse from the Action list, and click inside the Hotkey text box. Press Shift+C to create the hotkey for this shortcut (see Figure 3.21).

4. Click Assign to finish creating the keyboard shortcut. Shift+C now appears in the Shortcut column next to Collapse, as shown in Figure 3.22. Close the Customize User Interface dialog box when you're finished.

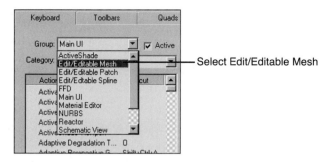

Select Edit/Editable Mesh

Figure 3.20 Selecting the different control groups in the Group menu allows you to access, modify, and create the keyboard shortcuts for your max interface commands and tools.

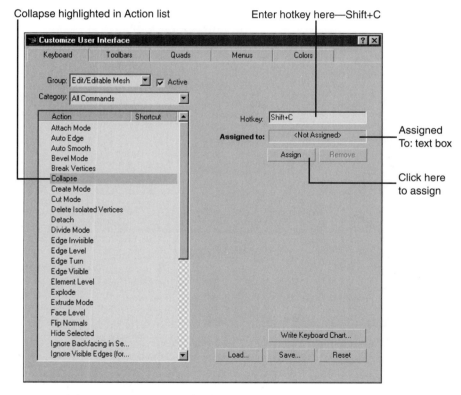

Collapse highlighted in Action list

Enter hotkey here—Shift+C

Assigned To: text box

Click here to assign

Figure 3.21 Be careful to pay attention to what's displayed in the Assigned To text box. It tells you whether you've chosen a keyboard shortcut already assigned to another key.

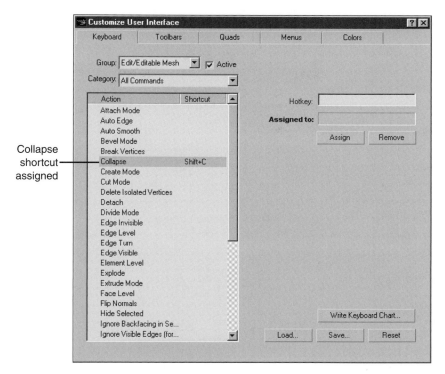

Collapse
shortcut
assigned

Figure 3.22 The changes you make to any of the user interface components can be saved under unique filenames. The Write Keyboard Chart button creates a printable text file showing all the hotkeys currently assigned in your interface.

Caution

Be careful. Max allows you to specify the same keyboard shortcut for use in different parts of the interface. Max will alert you if the shortcut is already assigned within a specific group but not if it's assigned in another group, such as the Main User Interface, for example.

The shortcut for the Collapse command you just created could have been a simple C instead of the Shift+C that was assigned as the hotkey. If you had used a simple C shortcut, you would have eliminated the use of the Camera view shortcut, which also uses the hotkey C during mesh editing.

Be aware of shortcut overlap by familiarizing yourself with all the major hotkey assignments outlined in your User Reference, the Customize User Interface dialog box, or on the inside of the front and back covers of this book.

To make the Collapse shortcut a permanent part of your user interface, use the user interface file controls (refer to Figure 3.19) to save this customized interface under a unique name.

You can also use these controls to load previously created and saved customized interfaces or reset the interface to max's default configuration. Resetting the interface without saving your changes will obviously wipe out any custom shortcuts you've created.

The flexibility of this aspect of the max interface allows you to create and use customized toolsets specifically designed for repetitive animation, rendering, or modeling processes. This powerful, unique feature is designed to sharpen your productivity saws.

The Cooling Tower Model

With your new keyboard shortcut in place, it's time to finish modifying the vertices of your model to create the rest of the triangular and trapezoidal polygons:

1. Select two vertices in the vertex row just above the trapezoidal polygon, as shown in Figure 3.23. You will be collapsing these vertices using your keyboard shortcut instead of clicking the Collapse command in the Modify command panel.

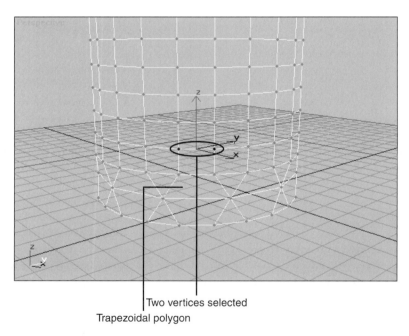

Two vertices selected

Trapezoidal polygon

Figure 3.23   When you think about the surfaces you'll create in max, learn to think about them in terms of how you can modify their subobjects to achieve your design.

2. Press Shift+C to collapse the selected vertices. Then select the next adjacent pair and repeat the process until you have completed this row.

3. Repeat the same process for the remaining rows of vertices. As you move up the form, be sure you start by selecting vertices just above the trapezoidal polygon in the preceding row. This will create a consistent trapezoidal pattern in the surface mesh.

4. Don't collapse any of the vertices on the top vertex row. When you are done, press F3 and F4 to change your viewport display mode to Smooth+Highlights and Edged Faces, as seen in Figure 3.24.

Leave top row as is

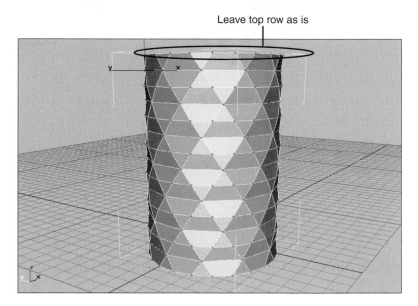

Figure 3.24 Changing to Smooth+Highlights and Edged Faces display mode allows you to see the facets of the surface you've just created more clearly. Use F3 and F4 to toggle these display modes on and off.

The basic surface of the cooling tower has been created. Now it's time to taper the form to create the sloped sides seen in the storyboard and design sketches.

Max Modifiers: Basic Form Refinement

Max uses a set of tools known as *modifiers* to change an object's form and shape. Max modifiers are divided into two basic types: Object Space Modifiers (OSM), which use an object's local coordinate system to modify its unique parameters or topology; and World Space Modifiers (WSM), which affect or modify an object using world coordinates. Max has more than 30 modifiers, organized into 11 modifier sets that are grouped according to functionality.

In this section, you'll learn how to apply modifiers and how max organizes and keeps track of the modifiers you apply. Remember that to see and use the modifiers in the Modify command panel, a max object must be selected.

Accessing and Applying Modifiers

There are three basic ways to access and use max modifiers. The first way is to use the Modifier list.

Select the Cooling_Tower_Master cylinder you've been working on and click the Modify command panel. Click the Modifier List text box to see a listing of all modifiers, as shown in Figure 3.25. Don't click any of the modifiers in this list right now. Just scroll down to see all the modifiers available.

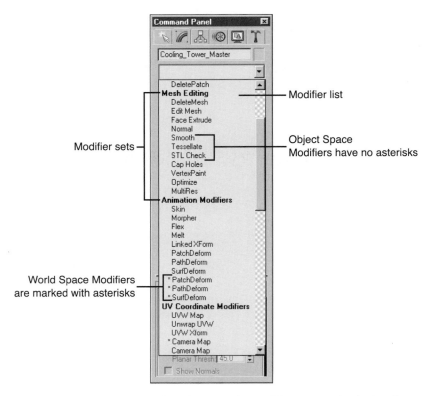

Figure 3.25   Selecting from the list of modifiers in the Modify command panel is the most basic way to access and use max modifiers.

Intermingled in the modifier sets are nine World Space Modifiers, which have asterisks beside their names.

Tip

If you want to know more about a specific modifier or modifiers in general, press F1 to access the max User Reference. Then type in the name of the modifier in the search or index tab for information on how it is used and what effect it will have on your max models.

A second way to access and use max modifiers is to configure the Modify command panel to show the buttons that correspond to each of the 11 main sets in the Modifier list. Click Configure Button Sets [icon] just below the Modifier list on the right side of the set of controls (see Figure 3.26).

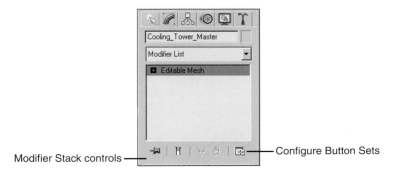

Modifier Stack controls ——————————— Configure Button Sets

Figure 3.26 The five Modifier Stack control icons in this row control different aspects of the appearance and function of the modifier stack.

The Configure Modifier Sets list shown in Figure 3.27 is divided into three main sections. The top section allows you to configure which modifiers appear in the respective button sets. The middle section controls which modifiers are displayed in the Modifier list and the button sets. And the bottom section allows you to select one of the 11 main modifier sets to be displayed in the button sets of the Modifier list.

Figure 3.27 The Configure Button Sets dialog box controls how the different sets of modifiers are displayed and accessed in the Modify command panel.

Select Parametric Modifiers from the list. The dialog box closes when you do this, so click the Configure Button Sets icon again. This time choose Show Buttons from the second section of the list—the buttons for the Parametric modifiers will appear in the Modify command panel below the Modifier list (see Figure 3.28).

3ds max 4

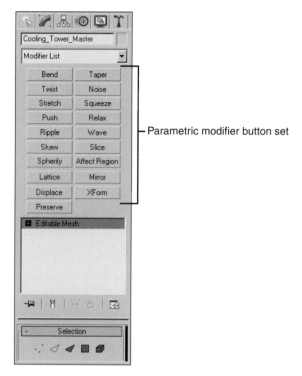

Parametric modifier button set

Figure 3.28 Button sets can be modified by adding or removing specific modifiers from the set. This allows you to create custom button sets designed to fit your personal process.

You'll be using a third way to access max modifiers so, before you move on, click the Configure Button Sets icon again, and deselect Show Buttons. This hides the button set and makes it easier to see the modifier parameters you'll adjust in the next section.

> **Note**
>
> From Dave Campbell, Technical Editor: You might find that you want to access specific modifiers without having to go to the Modify command panel. Adding frequently used modifiers and commands to your Quad Menus, Tab Panels, and floating toolbars will help customize max to fit your workflow. Open your max User Reference and consult the sections on Customizing the User Interface.

The best way, in my opinion, to access modifiers is by using the Quad Menu system by right-clicking selected geometry. Holding down the Ctrl key, Alt key, Shift key, and combinations of those keys while right-clicking will access alternative Quad Menus.

Hold down the Ctrl key and right-click your cooling tower. Then select Modifiers from the alternative Quad Menu, as shown in Figure 3.29.

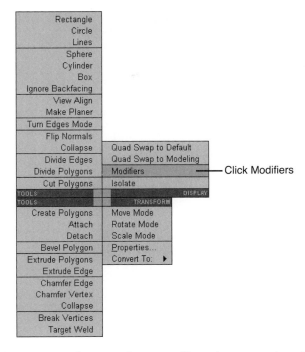

— Click Modifiers

Figure 3.29   Learning how to access and use Quad Menus will accelerate your learning process and increase your productivity. Use these shortcuts whenever you can.

Select the Taper modifier from the upper-right quadrant of the Quad Menu, as shown in Figure 3.30.

When you added the Taper modifier to the tower, the modifier appeared in the modifier stack, as shown in Figure 3.31. The next section helps you understand how the stack is organized and used.

Inside the Modifier Stack

Modifiers are applied to geometry in the Modify command panel, and max keeps track of them in a history list called the modifier stack. The original object sits at the bottom of the stack and the modifiers applied to it are added in order of their application from bottom to top (refer to Figure 3.31). Before you adjust the parameters of the Taper modifier, it's important to know a little bit more about the stack itself. Start with the five functional control icons just underneath the stack.

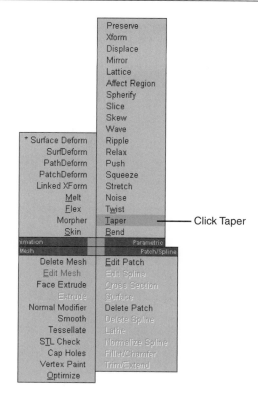

Figure 3.30   Adding a modifier to an object by selecting it from the Modifier list, from the appropriate button set, or from the Quad Menu are all valid ways to access the utility of max modifiers.

Stack Controls

The stack controls are used to organize, access, and change some of the more basic attributes of the modifiers applied to your models. The following definitions of the other four modifier stack controls will help familiarize you with their functions (Configure Button Sets was defined in the previous section):

- **Pin Stack**—Locks the stack and the Modify command panel controls to the selected object. This allows you to continue editing the "pinned" object's modifier parameters even if you select other objects in the viewport.

- **Show End Result**—Shows the effect of the entire stack of modifiers on the object that you are modeling when toggled on. When it's off, it shows the effect of the stack up to and including the current modifier.

- **Make Unique**—When you create an instanced copy of an object, the modifiers in its stack are also copied. Any change in the original modifier will affect the modifiers of all the other instanced copies. Make Unique allows you to convert an instanced copy of a modifier into a unique copy that will affect just the geometry to which it's applied.

- **Remove Modifier**—Deletes the currently selected modifier from the stack. This also deletes all the effects the modifier applied to the object.

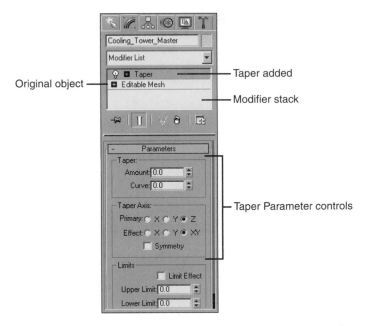

Original object

Taper added

Modifier stack

Taper Parameter controls

Figure 3.31 The Taper modifier is one of 19 parametric modifiers that can be used to effect subtle or radical changes in your model's surface geometry. The effects of modifiers, like every other max tool, can also be animated.

Modifier Subobjects

The modifiers in the stack, Editable Mesh and Taper, have plus signs just to the left of their names. Clicking these plus signs will open a list of the subobjects that are available for modification (see Figure 3.32).

The modifiers you apply to your objects have their own unique subobjects. These subobjects are selected by clicking their names in this list or by right-clicking selected geometry when the modifier is selected in the stack (see Figure 3.33). The Taper modifier's subobjects are Gizmo and Center.

Understanding the three basic modifier subobjects is important:

- **Gizmo subobject**—When you apply a modifier to an object, the Gizmo initially surrounds the entire object, like an envelope—it's the yellow wireframe box around the cooling tower in your viewport. The modifier's effect on the object's geometry relates to this envelope and you can move, scale, and rotate a Gizmo to change the effect of the modifier on the object.

- **Center subobject**—This is the center of the modifier's effect, and it's marked with a 3D coordinate axis and pivot point just like the other objects that you create in max. When Center is selected in the subobject list, you can change the origin of the modifier's effect by transforming the center in the X, Y, or Z axes.

- **On/Off Toggle**—Next to the Taper modifier in the stack is a light bulb. This is an on/off toggle. When the bulb is toggled on, the modifier will affect its associated geometry and vice versa.

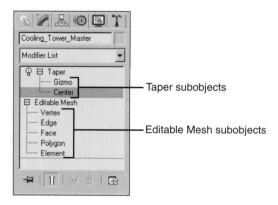

Figure 3.32   Modifiers have unique subobjects that control how the modifier affects the geometry to which it's applied.

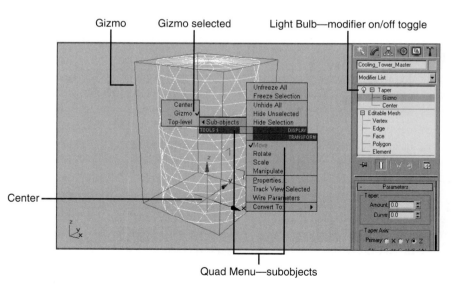

Figure 3.33   Transforming a modifier's Center or its Gizmo will change how the modifier affects the geometry.

Adjusting Taper Parameters

Every modifier has its own unique parameters to control how it will affect the geometry to which it's applied. The effect of Taper applied to the cooling tower model creates a sloping surface, which gives the form a cone-like or conical appearance. You can also add a curve to the Taper by adjusting the curve parameters.

Take some time and experiment with all the parameters for this modifier. When you're ready to move on, use the Undo command 🔄 to discard your experiments and change the Taper modifier parameters to the following settings: Taper Amount: -0.65; Taper Curve 0.20; and leave the other settings as they are—your cooling tower should look like Figure 3.34.

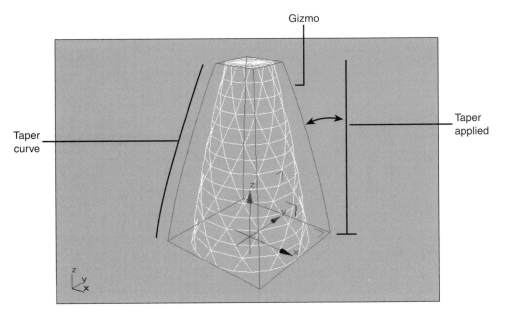

Figure 3.34   The sequence of the modifiers added to the modifier stack will yield different results in the modeling process. Max doesn't limit you to the sequence or to the number of modifiers you can use; that is left up to your knowledge, experience, and expertise.

The next step in the creation of the cooling tower model process is to divide the form.

Division of Form: Completing the Cooling Tower Form

The basic form of the cooling tower is complete but the top detail of the tower needs to be created. To accomplish this, you'll be scaling some of the vertices at the top of the tower to create the division of form seen in the pre-viz sketches and storyboards.

When you first created the cylinder for the cooling tower, you converted it to an editable mesh. You could do the same thing now, but if you do, you'll collapse the modifier stack. Collapsing the stack means that all the modifiers you've added will no longer appear in the stack where their parameters can be manipulated. Their effect on the geometry will be "baked" into the new editable mesh that you created through the conversion to editable mesh, but the individual modifiers and their parameters are gone.

So, instead of converting the cylinder, you'll add a new Edit Mesh modifier above Taper at the top of the stack. This will allow you to select and manipulate your model's subobjects, without altering your original geometry and without losing parameter control of the Taper modifier. Follow these steps to add an Edit Mesh modifier:

1. Click Taper in your modifier stack and Ctrl+right-click the cooling tower. Select Modifiers from the Quad Menu, and then choose Edit Mesh from the Mesh modifier set in the lower-left quadrant, as shown in Figure 3.35.

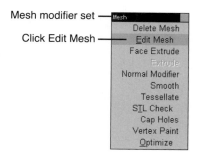

Figure 3.35 Adding an Edit Mesh modifier above the Taper modifier will allow you to manipulate the form of the cooling tower in reference to the tapered form at the subobject level.

2. Right-click the cooling tower model and select Subobjects, Vertex from the Quad Menu, as shown in Figure 3.36.

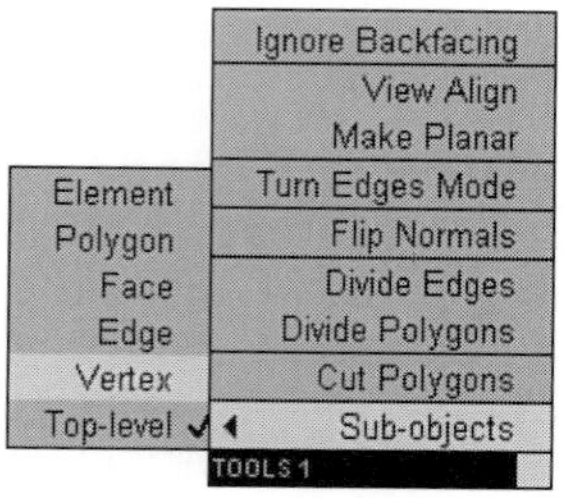

Figure 3.36 You can also access the vertex subobject by clicking the plus sign next to Edit Mesh in the modifier stack and selecting Vertex from the list.

3. Press R to change to Right view, W to maximize your viewport, and Ctrl+Alt+Z to center your geometry in the view. Be sure that Ignore Backfacing is off in your Modify command panel and drag a selection rectangle around the cooling tower's top three rows of vertices, as shown in Figure 3.37.

Selection rectangle

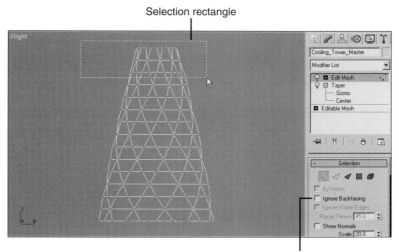

Ignore Backfacing off

Figure 3.37 Turning Ignore Backfacing off will allow you to select all the vertices within the boundaries of the selection rectangle, regardless of their position in the 3D surfaces of the model.

4. The top three rows of selected vertices will turn red. Right-click the vertices and select Scale from the Quad Menu Transform toolset, as shown in Figure 3.38.

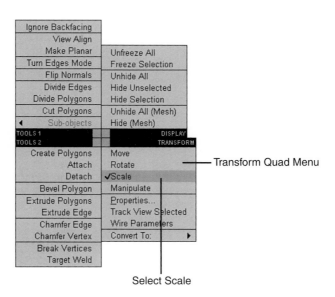

Transform Quad Menu

Select Scale

Figure 3.38 The transform tools—Move, Rotate, and Scale—are also available in the Main Toolbar.

5. Press F12 to open the Scale Transform Type-In dialog box. Type 130 in the Offset:Screen percent section shown in Figure 3.39. This will scale the vertices by 130%, creating the beveled detail at the top of the cooling tower.

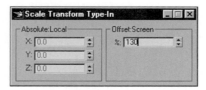

Figure 3.39   The Transform Type-In dialog box allows you to perform precise Move, Rotate, and Scale transforms.

6. Select the two top rows of vertices and use the Scale Transform Type-In dialog box to scale them to 85% (see Figure 3.40).

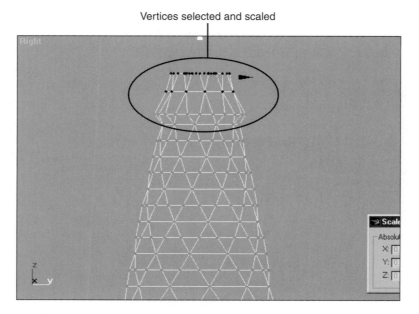

Figure 3.40   Selecting and scaling vertices is an effective way to create proportional division in the forms of your models.

7. The final step in this process is to select the top row of vertices and scale it down by 85% as well. This will create a smooth tapered form at the top of the tower, as shown in Figure 3.41.

Top row vertices selected and scaled

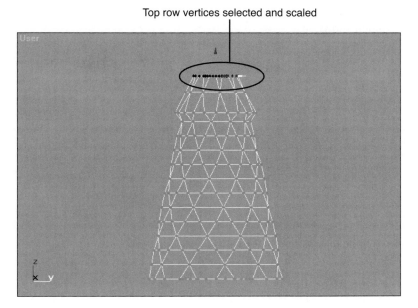

Figure 3.41 The intention of dividing a form this way is to create a more interesting and believable model and make the cooling tower look like the design sketches. Without this kind of detail, the cooling tower would be just a bland cone.

The third step in the modeling process is to add surface detail to the geometry. Adding surface detail can be accomplished by manipulating existing geometry subobjects, adding additional geometry, and using the texturing techniques you'll learn in Chapter 4, "Visual Touch: The Art of Material and Texture Development."

Details: Adding Doors

Effective and believable surface details are created through a combination of subobject manipulation, added geometry, and texture mapping. To complete the cooling tower, you'll create doors and a lattice superstructure.

Press P to change your viewport to Perspective view. Rotate your view and zoom in on the bottom of the cooling tower. Your viewport should look something like Figure 3.42.

Caution

A common problem when working with subobjects is to inadvertently transform (move, rotate, scale) them. Avoid this problem by being sure that you are in Select mode before you select any subobject. Click Select Object ▣ in the Main Toolbar to activate Select mode.

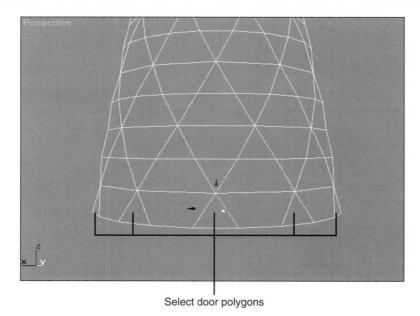

Select door polygons

Figure 3.42   To make these doors you can select, extrude, and bevel all these faces at the same time.

You are going to make doors in the tower by selecting, extruding, and beveling the triangular polygons at the bottom of the tower model:

1. Be sure the Edit Mesh modifier is selected in the modifier stack, and then right-click the cooling tower and select Polygon from the Subobjects section of the Quad Menu. Hold down the Ctrl key as you select all the triangular polygons on the bottom row of the cooling tower, as shown in Figure 3.43.

2. After the polygons are selected, use the Selection Lock Toggle at the bottom of the interface. Press the spacebar to activate this command or click the icon 🔒.

> **Tip**
>
> Use the Selection Lock Toggle to lock the selected max elements with which you are working. This will keep you from inadvertently selecting some other geometry or element in a complex scene. However, it's easy to forget that this toggle is on, so if you find that you want to select an object but can't, check to see if Lock Selection is on.

3. Scroll down to the Edit Geometry rollout in the Modify command panel and click the Extrude button. The button becomes highlighted and your cursor changes into the Extrude cursor, as shown in Figure 3.44.

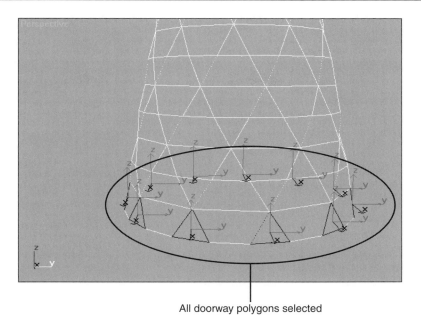

All doorway polygons selected

Figure 3.43 Any of the polygons in the surface mesh of this model can be selected to make windows, doors, or surface details.

4. There are several ways to use the Extrude and Bevel tools. The first way is to drag your cursor in the viewport. Dragging up in the viewport extrudes the polygons out from the surface. Dragging down extrudes them into the surface. Drag down in the viewport to create a shallow door about -1.0 deep. Watch the numeric box next to the Extrude button—it will show you the direction and the amount of the extrusion in positive or negative numbers (see Figure 3.45).

Tip

If you use the viewport cursor drag method or spinner drag input to extrude and bevel the selected polygons, you can cancel the action and return the faces to their starting position by clicking the right mouse button at any time during the drag action. To cancel the extrude/bevel action after you have stopped dragging, use the Undo command. Remember: A right-click during any drag/input action cancels the input, returning the object or subobject to its original position or parameter.

5. The door entryway has been extruded into the surface of the cooling tower. The next step is to use the spinner arrows next to the Bevel numeric control box to add a -.5 bevel to the doorway (see Figure 3.46).

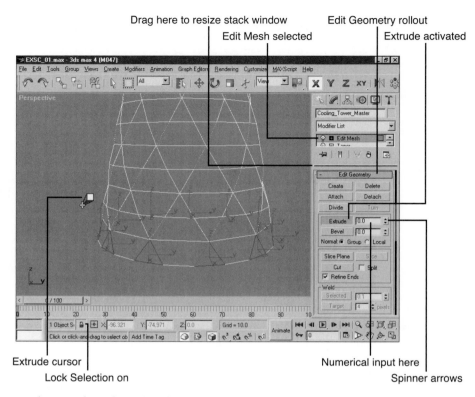

Drag here to resize stack window

Edit Mesh selected

Edit Geometry rollout

Extrude activated

Extrude cursor

Lock Selection on

Numerical input here

Spinner arrows

Figure 3.44   The Extrude and Bevel tools are interlinked and can be used by dragging in the viewport, using the spinner arrows, or inputting numbers.

6. Complete the doorway by extruding the selected polygons -10.0, and press R to change to Right view. Zoom in on the bottom of the cooling tower. You'll see that the selected polygons are overlapping the bottom of the cooling tower (see Figure 3.47).

7. Right-click anywhere in the viewport and select Move from the Quad Menu. Put your cursor over the y-axis of any one of the selected polygons and drag up in the viewport. This restricts the move to the y-axis only. Stop the move when the bottom edge of the door entryway created by the extruded polygons is parallel with the bottom edge of the cooling tower (see Figure 3.48).

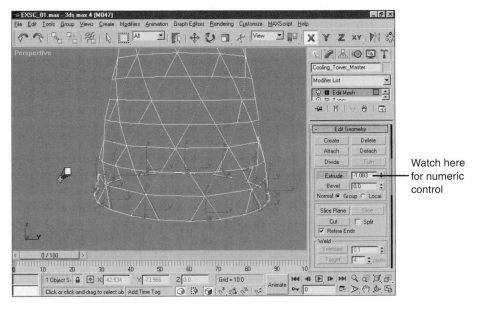

Watch here
for numeric
control

Figure 3.45 The spinner arrows next to the numerical input box can also be used to adjust the amount of the extrusion. Just click and drag in the desired direction—up for positive extrusion, down for negative.

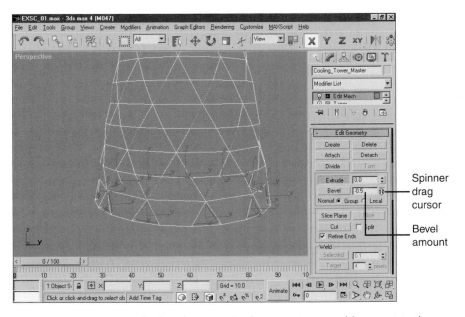

Spinner
drag
cursor

Bevel
amount

Figure 3.46 You can also type in the bevel amount in the numeric control box next to the Bevel button to achieve the same result.

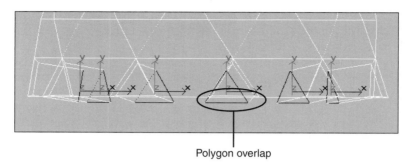

Polygon overlap

Figure 3.47 The polygons were extruded from a slightly angled surface so they are extruded at a 90° angle from that initial surface. Even though these faces are inside the tower and hidden from view, good modeling practice suggests that readjusting their position will help avoid any problems later on.

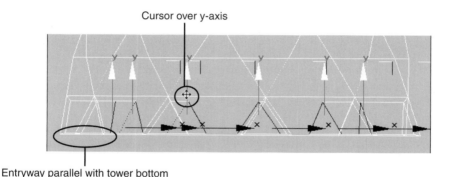

Cursor over y-axis

Entryway parallel with tower bottom

Figure 3.48 Selecting, modifying, and moving subobjects is the bread and butter of max modeling. You'll use these same basic techniques in every model you create in max.

Your doors and entryways should look something like Figure 3.49. The next step in this process is to create a more sophisticated surface appearance by adding a structural framework to the entire cooling tower.

Details: Making a Superstructure Using the Lattice Modifier

With the addition of the doors and entryways, the cooling tower is beginning to take on a more finished appearance. This is the intent of the third part of the modeling process. Adding a superstructure framework to the tower will create the next level of geometric detail. The final details will be achieved by the surface textures you'll create in Chapter 4.

Creating a superstructure can be accomplished in several ways. The simplest way is to add a Lattice modifier to a copy or clone of the cooling tower model.

Figure 3.49 The completed doors and entryways are a good example of the Extrude command at work. The Extrude command is one of the basic tools that you'll use frequently. Consider adding it to your default Quad Menu, the Tab Panel, or to a floating toolbar.

Max uses the term *clone* to refer to copying objects. Cloning can produce three different types of objects from an original: copies, instances, and reference objects:

- **Copies**—The most common and familiar kind of clone object. They are exact copies of the original and can be modified, transformed, animated, and so on independently of the original.

- **Instances**—A kind of connected clone of an original object. If you modify an original object, its instance changes automatically. Conversely, if you modify the instanced clone, it changes the original. Although instances share the same modifiers, materials, maps, and animation controllers as the original object, each individual instance can have its own set of transforms, unique position in 3D space, and object properties.

- **References**—Also called one-way instances. Although referenced objects are instanced clones of the original object, they can have their own unique modifiers. The one-way instance refers to the fact that any modification made to the original object is passed on to its referenced clones, but any modification made to a reference is not passed back to the original object. This allows a reference object to take on individual attributes, animation, and so on.

To clone an object, you must first select it. Then the Clone command can be accessed in one of two ways. The first way is through Edit in the Menu Bar. The second way, which you'll learn by following the next set of steps, is the one you will use for 99% of your max cloning activities.

Right-click your model and select Top-level from the Subobjects list in the Quad Menu. This will take you out of Subobject mode. Select your Cooling_Tower_Master model for the next step of the process:

1. While still in Move mode ![cursor], hold down the Shift key and click your cooling tower model. This will open the Clone Options dialog box. Leave the default Object mode set to Copy and change the name of this clone to Cooling_Tower_Lattice, as shown in Figure 3.50. Click OK to exit the dialog box and create the cloned copy of the tower.

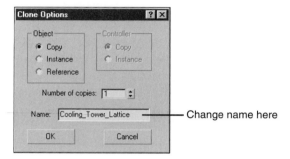

Change name here

Figure 3.50   You can also use the Shift key with the Rotate and Scale transforms to clone an object. Creating multiple clones of an object, by increasing the number of copies in the Clone Options dialog box, will result in cloned objects named Object 01, Object 02, and so on—the original name and an incremented number automatically assigned by max.

2. The cloned copy of the cooling tower is selected and sitting exactly on top of the original cooling tower. The Modify command panel shows the clone and its name at the top of the panel, followed by its modifier stack. You won't need to access the former modifiers for the purposes of this model, so select Edit Mesh at the top of the stack and right-click anywhere in the modifier stack window to open the Modifier Stack options list. Select Collapse All from the list, as shown in Figure 3.51.

3. Click Yes when the warning dialog box appears. This collapses the mesh, creating an editable mesh object.

4. Press the spacebar to lock the selection and Ctrl+right-click the Cooling_Tower_Lattice model. When the Quad Menu appears, click Modifiers and select Lattice from the Parametric Modifiers set in the upper-right quadrant of the Quad Menu. The model in your viewport will look like it just sprouted a gazillion jagged edges.

    The Lattice modifier adds a joint object to every vertex, which is in turn joined together by a strut along every edge of the surface mesh. This creates a Tinker Toy–like structure perfect for use as a framework for the cooling tower. The joint and strut parameters can be adjusted independently to create the look you are trying to achieve.

Figure 3.51   Collapsing the entire modifier stack in this way yields the same result as converting a model to an editable mesh.

5. Adjust the Struts parameters to the following settings or experiment with some of your own—Radius: 0.25; Segments: 1; Sides: 4. Check the box next to Smooth and leave the rest of the parameters as they are.

6. Change the Joints Geodesic Base Type to Icosa and adjust the Joints parameters as follows—Radius: 0.75; Segments: 2. Check the Smooth box and leave the rest of the parameter set to their defaults (see Figure 3.52).

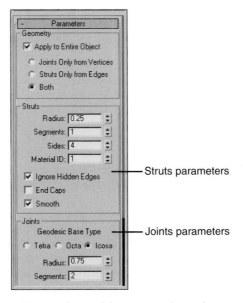

Figure 3.52   The Lattice Parameters rollout in the Modify command panel contains the parametric controls used to adjust the appearance of the joints and struts of the lattice structure.

Everything You Always Wanted to Know About Polyhedrals—But Were Afraid to Ask!

Polyhedrons are multi-sided geometric (geodesic) forms that max uses to define the form of the joints created by the Lattice modifier. A *regular* polyhedron (only five of these are possible) is a polyhedron whose polygonal faces are identical in both shape and size. In addition to the size, number, and shape of their polygonal surfaces, regular polyhedrons also have two spheres associated with the vertices and faces that define the polyhedron. The *circum-sphere*, measured by its diameter or circum-diameter, is the sphere that encompasses the polyhedron touching all its vertices. The *in-sphere*, measured by its *in-diameter*, is the sphere that fits inside the polyhedron touching all the faces. Polyhedrons are named by the number of faces they have and are defined by the number of faces, vertices, edges, and the angle (in degrees) between any two adjacent faces, which is known as the *dihedral* angle. Table 3.1 shows the big five.

Table 3.1   Regular Polyhedrons

Name	Faces	Vertices	Edges	Dihedral Angle
Tetrahedron	4	4	6	70.533
Cube	6	8	12	90
Octahedron	8	6	12	109.467
Dodecahedron	12	20	30	116.567
Icosahedron	20	12	30	138.183

Save your max file when you have finished! The superstructure is complete and should look something like Figure 3.53.

In the next section, you'll use the models you just made to begin production of Sc-01, the first scene you'll create for Area51.avi. The basic modeling process you have learned in this chapter provides a foundation for the subsequent techniques that will be introduced as you create the remaining scenes.

Each step along the way you'll also update the animatic you made in Chapter 2 to include the new imagery you'll create in each of the chapter Workshops in this book. And as always, experiment and try your own variations on the scenes, models, effects, and animation.

Figure 3.53   The completed cooling tower and superstructure models are a simple and effective introduction to basic modeling in 3ds max 4. Intermediate and advanced modeling are based on the same fundamental principles and techniques introduced in this process.

Max Workshop—Sc-01

In this section, you'll create the basic elements for Sc-01, including the camera and the sky used for the background. To begin the process, save your previous work as `Sc-01_Tower.max`, and then click File, Save As in the Menu Bar. When the Save File As dialog box appears, save this new file as `MAXWorkshop\Scene Models\Sc-01\Sc-01.max`.

> Saving your tower model as a separate file is an organizational safeguard that preserves its original geometry for use in other scene files. The complete model of scene Sc-01 can be found on the companion CD in the following directory: `MAXWorkshop\Help_Files\Chapter_3\EXSC_01.max`.

Tip

First Things First: Scene Setup

Before you begin the creation of any scene, two important parameters must be considered: the format of the rendered output and the scene length. In Chapter 2, you created an animatic that established both of these parameters. Setting up this new scene with the same settings requires a visit to the Render Scene and Time Configuration dialog boxes.

Configure Frame Rate and Animation Frame Count

Click Time Configuration ⌧ to open the Time Configuration dialog box. Change the settings in the Frame Rate section to Custom and set the FPS (Frames per Second) to 24. Change the Frame Count in the Animation section to 288, and set the Start Time to 1. This is the frame count you specified in the animatic created in Chapter 2 (see Figure 3.54).

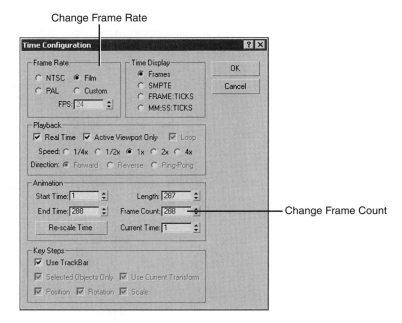

Change Frame Rate

Change Frame Count

Figure 3.54   The usefulness of an animatic is readily seen when you begin setting up the production scenes for Area51.avi. The pre-visualization process establishes all the scene parameters, such as Frame Count and output formats. This allows you to quickly and correctly set up each individual scene.

Specifying Rendering Output

Click Render Scene 🖼 in the Main Toolbar or press F10 to access the Render Scene dialog box. The only parameter you'll change at this time is the Output Size. Change the Width to 640 and the Height to 346 and lock the Image Aspect, as shown in Figure 3.55. When you are finished, click Close to close the dialog box and set the render output format.

Creating the background sky will introduce you to the Material Editor, which is the main texture creation and application tool in max. Chapter 4 goes into more depth about materials and textures and the specific use of this interesting and powerful part of max.

Sc-01: Background Sky

The gradient sky color for Sc-01 uses a procedural map applied in the Environment dialog box. Although these maps have some limitations, this is a simple and powerful tool to create exciting and fun BG (background) images. To evaluate the sky without seeing the tower models you've created, press Shift+O. This shortcut hides all geometry in your scene.

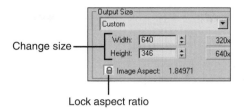

Change size

Lock aspect ratio

Figure 3.55 Locking the image aspect ratio allows you to quickly change the size of your rendered images for test renders.

Creating a Gradient Sky

At midday, the core of the sky directly overhead is a deep blue, which gradually lightens as your eye travels down to the horizon. This gradient effect is caused by the light energy that reaches your eyes from the distant horizon passing through many cubic miles of dust particles and gaseous smog vapors in the atmosphere. This is the atmospheric gradient effect you are trying to create for this scene and is why you use a gradient map for the BG sky.

Why the Sky Is Blue

If you've ever had a child ask this question, here's the answer. Every second, the sun converts about 4 million tons of its fuel into light energy. Each day, about 160 tons of that light energy falls onto the earth through our atmosphere. Some parts (wavelengths) of that sunlight are absorbed and diffused by the atmosphere. The sky is blue because that is the wavelength of light energy that is not absorbed by the atmosphere surrounding the earth. In a similar manner, you see an apple as green or red because the skin of the apple absorbs all wavelengths of light except that color, which is reflected back to your eyes.

You'll be using two parts of the max toolbox for this process: the Material Editor and the Environment dialog box. Follow these steps to create the background sky for Sc-01:

1. Press M to open the Material Editor. When it opens, move it over to the right side of your screen.

2. Select Rendering, Environment from the main Menu Bar. This opens the max Environment dialog box. Move it to the left of the Material Editor.

3. At the top of the Environment window in the section titled Common Parameters is a box titled Environment Map. This is where you will set up a background for your max scene.

4. Click the None button under Environment Map to access the Material/Map Browser. Scan this list of available material types and click Gradient. A gradient map appears in the upper-left corner preview window, as shown in Figure 3.56. Then click OK.

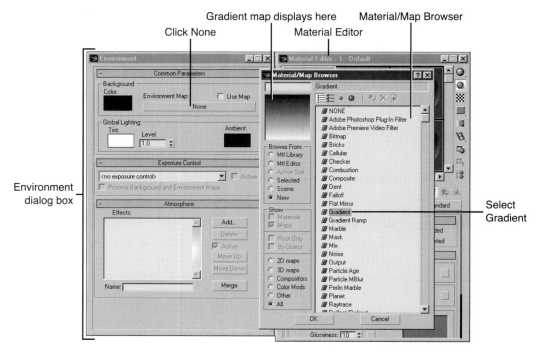

Gradient map displays here   Material/Map Browser

Click None   Material Editor

Environment
dialog box

Select
Gradient

Figure 3.56   Max 4 can use virtually any image or procedural map as a component of the materials you create. In this case, you are going to create a background using a Gradient map.

Map #0 (Gradient) appears in the Environment dialog box in the button that was previously titled None, and the box titled Use Map now has a check mark in it.

Using Drag and Drop to Move Map Files

Before you can use or modify the Gradient map in the background slot of the Environment window, you must put it into the Material Editor. Click the Gradient map title bar in the Environment menu. Without releasing the left mouse button, drag the map over to the upper-left material slot in the Material Editor, as shown in Figure 3.57. When you release the mouse button to drop the file, a window titled Instance (Copy) Map opens. Leave Instance as the default selection, and click OK.

The Gradient map from the Environment dialog box has been placed in the first map slot of your Material Editor (see Figure 3.58).

> To speed things along, the use of the drag-and-drop technique is described like this: "Drop file x onto the material slot y." The click-drag technique used to create geometry is described like this: drag, as in "drag in your window to create the box."

Tip

Drag-and-drop cursor

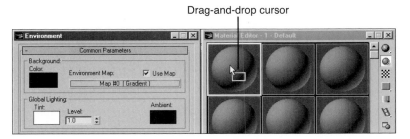

Figure 3.57 Drag and drop is the basic technique for moving many things, including material maps, in the max workspace.

Gradient map in place —

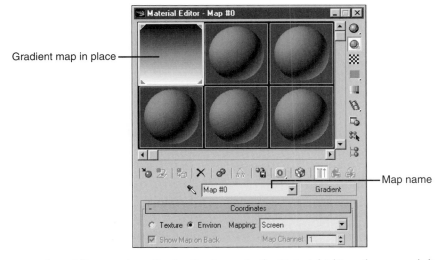

Map name

Figure 3.58 After you drag the Gradient map to the Material Editor, the upper-left preview window of the Material Editor shows the Gradient map from the Environment dialog box.

Editing the BG Sky

The Gradient map from the Environment dialog box is in the Material Editor ready for your modifications. You'll use the Material Editor parameter menus to modify this map. Close the Environment dialog box, and follow these steps:

1. Click in the text field that says Map #0 (in the middle of the Material Editor) and change the name to BG Sky (refer to Figure 3.58). Under the Coordinates slot, Environ is selected and Mapping is set to Screen. Leave these settings as they are.

> **Note**
>
> When a background uses Screen as its Coordinates setting, the map will always appear the same way in the screen regardless of the view in the viewport or how you move your POV. This screen map is not mapped onto any geometry; it's a software-generated or virtual image, also called a *procedural map*.

2. At the bottom of the Editor, Gradient Parameters is already open but you might not be able to see the entire parameter rollout. To scroll the window down to the Gradient Parameters portion of the rollout, place your cursor over a blank area of the rollout not occupied by a parameter control item. When you do this, the cursor turns into the helping hand cursor 🖑. Drag the cursor to scroll this window until you can see the Maps section's Gradient Parameters (see Figure 3.59).

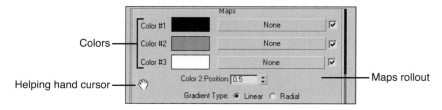

Figure 3.59 Max uses virtual windows within its menus to accommodate the complex and deep controls available for creating and modifying your images. To help you navigate these menus, the max cursor changes into a hand, allowing you to scroll the window to the place in the menu you want to use.

3. Click the white color field next to Color #3. The max Color Selector window opens (see Figure 3.60).

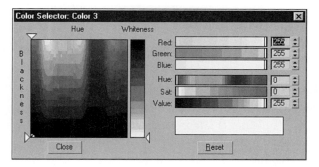

Figure 3.60 The max Color Selector is used to adjust the color parameters for everything that uses a color component in max.

4. In the upper-right side of this window are numerical input fields for the Red, Green, and Blue components of Color #3. Type 74 for Red, 159 for Green, and 128 for Blue. As you key in the values, Color #3 changes to the horizon color.

From here on, when there is a color to create, the RGB sequence will be given like this: 176,166,227. When you have multiple parameters to change, use the Tab key to jump between text-entry boxes to speed up your entry process.

5. Without closing the Color Selector, click the black field next to Color #1 and type 32,68,75 for its RGB value.

6. Select Color #2 by clicking the gray field next to its name and type 56,122,120. You now have a gradient sky. A few more adjustments and you'll render the result. Close the Color Selector dialog box.

7. Change the value in the text field titled Color 2 Position to 0.4. You can do this by typing the number or using the arrows to the right of the numeric field. The POV used in Sc-01 doesn't allow you to see much of the horizon color, so changing the Color 2 Position adjusts the position of Color #2 in the gradient to create just a blush of color at the bottom of the image.

When you are finished, close the Material Editor. The ability to evaluate your work as you go is important. Max provides several tools to allow you to see the animation, textures, and geometry you are creating. Rendering your imagery is a fundamental way to see your work and evaluate your creative process.

Test Renders: Seeing Your Progress

The *rendering* process in max is used to create image-output files. Preliminary or test renders are used for in-process evaluation of your max models, animation, lighting, and so forth.

Activate the viewport you want to render by clicking in it before you launch your render. In the case of the BG Sky, any viewport you render will create exactly the same sky image. This is because this BG is an environment screen map, which is a virtual part of the screen and not dependent on a specific POV viewport.

Press Shift+Q or click the Quick Render icon to render your scene and see the gradient sky you just created. After starting the render process, two windows open (see Figure 3.61). The window on the right is the Rendering dialog box, which shows the progress of the rendering process and all the other settings you've specified in the Render Scene dialog box. The window in the left of the figure is the Virtual Frame Buffer.

Virtual Frame Buffer

When the render is finished, the Render progress window disappears and the Virtual Frame Buffer remains open on your screen. The Virtual Frame Buffer (VFB) has some great features that are important to understand:

- **Save Bitmap**—Used to save the image as it currently appears in the VFB.
- **Clone**—Displays a new VFB containing a copy of the VFB contents.

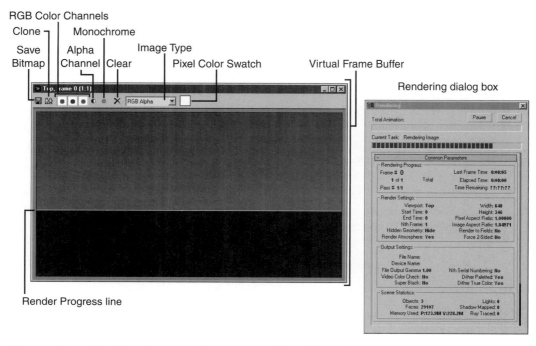

RGB Color Channels

Clone

Monochrome

Save
Bitmap

Alpha
Channel | Clear

Image Type

Pixel Color Swatch

Virtual Frame Buffer

Rendering dialog box

Render Progress line

Figure 3.61 The Virtual Frame Buffer is a powerful tool for evaluating and creating your scenes, and the controls and tools in it will become indispensable as you complete your production of the scenes for Area51.avi.

Tip

Clones of the VFB are useful when you want to do side-by-side comparisons of different lighting schemes, textures, or, in this case, a rendered BG. Use the Clone button to create a clone of the VFB. This copies the image into a new window. Then with both windows open, change the element attribute in your scene (lighting, texture, and the like) that you want to evaluate, and then re-render the scene. The new render is displayed in the original VFB, while the old image is still in the clone VFB window. Now you can evaluate the change by comparing both images side by side. Multiple VFB clones are useful for in-process evaluation of your shot images.

- **Enable RGB Channel buttons**—Toggle the color channels for the image off and on. This can be used to evaluate the RGB components of your image for certain types of image output.

- **Alpha Channel**—Shows the rendered object's alpha channel. When max renders an object, it also renders its alpha channel. In the case of your BG Sky, there is no alpha channel because no geometry is used to create the sky.

- **Monochrome**—Shows what the image looks like in grayscale. Although this changes the way your file appears in the VFB, it doesn't change your image into grayscale format.

- **Clear**—Empties the Virtual Frame Buffer, effectively deleting the image from its memory.

- **Pixel Color Swatch**—Opens the Color Selector: Pixel Color window. Use this window to specify and select specific colors that have been rendered in your scene.

Use your right mouse button and drag your cursor in the image. An eyedropper and the window shown in Figure 3.62 appear while you are dragging. As you drag, the eyedropper is sampling the colors of the pixels in the window and the Pixel Color window changes color to match the pixel you are sampling in the image. You can also drag the color in the Pixel Color window into your Material Editor to use as a map color.

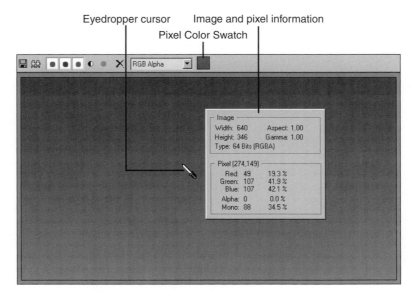

Figure 3.62   Hold down the Ctrl key and click in the VFB to zoom in on the image. Right-click in the VFB while pressing the Ctrl key to zoom out from the image. These image-navigation conventions can be used in the View Image File window, Asset Manager, and in viewports using ActiveShade mode.

Cameras and Camera View Controls

Cameras in max function in the same way as their real-world counterparts. Adding a camera or multiple cameras into your scenes allows you to accurately control and create the composition, POV, and camera movements specified in your storyboards. According to the Sc-01 storyboard, there is a zoom-out in this scene. You'll create that zoom in Chapter 4 by animating the camera that you'll create in this section.

The Sc-01 storyboard shows a worms-eye POV looking up the side of the cooling tower to the sky and clouds above. To place the camera correctly in the scene, you'll first need to unhide your geometry.

Using the Display Command Panel

The controls in the Display command panel are used to specify which max geometry, lights, cameras, and so on are displayed in your viewports. They are also used to freeze and unfreeze objects and alter an object's display characteristics.

Click the Display command panel icon ![icon] in your Command Panels and put your cursor over the left border. When the cursor changes to a double-ended horizontal arrow, drag the Command Panel window to the left to see an expanded view of the Display command panel (see Figure 3.63).

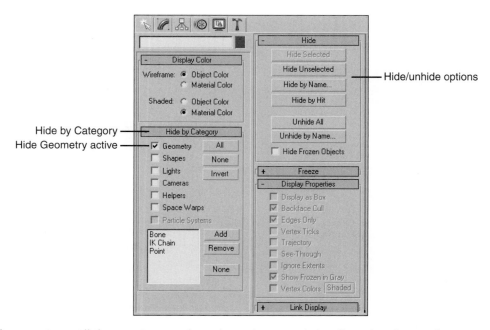

Figure 3.63   All the max Command Panels can be expanded or floated in the interface to provide easier access to their functional rollouts.

When you used Shift+O to hide the cooling tower geometry, you told max to invoke the hide Geometry selection in Hide by Category. To unhide your cooling tower, press Shift+O or uncheck the Geometry check box in the Hide by Category section.

Using the Shift+O keyboard shortcut is appropriate for scenes that have very few objects in them. For more complex scenes, a better way to hide and unhide objects is to use the controls found in the Hide rollout. Grab the left border of the Command Panel display and drag it to the right to return it to its default size.

When you hide any max elements using the Hide by Category controls, the items checked can be unhidden only if you uncheck the box next to them. So, if you can't find something that you know you just created, check this section of the Display command panel to be sure you haven't inadvertently hidden it.

Creating the Sc-01 Camera

Press R and W to change to the Right view and maximize your viewport. Click the Create command panel icon ![icon], and then click the Cameras icon ![icon] in that panel (see Figure 3.64).

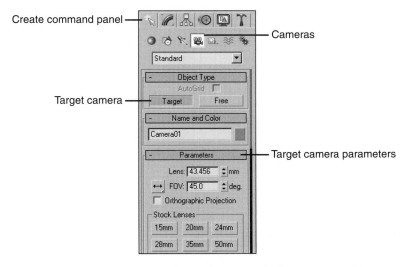

Create command panel

Cameras

Target camera

Target camera parameters

Figure 3.64   A Target camera gives you independent control of a camera and its target.

To create a Target camera, put your cursor just below and to the left of the cooling tower models and drag up in the viewport, angling toward the top of the tower. Then release the button to create the target (see Figure 3.65). Save your work.

Press C to change your viewport to Camera01. You are now looking at the cooling tower through the camera you have created. When you are in a Camera viewport, you can use the Camera view controls shown in Figure 3.66 to modify the camera's POV, or you can select the camera or its target and transform them independently in any of the Orthographic views.

The Camera Viewport Navigation Controls are different than the Perspective or Orthographic viewport controls you have been using. Here's a brief explanation of these important controls:

- **Dolly**—Moves the camera directly in or out along its line of sight. This is also called zoom in our storyboards.

- **Perspective**—Allows you to change the field of view and dolly the camera at the same time.

- **Roll**—Rotates a camera around its line of sight. In a Target camera, the line of sight is the line that connects the camera with its target.

- **Zoom Extents All**—Doesn't operate on the camera view itself. When selected, it affects all other noncamera viewports.

- **Min/Max Toggle**—Operates just like all the other min/max toggles. Clicking this icon changes the viewport configuration from a single maximized viewport to a multiple viewport configuration.

- **Orbit Camera**—Acts like Arc Rotate for noncamera views and moves the selected camera in an orbit around its target.

- **Truck Camera**—Similar to Pan and moves the camera laterally, parallel to the view.

- **Field of View**—Zooms you in and out of a scene while changing the field of view (FOV). Larger FOVs allow you to see more of the scene, creating a wide angle or fisheye lens type of image. Smaller FOVs create telephoto or closeup imagery, flattening the perspective in the scene as your FOV zooms in closer.

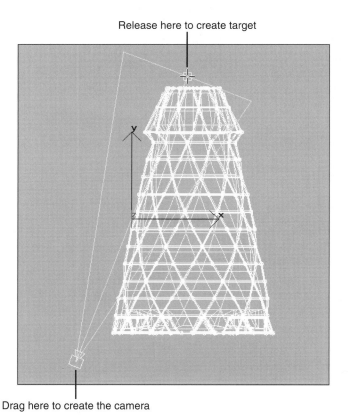

Release here to create target

Drag here to create the camera

Figure 3.65 Use the transform commands or the Camera view controls in the Viewport Navigation Controls to modify a camera's position after it has been created.

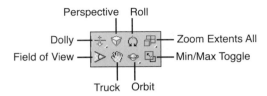

Figure 3.66   The Camera view controls are included on the tear card that comes with this book. Keyboard shortcuts for Camera view controls and all the Viewport Navigation Controls are also found on the inside of the front and back covers of this book.

Use the Camera view controls to adjust the POV to match the one shown in the storyboard. When you are finished, press Shift+Q to render your scene, which should look like Figure 3.67.

Figure 3.67   This image can now be placed in your animatic, taking the place of the Sc-01 storyboard image that is currently in the VP Queue.

Click Save Bitmap 🖫 in the Virtual Frame Buffer. When the Browse Images for Output window opens, browse to MAXWorkshop\Images_ArtWork\ and make a new folder titled animatic_Stills. Name this image Sc-01 and save it as a Targa image file, as shown in Figure 3.68.

When you click Save, the Targa Image Control window opens. In the Image Attributes section, leave the Bits-Per-Pixel set to 32 and uncheck the Compress box. This tells max to create a 32-bit uncompressed image. In the Additional Information section, enter your name and the name of this project, and add some comments identifying the purpose of this image (see Figure 3.69).

Update the Area 51 Animatic

The animatic you created in Chapter 2 is designed to be a work in progress that's updated every time you create a new section of the content. The preliminary image for Sc-01 is the first digital image that will replace the storyboard placeholder in the animatic. Here's how it's done:

1. Save your current max file, Sc-01, and open MAXWorkshop\Scene Models\Animatic\ Area51_Animatic.max. This is the file you used to create the animatic in Chapter 2.

2. When the file opens, click Rendering, Video Post in the main Menu Bar.

3. When Video Post opens, double-click Sc-01 Cooling Tower Upshot.tif in the VP Queue. This will open the Edit Input Image Event window. Make note of the VP Start and End Times: 191, 478. You'll need these numbers in a moment (see Figure 3.70).

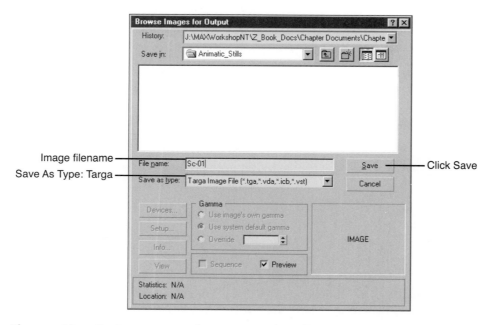

Figure 3.68   The Browse Images for Output window allows you to organize and save your rendered imagery and animation in virtually every common format used in digital content creation.

4. Click the Files button shown in Figure 3.70 to open the Select Image File for Video Post Input browser window.

5. Browse to MAXWorkshop\Images_Artwork\Animatic_Stills and load Sc-01.tga. This is the still image of the cooling tower you just created. Click Open and change the VP Start Time to 191 and the End Time to 478 for this new image.

6. Click Save Sequence ▣ and save this sequence in MAXWorkshop\Video Post\Sequences\ Area51_Animatic.vpx. Then save your max file.

7. Click Execute Sequence ▣ to render your animatic with the new still image in place.

Your modified Video Post Queue with the new image file in place adjusted to the proper length in the queue should look like Figure 3.71.

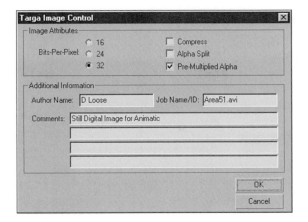

Figure 3.69   The Targa Image Control window is an important organizational tool that will help you annotate and keep track of your max images.

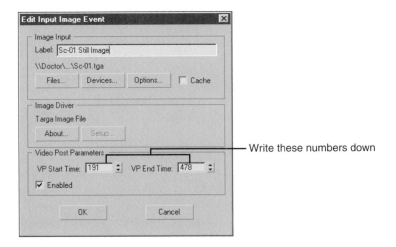

— Write these numbers down

Figure 3.70   Every time you replace an image in your animatic's Video Post Queue, you'll also need to reset the image's Start Time and End Time.

It should take no more than a few minutes to swap in a new animatic still image. Rendering the new AVI will take the same time as it did before: approximately 30 minutes. Keep up with this process and update your animatic whenever you've completed a new part of Area51.avi.

New still image in place

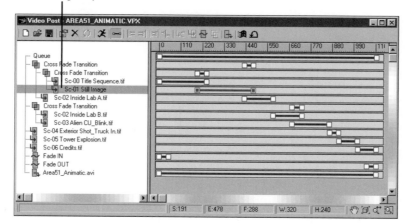

Figure 3.71 Updating your animatic each time you create new imagery is a great way to show your art director, producer, or clients exactly where you are in the production process.

Next Steps

The first next step would be to change the design of the cooling tower to something from your own imagination. Changing door details or experimenting with some of the other parametric modifiers to yield different results would also help you learn more about the concepts in this chapter.

The sky colors were chosen to go with the overall color theme used throughout the Workshop. A next step here would be to experiment with the gradient sky colors. If you find a combination that you like, use it throughout the Workshop whenever the color theme variations are applied to texture, lighting, or effects.

Lesson 4 of the prequel to this book, *3D Studio MAX 3.0 Workshop*, shows how to add a moon and star field to a background sky. By using the techniques discussed in that lesson, you can add similar finishing touches to Sc-01, creating more complex and sophisticated imagery.

In the next chapter, you'll be introduced to the basic techniques and processes of how textures and materials are developed, applied, and animated in max. And you'll create the animating cloud layer and tower textures needed to complete Sc-01.

MATERIAL DEVELOPMENT

PRINCIPLES / PROCESS

0-7857-2546-0

Visual Touch: The Art of Material and Texture Development

"Artists and Animators need to have a first-hand acquaintance with reality—a tactile, visual, auditory immersion in real things—in order to have a sense of what things are and what emotions they evoke in their raw form." - John Dykstra, Visual Effects Pioneer Extraordinaire, *3D Magazine*, January 2000

Like the parts of a body, wherein the head cannot say it has no need of the feet, no single part of a successful digital production can lay claim to being the most important part. Each discrete component, such as the story, animation, material development, lighting, effects, compositing, music, and so forth, all combine to create the holistic experience your audience expects.

When there is a problem in a scene, the most important component is the one that is causing the problem. For example, a beautifully designed and modeled character cannot compensate for poor animation, no matter how good the model looks. And, as you might have noticed, big-budget special effects cannot make up for the lack of a story or poor acting. When a specific digital content component isn't created correctly or at the appropriate level of production value, the quality of the entire production suffers.

Because the work you produce is primarily visual, you must access the imagination of your audience to help them understand the story you are telling. To facilitate suspension of disbelief, their eyes have to *visually touch* the atmosphere, the environments, and the surfaces of the objects in your scene.

The audience is your greatest critic and your most powerful ally. They are interested in your story and are ready and eager to believe what you place before them. Mastering the principles of art *and* science at the core of material development will help you create imagery that your audience can touch with their eyes.

Introduction to Material Development

"Fundamental art and science skills: drawing, color, composition, lighting, study of motion. Every Studio encounters people who think they can become an artist without developing those skills. Wrong." - Ed Catmull, Executive VP and Chief Technology Officer of Pixar Animation Studios, *3D Magazine*, January 2000

If you want to succeed as a max artist, you can't afford to be ignorant of the symbiotic relationship between science and art in digital content creation. Physics, kinesiology, anatomy, astronomy, and so forth all hold the keys to understanding principles that will guide your work. Learning the secrets of science is exciting, especially when you understand how the application of those secrets can change your work from mundane to magnificent.

How You See the World: Sight and Perception

Seeing is the physiological process of light entering the eye, stimulating the cells on the retina, and transmitting the resultant information to the visual cortex of your brain. Perception is the cognitive process you go through to decide what those images mean. The eye tells you what is out there; your perception determines the meaning and the reality of what you are seeing.

Everything you see in the world around you is made up of a complex physical structure of basic atomic and subatomic elements held together by electromagnetic energy. The vibration of the atoms in each object determines the visible, tactile, and physical attributes of its appearance, mass, weight, surface properties, and so forth.

To be an effective digital artist, you must begin to perceive each of the objects in the world around you in terms of how light falls on its surface, the reflection patterns that are produced by the form of the object, and its relationship to you in the environment.

Understanding Light—Object Interaction

The primary scientific principles of material development are centered around the physics of how light interacts with an object's surface. Although there are many ways to learn about these concepts, the most powerful teachers you have are your own eyes.

In the January 2000 edition of *3D Magazine*, Phil Tippett, special effects creator for *Star Wars*, animation supervisor for *Jurassic Park*, and co-director of the battle sequences in *Starship Troopers*, was asked: "What will be the most important skills for professional artists and animators to possess in the coming decade?" This is what he said:

> "Observation of the world around them. How they move in space, how light bounces off surfaces, how things look and feel and what the true relationships of things are. In a 2D medium like painting or drawing, a good artist will spend a lot of time out in the world observing and will bring that back to the studio."

Phil's statement is representative of the observation skills and basic scientific knowledge expected from you as a max artist.

Light Energy: Particles and Waves

Light particles move in waves that bounce off, move through, and bend around the objects in their path. The first law describing the wave-like behavior of light particles deals with reflection—how light bounces off an object. Reflected light creates the visible and distorted images that can be seen in the surfaces of all natural and manmade artifacts and objects.

Assume Nothing!

You might assume that max will take care of reflections for you. This is a dangerous assumption that, unfortunately, many digital artists make. Consequently, they fail to make full use of the principles of science, preferring instead to rely on the computer to do their work for them. And it shows in their work. Max is a powerful tool and can compensate for some deficiencies in your knowledge of the scientific principles governing the appearance of surfaces. However, in the long run, it is imperative to learn why surfaces appear the way they do and how you can use the principles of optics and physics to achieve your artistic vision.

The First Law of Reflection Theory

When a light wave approaches a surface, the angle at which the wave strikes that surface is equal to the angle at which the light wave leaves the surface. This is the basic law of reflection theory.

The approaching light wave is called the *incident ray*; the light wave leaving the surface is called the *reflected ray*. At the point where the incident ray hits the surface, an imaginary line perpendicular to the surface, known as a *surface normal* or *normal line*, is created.

The normal line divides the angle created by the incident and reflected rays of light into two equal angles. The angle between the incident ray and the surface normal is called the *angle of incidence*. The angle formed between the surface normal and the reflected ray is called the *angle of reflection*. Figure 4.1 shows a simple diagram illustrating this law.

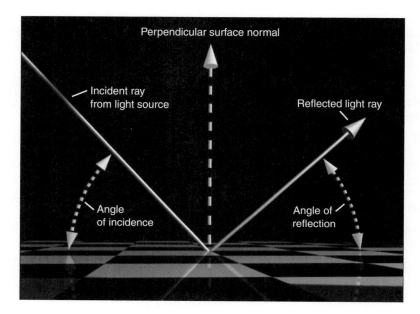

Figure 4.1   "The angle of incidence is equal to the angle of reflection" is the first law of reflection. This is a basic law that remains true under most lighting conditions you will encounter.

Understanding Surface Normals

The cooling tower model is a mesh made up of individual polygons. Each one of the faces that make up those polygons has a surface normal. Max uses surface normals to define, in part, how light interacts with your objects and to control the visibility and appearance of all the surfaces you create in your polygon models. Knowing how to access and modify the surface normals of your polygon objects is an important basic technique:

1. Press W and P to change to a full screen, perspective view and click the Cooling_Tower_Master model to select it.

2. Right-click the model and click Hide Unselected from the Display Quad Menu as shown in Figure 4.2.

3. Click the Modify command panel, right-click the cooling tower, and select Sub-objects, Polygon from the upper-left quadrant of the Quad Menu. Right-click the model again and select Ignore Backfacing at the top of the left side of the quadrant.

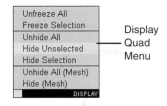

Figure 4.2   Hide Unselected can also be accessed in the Display Command Panel .

4. Click one of the polygons in the front of the surface mesh, press Z to access the Zoom command , and zoom in on the selected polygon. Click Show Normals in the Selection rollout of the Modify command panel. Your Perspective viewport and Command Panel should look like Figure 4.3.

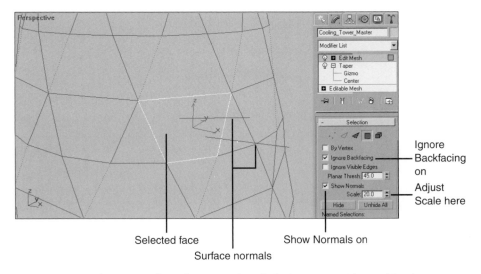

Figure 4.3   Max uses surface normals to determine how light interacts with an object's surface.

Two normals are shown in your viewport. That's because the selected polygon is made up of two faces, each one with its own surface normal. The orientation of the surface normals tells max which side of the face is to be visible in the viewport. The polygon faces of the cooling tower are visible because their surface normals are pointing out, perpendicular to the front side of their respective surfaces.

Note   Later in this Workshop you'll change the orientation of the normals in Sc-02's set models so that you can create the interior of the Alien lab inside the cooling tower. Changing normals is referred to as *flipping*.

Scroll down in the Modify command panel to the Surface Properties rollout shown in Figure 4.4 and click Flip. This will change the orientation of the surface normal for the selected faces.

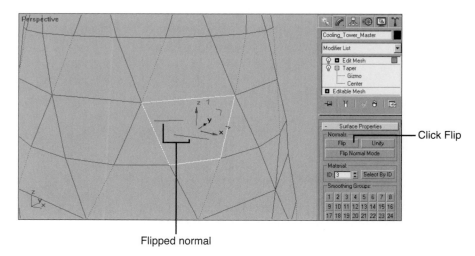

Click Flip

Flipped normal

Figure 4.4   Flipping a normal changes how a polygon is seen in the viewport and also affects how lighting interacts with the surface material.

The Surface Properties rollout contains some useful tools to modify surface normals and the appearance of the surfaces of your models when they are textured, lit, and rendered. Here are the definitions of these other parts of the rollout:

- **Unify**—Unifies the normals of selected polygons, causing them to face the same direction.
- **Flip Normal Mode**—Allows you to flip normals just by clicking the polygons in your viewport. Be careful with this command and be sure Show Normals is on when you use it.
- **Material: ID**—Selecting a set of polygons and changing the number in this box allows you to assign a unique material identification number to selected surfaces. Having different surfaces carry different ID numbers enables you to create materials that apply different textures to different parts of the model based on that surface ID.
- **Select by ID**—Allows you to select surfaces by their material ID number. This creates a selection set of subobject surfaces that you can use for modification, animation, selective smoothing, and texturing.
- **Smoothing Groups**—Allows you to independently select and smooth specific parts of an object's geometry. Selecting a set of polygons and clicking one of these numbered boxes assigns that number to the faces you selected, creating a smoothing group. You can use this tool in max to have smooth and faceted geometry within the same object.

You'll learn more about how these controls are used as you use them to create the scenes for Area51.avi. In addition to principles of reflection theory that you have seen so far, the concepts and science behind light-object interaction include refraction and diffraction. The underlying concept in all material development is that surfaces are like lenses. And the lens-like quality of a surface is created by both its form and material.

The Lens-Like Quality of Surfaces

The objects shown in Figure 4.5 distort and reflect light from their surfaces according to their unique shapes. All surfaces have this lens-like quality, which is produced because of the form of the object and its material. To create effective and believable materials, it is critical to understand that the shape *and* the material of an object determine the reflective patterns seen in its surface.

Figure 4.5   Curved surfaces distort the reflections of the objects seen in them. This capability of curved surfaces to compress, distort, and even magnify the reflected image of an object is akin to the physics of lens optics.

When light is reflected off a mirrored surface, the reflected light carries information back to your eyes. The brain then interprets the information and you see the visual memes you know as a chrome cylinder, sphere, and so on. It is the light that enters your eyes that tells you about the form and material of the objects in the environment.

Mirrored surfaces reflect virtually all the light that strikes them. When light waves strike identical forms made from different materials, the reflected light rays carry the information about the material differences. Figure 4.6 diagrams what happens when light strikes a smooth surface, such as a mirror or polished metal, and a rough surface, such as wood or rock.

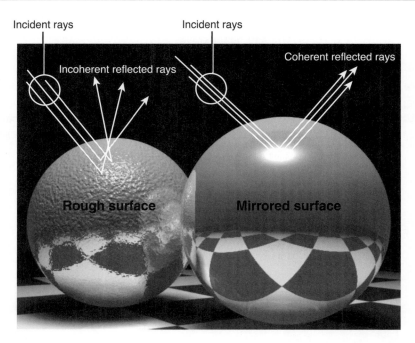

Figure 4.6   Reflected light rays become broken up or incoherent by their interaction with rough surface materials.

Incident light rays striking a polished surface remain *coherent* as they reflect off the surface. Coherent light rays carry a complete reflected image of the objects in their environment, including color, shape, spatial relationships, and so on.

Light rays reflect off a rough surface at all kinds of different angles. These light rays are called *incoherent* and can't carry the complete environment picture as a mirrored surface does. However, even though the image is broken up, the reflected light rays still carry some color and reflected-image information.

Figure 4.7 shows a comparison among three cooling towers that use the same metallic material. The difference between the materials is the relative roughness of their surface texture.

Materials and First Surface Reflections

At some time in your career as a digital artist, you will be asked to create materials that are both reflective and transparent. Water, glass, the clear-coat over the painted surfaces of most automobiles, polished or waxed surfaces of wood, transparent plastics, and common household mirrors are examples of materials that simultaneously exhibit these two attributes. All these types of materials create what is called *first surface reflections*.

First surface reflections occur when an object's surface is made from a material that is both transparent and reflective. When light waves strike a normal household mirror, some of the incident rays are reflected by the first surface of the glass, as shown in Figure 4.8. This creates a first surface reflection.

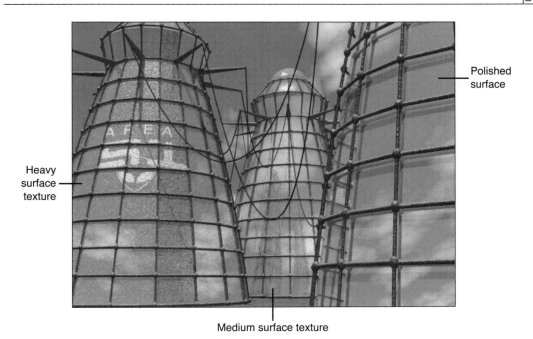

Polished
surface

Heavy
surface
texture

Medium surface texture

Figure 4.7   Although the complete image and color of the reflected environment can be seen only in the polished surface, notice that the same reflection patterns and colors are seen in the surfaces of the other cylinders.

Everyday First Surface Reflections

Windows in full sunlight reflect light just as a mirror would. This is because the relatively dark interior behind the windows creates a perfect background for first surface reflections of the outside world, sky, sun, buildings, and so on.

Any bright or light-colored object reflecting into windows on the shady side of a building or car will also create a mirror-like first surface reflection you can't see through.

First surface reflections also occur when a material is coated with another transparent material. Wood polish creates a reflective thickness of wax on top of the wood surface—the clear-coat paints used in automotive finishes do the same. Although these first surfaces are barely thousandths of an inch thick, the incident rays still follow the same rules of reflection.

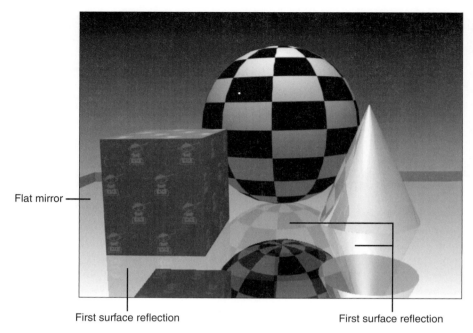

Flat mirror

First surface reflection

First surface reflection

Figure 4.8   Some of the light rays striking the first surface of a mirror are reflected immediately. The rest strike the mirror material at the back of the glass and are then reflected.

The Old Masters: Painting and Reflected Light

Artists, such as the Dutch master Jan Vermeer and the American master Andrew Wyeth, used the physics of first surface reflection to create the beautiful depth of color and vivid luminosity seen in their incredible paintings.

When light strikes the layered pigment surfaces of such a painting, some of the light is immediately reflected back to your eyes, carrying color and value information. The rest of the light continues through transparent glazes striking the layers of opaque pigment underneath. The light then reflects back out through the glaze layers, carrying color and value information to our eyes and giving the paintings their amazing inner glow of light.

Materials and Refraction

First surface reflections also occur in the water, except for those areas that reflect the dark underside of objects that aren't in direct sunlight. Shadows and reflections of dark or unlit objects seen in transparent and reflective materials, such as water and glass, make the surface more transparent and less reflective in those areas. In the case of water, if it's clear enough, the dark reflection allows more light to pass through, illuminating the rocks under the surface.

If you hold a stick upright in the water, you will see two distinct optical phenomena occur. You will see the stick's first surface reflection on the water and you will see the image of the stick under the water bend abruptly at the point at which it passes through the first surface. This optical illusion is a result of light refraction.

When light waves pass from one medium to another, the path of the wave bends at the boundary between the two media. The light rays, in the case of the water and the stick, are passing through air and water, which are separated by the water's surface—the boundary between the media. It's at that surface boundary that the incident rays of light bend, causing the stick to also appear bent below the surface of the water. In addition to bending light rays, refraction also distorts the image under the water, which causes the part of the stick under the water to appear shorter.

The amount of the refractive bend and distortion of the light passing through a material is known as the material's *index of refraction,* or *IOR.* Water, glass, air, transparent plastic, organic crystal elements such as diamonds, elemental gases, and ice are some of the materials that refract the light rays passing through them (see Figure 4.9).

Materials and Diffraction

The third type of light-object interaction is called diffraction. *Diffraction* describes how light waves behave as they pass through an opening in an object's surface or bend around the outside surfaces of an illuminated object. Diffraction causes shadows to look the way they do and is also responsible for the edge or rim lighting phenomenon seen in intensely backlit objects (see Figure CP.12 in the color section).

Diffraction is primarily generated by how you create and adjust your lighting in max. And it doesn't happen automatically; you might have to fake it. Materials can also be created in such a way to produce a diffraction effect in your imagery.

Light rays spread out from a light source in curved waves, not in straight lines. As light strikes an object, some of the rays are reflected. The rest bend around it and continue on their way—their direction and intensity slightly altered. Diffraction is the underlying science behind why objects far away from your POV appear blurred or fuzzy, which is also called *atmospheric perspective.* Creating materials, lighting, and effects based on the principle of diffraction will help you create depth and realism in your images.

Reflection, refraction, and diffraction are important scientific principles that reveal how light rays behave when interacting with the materials and surfaces of the objects you build in max. How you put these principles into practice is up to your own individual vision and an understanding of the basic material-creation tool in max—the Material Editor.

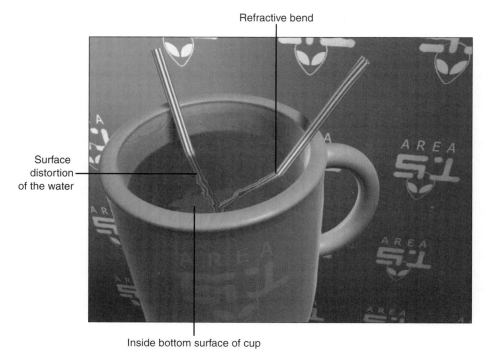

Refractive bend

Surface
distortion
of the water

Inside bottom surface of cup

Figure 4.9 Because the inside of the cup is not in direct light, the refracted image of the bottom of the container can be seen below the surface of the water.

Material Editor Basics

The look and feel of the materials you create in max is limited by three factors: your understanding of the software and the technical creative process, your knowledge of scientific principles, and your imagination.

These three factors are interdependent and synergistic. Your imagination can be stimulated by an understanding of how to use the tools and knowledge of the science behind your work. And your expertise with max can be magnified by imaginative and scientific experimentation.

In this chapter's Workshop, you'll create the textures for the cooling tower and the animating cloud layer. As you work through the process, you'll also gain more knowledge and understanding about the Material Editor.

The first section of this chapter introduced one of the three synergistic factors at the foundation of your material development work: knowledge of scientific principles. Expanding your mastery of the software and the technical creative process of the Material Editor also requires an understanding of its basic structure.

Anatomy of the Material Editor

Press M to open the Material Editor or click its icon ▨ in the Main Toolbar. Click the Map slot next to the BG Sky map. Change the name of this map to Cooling_Tower_Master, as shown in Figure 4.10. The following definitions will help you understand the anatomy of the Material Editor.

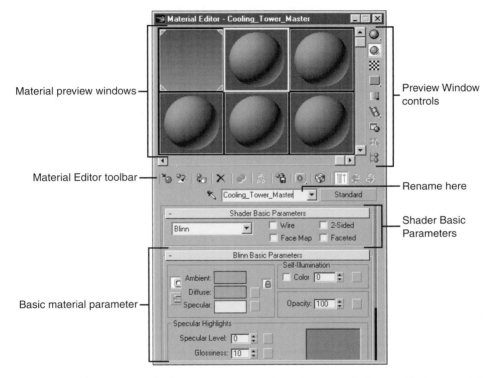

Material preview windows

Preview Window controls

Material Editor toolbar

Rename here

Shader Basic Parameters

Basic material parameter

Figure 4.10   The Material Editor is a miniature digital content design tool in its own right. Learning to use the depth of this powerful tool is an important step in your development as a max artist.

- **Preview window**—Shows you a preview of the material as it's created in the Material Editor. Any change you make as you develop the material is automatically updated in the preview window and also in the corresponding objects in the scene to which the selected material is assigned.

- **Preview window controls**—Determine how the preview window appears—its type of display, background, backlighting, and so forth.

- **Material Editor toolbar**—The controls in this section allow you to organize how materials are used in the scene.

- **Shader Basic Parameters**—Max's seven basic shaders are Anisotropic, Blinn, Metal, Multi-Layer, Oren-Nayar-Blinn, Phong, and Strauss. The other selections on the right side of this section allow you to specify four special rendering modes for the shader.

- **Basic material parameters**—Control the parameters used to define the color and value of reflected light seen in the materials you create. The Ambient channel controls the color of a surface not in direct light. The Diffuse channel creates the color of a surface in direct light. The Specular channel and Specular Highlights parameters determine the color and intensity of the reflected light and highlights seen in the material surface.

You'll be learning more about the specific controls in the Material Editor structure as you use them to create the materials for Sc-01. The next section introduces some of the basic terminology used in the Material Editor.

Basic Terms: Materials, Maps, Textures, and Shaders

Maps, materials, textures, and shaders are basic terms used in the max material-editing process. To understand the concepts behind material and texture design, here are some simple definitions of these terms:

- **Maps**—Procedural algorithms and 2D image files used to simulate the appearance of natural, synthetic, or imaginary surfaces. Max provides 32 different types of maps for use in the creation of materials. Appendix B, "Dr. D's Essential Guide to Standard Material Component Maps," shows the effects that can be achieved by adding maps to the material component channels.

- **Material**—The best generic term for the texture applied to the surface of max objects. It is a composite of several components, including maps and shader parameters. Max provides 10 types of basic textures to choose from: Blend, Composite, Double Sided, Matte/Shadow, Morpher, Multi/Sub-Object, Raytrace, Shellac, Standard (the max default material), and Top/Bottom.

- **Texture**—The physical characteristics of an object's surface. Textures can be interchanged with material to describe the surface appearance of an object. A simple example is the difference between sandpaper and a mirror. One is rough and the other smooth. The texture of paper is referred to as its *tooth*; of wood, it's referred to as its *grain*; of grass, its *fiber*; and so on.

- **Shaders**—A component of a material that attempts to re-create how light interacts with a surface. Shaders do this by using math and physics algorithms to simulate light refraction, diffraction, and reflection. Shaders are named after the scientists who wrote the algorithm or the light phenomenon the algorithm is re-creating.

First Things First: Applying UVW Mapping Coordinates

Mapping coordinates must be assigned to your models before you can properly apply a material. These specialized coordinates tell max how to apply materials to an object's surface. They are either generated at the time the object is created or are added later by the application of a mapping modifier. The Lattice modifier you used to create the exterior superstructure created mapping coordinates for the joints and struts when you applied it to the cylinder.

XYZ and UVW Coordinates

In 3D space, objects are oriented according to XYZ coordinates, which relate to their parametric height, width, and length. Max materials need similar coordinates to control the 3D spatial assignment of materials onto objects in your scene. Instead of using XYZ as the coordinate convention, mapping coordinates are referred to as UVW coordinates—U relating to the X-axis, V to the Y-axis, and W to the Z-axis.

The original cylinder of the cooling tower has been modified at the subobject level to create its final form. The mapping coordinates associated with its original primitive shape are no longer valid and can't be used by max to control the assignment of materials to its surface. Applying a UVW Map modifier to the cooling tower will solve this problem. This modifier is also used to apply mapping coordinates to objects without any mapping. Learning how to assign a UVW Map modifier is an important basic process, which you will use often:

1. Select Cooling_Tower_Master and open the Modify command panel 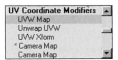.

2. Be sure the Edit Mesh Modifier at the top of the stack is selected, and click UVW Map from the UV Coordinate Modifiers set in the Modifier List to add it to the towers modifier stack (see Figure 4.11).

Figure 4.11 Use the UVW Map modifier to create and control the mapping type, size, and tiling parameters for your max models.

3. The UVW modifier appears in the stack list and an orange plane intersecting your cooling tower appears in the viewport. The intersecting orange plane is a gizmo that provides a visual representation of max's default Planar-mapping type (refer to Figure 4.11).

4. Change the mapping type from Planar to Cylindrical. The planar mapping gizmo changes to a cylindrical gizmo surrounding the entire cooling tower, as shown in Figure 4.12.

The single most important function of digital content creation is to support the story being told. Every component part of the objects in your scene, including their materials, establishes the visual words that support this goal.

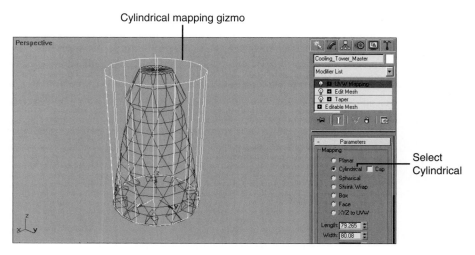

Cylindrical mapping gizmo

Select Cylindrical

Figure 4.12   Assigning a UVW Map modifier to an object gives you a lot more control over how the map appears in the surfaces of your objects. The Cylindrical mapping type was chosen because it's the mapping type closest to the shape of the cooling tower.

Area 51 Weathered Metal

Before you create a material, you must determine the story the material will tell about the object it's applied to and the environment it exists in. Here's the story about the material applied to the cooling tower.

Area 51, also known as Groom Lake, is a secret military installation in the desert about 400 kilometers northeast of Los Angeles. Its name is taken from the designation of the ordnance testing range next to Groom Lake: Bombing Range 51. The surfaces of the towers are weathered by the wind and sand blasting them; and they feel slightly alien in nature. They have a uniform sheen and strange texture, as if they are made from some kind of weird unpainted metal.

Using the Raytrace Material

Understanding a material's *story* helps you begin the material-creation process with the end in mind. So what material type should you begin with? Max loads the Standard material into the preview windows by default. Although it's a good texture to start with, it has some limitations.

Through experience, many max artists—including myself—have come to prefer using the Raytrace material instead of the Standard material as the basis for basic material development. It has become the de-facto "Standard" material for my work in max.

Tip

The Raytrace material is complex and advanced. It is worth a visit to your User Reference to learn more about it and how it differs from the Standard material. Use the keyword *Raytrace* in the Index or Search tabs.

Raytracing

Raytracing is a rendering algorithm used to simulate how light interacts with objects in the real world. It tracks and uses the incident rays of light from a light source and traces (calculates and follows) their paths through 3D space. When those rays strike a surface, the reflected and refracted rays are traced and the resulting shadows and reflections created by the light-object interaction are then formed in the image's mathematical model.

For all its power and resulting beauty, raytracing is not a complete simulation of real-world lighting. Another lighting and rendering algorithm called *radiosity* simulates the complete complexity of real-world lighting.

Basic Material Creation

Click the Cooling_Tower_Master material preview window in the Material Editor to select it for editing. Creating a basic material is a four-step process: Select the material type, select the shader type, adjust the Color component, and adjust the Specular components as shown here:

1. To change the material type from Standard to Raytrace, click Standard Standard in the Material Editor toolbar. When the Material/Map Browser opens, double-click Raytrace in the list to change the Cooling_Tower_Master material type to the Raytrace material type (see Figure 4.13).

Tip

☗ If you need help creating the materials for this chapter, the complete Sc-01 file, including the materials in the Material Editor, can be found in MAXWorkshop\ Help_Files\Chapter_4\EXSc_01.max.

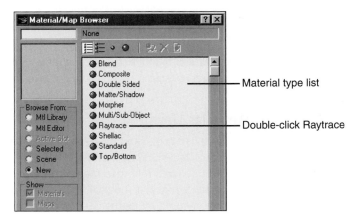

Figure 4.13 The Raytrace material reproduces real-world reflections, refractions, and Ambient, Diffuse, and Specular material components better than the Standard material. This results in richer and more realistic materials.

3ds max 4

> **Note**
>
> The Blinn shader is a variation of the Phong shader. Both are general-purpose shaders that use an adjacent-face averaging algorithm to interpolate light intensity across the faces in the surface mesh. The Blinn shader gives a more consistent highlight, especially when a light is striking a surface at a low angle of incidence.

2. Click Shading in the Raytrace Basic Parameters rollout and change the shading type to Blinn.

3. Click the color swatch next to the Diffuse color component. This will open the color selector. Change the RGB settings to 52,68,69.

4. In the Specular Highlight section of this rollout, click the color swatch next to the Specular Color component. Change its RGB color settings to 255,245,189. Change the Specular Level to 90 and the Glossiness to 38.

Click the Background toggle to change the material preview window background to a checkerboard. Your Material Editor should look like Figure 4.14.

> **Tip**
>
> Change the preview window to the checkerboard background to make the material easier to see in the preview window.

Raytracer Controls

The Raytrace material you are creating produces raytraced reflections and refractions. These functions are enabled by default in the Raytracer Controls rollout. The weathered metal you're creating doesn't need to have raytraced reflections to create a realistic appearance, so you'll turn raytracing off.

Scroll down to the Raytracer Controls rollout and click the plus (+) sign to open the rollout. Uncheck both boxes in the Raytracer Enable section to disable raytracing for this material and close the rollout (see Figure 4.15).

Adding Surface Details: Using Maps

The surface of the cooling tower has been sand blasted by the desert wind. You could use 2D images or 3D procedural maps to create this kind of dimensional surface texture. In this case, a procedural Noise bump map will be used to create the million little holes created by wind-driven rocks and sand striking the surface of the cooling towers. The term *procedural* is used for imagery or effects that are generated by mathematical algorithms.

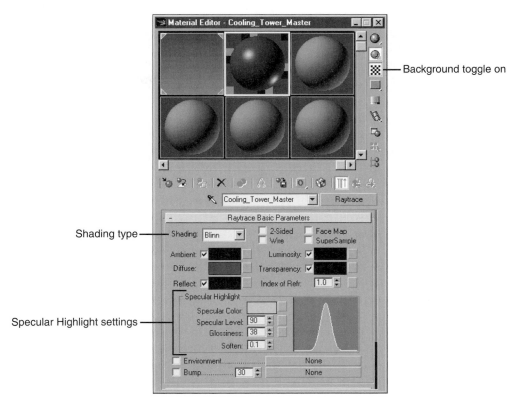

Background toggle on

Shading type

Specular Highlight settings

Figure 4.14 After a basic material color is created, the next step is to adjust the Raytracer controls and add surface detail to the material.

Click here to open and close rollout

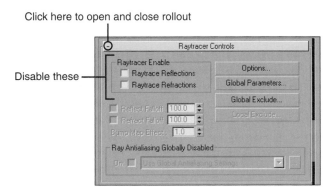

Disable these

Figure 4.15 Disabling the Raytracer function for materials that don't really need to be ray-traced will speed up your rendering process.

169

Procedural Noise

Learning how to add Bump maps to your materials will show you the basic procedure to add maps to the other material components as well. All the materials discussed in the Workshops in this book were created through experimenting with them in the Material Editor. The parameter values and adjustments indicated will enable you to duplicate the results seen in Area51.avi, but don't stop there! Try your own experiments with the materials. The following steps show you how to add a procedural noise map into the Bump component map slot of the Raytrace material that you are currently developing:

1. At the bottom of the Raytracer Basic Parameters rollout you'll see the Bump map amount control and component map slot. Click the empty Map slot titled None (see Figure 4.16).

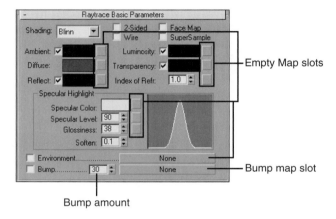

Figure 4.16   The rectangles and squares next to the component controls in the Basic Parameters rollout are Map slots. Clicking these slots allows you to assign 2D image maps or procedural maps to the material component channel.

Bump Maps

Bump maps use the grayscale of an image or procedural map to create the illusion of 3D textures in a surface. Both positive and negative numbers, depending on the effect you want to see in the surface, control the intensity of a Bump map.

Positive numbers in the Bump map channel mean that the darkest areas of the image will create the depressed areas of the surface, and the light areas will create the higher, debossed elevations of the surface texture. Using a negative number reverses the effect.

2. Double-click Noise in the Material/Map Browser to load the procedural Noise map into the Bump map slot. The Material Editor now shows the mapping coordinate and parameter controls for the Noise map (see Figure 4.17).

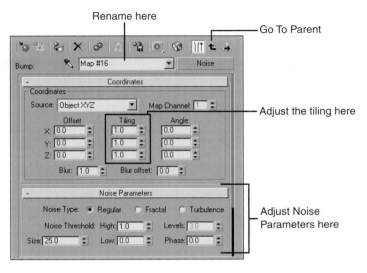

Rename here · Go To Parent · Adjust the tiling here · Adjust Noise Parameters here

Figure 4.17   Max uses a parent-child hierarchical paradigm for all its components' structural relationships. The Noise map you just added is considered a child of the cooling tower material because it is added as an additional map to the Bump map slot.

3. Rename this map Cooling_Tower_Noise and adjust the settings in the Noise Parameters rollout as follows: Noise Type: Fractal; Size: 0.5; Spread: 1.0; Bump Smoothing: .2. Leave the other settings as they are.

4. After you've adjusted the parameters, click Go To Parent ⬆, which will take you back to the parent Cooling_Tower_Master material. Change the Bump amount to 20.

Using Fractal as the noise algorithm creates a nonrepeating random distribution of the noise throughout the material. Adjusting the Noise Threshold values changes the value difference between the light and dark areas of the Noise map as they relate to each other.

Evaluating Your Work: Assign the Material

Effective materials can't be created based on how they look in the material preview windows—you need to see how they appear in a rendered image. To see the material in the rendered image, you must assign it to an object in the scene. Max provides two basic ways to assign material maps to the objects in your scenes. You can drag a material from the Material Editor and drop it onto the object you want to assign it to, or you can select the objects to which the map will be assigned and click Assign Material to Selection 🔲. Follow these steps to assign a material to an object:

1. Click the Map slot containing the Cooling_Tower_Master material. A white outline will appear around the preview window indicating that the material is selected and ready for assignment in your scene.

2. Select the Cooling_Tower_Master and the Cooling_Tower_Lattice models and click Assign Material to Selection 🔲, as shown in Figure 4.18.

White outline around active material

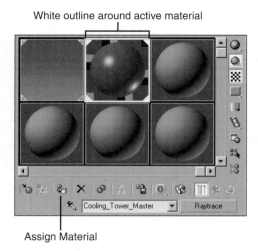

Assign Material

Figure 4.18 When a material is assigned to an object in the scene, the material slot in the Material Editor will have white triangles in the corners of its preview window.

The triangles in the corners of the Material Preview windows are visual indicators of which materials are *hot* or *cool*. There are three designations for hot and cool materials in your max scenes:

- **Cool**—A preview window with no triangles in its corners is cool—it hasn't been assigned to an object in the scene.

- **Hot**—White triangles in the corners indicate a hot material—it has been assigned to objects in the scene, and any changes you make in the Material Editor will change the appearance of all the objects that use the material.

- **Hot But Not Selected**—A preview window with gray corners, such as the BG Sky gradient map, indicates that the material is assigned to an object that is not currently selected.

Press C to change to Camera view and press Shift+Q to Quick Render your scene and see the weathered metal material applied to the cooling tower models (see Figure 4.19).

Surface Color: Using Image Maps

To create some variation in the surface color of the weathered metal material, a bitmap image will be used in the Diffuse channel. The colors and images in the Diffuse channel control the appearance of the surfaces of an object seen in direct light.

There are many ways to add color variation to the materials you create. Using a Noise map would work and would create a nice effect, but here you'll use a 2D image instead:

1. Click the Map slot next to the Diffuse color channel and select and load Bitmap from the Material/Map Browser. When the Select Bitmap Image File dialog box opens, browse to MAXWorkshop\Materials\Image_Maps\ and load Alien Metal.bmp from that directory (see Figure 4.20).

Figure 4.19 The Noise map adds a nice level of bump detail to the surface. All that's needed now is some surface color variation to create a more realistic appearance.

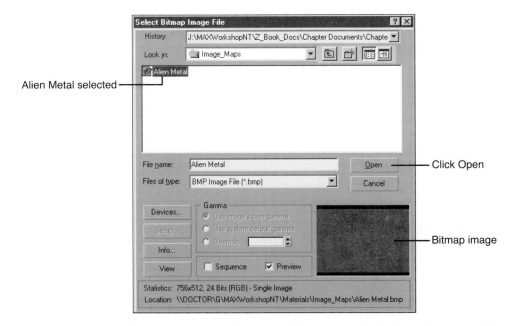

Alien Metal selected

Click Open

Bitmap image

Figure 4.20 The Select Bitmap Image File is basically the same dialog box that you used in Chapter 2, "Virtual Viz: The Art of Pre-Production for Digital Content Creation," to load the storyboard images for the animatic into the Video Post Queue.

2. After the image is loaded into the Material Editor, rename it Alien Metal and change the U and V tiling amounts to 2.0, as shown in Figure 4.21. When you're finished, click Go To Parent ⬆.

Rename here

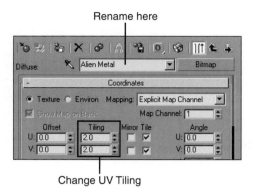

Change UV Tiling

Figure 4.21   Adjusting the UV tiling numbers of an image procedurally changes the size of the image as it appears in the material. It doesn't change the size of the original image or the surface mesh.

Understanding Tiling

UV tiling coordinate values specify the number of times an image will be repeated over the surface it's applied to. The default max value is 1.0, which means that a single Alien Metal image map is used to cover the entire surface of the cooling tower.

A UV tiling value of 2.0 means that the image will be tiled twice in the U and V dimensions—creating a tiled map that fits four images of the original map onto the model's surface. A UV value of 3.0 fits nine images onto the surface, and so on.

Tiling numbers less than 1.0 use less of the original image. For example, if you used a value of 0.5, only half of the original bitmap would be applied to the surface of the model. Using different numbers for the UV values will stretch the bitmap image according to the ratio of the UV numbers used.

Render your Camera viewport to see the result and save your work. The next section shows you how to create libraries to organize and store the materials you create for your projects.

Sharpen the Saw: Material Libraries

A lot of hard work and creative effort goes into creating materials. Max provides the tools to organize and save the materials from your individual scenes into libraries. Material libraries can be shared with other max users to provide consistency in a project team's production output. And as you master materials in max, you will create unique materials that you'll want to use again.

Setting up material libraries for specific projects is an important organizational habit that helps you keep track of those favorites.

Tip

 A complete material library for Area51.avi can be found on the CD in MAXWorkshop\Materials\Material Libraries\ExArea51.mat.

A material library stores the materials, maps, textures, and so forth that you are using in your scene. At this point, there are two materials in the Material Editor: the BG Sky gradient and the Cooling_Tower_Master material for the cooling tower models.

Max's default material library is a robust collection of textures you can use as a basis to develop your own materials. The max default library opens whenever you reset max to create a completely new workspace. Most artists switch between this default library and their own scene-specific libraries as they work. Follow these steps to create a new material library for `Area51.avi`:

1. Open the Material Editor and click the Get Material icon 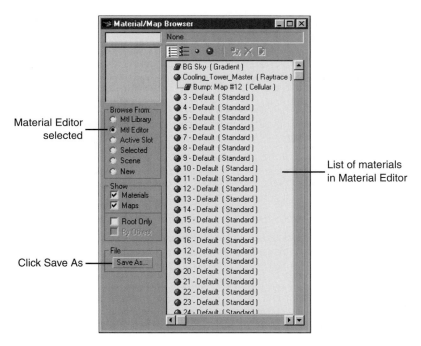. This opens the Material/Map Browser.

2. In the Browse From section of the dialog box, select Mtl Editor and then click Save As, as shown in Figure 4.22.

Material Editor selected

List of materials in Material Editor

Click Save As

Figure 4.22 Using existing materials from the default max material library or your own saved libraries as starting places for developing new materials will speed up your production process.

3. When the Save Material Library window appears, go to `MAX Workshop\Materials\ Material Libraries` and save this library as `Area_51`, as shown in Figure 4.23. Close the Material/Map Browser and the Material Editor, and save your file when you're done.

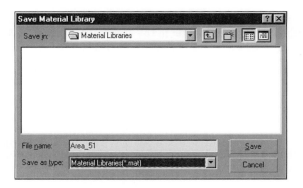

Figure 4.23   When you save your library, max applies the .mat suffix. You can share this library file with your co-workers and use it in your other max projects.

This is the process you will use to save your scene-specific material library. Organizing your max work in this manner is critical to your success as an artist working in a professional environment.

Max Workshop—Sc-01 Continued

The animating cloud layers in Sc-01, Sc-02, Sc-04, and Sc-05 were created using a fairly low-tech process—a plane and an animating Noise map. Unlike the incredible software programs available to make 3D volumetric clouds, the clouds created here won't cast or receive shadows. However, using the tools native to the max software and with a little bit of artistic and scientific thinking, clouds that look and move in a realistic manner can be created. In this part of the Workshop, you'll create the animating cloud layer for Sc-01.

Toxic Clouds

The clouds streaming over Area 51 are the toxic results of decades of industrial pollution. The intent of their appearance and animation is to create an ominous and somewhat surreal backdrop for the scenes in which they appear. And you certainly don't want to get caught in the rain they carry. First, you'll need an object that can be used to carry the animating cloud texture.

Creating a Cloud Plane

If you haven't done so, start max and load Sc-01.max. Click File, Save As in the Main Menu and rename this file Sc-01_Clouds.max. Renaming this file will enable you to work more efficiently when you render out the image layers for this scene later in the Workshop. Click Time Configuration ⊞ and be sure the Frame Rate is set to Film (24 FPS) and the Animation Start and End Times are set to 1, 288.

> **Tip**
>
> When you are creating image layer files, such as `Sc-01_Clouds.max`, it's always a good idea to delete any geometry, effects, and so on that aren't absolutely needed for the scene. Renaming the layer files by using the scene name first, followed by an easily remembered descriptor, will keep your process organized and efficient.

A simple plane above the cooling tower models is all that's needed to carry the animating cloud material. Before you create the plane, select the Cooling_Tower_Lattice model and delete it—it's not needed for the cloud layer. However, the Cooling_Tower_Master model is needed in the scene for reference and test renders to evaluate how your cloud layer will look in the final layer composite. Follow these steps to create the cloud layer plane for Sc-01:

1. Press T to change to the Top view and press Ctrl+Alt+Z to Zoom Extents your viewport. Use the Zoom navigation control to zoom out from the cooling tower model, making it smaller in the viewport.

> **Tip**
>
> ☀ If you need help, the completed cloud layer model can be found in `maxWorkshop\Help_Files\Chapter_4\EXSc_01_Clouds.max`.

2. Click the Create ▨ command panel and click Plane. Drag in the Top view to create a plane about 430 units square centered over the cooling tower.

3. Change the length and width segments of the plane to `10`. For primitive objects, such as this plane, max can generate mapping coordinates without the addition of a UVW Map modifier. So, be sure Generate Mapping Coordinates is checked, as shown in Figure 4.24.

4. Press R to change to Right view and right-click the plane. Select Move Mode from the Quad Menu and use the Y-axis to drag and move the plane above the cooling tower model to the approximate location shown in Figure 4.25.

5. The visible surface of the plane is pointing up and must be rotated 180° so that its surface will be visible in the Camera POV. Right-click the plane and select Rotate Mode. Press F12 to open the Rotate Transform Type-In dialog box. Type `180` in the Offset: World, Z box (see Figure 4.26).

6. Change to Camera view and render your scene. The BG Sky gradient can't be seen; it has been occluded by the plane you just created. Open the Modify command panel and change the name of the plane to BG_Clouds.

Noisy Clouds: The Base Material

Variations of the animating Noise map you'll create for the cloud image layer can also be used to make smoke, fire, and water. Experimenting with the basic technique coupled with Video Post effects can yield stunning imagery. The settings given here are the ones used to create the cloud layer for Sc-01; after you understand the basic process, try some settings of your own. The first step to create the cloud layer material is to copy and modify the Raytrace material you created for the cooling towers:

1. Click the Cooling_Tower_Master material preview window in the Material Editor. Make a copy of it by dragging it onto the empty preview window to the right (see Figure 4.27).

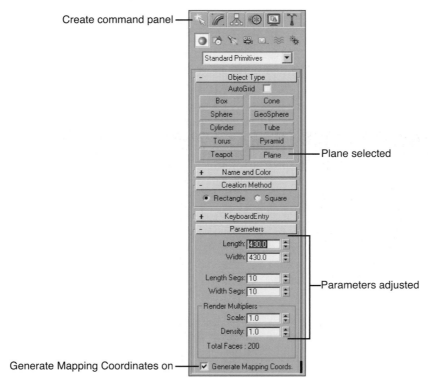

Create command panel

Plane selected

Parameters adjusted

Generate Mapping Coordinates on

Figure 4.24   The Plane object is a single-sided mesh surface. Materials and lighting only appear on the surface that faces the viewport POV.

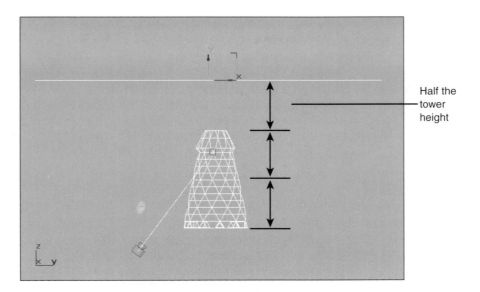

Half the
tower
height

Figure 4.25 The cloud plane's location above the cooling tower will be a minor but important factor in the final look of your clouds. Just be sure that it's centered over
the cooling tower in the Top view and about half the height of the tower above
the top of the cooling tower.

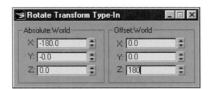

Figure 4.26 Rotating the plane will turn its visible side toward the camera POV. Press F12 to
use the Rotate Transform Type-In dialog box whenever precise geometry movements are needed.

BG Sky gradient   Drag and drop to copy Cooling_Tower_Master

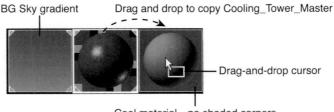

Drag-and-drop cursor

Cool material—no shaded corners

Figure 4.27 Starting with an existing material often saves you some steps in the material
creation process.

2. Rename this material BG_Clouds and make the following adjustments: Specular Color: 255,255,255 (white); Specular Level and Glossiness: 0.

3. Next to the Ambient color swatch is an empty Map slot. Drag it onto the Diffuse map slot just below it. This will delete the map in the Diffuse slot by copying an empty Map slot over the bitmap image from the old weathered metal material.

4. Click the Diffuse color swatch and change it to 0,0,0, or drag the Ambient color swatch onto the Diffuse color swatch.

5. Delete the Noise map in the Bump map slot by dragging the slot titled None onto it. The Material Editor should look like Figure 4.28.

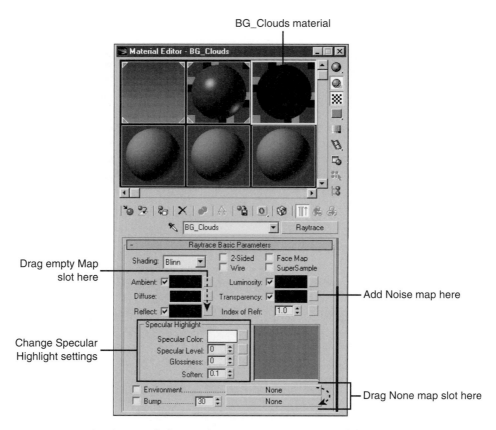

Figure 4.28 Using the drag-and-drop technique to move, copy, and delete materials, colors, and maps in the Material Editor is an essential max shortcut technique.

Sometimes, especially when working with transparent or refractive materials, it is difficult to see materials in the material preview windows. Changing the background color behind the material will help.

Sharpen the Saw: Modifying Material Editor Options

Changing the way materials are displayed in the preview windows can help you in your creative process. Here's how to do it:

1. Right-click any material preview window to access the menu shown in Figure 4.29.

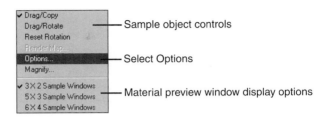

Figure 4.29 The preview window right-click menu allows you access to the most-used preview window controls and options.

2. Click Options in this menu to access the Material Editor Options window shown in Figure 4.30. Change the Background Intensity value to 0.6, click the check box next to Anti-alias to turn it on, and click Apply to effect the changes. Then close the window.

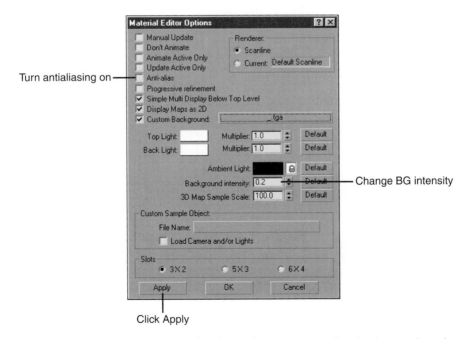

Figure 4.30 Changing the BG Intensity brightens the preview window background, and antialiasing smoothes the edges of your preview sphere. Both adjustments make it easier to see the Noise map as you develop it.

You'll revisit the Material Editor Options dialog box and adjust its settings as needed throughout the Workshop.

Adjusting the Noise Parameters

The official max definitions for what each noise parameter does are important to learn. However, understanding those definitions is difficult without a practical application of the actual effect that changing each parameter has on the specific map you are creating. Sometimes it's easier to tell you the *why* behind a particular parameter change than it is to give you a textbook definition.

The settings in the Cloud Noise map were arrived at by trial and error with some help from the User Reference and fellow max artists. Here are the reasons the specific noise parameters were chosen. Your max User Reference, keyword *Noise Map*, has all the complete official definitions. Some of the changes described here are subtle and might be hard to see in the figures. You should make the changes indicated in the figure callouts to see the effect on the material in your Material Editor as you read through the descriptions of the noise settings.

- **Fractal Noise**—I use Fractal for the majority of the elemental (fire, water, clouds) Noise maps I make. Fractal is a mathematical algorithm that creates a realistic randomness to the noise texture. Regular noise is essentially Fractal noise with a nonadjustable Level setting of 1.0.

- **Levels**—A level setting of 10.0 creates wispy cloud edges. A level setting of 1.0 (the lowest setting possible) smoothes out the edges, eliminating the wispy turbulent edges appropriate for clouds (see Figure 4.31).

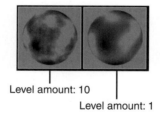

Level amount: 10

Level amount: 1

Figure 4.31   The level amount controls how refined and complex the edges of the clouds will be.

Experiment to Understand

You can't understand the official max definitions for the noise parameters (or any other parameter setting) without significant experimentation. One criticism of the User Reference is that the definitions are too esoteric and the examples (when they are given) are not always clear in how they are applied in practice by the artist.

- **Size**—Determines the scale of the noise. Higher values create the larger forms appropriate for clouds. Lower values create smaller details, such as flames or the pitted texture used in the cooling towers' weathered metal material (see Figure 4.32).

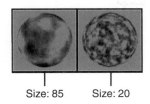

Size: 85   Size: 20

Figure 4.32   Size amount is actually controlling the scale of the noise.

- **Thresholds**—Work in synergy with the size and levels settings to control the shape and the relative value (light and dark) or grayscale of the clumps of clouds created by the noise. A good cloud setting, discovered by experimentation, is Low: 0.3 to 0.4; High: 0.9 to 1.0. Figure 4.33 shows a comparison between six different threshold settings with a common size of 85 and level setting of 10.

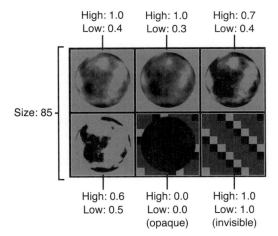

High: 1.0   High: 1.0   High: 0.7
Low: 0.4   Low: 0.3   Low: 0.4

Size: 85

High: 0.6   High: 0.0   High: 1.0
Low: 0.5   Low: 0.0   Low: 1.0
            (opaque)   (invisible)

Figure 4.33   All the Noise parameters can be animated to achieve various special effects.

- **Invert/Swap**—These commands reverse the opaque and transparent areas of the Noise map in two different ways. Swap reverses the order of the color swatches in the Map slots and Invert inverts the color of the swatch, changing it to its analogous complementary color. This means that black becomes white and an RGB value of 255,0,0 (Red) becomes an RGB value of 0,255,255 (Blue) and so forth (see Figure 4.34).

- **Output Amount**—Controls the contrast between the light and dark—transparent and opaque—areas of the map. You can use positive or negative numbers for the amount to create positive and negative imagery effects. Figure 4.35 shows how positive and negative Output Amounts affect a sample sphere of a Noise map with the following settings: Size: 85; Levels: 10; and High/Low Threshold: 1.0–0.4.

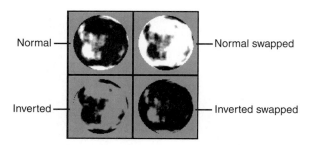

Normal — — Normal swapped

Inverted — — Inverted swapped

Figure 4.34 Don't confuse Invert with the effect the Swap button has on the imagery. They control different parameters. Try experimenting with different colors in the color swatches and the Invert command to see the effect that it has on the Noise map.

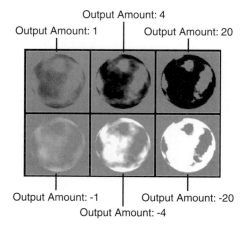

Output Amount: 4

Output Amount: 1 — Output Amount: 20

Output Amount: -1 — Output Amount: -20

Output Amount: -4

Figure 4.35 Changing the Output Amount can yield higher contrast noise effects. You'll adjust this parameter to make the cloud clumps more defined.

The rest of the parameters in these rollouts are worthy of your attention and experimentation, and some of them will be used and explained in later chapters. But for now, the clouds are waiting. Follow these steps to make the necessary adjustments to your cloud material:

1. Rename the Noise map `Cloud Noise` and make the following changes to the Noise Parameters rollout: Noise Type: Fractal; Noise Low Threshold: `0.4`; Levels: `10`; Size: `85.0`. Leave the rest of the settings as they are.

2. Scroll down and open the Output rollout. Click the Invert check box to invert the Noise map and change the Output Amount to `2.0`. Your Noise map and Material Editor should look like Figure 4.36.

Animating the Clouds

In this part of the process, you'll be using the animation controls at the bottom of the max interface, so reposition and resize the Material Editor dialog box to enable you to see both the editor and the animation controls.

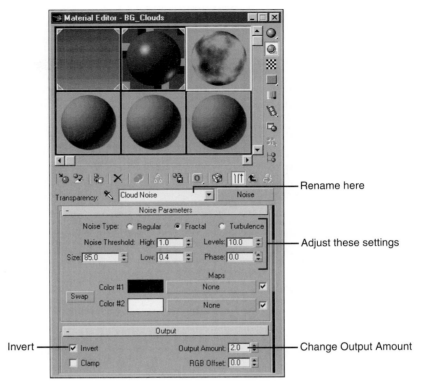

Rename here

Adjust these settings

Invert

Change Output Amount

Figure 4.36 Max can animate all the material parameters of your textures. The possibilities are limited only by your imagination!

Select the BG_Clouds plane and click Assign Material to Selection [icon]. Press Shift+Q to render the scene—nice stormy clouds. Making the clouds move will bring them to life.

Max uses a material's UVW coordinates to control its animation. UVW corresponds to the XYZ coordinates that the cloud plane uses to define its size and position in space. So, in this case, using the plane object as the source for the animation coordinates is appropriate. Scroll up to the Noise Coordinates rollout in the Material Editor (see Figure 4.37). The following steps show you how to animate the Noise map to simulate cloud movement:

1. Click the Animate button and change the frame number by typing 288. Or, drag the Time Slider all the way to the right to the end of the Track Bar (see Figure 4.38).

2. Change the X and Y values in the Offset section of the Coordinates rollout to X: 100; Y: 200. Change the Phase value to 0.5 (see Figure 4.39, a bit later in the chapter).

3. Click the Animate button to exit Animate mode and save your max file.

The X value creates a right-to-left horizontal movement from the camera's POV. The Y value moves the map up in the Y-axis. The Phase value controls the speed of the noise animation.

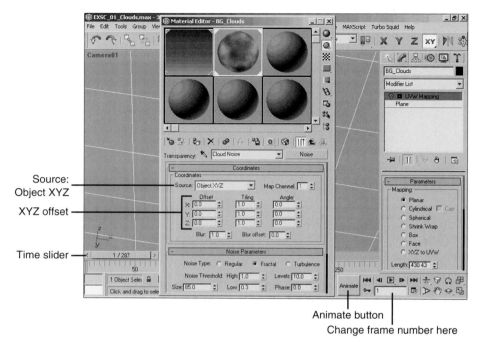

Source:
Object XYZ

XYZ offset

Time slider

Animate button
Change frame number here

Figure 4.37   The cloud map is animated using the XYZ coordinate values of the object to which it's applied and the Noise parameter's Phase amount.

You have just told max that beginning with frame 1, the map moves over the course of time to reach an X-coordinate value of 100, a Y-coordinate value of 200, and a Phase value of 0.5 at frame number 288. This is the fundamental basis of all animation—change over time.

Previewing Your Work

When Sc-01 is completed later in the Workshop, you'll render out all 288 frames of the cloud layer in preparation for effects and compositing. Before you render any final image sequence, it's important to view and evaluate the results of the animating material you just created.

Creating a Material Preview

A good way to evaluate your work is to create a half-size test render of the scene and save it as an .avi format movie. Or, you can create a preview of the material before the half-size test render. Follow these steps to create a material preview:

1. Select the cloud material and click and hold on the Sample Type sphere ⬤ in the controls on the vertical right side of your Material Editor. Select Box type ⬛ from the list to change your sample type to a box.

2. Right-click the BG_Clouds material preview window and select Drag/Rotate from the list. Your cursor changes to a rotation cursor similar to the viewport navigation Arc-rotate command.

Selected material—red frame

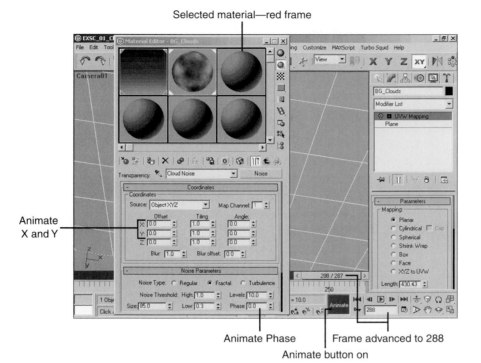

Animate X and Y

Animate Phase

Animate button on

Frame advanced to 288

Figure 4.38   Be careful! With the Animate button on, any changes you make to the map will be animated over time.

3. Drag in the material preview window and rotate the box until it can be seen straight on, as if in a front or side Orthogonal view (see Figure 4.40).

4. Click the Make Preview icon [image] in the controls on the vertical right side of your Material Editor. This opens the Create Material Preview dialog box, as shown in Figure 4.41.

5. In the Image Size section, change the Percent of Output to 200 and click OK. This starts the preview-creation process, creating a double-size .avi format movie of BG_Clouds. While the preview is being created, all other max functions are suspended.

> **Note**
>
> Max provides two ways to monitor the progress of the preview-creation process. As the preview is created, you can see the Time slider bar at the bottom of your viewport advance frame by frame, and there is a readout showing percentage completed. You can cancel the preview any time by clicking the Cancel button at the bottom of the interface. This will stop the process and allow you to view the rendered results up to the point at which you cancelled the process.

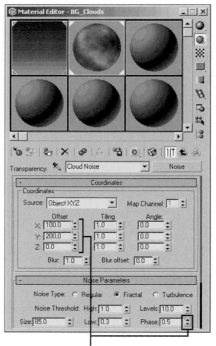

Red indicates animated parameters

Figure 4.39   When you change these parameter values, the spinner arrows next to them turn red as well, indicating that these values are now animated.

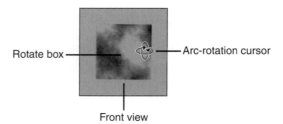

Rotate box

Arc-rotation cursor

Front view

Figure 4.40   Rotating the Sample Box in the preview window gives you a better view of the cloud layer map animation.

Depending on the speed of your machine, this can take up to five minutes. When the preview is finished, a media player window opens and plays the result. You will see the animating cloud material on the sample cube. You can use the media player controls to save this preview as an .avi movie if you want.

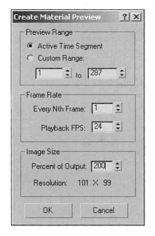

Figure 4.41 The Create Material Preview dialog box is an evaluation tool used to create simple previews of the materials you animate in max.

Creating a Half-Size Test Render

A half-size test render of your material applied to its object is a good way to see how your work is progressing. Follow these steps to create a half-size test render:

1. Click the BG_Clouds plane to select it and right-click to access its Quad Menu. Click Hide Unselected to hide the cooling tower.

2. Click Render Scene to open the Render Scene dialog box. Then click Range and change its start and end frames to 1 and 48. This makes your test render 48 frames or 2 seconds long—plenty of time to evaluate your progress.

3. The Output Size should be set at Width: 320; Height: 173. Then check the Save File box and click Files to specify the save location and file format.

4. When the Render Output File window opens, browse to MAXWorkshop\AVI's\Test and save this file as BG_Clouds.avi. If needed, click Setup to adjust the compression parameters of your AVI (see Figure 4.42).

5. Your Render Scene dialog box should look like Figure 4.43. Click Render to render your test AVI.

When the test render is complete, click File, View File and browse to MAXWorkshop\AVI's\Test. Select and open BG_Clouds.avi to view the clouds. The clouds are animating nicely and the Phase animation has created interesting secondary motion.

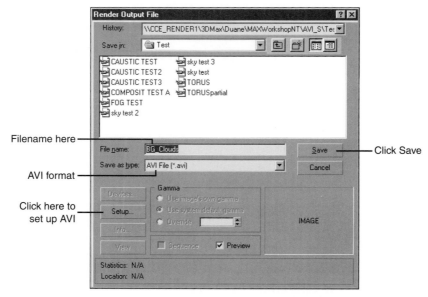

Figure 4.42 Save your test renders to give you and your production leadership a tool to view and evaluate your progress.

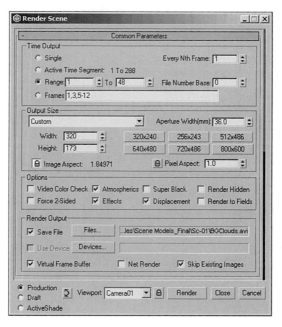

Figure 4.43 Watching the first few frames of your test render will give you immediate feedback. If the test doesn't look correct, click the Cancel button in the Rendering-BG_Cloud progress window, make your adjustments, and re-render the test.

Next Steps

The next steps for you in this chapter include additional experiments with the BG_Clouds material:

- Adjust the diffuse color and the self-illumination levels of the BG_Clouds material for brighter glowing clouds.

- Add image or procedural maps into the Map slots next to the black-and-white color swatches in the Noise Parameters rollout to experiment with the way maps change the look of the noise.

- Try different combinations of color in both the cloud material and in the BG_Sky gradient to create the feeling of dawn, high noon, or the night sky.

Changing the BG_Sky gradient map by swapping the positions of color numbers 1 and 3 is an interesting experiment:

1. Click BG_Sky gradient map in the Material Editor. Drag color #1 down onto color #3.

2. When the Copy or Swap Colors dialog box opens, select Swap from the options, as shown in Figure 4.44.

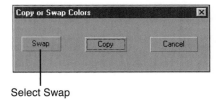

Select Swap

Figure 4.44 Swapping the gradient colors in the BG_Sky material also creates a suitably alien and eerie appearance in the clouds and sky.

3. Click Render Scene and save this file as MAXWorkshop\AVI's\Test\BG Clouds_2.avi.

At some point in your development as a visual artist, you will come to the understanding that creating great images is fundamentally and solely about re-creating the phenomenon of light.

It's easy enough to understand that if there is no light, there is nothing to see. But what kind of light are you trying to create; what color should it be, where should it be placed, and so on? These are important questions and, in the course of time and experience in max, you will create your own approach to the answers. Your goal as a digital content artist is the creation of sophisticated illusions that are designed to support and elicit emotional responses from your audience. Lighting is a core component of that illusion.

3ds max 4

In *3D Studio MAX 3.0 Workshop*, I referred to the lines from the Moody Blues song "Nights in White Satin" to illustrate fundamental lighting concepts. If you want to be successful in your lighting endeavors, study this poem—and read the next chapter. Here's the poem:

> "...Cold-hearted orb that rules the night,
> Removes the colors from our sight.
> Red is gray and yellow white.
> But we decide which is right.
> And which is an illusion?"

—from "Late Lament" by Graeme Edge of the Moody Blues on the album *Days of Future Past*, 1967.

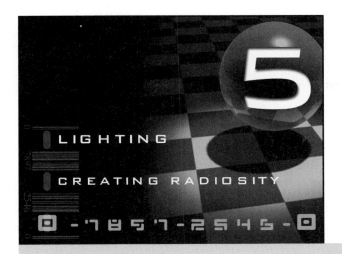

LIGHTING

CREATING RADIOSITY

0-7857-2546-0

Photon Paint: The Art of Lighting

"...the object of art is not to reproduce reality, but to create a reality of the same intensity." - Alberto Giacometti

The fundamental intent of the lighting process is to create a synthetic visual reality that captures the emotion and atmosphere of the story. Augmenting reality to create imagery that appears real to your audience requires a shift in your perception of light and lighting in the world around you. Simply reproducing what you see isn't enough.

Vincent Van Gogh said, "I often think that the night is more alive and more richly colored than the day." To Van Gogh, the night sky was not simply black; it was full of brilliant and deep blues and purples, patterned with glowing yellow stars. His perception of the color and play of light in the night sky wasn't based on an uneducated guess; it was an insight earned through dedicated observation and artistic experimentation.

3ds max 4

Your path to learning the language of light starts in your own observation of nature and ends when you can create a reality of the same intensity. Your task as a digital artist is to create images that are *more real than real*.

This chapter introduces you to one of the most amazing and creative parts of digital content creation: how light affects the appearance of the materials used in your models and how to use lighting to create depth, mood, and atmosphere in your visual imagery.

Introduction to Lighting Theory, Principles, and Practice

"The finest thing we can experience is the mysterious. It is the fundamental emotion, which stands at the cradle of true art and true science. He who does not know it and can no longer wonder, no longer feel amazement, is as good as dead, a snuffed-out candle."
- Albert Einstein

Einstein's powerful words establish a common origin for both science and art—the exploration of the mysterious. The goal of lighting design is to help create amazement and wonder in the audience. The audience wants to experience the mysterious, and lighting is a powerful tool to help you accomplish that task.

This Workshop contains only a small portion of all there is to know about lighting. However, there are some fundamental theories, principles, and processes that must be presented to establish your foundation of basic lighting principles, theory, and technique.

Tip

 If you want a more in-depth treatise on lighting, I recommend Jeremy Birn's excellent book *Digital Lighting and Rendering*, published by New Riders in July 2000.

During your career as a max artist, you will be asked to create the lighting for many diverse scenes. Knowing how to light a room at twilight, a desert under a full moon, or a rainy night on the docks in San Francisco is based on an understanding of why light behaves as it does and the principles governing the artistic use of lighting in your scenes.

Radiosity: Creating the Illusion of Reality

"In order to paint absolute truth, you must lie a little." - Monet

Raytracing is a rendering algorithm that partially simulates real-world lighting by tracing the paths of incident rays of light from a light source through 3D space. Although raytracing results in a realistic reflected and refracted light phenomenon, it doesn't create the complete complexity of real-world lighting known as *radiosity*.

Radiosity plug-ins are available for 3ds max 4 that can create radiosity lighting and rendering for your scenes; however, they come with a cost, both in terms of money to purchase the software and the magnitude of time it will take your system to render each frame of a shot. Radiosity rendering algorithms are good at reproducing reality, but they cannot replace the experienced eye of an excellent artist. When you understand the basic principles behind radiosity, you'll understand that the lighting effect can easily be created using the basic lighting tools and material options available in 3ds max 4. You can fake it! Or as Monet says, you can "lie a little." The first step in learning to fake radiosity is to understand some of the science at the core of lighting and color perception.

Light Bounces

"Science is spectral analysis. Art is light synthesis." - Karl Kraus

The side of an object facing a light source is illuminated by direct light. This direct light is also referred to as *key light*, a photography term used to designate the main lighting source of your scene. Raytracing calculates the effect of direct lighting very well, accurately creating surface reflections, value gradations, cast shadows, and so forth.

The surfaces of an object that aren't in direct light are illuminated by light bouncing off of all other surrounding surfaces. Bounced or reflected light can also be referred to as *ambient* light. A photographer would call this light *fill* or *back light* because it fills in the back surfaces of objects away from the main source of illumination. Radiosity, like raytracing, is based on a mathematical algorithm, which, in addition to tracing the paths of the light rays from the light source, also traces the paths of the reflected rays of light bouncing around your scene. Figure 5.1 illustrates a synthesized radiosity effect of light bouncing around in the environment.

 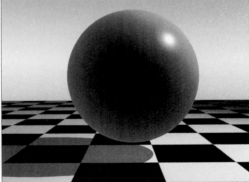

Figure 5.1 Simulating the effects of radiosity in your imagery emphasizes the 3D form of your models and creates the illusion of depth and ambient lighting in your scenes.

No Shortcuts to Excellence

In the hands of an experienced artist who understands the underlying principles, automated processes, such as radiosity rendering or motion capture, are fantastic and powerful tools. However, these tools aren't shortcuts, and artists who use them in ignorance of principle produce me-too imagery. Van Gogh said, "Do not quench your inspiration and your imagination; do not become the slave of your model." That goes for tools, too! Allow your imagination to dictate the end result you are seeking and use knowledge of the principle behind the tool to bend it to your artistic will.

Both spheres shown in Figure 5.1 are mapped with a shiny nonreflective material and have strong highlights that help define their spherical form. The difference between the two is seen in how the light reflects onto the side of the sphere away from the key light source. No fill light can be seen in the back-bottom edges of the sphere on the left. This creates a visual problem—the bottom and side edges of the sphere are undefined and are visually lost in the checkerboard of the ground plane.

The back and bottom edges of the sphere on the right, however, are reflecting bounced light—simulating the ambient light effect of radiosity. Synthesizing radiosity can be accomplished by adding additional fill lights to your scene or by adjusting specialized parameters in your object materials. In the case of the sphere on the right in Figure 5.1, an extra light in the scene did not light its edges. The ambient light radiosity effect was achieved by adjusting the parameters of the material applied to the sphere.

Light Energy and Color Perception

"Yes, I answered her last night; No, this morning, sir I say, Colours seen by candlelight, will not look the same by day." - Elizabeth Barrett Browning

One of the most important factors to understand about creating your scene lighting is the relationship between light energy and color. Lower light energy results in a corresponding reduction in reflected light and a subsequent reduction in your eye's physical ability to see color and value.

Filmmakers and lighting designers have grappled with the chronic challenge of how to effectively create night scenes and other low-level lighting conditions. The solutions have been varied, somewhat crude and often ingenious. In the 1950s, filmmakers would just use a dark filter on their camera lenses and shoot their night shots in broad daylight. This was the reality of the technical limitations of film, film processing, and available technical lighting at the time. Although the audience accepted the imagery then, it is doubtful that such a solution would be viable today.

The triumph of the digital artist is the ability to use imaginary color and lighting to simulate the effect of night without losing important image elements to the shadows. Understanding exactly what's happening under different lighting conditions and why "...colours seen by candlelight, will not look the same by day" is critical to your mastery of digital lighting.

The visible spectrum of light is a small part of the vast electromagnetic energy surrounding you. Light that cannot be seen, such as X-rays, radio waves, ultraviolet light, and infrared light, lies outside the boundaries of the visible spectrum.

Your eye processes light information by using specialized cells called *rods* and *cones* found in the retina. The retinal membrane in your eye is approximately the size of a postage stamp and contains 100 million rods and 3 million cones. The rod cells are sensitive to differences between light and dark and help you see and interpret object shape and movement. Cones are the color-sensing cells in the retina and require more light energy to be activated.

During the middle of the day, the sun's direct light is at its most powerful—illuminating everything in its path. Under such powerful illumination, all the colors in the visible spectrum can be seen. On an overcast day, when light energy is reduced through atmospheric conditions, object colors appear less vibrant or even colorless. During twilight, colors at the red end of the spectrum become gray, blending in with the shadows in the environment, and becoming almost impossible to see.

Depth Perception and Color

Depth perception is partially created by your ability to see patterns of light and shadow, which give you visual cues regarding your relative position to objects around you. During twilight, the sun is no longer directly illuminating the world, so your ability to see color and gauge depth is reduced dramatically. This is one of the reasons twilight is the most dangerous time of day to drive.

After a long history of twilight accidents, many emergency vehicles are now painted in optic yellow or optic green instead of traditional red. Optic green and yellow appear white under low and indirect lighting conditions, making them easier to see at night. This is also one of the reasons fluorescent green and orange tennis balls were created—they are easier to see during twilight, a favorite time of day for recreational tennis.

The excerpt from the poem "Late Lament" by Graeme Edge of the Moody Blues given at the end of Chapter 4, "Visual Touch: The Art of Material and Texture Development," illustrates the basic relationship between color perception and light. The "Cold-hearted orb that rules the night" is the moon, which reflects about 10% of the sunlight striking it. The moon provides enough light to allow your eyes to recognize shapes and perceive motion. However, there isn't enough light to activate the cone cells in the eyes, thus removing "the colors from our sight." Under such low-level lighting, the color red is seen as gray and yellow appears white. Other colors exhibit similar perceptual changes under low lighting and indirect light levels.

Creating the Emotional Context of Lighting

"A work of art which did not begin in emotion is not art." - Paul Cézanne

To understand light and lighting, you must study the scientific basis of its creation. But your task as an artist is to bend, break, or make up new rules as you go to achieve the atmosphere and emotion of the story—to "create a reality of the same intensity," as Giacometti said.

The movies *The Matrix* and *Saving Private Ryan* are great examples of how light and color are used to create a visual reality that taps into the emotions of the audience. They are also great examples of the intentional use of lighting to capture and convey emotional content. Consider the opening scene of *Saving Private Ryan* and the lighting design of *The Matrix*.

Saving Private Ryan

Director Steven Spielberg and cinematographer Janusz Kaminski wanted to capture the terror, slaughter, and chaos of the invasion at Omaha Beach, D-Day, June 6, 1944. To accomplish this technically, they used handheld cameras with lenses that had been modified by stripping out the black coating on the interior of the lens bodies. The interior surfaces of modern cinematography lenses are coated with a nonreflective matte finish to eliminate internal light reflection.

Modifying the lens in this way created a higher contrast image reminiscent of the black-and-white newsreels seen during World War II. The overcast indirect natural light of the French oceanside, coupled with the high-contrast images produced by the lenses, enhanced the viewer's perception of motion in the scene. This is a masterpiece of value contrast and the use of lighting to capture story and emotion.

The Matrix

Bill Pope was the director of photography on *The Matrix* and had this to say about the lighting, color, and emotion they were trying to create.

"To distinguish the Matrix from 'reality,' from the Nebuchadnezzar and the pods, 'reality' was given a cooler look, a bluer, more normal, less sickly look. The future in the film is cold, the sun is blotted out, there is no real warmth unless it is artificial heat, so that is why they went for the cool side.

"Whereas the Matrix, created by the computers, is a decadent, decaying world, so it has a green hue. These are the two different colors—green and blue. The Matrix should make you feel sick, and in 'reality' you should feel a little more at home, but never comfortable. If you make it gold and warm you know that it is home, a safe haven. The other day I started using warm lights—I did this unconsciously for the first time in Neo's bedroom. It just felt right that it should be slightly warm. As harsh as that bunk is, it is the only home he has got." (from an interview published on the official *The Matrix* Web site).

This reveals the consideration given to creating the differences between the reality Neo finds himself thrust into and the unreal world of the Matrix. The use of some warm light in Neo's apartment to create the feeling of home is a subtle and powerful example of how lighting is employed to reinforce the feelings naturally occurring in the hearts of the audience: Home should be warm, comfy, and safe.

Color and Light Memes

The "sickly" green color and lighting in the Matrix cyberspace are visual memes intentionally chosen to affect the emotions of the audience. In the Western culture, yellow-green is associated with sickness, just as black evokes death and red evokes evil. The green tone of the Matrix was further enhanced during the chemical processing used to develop the final negative cut, giving the shots and scenes in the Matrix a glowing greenness that punches a hole through the psyche into the emotional basement of the audience. This is what lighting and color can do. Very powerful!

Painting with Light

"...instead of trying to reproduce exactly what I see before my eyes, I use color more arbitrarily so as to express myself forcibly." - Vincent Van Gogh

A single Workshop like this can't contain an exhaustive treatise on color theory and how to paint with light. But a simplified explanation of the basic approach taken when lighting a scene will set the foundation for your own experiments. For greater detail on lighting, read Jeremy Birn's *Digital Lighting and Rendering*. The following sections detail the basic concepts to keep in mind when lighting a scene.

Tip

 For more information on color theory, read *Elements of Color* by Johannes Itten and Faber Birren, *The Art of Color: The Subjective Experience and Objective Rationale of Color* by Johannes Itten, and the classic *Painting with Light* by John Alton.

Light Color and Material Color Interaction

The color of the light in your scenes changes the color of the material it is illuminating. For example, a red light turns a light-colored material red and turns a bright green material black. Multiple lights in a scene also add their color to each other. For example, overlapping red, green, and blue spotlights creates white light at the nexus of their intersection.

Plan for this in advance by choosing material colors that work with the lighting color design of the scene.

Lighting and Painting Analog

"My choice of colours does not rest on any scientific theory; it is based on observation, on feeling, on the very nature of each experience." - Henri Matisse

In traditional painting techniques, opaque paint is used to model the forms of the objects seen in the image. The term *model* in this context means to render the contours of the form using only light and dark tones. After the light and dark values are completed, transparent color glazes are applied to create the color seen in the image. The process continues in a cycle of building up opaque value layers and glazing for color until the painting is complete.

You Know More Than You Think You Do

In the transition from traditional art to digital content creation, the principles you learned in design, painting, and illustration will be extremely helpful in formulating a lighting process. When you are able to find the analog between what you know and what you are trying to do in max, the results you'll achieve will be even better than if you just rely on the dry, didactic formulas of tutorials and user manuals. Whatever your background, strive to relate what you know to what you are trying to achieve in max and realize that you know more about lighting than you might think you do.

The analog to this technique in digital content creation is to use the diffuse and ambient color components of the materials to model the light and dark values of your objects. Then use lights to create glazes of color for your objects. This is the main principle behind using color in lighting.

Sometimes the diffuse color of the material needs to be less intense and more neutral (less colorful or saturated) to allow the color of the light to create the color seen on the object. You won't see the need for this kind of adjustment to your object material until you are lighting your shot. Using layers to create your scenes enables you to easily accommodate this kind of change to achieve the lighting effect you desire.

Lighting Basics

"What good are computers? They can only give you answers." - Pablo Picasso

Picasso's quote suggests that the ability to ask questions is the important thing, not the answers. Indeed, it is our curiosity and ability to form relevant questions that elevates us above the mighty digital tools at our disposal. The important question is, "Light we must, but what kind of lighting?"

At the end of this chapter, you'll have completed the lighting, materials, animation, layer rendering, and compositing for Sc-01—your first complete scene for `Area51.avi`. This section, "Lighting Basics," focuses on helping you understand the different kinds of lights in max and how each one can be used in your scenes. You'll also learn how to adjust the parameters controlling the attributes common to all lighting, such as color, shadow casting, and so on.

> ☮ "One must from time to time attempt things that are beyond one's capacity."
> - Auguste Renoir
>
> If you find that this section stretches you beyond your capacity, the complete
> scene with all the lighting and material changes for Sc-01 can be found in
> MAXWorkshop\Help_Files\Chapter_5\EXSc_01.max.

Tip

Up to this point, you have created three max files: Area51_Animatic.max, Sc-01.max, and Sc-01_Clouds.max. You'll be accessing all three files to finish the scene.

Start by opening Sc-01.max. This file contains the cooling tower models and the camera that you created in Chapter 3, "Giving Form to Feeling: The Art of Modeling." When max opens, click the Create command panel and select the Lights icon ◼️. 3ds max 4 provides three standard types of lights to work with. Two of them, Spot and Direct, also have a target version (see Figure 5.2).

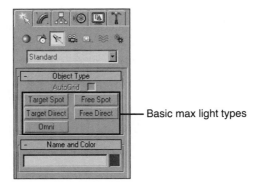 —— Basic max light types

Figure 5.2　The basic light types in max have unique capabilities and lighting effects modeled after their real-world counterparts.

Until you create your first light in a scene, max uses an invisible default lighting system to temporarily illuminate your models. Max's default lighting is the equivalent of one or two omni lights set in front and to the left of the scene and behind and to the right of your objects in the workspace. These omni lights turn off when you create your first light in max, so they won't interfere with your lighting process.

Although each standard type of light in max has its own unique properties and effect, they share some common attributes and controls. An understanding of which light to use and when to use it will come as you experiment with each type of light. The following section provides an overview of max lights and some generalized rules of thumb to guide how they are used in your scenes.

☟ Press F1 to access your max User Reference and type in the keyword *Lighting*. There are six topic titles that you should access and study: Guidelines for Lighting, Working with Lights, Properties of Lights, Lights, General Lighting Parameters, and Lighting in 3ds max.

Direct, Omni, Spot: Which One to Use?

Sc-01 takes place outside. Its key light source is the sun, which sits low on the horizon shining through the ominous clouds roiling overhead. Because the sun is shining through the clouds, its light isn't constantly illuminating the cooling tower, and the shadows cast by the clouds can be seen moving across the front face of the tower. In consideration of these factors, a Target Direct Light was chosen as the light source in this scene.

Direct Lights: Coherent Light

I use direct lights almost exclusively for simulation of any type of outside light source, including sunlight and moonlight. The light rays from a direct light source are coherent, meaning they travel in the same direction parallel to each other. This simulates the way light rays from an extremely large and distant light source, such as the moon or sun, travel and illuminate the objects in their paths (see Figure 5.3).

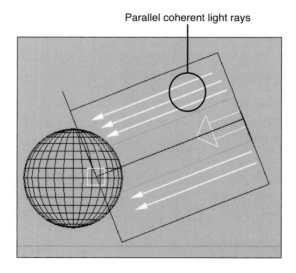

Parallel coherent light rays

Figure 5.3 A direct light can also be used to create the light from laser beams and powerful focused flashlights and spotlights.

Omni Lights: Incoherent Light

The light from an omni light is incoherent and radiates spherically in all directions. The light from a normal light bulb is a good example of an omni light application and incoherent light. I use omni lights mostly as fill lights—they are especially good at creating the kind of fake radiosity and soft, glowing ambient light needed to simulate night shots. The shot created in *3D Studio MAX 3.0 Workshop* used 17 omni lights at one point to achieve the correct radiosity (see Figure 5.4 and Figure CP.12 in the color section).

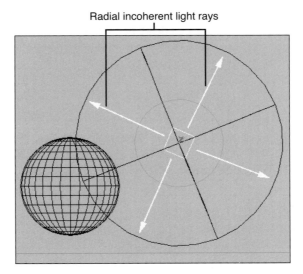

Radial incoherent light rays

Figure 5.4 Use omni lights as fill lights and to help simulate radiosity and ambient light in your scene.

Spotlights: Coherent Incoherency

Spotlights work well for simulating artificial lighting such as street lamps, work lights, vehicle headlights, and so on. Spotlights are used for interior lighting in most cases and also in conjunction with omni lights to achieve the appearance of radiosity.

The light rays from a spotlight are emitted in a cone-shaped pattern. The light rays aren't parallel but they are semicoherent—contained within the cone angle of the light specified in the lighting falloff parameters (see Figure 5.5).

Whatever lights you choose to use, give yourself time to experiment, and when you have found a combination that works, refine it and see whether you can achieve the same effect with fewer lights. Sometimes that is impossible and, fortunately for those of us who love lights, max doesn't limit the number of lights you can use in your scene.

Conic semicoherent light rays

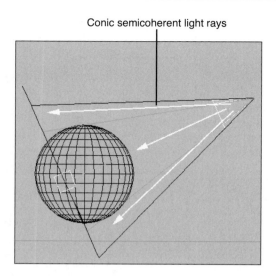

Figure 5.5 Use spotlights to create the light from artificial light sources.

Ambient Light: Global Illumination

Ambient light is another type of lighting effect that is an important element for achieving the effect of radiosity in your scenes.

Creating the appearance of radiosity in your lighting requires that you simulate how an object's reflected light illuminates other objects in the environment. Ambient light can be thought of as the sum total of all that reflected light bouncing around your scene. The lighter or more reflective a surface is, the more light energy it contributes to the total ambient light in your shot. Ambient light uniformly illuminates an environment; you can't tell where it's coming from, and it doesn't have an identifiable direction. There are two specific ways to add ambient light into your scene. You can add more lights into the environment or you can use the max global ambient light setting, which is turned off by default in max4.

I prefer to use additional lights to create ambient radiosity and rarely use the global ambient light setting in max. However, it does work well when trying to create the diffused light effects seen in mist or fog in broad daylight, such as the foggy morning shown in Figure 5.6. Ambient light also works well when trying to create special effects, such as a flash of lightning that washes out the scene with an arc of bright white illumination. Think of using the ambient setting for experimental and special effects, and keep it turned off completely when you begin lighting in max (see Figure CP.13 in the color section).

Figure 5.6   Ambient light is created when light is reflected and scattered uniformly by the fog in this environment. The ambient light bouncing around an environment is the reason shadows are not really black and the ground shadows on a bright snowy morning are deep blue.

Start in the Dark

A watercolorist begins the painting process by preserving and using the white of the paper and then painting with transparent color washes, building layer upon layer to create increasingly darker areas of the composition; in other words, the artist paints light to dark.

Lighting in max is exactly the opposite. You start with all the lights turned off, completely in the dark, and build up the lighting layer by layer; color by color; brighter and brighter—you'll light the scene (paint with light) dark to light, until you've achieved the desired atmosphere and mood.

In Sc-01, you are trying to create an ominous alien environment. The first step is to establish the main or *key* light of the shot—in this case, the sun at the horizon. The next step is to fake the radiosity effect by modifying the cooling tower material to add some of the sky color into its surfaces. Adding sky color into materials in daylight shots helps objects match the color and atmosphere of the other composited layers.

The Anatomy of a Target Direct Light

When you are finished with this part of the lighting, your cooling tower will look like the image for Sc-01 (see Figure CP.11 in the color section). You can also find the image on the CD in MAXWorkshop\Area51Final Targas\Sc-01. Target Direct Lights and Target Spotlights have three component parts: the light object, the target object, and the line that connects the two.

Creating a Target Direct Light is similar in process to the camera you created in Chapter 4. You'll choose the kind of light you want to create and drag in the viewport. The initial point of the drag defines the location of the light, and the point where you release the mouse establishes the location of the target object. The following steps create the Target Direct Light for Sc-01:

1. Change to Right view and maximize your viewport. Zoom out from the tower and camera so that you have some room to create the light (see Figure 5.7). Click the Lights icon ⬚ in the Create command panel ⬚ and select Target Direct.

2. Click in the viewport to the left and slightly above the cooling tower model, and drag the mouse to the right at a slight downward angle. Release the mouse to define the target position in the center of the cooling tower just below the top section. Your viewport should look like Figure 5.7.

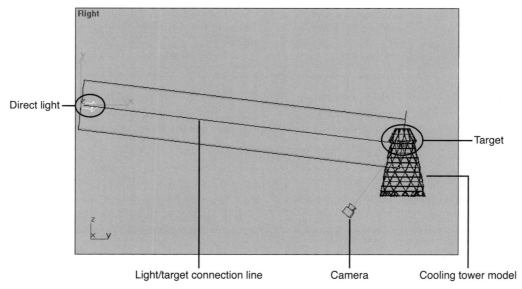

Figure 5.7   The Target Direct Light for Sc-01 is slightly above the tower and its light is coming from the horizon just as the sun's light would be at dusk.

3. Change to Top view and click the line that connects the light and its target. Select Move from the right-click Quad Menu and move the sunlight and its target using the X-axis. Center it over the cooling tower, as shown in Figure 5.8.

To see how the light is currently affecting your cooling tower, press C and Shift+Q to change to Camera view and render your scene. The light illuminates the front of the tower, creating a hotspot of light in its middle. The bottom and sides of the tower fade off into darkness. After a light is created and positioned correctly, the next step is to adjust the general parameters that create its color, shadows, and so on.

Light and target selected

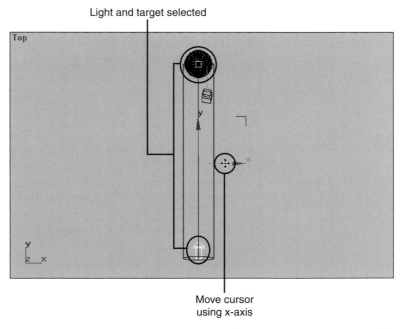

Top

Move cursor
using x-axis

Figure 5.8 Selecting the line that connects the target to the light will simultaneously select both elements. The same holds true for Target Cameras.

Adjusting General Lighting Parameters

All lights in max use the same general parameters to control how the light affects the scene. With your light selected, click the Modify command panel and change the name of this light to Sun Light. Then look at the General Parameters rollout, as shown in Figure 5.9.

Note

It's important to note that the location and parameter adjustments for the Sun Light were arrived at through several rounds of experimentation. To achieve exactly the right lighting for a scene, adjustments are made to the lighting during the entire scene creation process. This is why using layers is so effective—it allows you to tweak lighting and color independently for each layer in your composited imagery.

When I started using max it took a long time to learn how each of these interrelated parameters affected the lighting design I was creating. It's important to take the time and experiment with all the settings to discover exactly what they do, and a brief overview of the parameters will help you begin the process of discovery. As you read about the parameters, change the settings for the Sun Light as listed in the following sections.

3ds max 4

Modify command panel

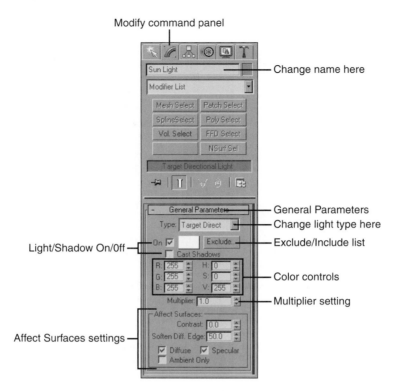

Change name here

Change light type here

General Parameters

Exclude/Include list

Light/Shadow On/Off

Color controls

Multiplier setting

Affect Surfaces settings

Figure 5.9 General Parameters control the basic parameters common to every type of max light object. These parameters are often misunderstood and therefore underused. Learning the function of each of these parameters will help you use the lights in your scene more effectively.

Type List

The Type list contains all the light types available in max. If you want to change the light type of a light you are modifying, just select the new light type from this list. Leave this setting as is for the lighting in this scene.

Exclude/Include List

Max gives you the capability to exclude and include specific objects from light and/or shadows cast by any light in the scene. This is especially important when you are trying to achieve the appearance of radiosity in your scene. *Including* an object is equivalent to *excluding* all the other objects in the scene; and, conversely, *excluding* objects is equivalent to *including* the remaining objects.

Light and Cast Shadows On/Off Check Boxes

When both of these boxes are checked, the light is on and it will cast shadows. When Cast Shadows is unchecked, the light won't cast shadows in the scene. When an unattenuated light doesn't cast shadows, it lights up all the objects in its path regardless of whether the object is sitting behind another object. When a light is turned off, its wireframe image turns black in your viewport and no shadows are cast regardless of the on/off status of the Cast Shadows check box. Max lights are on and Cast Shadows are off by default. The Sun Light in Sc-01 will cast shadows, so check the Cast Shadows box to turn it on.

Light Color Controls

There are three ways to adjust the color of your lights in max. You can click the color swatch next to the On check box and adjust the color using the color selector dialog box, you can change the RGB values, or you can change the HSV values.

HSV is another way of describing color, and its values and spinners are interdependent with the RGB settings. HSV controls the hue, saturation, and value of a light's color. Hue is another name for the color—red, green, and so on. Saturation determines how much of the pure hue is present in the color. Value determines the brightness of the color. Adjust the Value setting to make a color darker in value without diminishing its saturation. Change the HSV value of this light to 105,199,199 to add a green tint to the light to go with the sky gradient.

Multiplier Setting

Adjusting the Multiplier value enables you to increase or decrease the brightness of a light beyond its normal range. The max default Multiplier setting is 1.0. Increasing the Multiplier value above the default setting intensifies the brightness of the light, tending to create glare and washed-out images. Decreasing the Multiplier to values less than 1.0 diminishes the intensity of the light. Negative multiplier values create dark areas in the shot as if the light is removing light from the surfaces in its path. This comes in handy when you are trying to consciously create more contrast by darkening specific areas in your composition. Using a negative light value also changes the color of the light to its complementary color. When creating the projector map for the cloud shadows, which you will do in moment, the Sun Light needed more intensity to be able to "burn" through the clouds. So, change the Sun Light Multiplier value to 2.0.

Affect Surfaces Section

The controls in this section enable you to specify the specific part of a material's ambient, diffuse, and specular components that will be affected by the selected light. In general, I prefer to soften the blend between the diffuse and ambient material components by increasing the Soften Diff. Edge value to its maximum setting of 100. Leave the Diffuse and Specular check boxes as they are for now.

Sun Light General Parameters Recap

Here's a recap of the General Parameters settings for the Sun Light. Type: Target Direct Light; Light and Cast Shadows: On; Exclude: None; HSV Values: 105,199,199; Multiplier: 2.0; Affect Surfaces: Soften Diff. Edge: 100. The General Parameters rollout for the Sun Light should look like Figure 5.10.

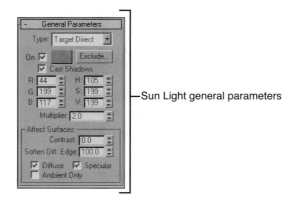

Sun Light general parameters

Figure 5.10   Adjusting a light's General Parameters is just the tip of the lighting iceberg. Understanding how these parameters affect your lighting lays an important foundation for adjusting the deeper lighting controls in the other rollouts.

Adjusting Directional Parameters

The controls in the next rollout specify how your light appears in the scene. You can specify the shape of the light, its hotspot, and Falloff amount, and add projector maps; a great feature that you'll use for the animating cloud shadows (see Figure 5.11).

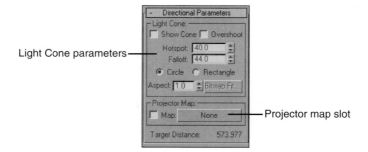

Light Cone parameters

Projector map slot

Figure 5.11   Directional Parameters allow you to fine-tune the display, appearance, and effect of the lights in your scene.

> **Tip**
>
> ⬇ Press F1 to access your max User Reference and type in the keyword *Directional Parameters* for a comprehensive explanation of this rollout.

Light Cone Settings

The settings in the Light Cone section of the Directional Parameters rollout control how the light is displayed in the scene and how it affects the environment it's placed in. The Projector Map section enables you to use a special light effect called projector map. As you read these definitions, make the indicated adjustments to this rollout:

- **Show Cone**—When the box next to Show Cone is checked, the light cone, determined by the falloff size, always appears in your scene. When it's unchecked, the cone appears only when the light is selected. Check this box to display the cone of the Sun Light.

- **Overshoot**—When Overshoot is checked, a light casts light in all directions like an omni light. However, the light's projection maps and shadows occur only within the light's cone. Leave Overshoot unchecked.

- **Hotspot and Falloff**—Falloff is the diameter of the cone of the light that determines how big an area of light will illuminate. The size of the hotspot relative to the falloff controls how soft the edge of the falloff diameter appears in the scene. The size of the hotspot determines how intense a highlight the light creates on the surfaces of the objects it's illuminating. Change the Falloff amount for the Sun Light to 82 and the Hotspot amount to 35.

  Figure 5.12 shows the effect that changing the relative value of the Hotspot will have on the appearance of the falloff. A direct light with a Falloff amount of 70 lights all three spheres.

- **Circle/Rectangle**—The falloff shape of spotlights and direct lights can be a circle or a rectangle. The rectangular shape is useful for light and shadows created by doors, windows, or the flat surfaces of buildings. Leave the Sun Light set to Circle.

- **Aspect/Bitmap Fit**—When you select Rectangle for your light shape, you can adjust its width-to-height proportion by using the Aspect spinner. An aspect value of 1.0 creates a rectangle whose height is equal to the width. A value of .5 means that the rectangle is half as high as it is wide. Bitmap Fit is used to match the aspect ratio of a rectangular spotlight or direct light to the aspect ratio of the bitmap image used as a projector map. This ensures that the projection appears correctly in the scene. These controls don't work with the Circle selection.

- **Target Distance**—Shows you the distance from the light to its target.

Sun Light Directional Parameters Recap

The Directional Parameter settings for the Sun Light are as follows: Show Cone: On; Overshoot: Off; Hotspot: 35; Falloff: 82; Circle is the selected light shape; leave the rest of the parameters as they are. Your Directional Parameters rollout should look like Figure 5.13.

The Sun Light in Sc-01 isn't attenuated, so the Workshop at this point will skip Attenuation and move on to the Shadow Parameters rollout. For a complete explanation of Attenuation, visit the max User Reference. After you learn about shadow parameters, you'll return to the projector map and create the animating map used to simulate the clouds passing in front of the sun.

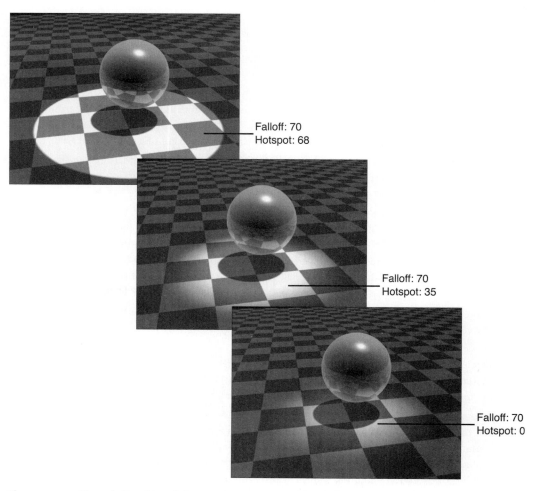

Falloff: 70
Hotspot: 68

Falloff: 70
Hotspot: 35

Falloff: 70
Hotspot: 0

Figure 5.12 The relationship of the Hotspot amount to the Falloff amount determines how soft the edge of the area illuminated by the light will be.

Figure 5.13 The Directional Parameters settings for the Sun Light were chosen to create a softer falloff edge without a strong highlight.

Adjusting Shadow and Shadow Map Parameters

Scroll down in the Command Panel and open the Shadow Parameters rollout. This rollout has two sections that control the general parameters of object and atmospheric shadows cast by your max lights (see Figure 5.14).

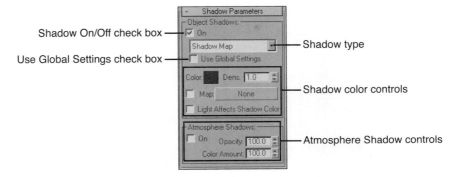

Figure 5.14 The parameter settings in this rollout will be fine-tuned in the Shadow Map Parameters rollout.

>
> **Tip**
>
> 🖤 Your max User Reference has a comprehensive explanation of the Shadow Parameters rollout that you should check out. Use the keyword *Shadow Parameters* in the Search tab.

Cast Shadows is already turned on for Sun Light in the General Parameters rollout. The On check box in this rollout and the Cast Shadows check box in the General Parameters rollout are linked—turning off shadows here will turn them off there, and vice versa.

Shadow Map and Raytraced Shadows

Two types of shadows can be created in 3ds max 4: Shadow Map and Raytrace. Raytraced shadows take longer to render, and with some creative adjustment, Shadow Map shadows can achieve the look of Raytraced shadows. Both shadow types can be used in your scenes because the shadow type for every light can be set independently. Common shadow parameters can also be applied to several lights at the same time using the Global settings.

You can mix shadow types according to where the shadow appears in the composition: Raytraced shadows in the foreground to emphasize detail and Shadow Map shadows in the imagery far away from the camera where a low level of detail is required. It's important to experiment with both types of shadows to learn their limitations and how each one affects scene imagery and rendering time. Figure 5.15 shows the difference between Raytraced shadows and Shadow Map shadows set at their default max settings. You can leave the shadow type for the Sun Light set to Shadow Map; its quality is sufficient for Sc-01.

Shadow Map shadows

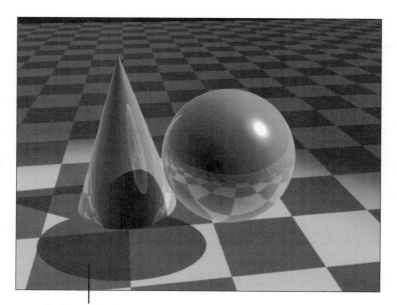

Raytraced shadows

Figure 5.15 Raytraced shadows create accurate shadows of a high quality. The only downside is that they can take longer to render. Furthermore, Raytraced shadows only accurately simulate shadows of harsh lighting conditions, giving the shadow a sharp edge. Shadow Map shadows allow for feathered shadow edges—thus, it is in combination that reality can be replicated.

The Shadow Map shadows took 47 seconds to render; the Raytraced shadows were rendered in 54 seconds. That doesn't seem like too big of a difference, but the more complex a scene, the greater the differential will be between the two rendering times.

Using Shadow Map shadows for the Sun Light shadows in Sc-01 produced a rendering time of 36 seconds per frame; Raytraced shadows were rendered in 50 seconds per frame. The difference between the two is just 14 seconds. However, when you multiply the difference by the scene length of 288 frames, the total rendering time difference is over 65 minutes. That's not insignificant. Using multiple lights following the advice given by Dave Campbell can help you optimize your rendering times. Keep these factors in mind as you design the lighting for your scenes.

A good way to get around this problem is to fool the audience into thinking that a scene is raytraced (both shadows and reflections) by putting a Raytraced image layer in the extreme foreground. The eye sees the higher image quality and fools the mind into thinking that the entire scene is raytraced also. This is especially effective in shots using animated cameras. Figure 5.16 shows an image that uses this cheap trick.

Global Settings

The Use Global Settings check box allows lights in a scene to use the same shadow and Shadow Map parameters. When this box is checked, you can control the shadows of all lights that also have this box checked using one set of parameters. Changing the parameters of one light in the global settings group changes all the rest. When global settings are used, the Shadow Map Parameters rollout changes to show the parameters for all lights that are using global settings.

Adjusting Shadow Color and Density

The color swatch next to Color and the Density amount (the Dens. box) are used to specify the color and intensity of the shadows cast by your lights. When you click the color swatch, the Color Selector dialog box opens for you to specify the RGB or HSV values of your shadow color. The Sun Light shadow color can remain set to black. Color will be added into the shadows in another way later in this chapter.

Foreground Raytraced layer

Figure 5.16 Use Raytraced reflections and shadows wisely by creating limited Raytraced layers that can fool the eye into thinking the entire scene is raytraced. The color version of this image can be seen in Figure CP.7 in the color section of this book.

Density controls the value of the shadow. The default Dens. amount is 1.0, which creates the darkest value of shadow possible. Lower values create less dense or lighter shadow values and allow the color of the object material that the shadow is being cast on to show through. Leave the Sun Light shadow Density value set at 1.0 for now.

Shadow Parameter's Map Option

When a bitmap image or procedural map is put into the Map slot, it will be seen in the shadow cast by the light. This can result in some really interesting effects that allow you to create patterned and animating shadows images (see Figure 5.17).

Light Affects Shadow Color Parameter and Atmosphere Shadows Section

The Light Affects Shadow Color parameter is another feature of max lighting that helps simulate radiosity in your scenes. Under realistic lighting conditions, shadows are never truly black. Their color is created by three factors: the intensity and color of the light creating the shadow, the color and surface properties (reflective and nonreflective) of the material the shadow is being cast on, and the intensity and color of the ambient light bouncing around in the scene.

Bitmap image map added to shadow

Figure 5.17 Adding bitmap and procedural maps to the Map slot of the Shadow Parameters creates images and effects inside cast shadows.

Allowing the light to affect the color of the shadows will essentially blend the light color with the shadow color. This simulates the way shadows look in the real world. Later in this chapter, you'll adjust the cooling tower material to create a fake radiosity effect. This will negate most of the effect that using the Light Affects Shadow Color will have in the imagery, so leave this box unchecked.

Note Max's atmospheric effects can also cast shadows, but only when the light shining through the effect has the On box checked in this section of the rollout. This effect won't be explored in this Workshop.

Adjusting Shadow Map Parameters

Shadow Map parameter settings are used to fine-tune the quality of the shadows cast by your lights. In Figure 5.15, shown previously, the Shadow Map shadows appeared a bit rough around the edges because of the default settings shown in Figure 5.18.

Figure 5.18   Shadow Map Parameters fine-tune the location and quality of Shadow Map shadows.

Your max User Reference provides a comprehensive explanation of the Shadow Map Parameters rollout. Use the keyword *Shadow Map Parameters* in the Search tab.

Map Bias controls how close the shadow is to the shadow-casting object. Higher Bias values can result in shadows that don't look like they are *attached* to the object correctly. A map Bias of less then 1.0 creates a shadow that looks correctly attached to the object.

Map Size determines the quality of the shadow image. Lower values create jaggy edges. Higher values create near-raytrace-quality shadow maps.

Sample Range determines how soft the edge of the shadow is. Higher values produce softer edges that simulate diffraction. Lower values create hard shadow edges. Figures 5.19 and 5.20 show two images rendered with different shadow bias, map size, and sample range settings.

Note

A note from Dave Campbell: It's important to realize that Raytraced shadows aren't intrinsically *better* than shadow maps—both are very useful and must be used according to the benefit they bring to your scene lighting. Beginning users of max sometimes try to crank up the quality of shadow maps to achieve Raytraced quality. However, shadows maps are so much more useful because of their soft edges, and motion blur can be applied to them as well. In general, Raytraced shadows works best for high-intensity scenes; shadow maps work for lower lighting conditions when diffused shadows are needed.

Raytraced shadows use two parameters to control their appearance: Bias and Max Quadtree Depth. Raytrace Bias functions in a similar manner to the Bias setting for Shadow Map shadows. Higher values move the shadow away from the shadow-casting object, and lower values create a more correct connected shadow. Raytraced shadows always have a hard-defined edge.

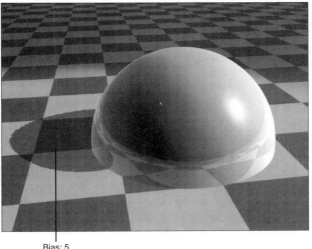

Bias: 5
Map size: 512
Sample range: .1

Figure 5.19 High bias values make shadows appear disconnected from the shadow-casting objects. Low map sizes reduce the quality of the shadow map and, coupled with low sample ranges, create jagged shadow edges.

Bias: .75
Map size: 2000
Sample range: 30

Figure 5.20 Bias values less than 1.0 generally make shadows appear correctly connected to the shadow-casting objects. High map size improves the quality of the shadow map and, coupled with high sample ranges, create near-raytrace-quality imagery; however, it takes just about the same time to render.

> **Note**
>
> A *quadtree* is the data-handling algorithm used by 3ds max 4 to control the ray-tracing process. Max (short for maximum) Quadtree Depth controls the quality and subsequently the rendering speed of Raytraced shadows. Higher values speed up the raytracing process, but at the cost of using more memory (RAM). Your max User Reference gives a warning worth mentioning: "An omni light can generate up to six quadtrees, so omni lights that cast raytraced shadows use more memory at render time than spotlights do." The point is to know what these parameters do and how they are interrelated. This will reduce a lot of frustration wondering why it's taking forever to render your scene.

Figure 5.21 shows Raytraced shadow using a Raytrace Bias of .5 and a Max Quadtree Depth of 10. This resulted in a rendering time of 43 seconds—an acceptable rendering time comparable to 42 seconds for Shadow Map images of similar quality.

Figure 5.21 The choice between Shadow Map shadows and the crisp, realistic Raytraced shadows shown in this image becomes a matter decided by the needs of the scene, the visual language of the production, and the production schedule.

Projector Map: Creating Animated Cloud Shadows

The clouds you created in Chapter 4 for Sc-01 are not real 3D volumes of simulated water vapor and can't cast shadows or be realistically lit in their current form. Real clouds passing in front of the sun sitting low on the horizon would cast shadows into the environment the sun is illuminating. And the light illuminating them would light up the surfaces of the clouds closest to the sun. To create the shadows of the clouds that are moving across the face of the cooling tower, you'll make a Noise map similar to the one you used to create the overhead clouds and use it as a projector map.

Creating the Cloud Shadow Projector Map

Follow these steps to create the projector map:

1. Press M to open the Material Editor and position it in your viewport just to the left of the Command Panels.

2. Select the Sun Light and click the Modify command panel. Scroll down to the Directional Parameters rollout and click the Map slot marked None in the Projector Map section.

3. When the Material/Map Browser opens, double-click Noise to close the browser and add the Noise map into your Projector map slot.

4. Drag the Noise map and drop it onto an empty material preview window in the Material Editor. Select Instance as the Clone type when the Clone/Copy dialog box appears, and click OK. Your Material Editor and Directional Parameters rollout should look like Figure 5.22.

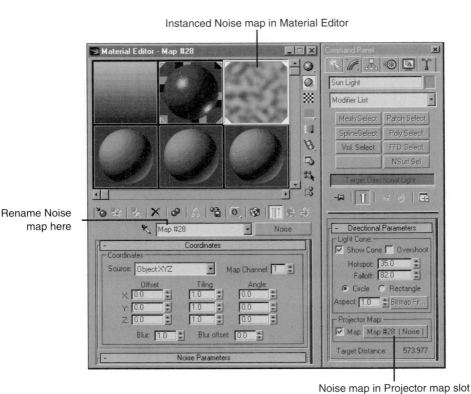

Instanced Noise map in Material Editor

Rename Noise map here

Noise map in Projector map slot

Figure 5.22 The drag-and-drop process is the same one you used to create the BG Gradient map in Chapter 3.

5. Change the name of the Noise map to Cloud_Shadows and scroll down to the Noise Parameters rollout in the Material Editor.

6. Change the Noise Parameters to the following: Noise Type: Fractal; Noise Threshold— High: 0.6; Low: 0.4; Levels: 3.0; Size: 50.0 (see Figure 5.23).

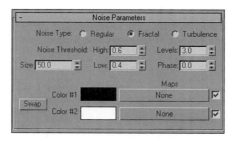

Figure 5.23   The settings for the projector map were developed through a lot of experimentation with the look of the cloud shadows and how they animated across the face of the cooling tower.

7. Scroll down and open the Output rollout and click Invert; leave the rest of the output parameters set to their default values, as shown in Figure 5.24.

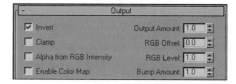

Figure 5.24   Every map created in the Material Editor has an Output rollout, which gives you control over the major factors affecting the appearance of the map in your scene. It's a fun and powerful set of parameters that can be used to affect subtle and intense changes to basic bitmap and procedural map imagery.

As you did with the cloud plane in Chapter 4, you'll be using the X- and Y-axis Offset in the Coordinates rollout to animate the cloud shadows.

Animating the Cloud_Shadows Projector Map

Clouds are found almost exclusively in the troposphere, which starts at sea level and extends up to approximately 15 kilometers above the earth's surface. Because of their enormous size and distance from our earthbound POV, the speed at which clouds move is difficult to gauge by eye. The one way to gauge their speed accurately is by measuring the ground speed of the shadows the clouds cast on the ground. Visually the shadows and the clouds will appear to travel at different speeds—a type of parallax effect created by relative distance of the clouds, which are far away, and their shadows, which are very near.

To create realistic-looking animating shadows on the cooling towers, and taking the parallax effect into account, the shadows moving across the face of the cooling tower will move faster than the clouds seen in the cloud plane. The cloud shadows also need to move up and to the right over the face of the tower to relate to the movement of the cloud layer:

1. Scroll up to the Coordinates rollout and click the Animate button ⬚ to enter Animate mode. Move the time slider to frame number 287 at the end of the Track Bar.

2. Change the X Offset value in the Coordinate rollout to -400 and the Y Offset value to -200. Click the Animate button to exit Animate mode, save your file, and render the Camera view to see the shadows cast by the projector map. Your Coordinates rollout should look like Figure 5.25.

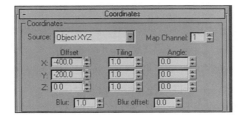

Figure 5.25   When you are designing your effects animation, consider the power of animating materials to create the imagery you are trying to achieve.

Note

The coordinate values for the cloud shadow map are expressed in negative numbers. This is different than the positive numbers used to animate the cloud layer. The difference comes from the fact that the relative XYZ coordinates of the object to which they are applied are oriented differently in space relative to the camera POV.

After you have modified the cooling tower material and created the camera animation, you'll render the sequential images of the cloud shadows on the cooling tower. The images will be composited with the cloud layer you created in Chapter 4 and the BG Sky from Chapter 3.

Faking Ambient Radiosity

The technical director at our studio, Dave Otte, and I have a lot of discussions about lighting, material development, scene complexity, and so on. Technical directors like Dave are excellent artists who also have expertise in the more technical aspects of modeling, lighting, animation, scene development, and production rendering. Their job is to work with the art director to establish the visual language and invent the processes that implement the visual language into the production pipeline.

3ds max 4

Achieving the look and feel of radiosity in production imagery without having to resort to dozens of lights or radiosity rendering plug-ins has been an ongoing project of Dave's. He's come up with several techniques that are fun, easy to use, and creative. You'll be learning about one of the techniques in this scene.

Nonlinear Thinking

Creating light without actually using lights in your scenes is a great example of the type of nonlinear creative thinking needed in your max work. This is also the basis for some amazing next-generation radiosity rendering technology being invented for max, such as the Arnold Messiah rendering system by Marcos Fajardo and the Ghost renderer being developed by Blur Studio. The intent of using materials to achieve radiosity is to simplify the lighting of a scene and gain more control over the rendered image layers. And the results can be stunning. Check out Blur's Ghost Web site at `www.blur.com/blurbeta/ghost`.

Adding a Falloff Map

The following steps will show you how to use a Falloff map to fake radiosity in the cooling tower material:

1. Click the Cooling_Tower_Master material preview window in your Material Editor. Scroll down in the editor until you see the Maps rollout (see Figure 5.26).

2. Click the Map slot next to Extra Lighting and select Falloff from the Material/Map Browser. Click OK to load the Falloff map into the Extra Lighting map slot.

Tip

 In addition to being used to create ambient radiosity, Falloff maps can be used to create some cool X-ray–type material effects. Use the keyword *Falloff Map* in your max User Reference to learn more. There's also a great book, *3D Studio max R3, f/x & Design* by Jon A. Bell (published by Coriolis), that goes into some fun and creative uses of this map. The entire book is a worthwhile investment.

Using this map allows you to specify a color for all the shadows seen on the cooling tower form, including those cast by the Sun Light and its projector map.

Adjusting the Falloff Map

When you add the Falloff map into the Map slot, the Maps rollout window changes to the Falloff Parameters window shown in Figure 5.27.

Cooling tower master material selected

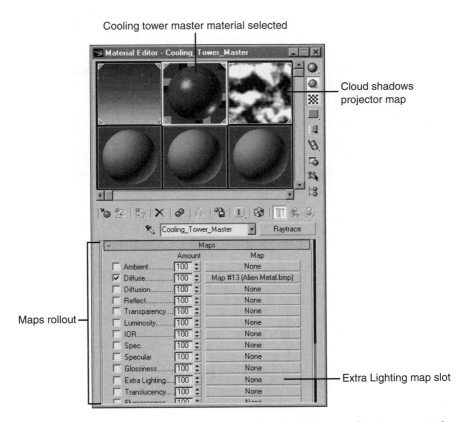

Cloud shadows
projector map

Maps rollout

Extra Lighting map slot

Photon Paint: The Art of Lighting

Figure 5.26 The Maps rollout provides a comprehensive list of all the Map slots in a material and the maps assigned to them.

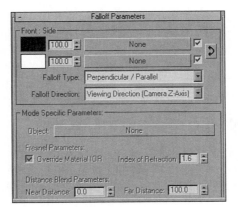

Figure 5.27 Falloff maps can be used to control reflection, material color, transparency, and so on. A Falloff map can be used in any of the material Map slots.

Finding the right combination of falloff settings, background gradient color, cloud layer color, and cooling tower material color was accomplished with a lot of test renders and experimental failures. Here are the settings that worked with the lighting scheme created for Sc-01. If you are trying a lighting and color scheme of your own, experiment with the settings until you get the look you want:

1. Click Falloff Type and select Shadow/Light from the list. This is the type of falloff that enables you to create a different color or even material for the surfaces of an object that are illuminated and those in shadow.

2. Click the black color swatch under Shaded:Lit in the top-left corner of the rollout. Change the color values to HSV: 150,191,100. This specifies that the color seen in the shadows of the material will be a deep blue. This color was chosen to go with the color scheme of the scene and to fake radiosity by creating shadows that aren't black.

3. Scroll down to the Mix Curve rollout and drag the point on the left down about halfway in the graph window (see Figure 5.28).

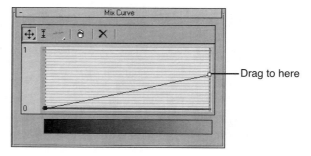

Figure 5.28   The Mix Curve graph controls the gradient produced by the falloff. The gradient bar below the graph shows the result of the adjustments you make to the curve.

4. Open the Output rollout and change the value in Output Amount to 2.0. This intensifies the color seen in the shadows. Close the Material Editor when you're finished.

When you render your scene, you can see the dark blue color specified by the Falloff map in the shadows of the cooling tower. This color will blend perfectly with the rest of the finishing touches you'll make to complete the scene.

Max Workshop: Completing Sc-01

This section takes you through the final steps needed to complete Sc-01. All the techniques and processes in this chapter and the ones preceding it will be used to create the rest of the scenes for Area51.avi. An interesting part of this section will be animating the field of view of the camera to create the zoom specified by the storyboard for Sc-01.

Animating the Camera Field of View

Camera moves, as discussed earlier in this Workshop, are an integral part of your toolbox for creating dynamic imagery to entertain your audience. The camera movement for Sc-01 doesn't require any actual movement like some of the other scenes. Instead, you'll animate one of the camera's parameters—the field of view. This is a variation of a technique used in mystery and suspense movies and will help create an interesting depth effect to the scene.

> **Note**
>
> Inspiration for cinematic camera effects comes from observing and copying the work of master cinematographers. The push pull camera move for Sc-01 is a subtle variation of the kind of camera work pioneered by Alfred Hitchcock in his movies *Vertigo* and *Psycho* and the multi-plane camera used by Walt Disney.

1. Press H to open the Select Objects dialog box and choose Camera01 from the list, as shown in Figure 5.29.

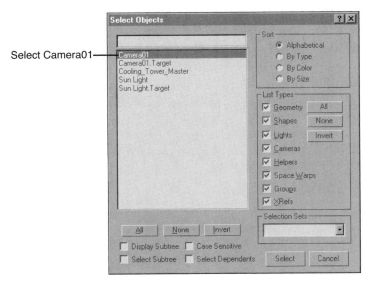

Select Camera01

Figure 5.29 The Select Objects dialog box is an indispensable tool, especially when you want to select an object that is not currently in the viewport or when you are working with a complex scene and need to find a specific object easily and quickly.

2. Click the Modify command panel to see the Parameters rollout for the camera, and adjust the FOV to 42, as shown in Figure 5.30.

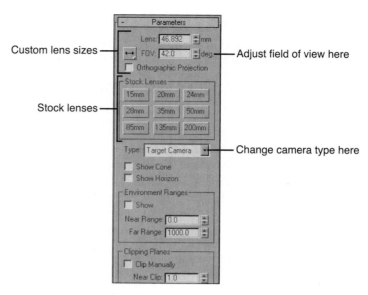

Custom lens sizes — Adjust field of view here

Stock lenses

Change camera type here

Figure 5.30 The basic camera control parameters enable you to adjust lens and FOV settings, change camera types, and modify certain camera viewport display components.

3. Click the Animate button to enter Animate mode and move the Time Slider to frame 287 in the Track Bar. Change the FOV setting in the Modify command panel to 35 and exit Animate mode. Click Play Animation ▶ to view the animated effect—a slow dolly move closer to the tower. You can also see the FOV value in the Modify command panel change over time as the animation is played.

Save Sc-01.max and open Sc-01_Clouds.max. All that's left to do for this scene is adjust the cloud layer material and animate the FOV camera move for the clouds.

Adjusting the Cloud Plane Material

Although the clouds created in Chapter 4 are suitably ominous, their black color is a bit too stark. A dark blue or green would be a better choice because it will blend with the scene ambient color and still provide a dark background for the cooling tower in the foreground.

1. Press M to open the Material Editor and click the BG_Clouds material preview window.

2. Click the color swatch next to Luminosity in the Raytrace Basic Parameters rollout. Add a deep blue color to this material by changing the HSV values of the Luminosity color to 158,212,53. Adding the color changes the cloud color to dark blue, which will help the image layer blend with composition and the cooling tower material.

3. Click the Map slot next to Transparency to access the Noise map used to create the clouds. Change the Threshold Low Noise value to 0.3 to soften the clouds.

4. Open the Output rollout and change the Output amount to 1.6 to soften the visual intensity of the Noise map. Invert should be checked in this rollout; the rest of the parameters are left at their default settings.

Adjusting the Sc-o1_Clouds Camera Animation

You've animated the Sc-01 camera to create a subtle dolly-like move toward the cooling tower. For the cloud layer imagery, you are going to animate the camera FOV to move the camera in the opposite direction—away from the clouds. This will create a dual camera move in the same scene, emphasizing the weirdness of Area51.avi that will also enhance the perception of depth in the shot.

1. Select the Camera, open the Modify command panel as you did in the previous section, and change the FOV to 38.

2. Click the Animate button to enter Animate mode and move the Time Slider to frame 287 at the right end of the Track Bar.

3. Change the Camera FOV to 50 and click the Animate button to exit Animate mode. With the Time Slider set to frame 287, your Modify command panel should look like Figure 5.31.

Figure 5.31   Relating your max camera work to traditional cinematography is an important element in your education as a digital artist.

Save your work and open Sc_01.max to begin the layer rendering process.

Rendering Sc-o1 Layers

Sc-01 is composited from three image layers: the BG_Sky, the BG_Clouds, and the cooling tower in the foreground. Rendering these layers will show you the basic render-and-save process you'll use for the rest of the Workshop. A simple file structure and naming convention will also help you keep track of the image files. This is important because working with layers can get a little complicated and it's easy to get confused if you haven't organized yourself effectively.

Sc-o1 BG_Sky

The first layer you'll create is the BG_Sky layer. This is an easy one because it's only one image:

1. After SC_01.max opens, select and hide the cooling tower models. Click Rendering, Environment to access the Environment dialog box you used to create the BG Sky map. The BG Sky (Gradient) map is in the Environment map slot. Leave this window open until after you have rendered the BG Sky layer (see Figure 5.32).

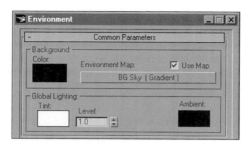

Figure 5.32   The BG Sky is a still image that will be composited as the background image for the other two layers of Sc-01. Using the Video Post Event Track Area, you'll adjust its frame length to appear as the BG for the entire 288-frame scene.

2. Click the Render Scene dialog box icon 🔲 in the Main Toolbar. When it opens, be sure the Time Output is set to Single and the Output Size is 640×346. Leave this window open (see Figure 5.33).

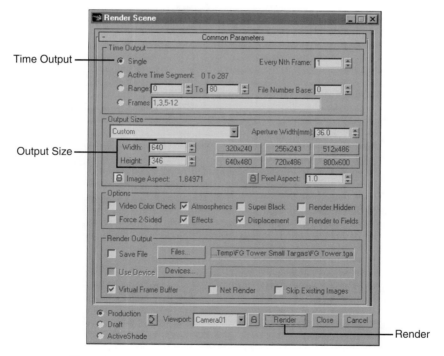

Figure 5.33   You'll use the Render Scene dialog box to organize how and where you'll save the layer images for all the scenes in Area51.avi.

3. When you have confirmed that the settings are correct, click the Render button at the bottom of the Render Scene dialog box.

4. When the image is finished rendering, click the Save Bitmap icon in the toolbar at the top of the Virtual Frame Buffer (see Figure 5.34).

Save Bitmap button

Figure 5.34 Using the Save Bitmap command in the Virtual Frame Buffer for single images such as the BG Sky is often easier than using the Save File function in the Render Scene dialog box.

5. When the Browse Images for Output window opens, browse to your MAXWorkshop master directory and create a new folder titled Area 51 Final Targas. Create another new folder inside Area 51 Final Targas and name it Sc-01. Save the BG Sky image in this folder as Sc-01_BG_Sky.tga. The Browse Images for Output window should look like Figure 5.35.

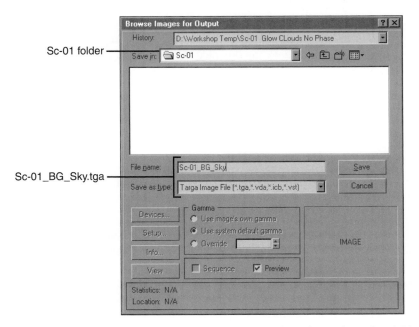

Sc-01 folder

Sc-01_BG_Sky.tga

Figure 5.35 Because the BG Sky is a single image, it doesn't need another folder of its own as the other two layers will. Being this organized is imperative—it will save you headaches, embarrassment, and frustration.

6. Click Save when you are done. When the Targa Image Control window opens, fill in all the additional information and be sure that 32 Bits-Per-Pixel and Pre-Multiplied Alpha are selected. Your window should look like Figure 5.36.

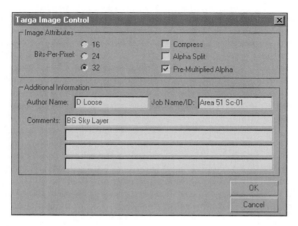

Figure 5.36 Your information will, of course, be different, but follow the basic guide shown here and add any other comments you deem necessary.

7. Click OK to save the image and close the Targa Image Control window. Then close the Virtual Frame Buffer. You won't need the BG Sky map in the layer images for the foreground cooling tower layer, so uncheck the box next to Use Map in the Environment dialog box.

Close the Environment dialog box when you're finished and save your file. The next two image layers will use the Render Scene dialog box commands to set up the location and information for the rendered images before you render them.

Sc-01 FG Tower

The first step to render this layer is to unhide the Cooling_Tower_Master and Cooling_Tower_Lattice models. Be sure your Camera viewport is active and the Render Scene dialog box is open. Make the following adjustments to the Render Scene dialog box settings:

1. Change the Time Output selection to Active Time Segment: 1 to 288; leave the Output Size set to 640×346; and click Files in the Render Output section, as shown in Figure 5.37.

2. The Render Output File dialog box that opens does the same thing as the Browse Images for Output dialog box you just used. Browse to MAXWorkshop\ Area 51 Final Targas\Sc-01 and create a new folder named Sc-01FGTower. Inside the Sc-01FGTower folder, name the targa images for this image layer: FGTower.tga. Before you click Save to exit this dialog box, click Setup (see Figure 5.38).

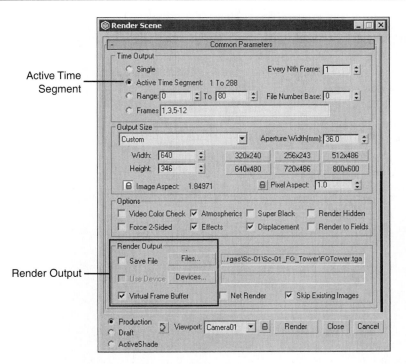

Active Time Segment

Render Output

Figure 5.37 After you click Files, the process to save and organize your images is the same in function as the process used when you saved the BG Sky image using the commands in the VFB.

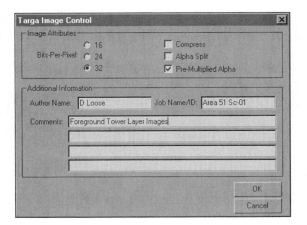

Figure 5.38 Setup also takes you to the Targa Image Control dialog box in which you'll enter all the important organizational information for these images.

3. Click OK to exit the Targa Image Control dialog box, and then click Save to exit the Render Output File dialog box. When you specify a name, such as FGTower, for a sequence of images, max adds sequential numbers after the name you specify to the image files when they are rendered. The rendered image filenames for FGTower will be FGTower0000.tga, FGTower0001.tga, and so on.

4. When you return to the Render Scene dialog box, click Render to start the rendering process. If you don't want to render at this time, click Close. This will save the settings and image path you've set up during this process. To begin the rendering process, return to the Render Scene dialog box and click Render or press Shift+Q (see Figure 5.39).

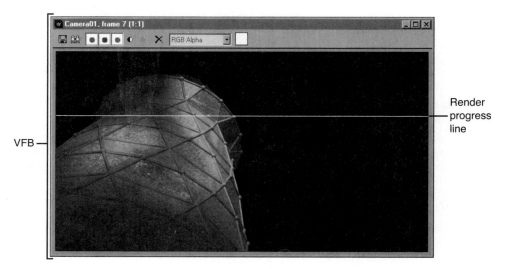

Render progress line

VFB

Figure 5.39 The images for this layer took about 35 seconds per frame. Total rendering time was two hours and 40 minutes on a Dual P3 450, Windows 2000 machine with 390MB RAM.

Tip

The settings you establish in the Render Scene dialog box will be used whenever you use any keyboard shortcut or UI command to start the rendering process. If you have forgotten that you had a render process set up and start to render a new layer without changing the Render Scene dialog box settings, max will always alert you that you are about to overwrite any saved images.

After the FGTower images are rendered, save SC_01.max and open SC_01_Clouds.max to repeat the rendering process for the cloud image layers.

Sc-01 Clouds

The process to render the cloud layer is basically the same as the one used for the FGTower images. When you render the images for this layer, they will appear black in the VFB because there is no sky gradient behind the cloud layer. Don't be alarmed, the images are there. Here's a recap of the steps to take to render the cloud layer images after you've opened SC_01_Clouds.max:

1. Open the Environment dialog box and uncheck the Use Map option to turn the BG Sky map off.

2. Change to the Camera viewport and hide the cooling tower that was used for reference.

3. Open the Render Scene dialog box and be sure the Time Output and the Output Size are correct. Then click the Files button in the Render Output section, browse to MAXWorkshop\Area 51 Final Targas\Sc-01, and create a new folder named Sc-01Clouds. Name the image files Clouds.tga and access the Targa Image Control to annotate the files and set up the image quality parameters.

4. Return to the Render Scene dialog box and render the images.

> **Tip**
>
> 🔅 These are the basic steps you'll use to render all the image files for the rest of the scenes in this Workshop. If you need help, just come back to this section for a quick review.

Compositing Sc-01

The compositing process follows the same basics that you learned in Chapter 2, "Virtual Viz: The Art of Pre-Production for Digital Content Creation," when you created the animatic for Area51.avi. You'll use Video Post to create a single composite image of all three Sc-01 image layers. That single image will be used in the animatic taking the place of the placeholder images in that file.

It's easier to create a separate max file to use for compositing each scene. This keeps all the compositing processes organized and makes any changes easy.

Sc-01_Compositor.max

Click File, Reset. When the alert window opens asking whether you want to save your changes, choose Yes if you haven't already saved Sc_01_Clouds.max. If you have saved, then click No. When the next alert opens asking, "Do you really want to reset?" resist the urge to curse and click Yes. Save this new file as Sc_01_Compositor in MAXWorkshop\Area 51 Final Targas\Sc-01.

Setting Up the Video Post Queue

Click Rendering, Video Post to open the Video Post Editor window and follow the next steps to composite the image layers for Sc-01:

1. Click Add Image Input Event 🔲. This opens the dialog box shown in Figure 5.40.

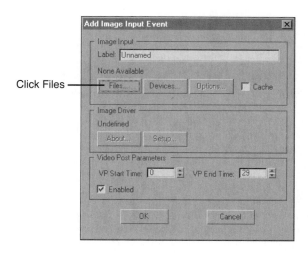

Click Files

Figure 5.40 The Add Image Input Event dialog box is the gatekeeper of the Video Post Queue. It controls how and when the images added to the queue are used.

2. Click Files to open the Select Image File for Video Post Input dialog box. Browse to MAXWorkshop\Area 51 Final Targas\Sc-01 and select Sc-01_BG_Sky.tga. Then click Open to return to the Add Image Input Event dialog box.

3. Change the VP End Time to 287, and then click Options, as shown in Figure 5.41.

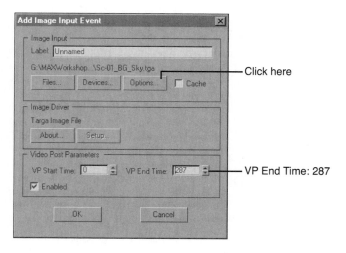

Click here

VP End Time: 287

Figure 5.41 Changing the VP End Time to frame 287 tells Video Post to make the BG Sky image last for the entire length of the scene.

4. When the Image Input Options dialog box opens, first select Do Not Resize in the Size section, and then click the center box in the Alignment section. Then click OK to return to the Add Image Input Event dialog box (see Figure 5.42).

Alignment: centered

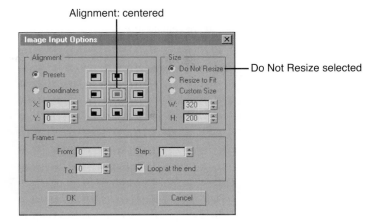

Do Not Resize selected

Figure 5.42 The rendered output format for Area51.avi is 640×480. The images used in the movie are letterbox format 640×346. The Image Input Options dialog box allows you to specify where the images will be placed within the larger format and their size in the rendered imagery.

5. After the Options are changed for this layer, change the label for this image to BG Sky and click OK. Video Post loads the image file into the queue, as shown in Figure 5.43.

BG Sky layer in queue

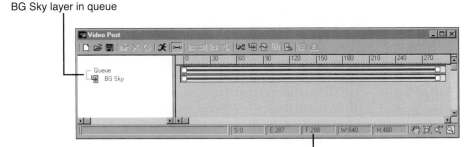

Image length: 288 frames

Figure 5.43 You might prefer to use the real name of the image file instead of a label. Sometimes a label can be more descriptive of the image and its function in the compositing process.

6. Click Add Image Input Event and click Files when the dialog box opens. Browse to MAXWorkshop\Area 51 Final Targas\Sc-01\Sc-01_Clouds and click the first Cloud image in the folder: Clouds0000.tga.

7. When you click the file, a preview image appears in the bottom-right corner of the browser window. To the left of that image is a check box titled Sequence. Click that box to select all the sequential files for the cloud image layer (see Figure 5.44).

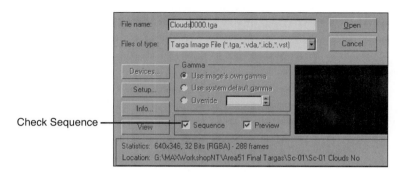

Check Sequence

Figure 5.44 The single selected image will be the only image file loaded if you don't check the sequence box to specify that a sequence of images be loaded.

8. When you click Open, the Image File List Control dialog box opens. All the settings are correct; click OK to load the images and return to the Add Image Input Event dialog box. Label this sequence: Clouds (see Figure 5.45).

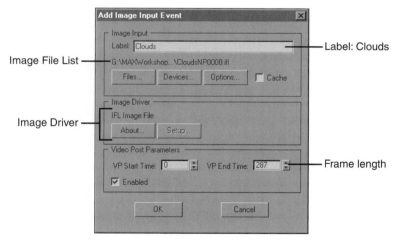

Image File List

Image Driver

Label: Clouds

Frame length

Figure 5.45 Max uses Image File Lists—also called IFLs—to control sequential images. Image File Lists are text files that can be edited to combine images from different source files. You'll learn more about IFLs in Chapter 9.

9. Click Options and click Do Not Resize first, and then align the image to the center just as you did with the BG Sky image.

> **Note**
>
> Notice that the VP Start and End Times are set to 0, 287. This yields a 288-frame sequence and differs from the setup in the max scene files where you specified your start frame as frame 1. The important number, in this case, is the total frame count regardless of the start frame number.

10. Click OK to exit the Image Input Options dialog box and click OK to exit the Add Image Input Event dialog box. The Cloud sequence is now loaded into the queue.

11. Repeat the same process to add the FGTower IFL to the VP Queue. Remember to adjust the settings in the Image Input Options dialog box. Label this layer Tower. Your VP Queue should now have all three image layers in place (see Figure 5.46).

Image layers added ———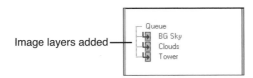

Figure 5.46   Compositing the image layers together will use an Alpha Compositor. This is an Image Layer Event that uses the alpha channel of Targa files to create composited imagery.

Adding the Alpha Compositor Layer Event

The next step in this process will use the alpha channels of the targa images you've created to combine the sequential images into a single layer. The following steps show you how to add the Alpha Compositor Layer event to the VP queue:

1. Hold down the Ctrl key and select the first two image layers in the VP Queue. This will activate the Add Image Layer Event button 🔲, as shown in Figure 5.47.

Add Image Layer Event button

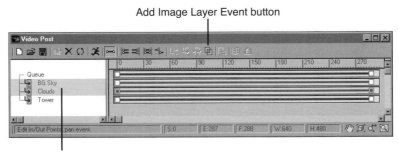

First two layers selected

Figure 5.47   Alpha channels are an integral part of the data structure of 32–bit Targa images. Without them, compositing doesn't work.

2. Click the Add Image Layer Event button, choose Alpha Compositor from the list shown in Figure 5.48, and then click OK.

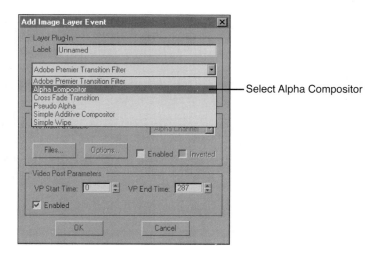

Select Alpha Compositor

Figure 5.48   Compositing these layers takes two Alpha Compositor Layer Events. Later in the Workshop, you'll learn more about the specifics of alpha channels and how they work.

3. Hold down the Ctrl key and select the Alpha Compositor Layer Event you just created and the Tower layer, as shown in Figure 5.49.

Alpha Compositor Layer Event selected

Tower selected

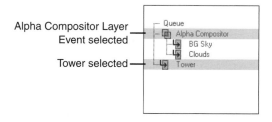

Figure 5.49   The length of the Alpha Compositor Layer Events is derived from the images they are compositing.

4. Click the Add Image Layer Event button, choose Alpha Compositor from the list, and then click OK. Your VP Queue should look like Figure 5.50.

Adding the Image Output Event

The final component of this VP Queue is an image output event to create the composited sequential targa images for the animatic. Be sure none of the existing layers or events are selected when you add the output event to the queue.

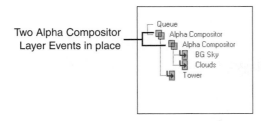

Two Alpha Compositor
Layer Events in place

Figure 5.50 An image output event is necessary to complete this queue and render the composited images.

Click the Add Image Output Event button ![icon], browse to MAXWorkshop\Area 51 Final Targas\ Sc-01, and create a new folder titled Sc-01 Composite. Open this folder and save the images as SC_01.tga. Click Save and fill out the information in the Targa Image Control dialog box when it opens. The VP Queue should now look like Figure 5.51.

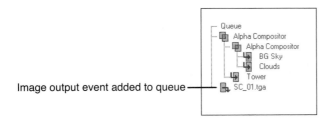

Image output event added to queue

Figure 5.51 The Video Post Queue now contains all the events needed to render and composite the image layers for Sc-01.

Render the Images

Now that the images are configured correctly for compositing, the next step is to tell max to render the combined sequential layers into a new sequence of combined images. Be sure nothing is selected in the VP Queue before continuing. Save your max file.

Click Execute Sequence ![icon] to open its dialog box. Click the Range radio button to select the frame range of 0 to 287. Leave the size set to 640×480 and leave the other settings as they are. Your Video Post Queue and the Execute Video Post dialog box should look like Figure 5.52. Click Render to render the composites.

Updating the Area 51 Animatic

When the Sc-01 composite images are finished rendering, you can add them to the *Area 51* animatic. Save and close Sc_01_Compositor.max and open Area51_Animatic.max. When it opens, click Render, Video Post to open the VP Editor window (see Figure 5.53).

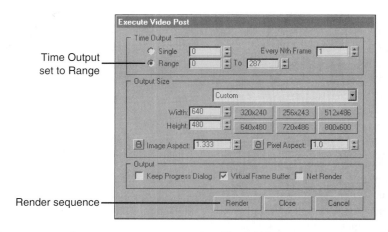

Time Output set to Range

Render sequence

Figure 5.52 The compositing process should take about 45–60 minutes, depending on the speed of your system.

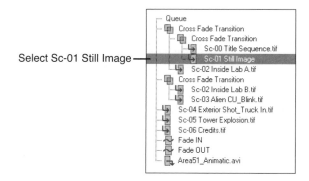

Select Sc-01 Still Image

Figure 5.53 The queue you just created for Sc-01 was simple compared to this monster. This is where the intense organization of the animatic you created in Chapter 2 begins to pay off.

Follow these steps to add the combined Sc-01 images, which you just created, to the VP queue:

1. Double-click Sc-01 Still Image to select it for modification. When the Edit Image Input Event dialog box opens, make a note of the VP Start Time: 191 and VP End Time: 478. The sequential images you'll be adding create the correct length but they will need to be positioned in the queue at the correct location.

2. Click Files, browse to MAXWorkshop\Area 51 Final Targas\Sc-01\Sc-01 Composite, and select and load the sequence of composite images you just created: Sc_010000.tga to Sc_010287.tga.

3. When you return to the Edit Input Image Event dialog box, click Options and select Do Not Resize. The alignment selection should already be set at the center position. Click OK to exit the Image Input Options dialog box and adjust the VP Start and End Times to 191 and 478, respectively.

Sc-00

Sc-01

Sc-02

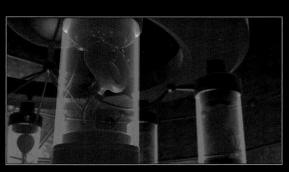

Sc-03

Sc-04—Sc-05

Sc-06

Figure CP.1   3ds max 4 Workshop explores the fundamental tools and techniques necessary to create six scenes for a short movie titled Area51.avi. As you create the scenes, you'll be introduced to the basics of pre-production design, modeling, material development, lighting, special effects, and compositing in 3ds max 4. **Area51.avi images by Duane Loose, © 2001.**

Chapter 2—Visual Language

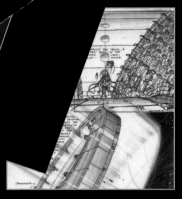

Pre-Production Sketch

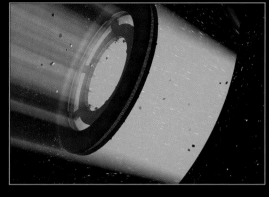

Concept Art

Figure CP.2　Concept Development begins in the mind of the artist/storyteller. Concept sketches are created to develop the visual language of color, detail, and form used in the imagery of the story. Color illustrations are created to bring the concept sketches to life and communicate the visual language of the story to all members of the production team. **Intergalactic Bounty Hunter sketch and concept art by Duane Loose, © 2001 Pan Interactive—Creative Capers Entertainment, Inc.**

Figure CP.3　Pre-production artists develop the visual language of a production by researching architecture, fashion, design, fine art, and archeological and mythological imagery from the past and present. Using the needs of the story as a guide, they create images to guide the production artists as the digital story is created. Nuclear power plants, the invention of Nikola Tesla and Robert VandeGraaff, inspired the visual language for the Alien power plant at Area 51. **Area51.avi image by Duane Loose, © 2001.**

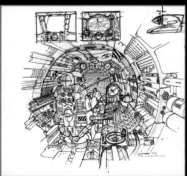

Figure CP.4　Memes are universal images, ideas, and concepts that are shared across time and cultures. Memes are also called mental viruses because of the infectious way they are passed from culture to culture in the form of stories, ideas, images, and so forth. The **Star Wars** phenomenon is a good example of how ancient memes of good and evil are universally propagated throughout the modern world. Imagery developed using memes feels familiar and is more easily understood by your audience. The visual memes in this concept sketch are taken from a World War II bomber cockpit. **Sketch by Duane Loose, © 2000 Creative Capers Entertainment, Inc.**

Area51.avi—Telling the Visual Story: Storyboards

Figure CP.5   Storyboards are used to pre-visualize each scene and shot of a production. Important elements of action, special effects, sound effects, camera movements, and so on are explored in storyboard form before any production imagery is created. Storyboards can be simple or complex depending on the needs of the production team. These storyboards for an animated feature about the boy-king Tut were created in a stark black and white comic book style to emphasize the mood and atmosphere of the story being told and to explore the cyclopean scale of the world seen from the POV of an 8-year-old boy. **King Tut storyboards by Duane Loose, © 2000 Creative Capers Entertainment, Inc.**

Figure CP.6   Storyboards for live action, animation, and television use different symbols and terminology to specify point of view, camera movement, character action, and so on. The storyboard for Sc-oo and Sc-oi of this Workshop's short movie titled **Area 51** were created using TV Animation style storyboard symbology. The storyboard frame on the right shows how the specified cloud layers, tower model, camera POV, and zoom movement relate to the completed imagery. **Area 51 storyboard and image by Duane Loose, © 2001 Que Corporation.**

Basic modeling in 3ds max 4 begins with concept sketches and storyboards to guide your work. Max provides several modeling toolsets to help you create the models needed for your scenes, including polygon-, spline-, and NURBS-based modeling. The environment models for these scenes were created using basic polygonal primitives[md]a perfect choice based on the visual language required for both projects. When you model in 3ds max 4, it's important to understand and choose the modeling tools that are appropriate for the models and animation you'll be creating. **Images by Duane Loose, © 2000 Creative Capers Entertainment, Inc.**

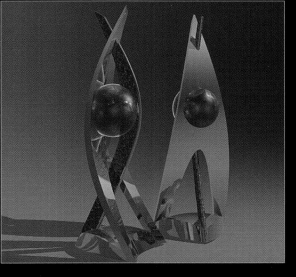

AIAS Award

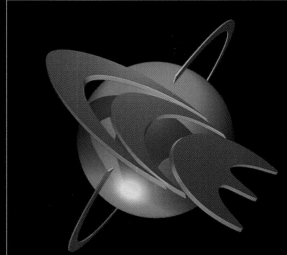

CCE Logo

Figure CP.8 More complex models can be created in max 4 by using the Compound object tools, mesh modifiers, and 2D spline shapes. The model for the Academy of Interactive Arts and Sciences Award statue was created using a basic sphere, lofted surfaces, the Bend modifier, and Boolean functions. The logo model for Creative Capers Entertainment was created using extruded splines, a sphere, and tube primitives. The speed shape was created using a box primitive and the MeshSmooth modifier. The wireform box next to speed shape in the foreground is the low polygon box that was used to create the smooth organic form. Using polygon-based meshes to create organic forms has some limitations, but it can create some very sophisticated models. **Academy of Interactive Arts and Sciences award designed by Duane Loose, David Otte, and Sue Shakespeare of Creative Capers Entertainment, Inc. Logo and speed shape by Duane Loose, © 2000 Creative Capers Entertainment, Inc. and AIAS.**

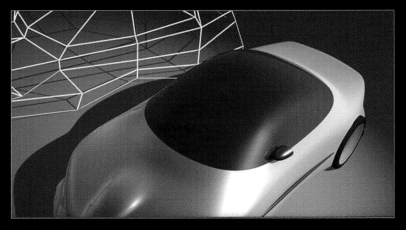

Speed Shape

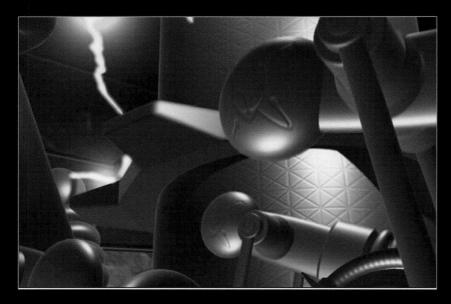

Figure CP.9 Using the MeshSmooth modeling technique outlined in Chapter 6 and Appendix E of this Workshop, you'll create the models for Area51.avi. This image from Sc-02 shows the interior of the Alien power plant, which was modeled using simple primitive shapes to which the MeshSmooth modifier was applied.

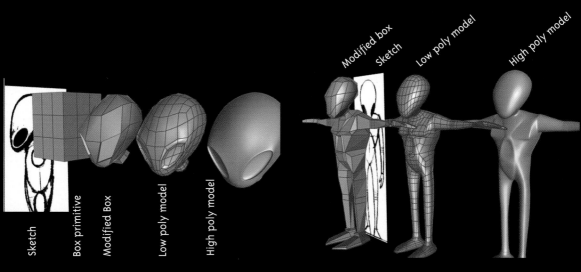

Figure CP.10 In its advanced applications, the MeshSmooth technique can be used to create the character models for your max scenes. Starting with a sketch and a box primitive, the Alien head and body shown in this image were shaped by moving, scaling, and extruding subobject vertices, edges, and polygons. This technique is known as box modeling—it's used to create the contiguous mesh surface required for character animation techniques.

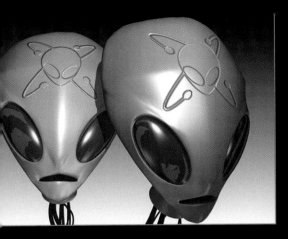

Bump Component Map

Opacitiy Component Map

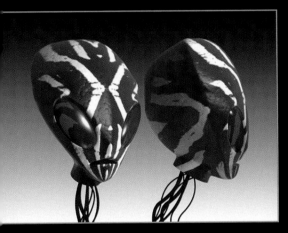

Diffuse Component Map

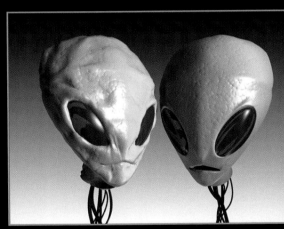

Displacement Component Map

Figure CP.11 Material and texture development in 3ds max 4 is based on some of the most advanced shader and raytrace technology available. Max allows you to specify which materials in your scene will be ray-traced, giving you control over the balance between rendering time and image quality. Selective ray-tracing was pioneered by 3ds max and is a powerful component of your material development process. Appendix B takes an in-depth look at the component map channels for a standard max material. Understanding max 4's material types and shaders and learning how to use material com-

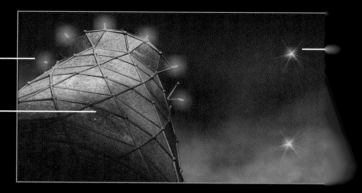

Sc-oı

Materials are a major component of the special effects tools in 3ds max 4. Ju
specify which materials will be raytraced in your final images, you can also

TheEnd.avi—Warm and Cool Contrast

oggy Morning—Atmospheric Perspective

ghting is the heart and soul of the atmosphere and mood of a scene. Underst
ght—object interaction and the principles of reflection theory—will enable you
ents that invite your audience to feel the story, capturing their hearts and mi
es, such as warm and cool contrast, atmospheric perspective, light and shad
nspire to create the emotion of the story you are trying to tell. **Images by Du**

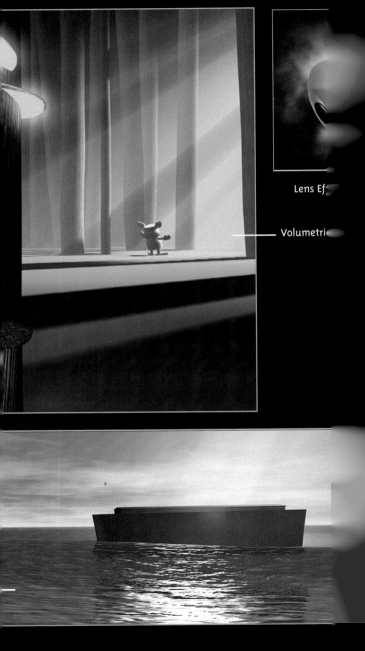

Lens Ef

Volumetri

lghting effects, such as volumetric effects, lens flares, glows, fire and pl
n, can be created using max lights and the built-in render effects availa
n the Ark shot uses a Fresnel falloff component to create the dappled li
is is a good example of how lights and materials can work synergistical
scenes. **Images by Duane Loose. © 2000 Creative Capers Ente**

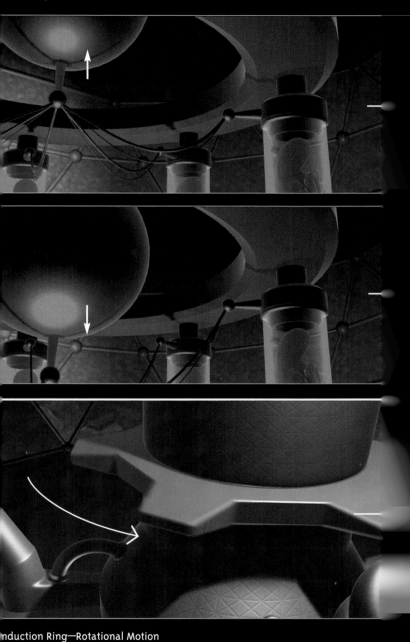

nduction Ring—Rotational Motion

orward and Inverse kinematics (FK/IK) techniques and tools are used to bring you
fe. Learning the fundamentals of hierarchies and the new 3ds max 4 IK solvers wi
o animate everything from machines to monsters. Basic keyframe animation and
f Range types are used to animate simple rotational movement like that seen in t
andeGraaff generator induction ring or the linear movement of the Sc-03 contair
on. When machines move, their movement can become blurred. Adding motion b
achines and all other animation will create more believable imagery

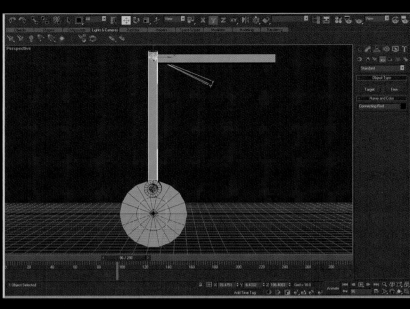

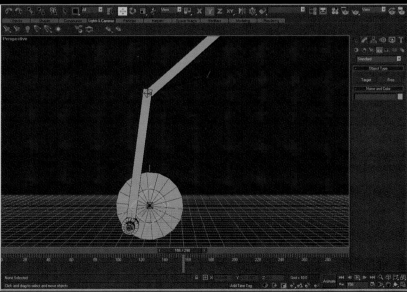

The coolant pump seen in Sc-02 is an example of a convergent process. First, create a te[...]
motion you want to create. Then, make the final model to fit the IK/FK solution you ach[...]
animation, like character animation, must be based on real engines, pumps, levers, pis[...]
forth. The real pumps, which inspired the Area 51 coolant pumps, are the ubiquitous oil [...]
late the western United States and Canada. The screen shots of the test model show max[...]
tomized user interface—creating your own UI is one of the new and enjoyable parts of [...]

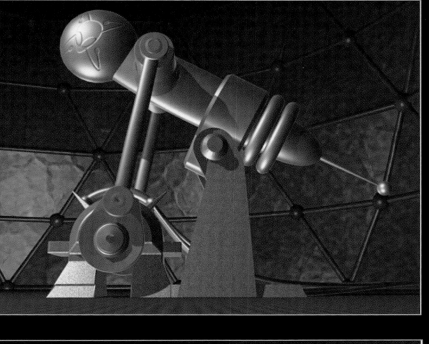

Final Pump

Blended FK
and IK
Animation

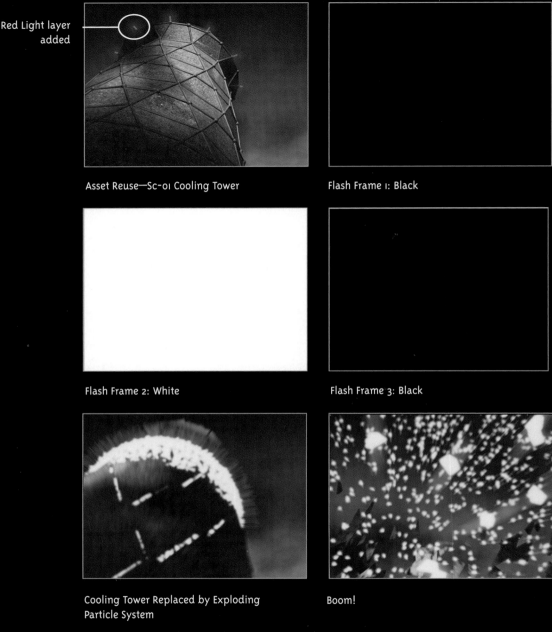

Red Light layer added

Asset Reuse—Sc-01 Cooling Tower

Flash Frame 1: Black

Flash Frame 2: White

Flash Frame 3: Black

Cooling Tower Replaced by Exploding Particle System

Boom!

Figure CP.17 In addition to the high-voltage arcs seen in Sc-02, you'll learn how to use a particle system to blow up the cooling tower. You'll also learn how subliminal flash frames can be used to emphasize the start of the explosion. Special effects are the nexus of all the techniques and tools in max. Motion, blur, glow, creative compositing, animation processes, and so on, all come together to create the effect you have in your imagination.

Groom Lake : Western Nevada Badlands

[3ds max 4 workshop]

Sc-oo—Opening Graphics

[3ds max 4 workshop]

Customized Screen Format

Sc-06—Credit Crawl

Sc-06—End Title

Figure CP.18 Onscreen graphics, such as titles, credits, and customized formats for your reel, are as much fun to create as the scenes for which they are created. Chapter 9 shows you how to use the tools and techniques from the previous chapters in the book to create Sc-00, Sc-06, and a personalized format for your version of Area51.avi.

4. Label this sequence Sc-01 Final. The Edit Input Image Event dialog box is now complete (see Figure 5.54). Click OK to exit and return to the VP Queue.

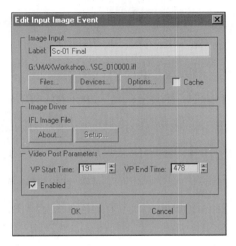

Figure 5.54 This is the process you'll use from now on when you want to add final imagery to the Area 51 animatic.

5. The last step to update the animatic is to execute this sequence and render out the animatic .avi.

This chapter's Workshop and Sc-01 are now complete. The beauty of the layering process is in how easily image layers can be added into the composite process. As you work through the rest of the scenes for Area51.avi, you might want to create some additional effects of image layers to make Sc-01 even more interesting.

Next Steps

"The source of genius is imagination alone, the refinement of the senses that sees what others do not see, or sees them differently." - Delacroix

Because of the flexibility of the layering process, you can add as many layers into this scene as you want. For example, a second cooling tower in the distance would create another level of depth in the composition. This would make the buildings seem like they were a part of a larger complex and not just a single cooling tower standing alone.

Another layer to add to this scene would be a flying debris or windblown sand effect. This is easily achieved using the particle systems you'll learn about in Chapter 8, "Trompe L'oeil: The Art of Visual Effects."

The clouds in this scene are nice but bland. Some experiments with a Video Post or Render Effects glow effect could yield a more intense or weird alien appearance. Of course, a glowing UFO flying through the background sky would be appropriate to this project (see Figure CP.12).

All these layer options can be achieved by using the techniques described in this Workshop coupled with the power of your own imagination. Chapter 6, "Machines in Motion: Modeling and Kinematics," is next. You'll learn how to create and animate a simple machine using max's IK system. You'll also learn a powerful modeling technique used to create the interior environment of the power plant inside the *Area 51* cooling tower.

ORGANIC FORM

KINEMATICS

0-7857-2546-0

Machines in Motion:
Modeling and Kinematics

"What I cannot understand, I cannot create." - Richard Feynman quoted in *Genius, the Life and Science of Richard Feynman*, by James Gleick.

Character design and animation can be the most visible stars of digital-content creation. Perhaps it's because of the complex technical challenges inherent in modeling and animating characters that will be accepted by an audience. Indeed, the same visual standards of quality apply regardless of whether the actor is a digital or a living human being. However, modeling and animating the machines in your digital worlds is a challenge that is equally demanding and often more unforgiving.

Animating believable machines requires that you understand the properties and effects of gravity, momentum, inertia, friction, fluid dynamics, and so on. Engineering the virtual machines that live in your imagination requires you to learn the animation and modeling techniques necessary to bring an organic level of realism to your models.

This chapter introduces you to the basics of Inverse Kinematics and intermediate-level modeling using the MeshSmooth modifier. Gaining an understanding of these tools and techniques is critical to your progress as an animator and modeler. To help you learn these tools, three additional instructional files have been prepared in Adobe Acrobat .pdf file format and can be found on the CD in MAXWorkshop\Help_Files\:

- **How to Make the Cooling Tower Interior.PDF**—Takes you through the process to change the Sc-01 cooling tower model into the interior set for Sc-02.

- **How MeshSmooth Works.PDF**—Shows you how MeshSmooth works on the surfaces you create and how its effect can be controlled using subobject manipulation and the vertex and edge weights tool and the crease tool.

- **Animation Principles in Practice.PDF**—An excerpt from *3D Studio MAX 3.0 Workshop* that shows you how to use basic animation tools. This tutorial leads you through a fundamental animation exercise: creating a bouncing ball.

Beginning with this chapter, only the new techniques and tools that you haven't used before will be presented in step-by-step detail. This will give you more freedom to experiment and create your own version of Area51.avi based on the concepts you'll be learning.

But you won't be left on your own! Every model needed to complete the Workshop can be found on the CD so you can decide what you want to build and what you want to use from the files that have been provided.

Sc-02—Setting the Stage

Sc-02 is made from six composited image layers: a gradient sky background, the clouds from Sc-01, the cooling tower interior, the VandeGraaff generator, Tesla coil towers, and the coolant pumps (see Figure 6.1).

Sc-02 File Setup

You'll be assembling the final set for Sc-02 in Chapter 8, "Trompe L'oeil: The Art of Visual Effects," after you've created the special effects layers for the scene. You can create models of your own design or use the premade models that are referred to in this chapter. If you make the models yourself, be sure that you name your models following the conventions outlined in the following sections of the Workshop.

The model assets for Sc-02 were each created in their own separate max files. This enables you to access and control the shot models independently and facilitates the use of the XRef and Proxy object system you'll use to assemble the scene. To set up your files correctly, create a new folder named Sc-02 in your MAXWorkshop\Scene Models directory—this is where you'll save the model files for Sc-02. The premade models are included on the CD in MAXWorkshop\Help_Files\Chapter_6. They're titled EXSc-02_Interior.max, EXSc-02_VandeGraaff.max, and so forth. A brief overview of how these models were created will be given later on in this chapter.

Sc-02 BG gradient and clouds (from Sc-01)

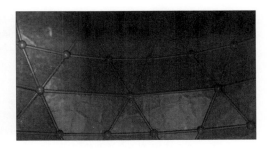

Sc-02 cooling tower interior

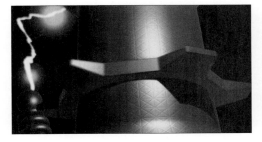

Sc-02 VandeGraaff generator

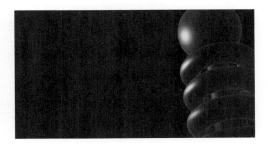

Sc-02 Foreground Tesla coil towers

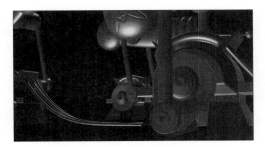

Sc-02 coolant pumps

Figure 6.1   Sc-02 is a 14-second scene made up of 336 frames and 6 image layers.

If max is open, be sure your work from Chapter 5, "Photon Paint: The Art of Lighting," is saved, and then click File, Reset to create a new workspace and save this new file as `Sc-02_VandeGraaff.max` in the Sc-02 folder you just created.

Working Smarter: Asset Re-Use Using the Merge Command

Production design is an important part of the pre-production process. The production designer's task, in part, is to design the schedule and flow of the scenes and shots that are to be created.

The PD will also look for ways to simplify the process and re-use scene and shot elements whenever possible. Asset re-use must be considered in the beginning of a production so that an asset can be created with re-use in mind—it's a critical part of working smarter in the production process.

Production Process: Re-Using Assets

Digital content production requires cooperative and coordinated efforts from all the members of the studio. The individual creative efforts of one artist can be re-used as the basis for the work of another artist tasked with a different part of the production process. This is called *asset re-use* and is a common and expected practice in a large production.

Creating separate files for your scene and shot assets will ensure that everyone on the production team has access to the specific asset required for their work without impacting the workflow of their fellow artists. It also allows models under development to be used as placeholders before they are completely finished. The advantage of this is that production can proceed according to schedule in a non-linear fashion while models, effects, animation, and so on are being created and perfected.

In Area51.avi, you'll re-use several model and image assets throughout the different scenes of the movie. The cloud image layers from Sc-01, for example, will be used for the sky in Sc-02, Sc-04, and Sc-05. The cooling tower model from Sc-01 has also been re-used and modified to create the interior set for Sc-02. And you'll get to blow it up when you create Sc-04 and Sc-05 in Chapter 8.

One of the max commands that makes it easy to re-use assets is the Merge command, which enables you to add objects from one scene into another. The following steps outline how max 4's Merge command is used to merge the modified cooling tower model from the CD:

1. Click File, Merge to open the Merge File browser. Browse to the CD directory MAXWorkshop\ Help_Files\Chapter_6\EXSc-02_Interior.max. This will open up the Merge - EXSc-02_Interior.max dialog box, as shown in Figure 6.2.

2. Select the Cooling_Tower_Interior model and click OK to merge it into your scene (see Figure 6.3).

The cooling tower model has been simplified and all its polygon normals have been flipped to create the interior walls. It has also been scaled up in size by 300% to accommodate a better scalar relationship for the creation of the set models.

If you want to go through the steps to modify the Sc-01 cooling tower and create your own interior model for Sc-02, the CD has an Adobe Acrobat file containing complete instructions. Open MAXWorkshop\ Help_Files\Appendix_D\Appendix_D.PDF.

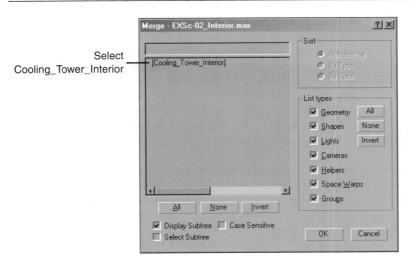

Select
Cooling_Tower_Interior

Figure 6.2   The Merge command enables members of a production team working with different elements of the same shot to share and re-use scene elements such as geometry, cameras, lights, and so forth.

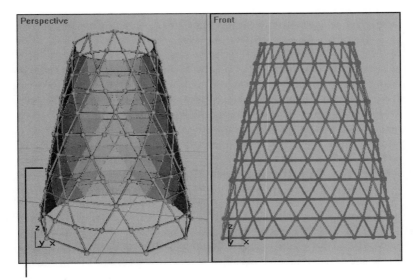

Model merged into workspace

Figure 6.3   Elements that are merged into your scene appear in the same world space location and orientation that they were in their original file.

Note

It's important to note that the changes you make to a merged object won't affect the original model or the original max file from which it was merged. If you make a mistake, you can always re-merge the model and begin again.

The Cooling_Tower_Interior model is the stage that provides the backdrop for all the other layers in Sc-02A and Sc-02B. Merging the Cooling_Tower_Interior also provides the necessary reference for both the proper scale and placement of the scene models and layer creation.

The next section in this chapter introduces you to one of the most enjoyable and powerful modifiers in 3ds max 4: MeshSmooth. The MeshSmooth modifier makes complex surface modeling as easy as playing with clay and enables you to produce virtually any kind of shape you can imagine.

Introduction to Organic Form: Concepts and Elements

"An artist is not paid for his labor but for his vision." - James McNeill Whistler

The polygon primitive modeling process you learned in Chapter 3, "Giving Form to Feeling: The Art of Modeling," was the first step to mastering max 4's modeling tools and techniques. But not all objects are as simple as the forms you've been working with so far, and learning how to create complex organic forms is the next step.

Organic forms are created from softer contours and blended surfaces; they're more realistic and accurate representations of natural and man-made objects in the real world. Many artists associate the term *organic* with models that are developed to re-create natural animal, vegetable, and mineral creations. However, it's important to realize that all objects are organic in some measure. Your models of rectilinear objects will benefit from the application of organic modeling concepts just as much as the trees, vehicles, and creatures you'll create.

Organic Form: An Expanded Definition

Organic as a descriptive term has become so overused that a clear definition has become lost in the rhetoric of technology. The truth is that every form, simple and complex, should have organic elements to make it look more real and less digital. This means that the line drawn by some artists between organic forms and everything else is an artificial division—all three-dimensional forms are organic. Understanding the definitive elements of organic form and how they are applied to your mastery of max modeling is an important quest.

The first place to look for an expanded definition of the term organic is in the intra-relationship of an object's surfaces—the transitional surfaces that are created between one surface as it intersects or blends with another.

Primitive Surface Types

When Whistler said that artists "*are not paid for our labor but for our vision,*" he was referring to the artist's ability to see the way things are formed by nature *and* by the hands of artisans.

He was also referring to the artist's ability to imagine new things of the same or similar pattern as those objects the artist observes and seeks to simulate.

Direct observation of the surfaces surrounding you will show that the reflections seen in a flat mirror are different than those seen in convex, concave, or spherical surfaces. You can also see that slight changes in the curvature of an object's surface will create analogous changes in the shape of the surface reflections. That's the fundamental principle at the core of surface development.

Just as there are primitive objects such as sphere, cylinder, box, and so forth, there are also primitive surface types that define the primitive shape. Primitive surfaces can be categorized into four types: flat, convex, concave, and spherical. The holistic combination and manipulation of these four primitive surface types is what many artists refer to as organic form, such as the aircraft speed shape shown in Figure 6.4.

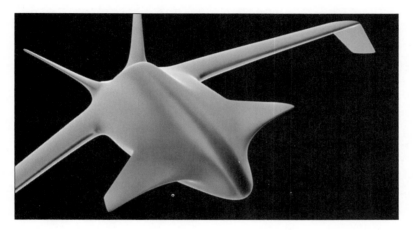

Figure 6.4   Speed shape studies are a perfect way to explore and understand how primitive surfaces are transformed into sculpted forms. After this chapter, you'll know how to develop your own complex surfaces using the MeshSmooth modifier.

Transitional Surfaces

The surfaces that are created when dissimilar surface types come together in the three-dimensional form of an object are called *transitional surfaces*. Figure 6.5 shows the transitional surface created when a square surface cross section is developed into a circular surface cross section.

The definable boundary at which one surface begins and ends its transition into the next surface is referred to as a *surface tangent*. Surface tangents define the edges and corners in the surfaces of your max models.

Transitional Surfaces: Primitive Edge Types

Edges are a type of transitional surface that are created when surfaces intersect. One of the common mistakes that an artist makes when modeling is to place too much attention on the overall form of a model and neglect the development of the transitional edges. This mistake can be seen when a model uses the default sharp edges of one of the many premade objects in the max toolbox (see Figure 6.6).

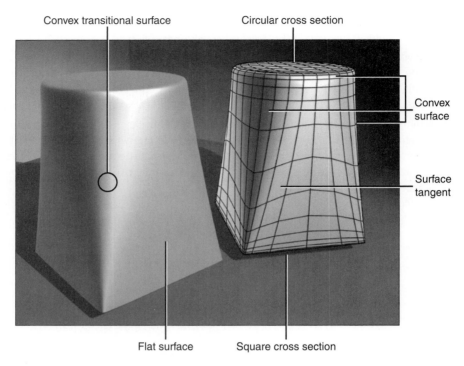

Convex transitional surface   Circular cross section

Convex surface

Surface tangent

Flat surface   Square cross section

Figure 6.5   The transitional surface created at the four edges of the form shown in this image is actually a cross section of a cone—a variant of the convex primitive surface type.

Sharpened metal, glass shards, thin plastic, and so forth are a few of the types of objects for which sharp-edged models would be appropriate. Edge surfaces that aren't intended to convey sharpness need to be developed by using variations and combinations of three primitive edge types: fillet, radius, and chamfer. Figure 6.7 shows an example of each primitive edge as defined in the following list:

- **Fillet**—Also called an "inside" or "reverse" radius. It can be thought of as a concave cylindrical section and is defined by a radial dimension. Fillets are used as transitions between adjacent and intersecting surfaces.

- **Radius**—A convex cylindrical section of a cylinder and, like the fillet, is also defined by a radial dimension. Using a radius along the outside edges of an object gives the object a more realistic developed appearance. Radius edges are used as transitions between adjacent and intersecting surfaces.

- **Chamfer**—A flat, transitional surface (usually at a 45° angle) between two adjacent or intersecting surfaces. It's used to give an object a sharper or more chiseled appearance and can be used in the same locations as a fillet or radius.

Transitional surfaces—Realistic detail

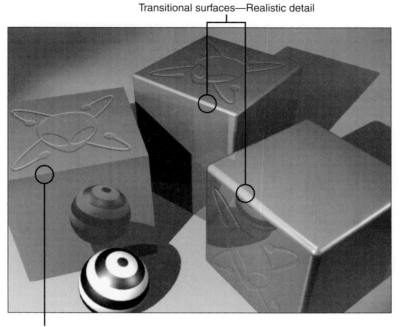

No transitional surfaces—Poor detail

Figure 6.6   Transitional edge surfaces are important organic elements that will enhance your model's visual appeal and realism.

Edges and Highlights

To create believable digital reality, the objects in your scene must reflect the surrounding environment, including the light sources. When the edges, corners, or surfaces of your objects reflect a light source, highlights are created. The size and shape of the highlight tells a lot about the object's surface development, including the relative dimension of the radius, fillet, and chamfered edges. In general, thin highlights are created by smaller radii and indicate sharp-edge transitions. Conversely, thick highlights are created by larger edge radii and indicate softer transitional edges and surfaces.

Understanding how surfaces are developed makes the step from primitive transitional surfaces into more complex organic surfaces a lot easier. Fortunately, many of the modeling tools in max have been specifically created to deal with compound curves and sophisticated transitional surfaces.

The workhorse of the toolset is the MeshSmooth modifier. Figure 6.8 shows the result of a few hours of MeshSmooth work. Well-developed transitional surfaces combine to create a quintessential organic form.

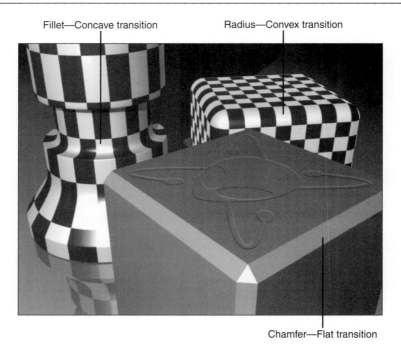

Fillet—Concave transition

Radius—Convex transition

Chamfer—Flat transition

Figure 6.7   Radius and fillet transitional surfaces are actually sections of a concave or convex cylindrical surface. This is an important detail to remember because it explains how highlights and reflections are created by the edges where surfaces meet.

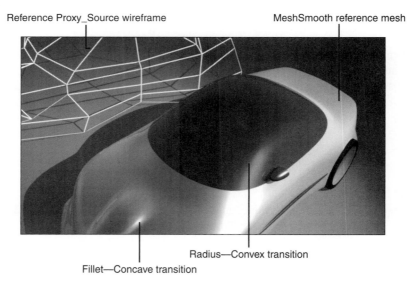

Reference Proxy_Source wireframe

MeshSmooth reference mesh

Radius—Convex transition

Fillet—Concave transition

Figure 6.8   The subobject vertices and polygons of the crude wireframe in the upper-left corner of this image were manipulated to make the automotive form. That's the power and magic of MeshSmooth!

Introduction to MeshSmooth: Digital Clay

Using the MeshSmooth modifier is a lot like using clay to sculpt your models. MeshSmooth surfaces can be pushed, pulled, blended, and so forth using techniques you've already learned in this Workshop. You'll learn the basics of this process and technique by creating the VandeGraaff generator that dominates the interior space of the cooling tower interior.

Before you move on, you should read `AppendixE.PDF` found in `MAXWorkshop\Help_Files\Appendix_E` on the CD for this book. This appendix gives you some more insight into the workings of MeshSmooth and the surface development concepts you've just learned.

Starting with a Primitive Object

Models created with the MeshSmooth technique usually begin with a parametric primitive object. In this case, you'll start with a cylinder because its symmetrical form best matches the intended shape of the VandeGraaff generator:

1. Change to Top view and click Cylinder in the Create command panel ![icon]. Drag a cylinder of any radius and height in the viewport to the right of the Cooling_Tower_Interior.

2. Change to Front view and move the cylinder down so that its base lines up with the bottom of the cooling tower. Open the Modify command panel and rename this cylinder `VandeGraaff Proxy_Source`.

3. Change the cylinder's parameters to Radius: `26.0`; Height: `135.0`; Height Segments: `10`; Cap Segments: `1`; Sides: `6`; Smooth, Slice, and Generate Mapping Coordinates: Off (unchecked) (see Figure 6.9).

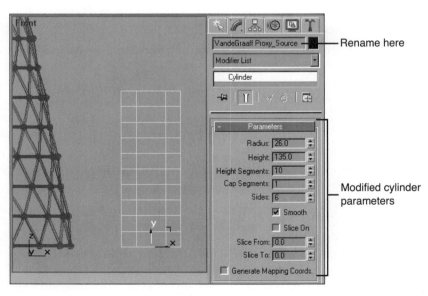

Figure 6.9   All the primitive shapes in max will create different results when used as the source objects for the MeshSmooth technique.

4. Right-click to access the Quad Menu and select Convert To, Convert to Editable Mesh.

Creating a Reference Clone

The next step is to create a special type of one-way instance clone called a *reference*. You'll recall from Chapter 3 that a reference is an instance that can have its own unique modifiers applied to it without affecting the original object. Using a reference as a source object for the MeshSmooth process allows you to affect changes in the reference surfaces by manipulating the parameters and subobjects of the source mesh.

Hold down the Shift key and use the X-axis to drag the proxy_source to the right. When the Clone Options dialog box opens, select Reference as the Object type and change the name to VandeGraaff Generator (see Figure 6.10).

Figure 6.10   Any change you make to the surface of the VandeGraaff Proxy_Source object will affect an analogous change on the surface of the reference object.

Adding the MeshSmooth Modifier to the Reference Object

Now for the magic ingredient: the MeshSmooth modifier. MeshSmooth is applied to the reference object and will create the smooth transitional surfaces needed for organic forms. Subdivision surface modifiers such as MeshSmooth are used to refine and smooth polygon models by subdividing a surface into increasingly finer increments:

1. Select the VandeGraaff generator, open the Modify command panel, and click the Modifier List window. Scroll down to the Subdivision Surfaces set and select MeshSmooth from the list (see Figure 6.11).

2. The Subdivision Method default setting is NURMS. Leave this at it is and change the settings in the Subdivision Amount to Iterations: 2, Smoothness: 1.0.

> **Tip**
>
> NURMS is the acronym for Non-Uniform Rational MeshSmooth. NURMS surfaces allow you to control an object's shape and detail by adjusting the weight and crease values of the vertices and edges that define the surface. The max User Reference has a complete overview of MeshSmooth and NURMS. Use the keyword *MeshSmooth* to find the information.

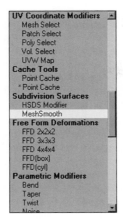

Figure 6.11   Think of your objects as clay and the MeshSmooth and HSDS modifiers as the clay-modeling tools that create form and surface details by giving you the ability to push, pull, and subdivide the mesh surface.

3. Check the Iterations box in the Render Values section and change the Iterations amount to 4. This tells max to increase the subdivision iterations for rendered images only, which will result in higher-quality images and slower rendering times (see Figure 6.12).

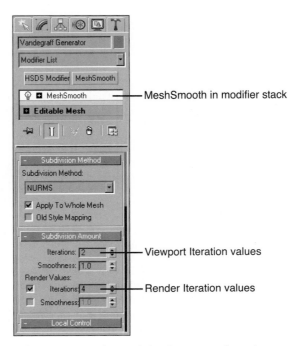

Figure 6.12   Higher viewport and render iteration values subdivide your surfaces into increasingly smaller polygons. This will have an impact on max performance, rendering time, and your productivity.

Be careful when you are adjusting iteration values. When MeshSmooth is applied, it increases the complexity of the surface mesh by adding extra faces at every edge and vertex. The higher the iteration value, the denser the mesh and the higher the polygon count, which will significantly impact your viewport navigation and rendering performance. Fortunately, max allows you to specify lower iteration values for the mesh seen in the viewport and higher values for the mesh seen in the rendered images. This keeps your creative process moving along quickly while delivering superb rendered images.

The MeshSmooth rollouts contain other powerful commands and tools, such as the Crease and Weight controls. You can learn more about the vertex weight and crease tools in AppendixE.PDF on the CD. The important concept to understand at this point is the effect that the MeshSmooth modifier has on the form of the object to which it's applied. Your source cylinder and the reference clone should look like Figure 6.13.

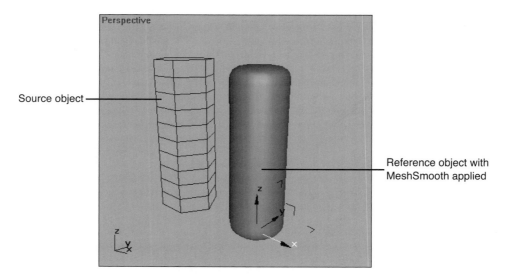

Figure 6.13 MeshSmooth has converted the hard linear edges of the cylinder primitive into smooth transitional surfaces.

The MeshSmooth algorithm and the parameters of the original cylinder control the MeshSmooth effect. The original transitional surfaces from the side of the cylinder to its top surface are right-angle edges with no radius surface to ease their transition. When MeshSmooth is applied, it creates a smooth transitional surface between the sides and top of the cylinder (see Figure 6.14).

Original hard edge, no transitional surface

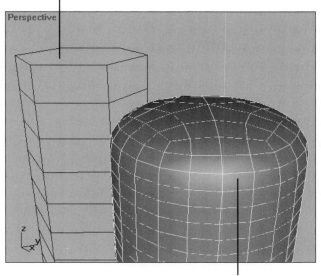

Faces added, smooth transitional surface created

Figure 6.14 The next step in the MeshSmooth process is to modify the VandeGraaff Proxy_Source object at the subobject level.

Modify the VandeGraaff Proxy_Source Model

The last step to create the VandeGraaff generator combines the subobject modification skills you learned in Chapter 3 with the magic of the MeshSmooth modifier. Select the VandeGraaff Proxy_Source model and open the Modify command panel. As you select and modify the vertices and faces of the source object, you'll see the effect of the modification immediately in the surfaces of the reference clone.

Tip

The steps presented for the exact numeric process to create the VandeGraaff generator are given for the sake of the instruction in this chapter. If you follow those values, you'll end up with the same form I did. However, this is not the way the form was developed initially—I eyeballed it.

MeshSmooth is an interactive and iterative process—you can immediately see the effect of any change you make in the form of the reference object. This enables you to eyeball the subobject transforms, adjusting the surfaces of your model as you go.

Creating the Basic Form

As you follow these steps to create the VandeGraaff generator form, feel free to create your own version of this model:

1. Change to Front view and choose Vertex 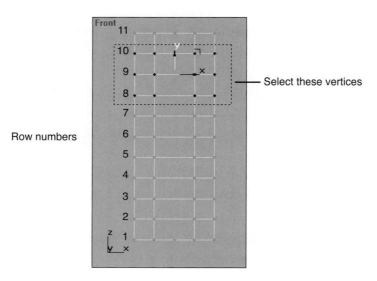 on the Editable Mesh Selection rollout in the Modify command panel. Be sure that Ignore Backfacing is not checked.

2. Select all the vertices in row numbers 8–10 in the source model, as shown in Figure 6.15. You'll scale these to make the spherical form at the top of the VandeGraaff generator.

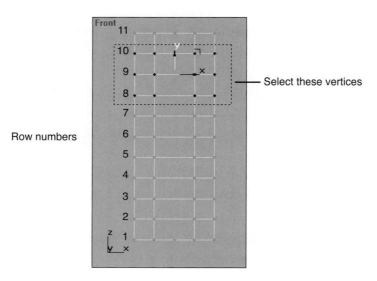

Figure 6.15   Move and Scale are the main transform tools you'll use to modify the VandeGraaff Proxy_Source subobjects.

3. Select Scale Transform mode and click the Absolute Mode Transform Type-In button at the bottom of the interface to change to Offset Mode Transform Type-In.

4. Change the X value in the Transform Type-In section to 220. This scales the vertices and simultaneously modifies the source and reference mesh, as shown in Figure 6.16.

5. Click and hold on the Uniform Scale icon in the Main Toolbar and select Non-uniform Scale from the drop-down list. Notice that the input fields next to X, Y, and Z in the Transform Type-In are now active. Change the Y value to 50 to create a more spherical shape (see Figure 6.17).

6. Hold down the Alt key and drag a selection rectangle around vertex row number 9. This deselects the vertices in row 9.

7. Click and hold on Non-uniform Scale in the Main Toolbar and select Uniform Scale. Scale the vertices in rows 8 and 10 by changing the X value in the Offset Mode Transform Type-In to 95 (see Figure 6.18).

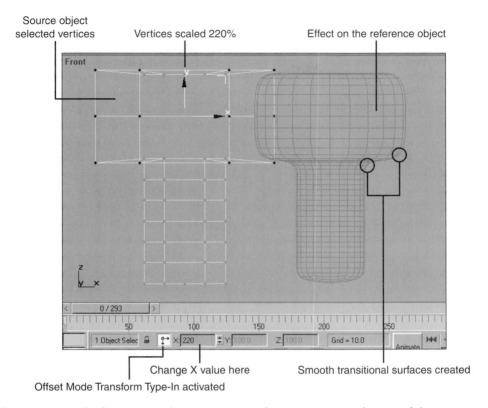

Source object selected vertices

Vertices scaled 220%

Effect on the reference object

Front

0 / 293

50   100   150   200   250

1 Object Selec   X: 220   Y: 100.0   Z: 100.0   Grid = 10.0

Animate

Change X value here

Offset Mode Transform Type-In activated

Smooth transitional surfaces created

Figure 6.16 The first vertex adjustment creates the extreme circumference of the generator. The next adjustments will refine the surface into a spherical shape. Notice the smooth transitional surfaces being created between the center support cylinder and the beginning of the sphere at the top.

8. Select the vertices in row 7 and change to Move transform mode 🔷 . Use the Y-axis to move the row down until it's just above row 6, as shown in Figure 6.19. This tightens the fillet transition between the sphere and the base column.

Creating the VandeGraaff Generator Base

The following steps show you how to manipulate the mesh subobjects to create the base of the VandeGraaff generator:

1. Select the vertices in rows 2 through 4 and use the Y-axis to move them down until row 2 is just above row 1, as shown in Figure 6.20.

2. Select the vertices in row 5 and move them down until they are just above row 4—about the same distance that row 7 is from row 6 (see Figure 6.21).

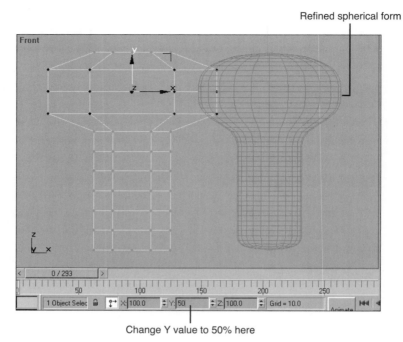

Refined spherical form

Change Y value to 50% here

Figure 6.17   Scaling the second and fourth rows of vertices turns the flat sides of the sphere into curved transitional surfaces.

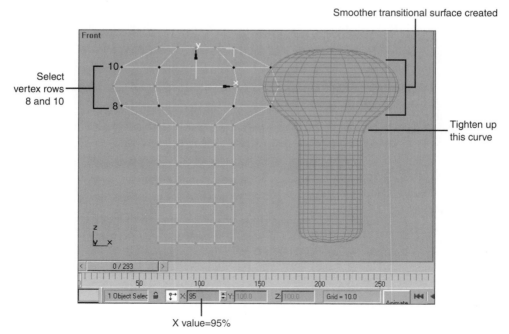

Smoother transitional surface created

Select vertex rows 8 and 10

10

8

Tighten up this curve

X value=95%

Figure 6.18   The next subobject manipulation adjusts the proportional relationship of the base cylinder to the upper sphere and tightens some of their transitional surfaces.

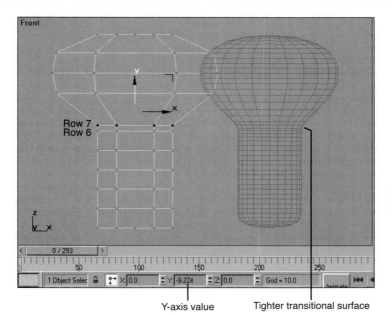

Y-axis value   Tighter transitional surface

Figure 6.19   Creating the final three surface details to complete the generator form uses the extrude command you learned about in Chapter 3. Adjusting the form of the base column is the next step.

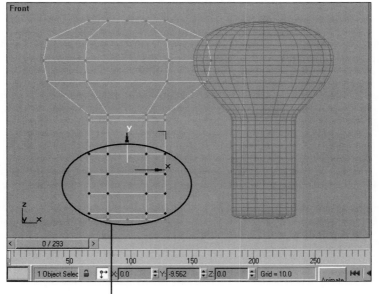

Rows 2-4 selected and moved down

Figure 6.20   Adjusting the relative location of the vertex rows creates the proportional relationship for the base of the column.

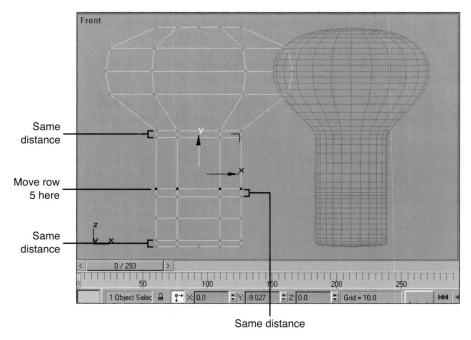

Front

Same distance

Move row 5 here

Same distance

Same distance

0 / 293

1 Object Selec   X: 0.0   Y: -9.027   Z: 0.0   Grid = 10.0

Figure 6.21   Using the MeshSmooth/Reference Clone process follows the basic modeling sequence of Form, Division of Form, and Detail outlined in Chapter 3. Now that the form of the base is proportionally divided, the remaining details can be created.

3. Change to Uniform Scale transform mode, select the vertices in rows 1 and 2, and scale them up approximately 120%. This creates the flare in the form at the column's base (see Figure 6.22).

4. Change the subobject selection mode to Polygon ▣. At the bottom of the max 4 interface just below the Transform Type-In section is the Crossing Selection button ⬚. Click it and change it to Window Selection ▦.

Crossing Selection mode ⬚ selects all objects and subobjects that the selection rectangle touches in the viewport. Window Selection mode ▦ selects only those objects or subobjects that lie completely withinselection rectangle. This is a useful tool when working with multiple objects and subobjects.

Tip

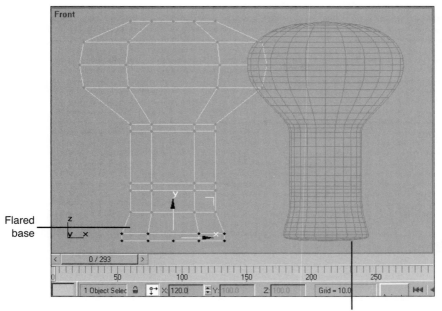

Flared base

Incorrect transitional surface

Figure 6.22   The flare in the form of the base looks correct, but the bottom of the base itself needs to be flattened to allow it to sit firmly on the floor of the cooling tower. Adjusting the transitional curve between the first row of polygons and the bottom/underside of the base will fix the problem.

5. Drag a selection rectangle around the bottom of the VandeGraaff source object, as shown in Figure 6.23. This selects only the bottom underneath polygons of the column base that lie within the boundaries of the selection rectangle.

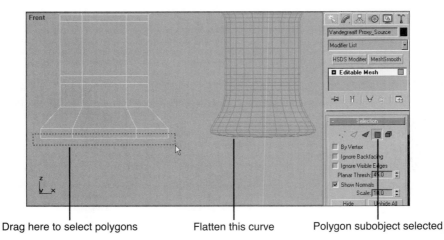

Drag here to select polygons   Flatten this curve   Polygon subobject selected

Figure 6.23   If the selection mode was set to Crossing Selection, all the faces that the selection rectangle touched would be selected.

A simple way to flatten the transitional surface between the side of the column's base and its underside is to extrude the underside surface of the source object. This adds additional faces to the bottom surface of the column, which MeshSmooth will use to develop a small radiused edge.

6. Scroll down in the Modify command panel to the Edit Geometry rollout and type 0.5 in the amount box to the right of the Extrude button, as shown in Figure 6.24.

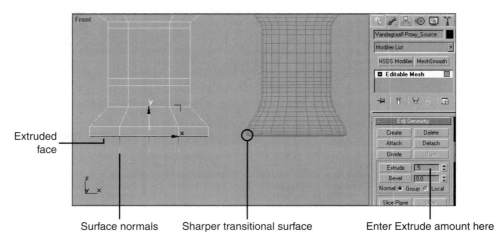

Figure 6.24 If you extrude this face two or three more times with increasingly small increments such as .25 or .125, the transitional surface will flatten out even more.

7. Extrude the selected polygon one more time using an extrude amount of .25. This creates a sufficiently flat surface and completes the base of the VandeGraaff generator.

Final Details: Creating the Perimeter Groove

In the final model, an animating ring will be placed around the perimeter of the generator. Creating an indentation for the ring gives it a place to sit within the form:

1. Select the polygons shown in Figure 6.25. You'll use these to create the groove around the circumference of the tower.

2. Select Local in the Normal section of the Edit Geometry rollout. To extrude the polygons correctly, you must use the local coordinate systems of the selected polygons for the extrusion process (see Figure 6.26).

Note

When Group (max default selection) is checked, extrusions take place along the averaged normal direction of the selected contiguous faces. When Local is checked, the extrusion takes place along the relative normal direction for each selected face.

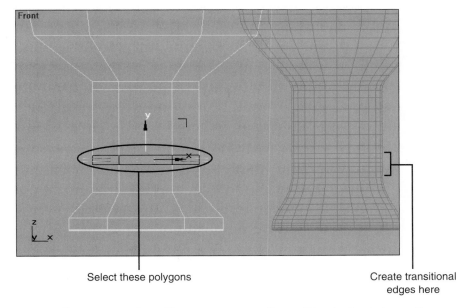

Select these polygons   Create transitional
                                  edges here

Figure 6.25   A small extrusion value will create a very small transitional edge between the outer surface of the base cylinder and the inside surface of the groove.

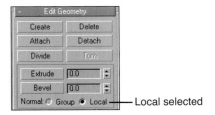

Local selected

Figure 6.26   The Group and Local selections determine how the Extrude and Bevel commands will be executed.

3. Extrude the selected polygons -.1 to create a small transitional edge on the outside surface of the generator.

4. Extrude the selected polygons -6.0. This extrusion creates the depth of the groove.

5. The third and final extrude amount is -.1, which creates a fillet between the inside surfaces of the groove. The sequence and size of these extrusions combines to create the crisp indented groove detail shown in Figure 6.27.

The next section provides a brief description of how the remaining set models for Sc-02 were made. As you read through the descriptions of how the models were built, pay close attention to the consistent naming conventions used for the source and proxy_source objects and their reference clones. These are important to the discussion of how to use XRef and Proxy objects in AppendixH.pdf on the CD.

Machines in Motion: Modeling and
Kinematics

3ds max 4

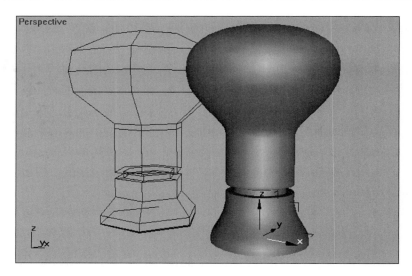

Figure 6.27   The indented groove is created with three separate extrude commands.

 If you need help, all the models with their related materials can be found in their individual files on the CD in MAXWorkshop\Help_Files\Chapter_6. Use the files as a guide to create your own models, modify them to create a variation for the scene, or use them without modification.

Tip

How the Sc-02 Models Were Made

The models created for Sc-02 have two versions: a source model and a reference clone. The specific names used for the models aren't important; however the creation of a consistent naming convention is. This will allow you to quickly identify the models that will be used as the proxy sources in the final scene.

Process Review

All the models were created in a process similar to the VandeGraaff generator you just completed. A review of the basic steps now will help as you create your own versions of the Sc-02 models:

1. Make sketches or storyboards to understand your model's form and function.

2. Create a primitive object—sphere, cone, box, and so on—that approximates the size and shape of your intended design. Be sure that its scale is correct by using other objects in the scene as reference.

3. Name the primitive *(Descriptive Name)_*Source. For groups of objects or single non-grouped objects, use *(Descriptive Name)_*Proxy_Source.

4. Convert the primitive to an editable mesh or add an Edit Mesh modifier to it to access the mesh subobjects: Vertex, Edge, Face, and Polygon.

5. Make a reference clone of the proxy_source object. Name the reference clone using the same descriptive name used for the proxy, but leave off the Proxy_Source suffix.

6. Add the MeshSmooth modifier to the reference clone. Start with an Iterations value setting of 2 and Render iterations set to 4. Adjust these values as needed for optimum max performance and model appearance.

7. Follow the three-step modeling process: Form, Division of Form, and Detail. Adjust the basic form of the model by using the transform commands (Move, Rotate, Scale) to manipulate the subobjects of the proxy_source mesh.

8. Divide the form and fine-tune the transitional surfaces of the reference clone using the commands in the Edit Mesh rollouts on the Modify command panel. Use Extrude and Bevel on selected polygons, faces, and edges of the proxy_source mesh.

9. Create detail by the same subobject manipulation process and by adjusting the vertex and Edge, Crease, and Weight values in the MeshSmooth Local Control rollout on the Modify command panel.

10. When the model is complete, add a UVW Mapping modifier and assign the material you've developed for the object.

Note

To refresh your memory about using the UVW Mapping modifier, see "First Things First: Applying UVW Mapping Coordinates" in Chapter 4.

Cooling Tower Interior

The proxy object for this model is called Cooling_Tower_Interior_Proxy_Source and the reference object is a group named Cooling_Tower_Interior, which contains the interior surface and the lattice framework models (see Figure 6.28).

Tip

 An Adobe Acrobat PDF file containing the complete step-by-step instructions to create the model for the cooling tower interior set can be found on the CD in MAXWorkshop\ Help_Files\Appendix_D\AppendixD.PDF.

VandeGraaff Generator—Tesla Coil Towers

The Tesla coil towers collect the high-voltage power from the VandeGraaff generator and condition it for transmission into the power distribution grid controlled by the Western Systems Coordinating Council (WSCC). The local Area 51 Independent Systems Operator at Groom Lake controls the feed of the Alien-generated power into the Nevada regional grid. They don't share it with California—it all goes to feed the massive nightly demand for power in Las Vegas.

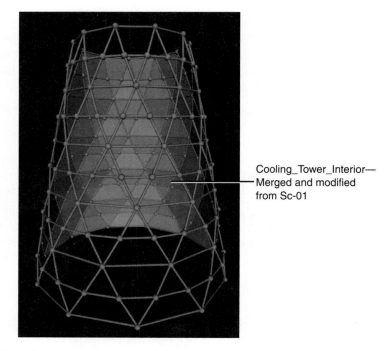

Cooling_Tower_Interior—
Merged and modified
from Sc-01

Figure 6.28   Completed Cooling_Tower_Interior model.

This model can be found on the CD in MAXWorkshop\Help_Files\Chapter_6\ EXSc-02_Tesla_Coil_Tower.max. The proxy_source model group in this file is Tesla_Coil_Tower_Proxy_Source and the reference model group is Tesla_Coil_Tower (see Figure 6.29).

Induction Globe—Sphere Primitive

The *induction globe* is a Sphere primitive 🔘 with the following parameters: Radius: 6.0; Segments: 32; Smooth: On; Generate Mapping Coordinates: On. The source object is named Induction Globe_Source and the reference model is Induction Globe.

Tesla Coils—Torus Primitive

The four Tesla coils are instanced clones of a Torus primitive 🔘 with the following parameters—Radius 1: 5.0; Radius 2: 1.75; Segments: 50; Sides: 18; Smooth: All; Generate Mapping Coordinates: On. The source object is named Tesla Coil_Source and the four reference models are Tesla_Coil, Tesla_Coil01, Tesla_Coil02, and Tesla_Coil03.

Tower/Base—Cylinder Primitive

The tower body and base were developed with the MeshSmooth technique from a Cylinder primitive 🔘 named Tower/Base_Source, created with the following parameters: Radius: 4.75; Height: 13; Height Segments: 5; Sides: 18; Smooth: On. The reference clone is named Tower/Base.

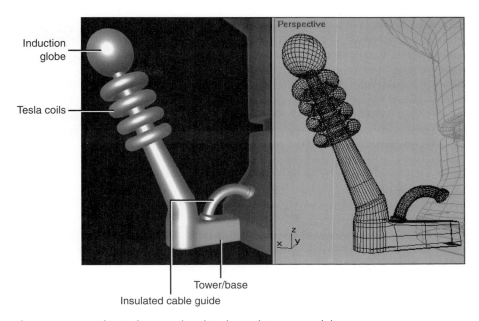

Induction globe

Tesla coils

Tower/base

Insulated cable guide

Figure 6.29   This is the completed Tesla_Coil_Tower model.

Insulated Cable Guide—Torus Primitive

The insulated cable guide was also developed with the MeshSmooth technique using a Torus primitive as the source object. The model is named Insulated Cable Guide_Source and was created with the following parameters: Radius 1: 8.5; Radius 2: 1.6; Segments: 8; Sides: 18; Smooth: All; Slice: On; Slice From: 27; Slice To: -78.0; Generate Mapping Coordinates: On.

The reference clone is named Insulated Cable Guide. Vertices and polygons in the source torus were manipulated to create the flanged ends of the model (see Figure 6.30).

Induction Ring—Tube Primitive

The *induction ring* is the rotating ring that fits in the groove you created around the perimeter of the generator. The model is named Induction Ring and is included in MAXWorkshop\ Help_Files\Chapter_6\EXSc-02_VandeGraaff.max.

The ring is made from a Tube primitive created with the following parameters: Radius 1: 27.0; Radius 2: 12.0; Height: 4.0; Height and Cap Segments: 1; Sides: 12. An Edit Mesh modifier was applied and alternating polygons on the outer perimeter were extruded and beveled to make the gear-like projections (see Figure 6.31).

Applying a .2 chamfer to the edge subobjects of the model created the chamfered edges of the induction ring (see Figure 6.32).

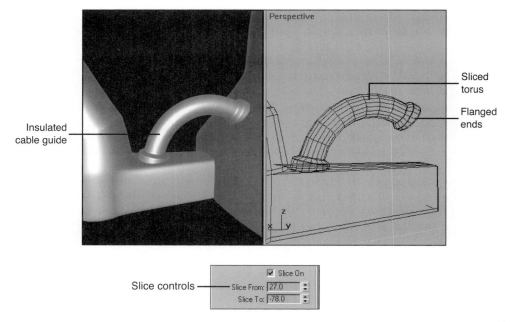

Insulated cable guide

Sliced torus

Flanged ends

Slice controls

Figure 6.30   Some parametric primitive objects have a Slice parameter, which allows you to create a sectional piece of the primitive using the Slice From and Slice To values—like slicing up a pie or an apple.

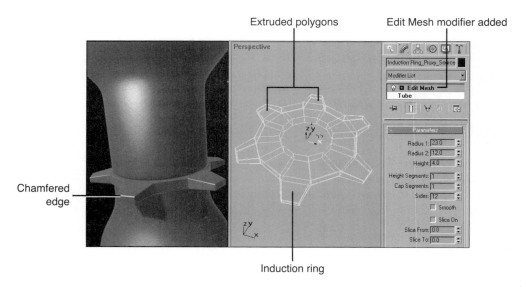

Extruded polygons

Edit Mesh modifier added

Chamfered edge

Induction ring

Figure 6.31   The induction ring's transitional edges were created using the Chamfer command in the Edit Mesh modifier command panel.

Edge subobject selected

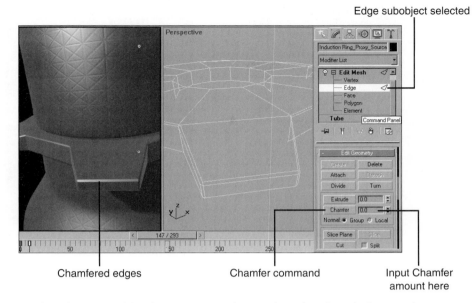

Chamfered edges   Chamfer command   Input Chamfer amount here

Figure 6.32   Chamfer is available when Vertex or Edge is selected as the subobject and is another way to create transitional edges in your model's surfaces development.

Coolant Pump

The *coolant pump* shown in Figure 6.33 keeps the VandeGraaff generator running at peak performance by pumping liquid oxygen through the Tesla coil towers. It also makes a good example to introduce you to the basics of Inverse Kinematics (IK). The models can be found on the CD in `MAXWorkshop\Help_Files\Chapter_6\EXSc-02_Coolant_Pump.max`.

The coolant pump was created using all the basic techniques presented in this Workshop—MeshSmooth, chamfered edges, extruded polygons, scaled vertices, and so on.

Learning to create great models in max is a wonderful journey into experimentation and discovery. I wish that there was room in this Workshop to explore all the fantastic modeling tools and techniques that max offers—so many tools, so few pages! If you want to explore all the modeling tools available in max4, read Chapters 6 and 7 in Volume 1 of your max User Reference.

> **Tip**
>
> ☗ If the basic animation tools in 3ds max 4 are unfamiliar to you, this would be a good time to read and complete the tutorial "Animation Principles in Practice"—`AppendixF.PDF`—provided in `MAXWorkshop\Help_Files\Appendix_F\` on the CD.

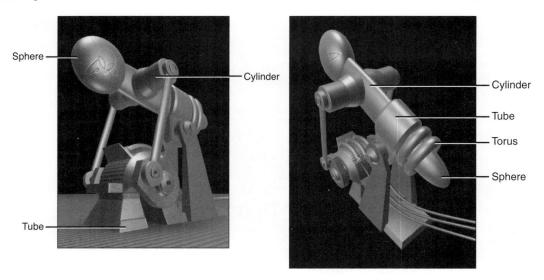

Figure 6.33   The coolant pump was first created in rough form to work out the animation and geometric relationships. Bringing machines, such as this pump, to life is made possible by the Forward and Inverse Kinematics tools in max.

Max Workshop—Introduction to Kinematics

Max has a robust set of animation tools that you can use to bring your models to life. Some tools, such as expression-controlled animation, are more geared to artists with a little bit of computer scientist lurking in their psyche. Other tools, such as Inverse and Forward Kinematics, rely on a sophisticated set of controls and an exacting process to achieve the illusion of life.

However, regardless of the complexity of the tool or technology, the primary power behind animation in max is your artistic vision and the processes you'll invent to bring that vision to life. Knowledge is the food of the imagination and the engine of invention—the more you know about animation in max, the more you'll be able to do with the tools.

All the animation tools in max are powerful, effective, sometimes complex, and often difficult to master. It takes practice, dedication, and more time and effort than one meager chapter to understand the universe of effects waiting for you to achieve and how the tools work. But you have to start somewhere and that's the express intent of this final section.

Using the coolant pump as the basis for a discussion of Forward and Inverse Kinematics, the next sections will introduce you to the fundamentals of animating machine motion in max. Save your work and reset max—you'll start from the beginning and build a rudimentary pump mechanism to illustrate the process.

Machines in Motion—Interrelated Movement

Machines are an assemblage of interrelated moving parts working synergistically to fulfill the intended function of the machine. The primary task of animating the machines you make in max is to accurately portray how the movement of one part of the machine affects the other parts.

A good example of interrelated motion is an automobile engine. As the pistons, constrained by the cylinder, move up and down, the camshaft translates their linear motion into rotational movement. The eccentric rotational movement of the camshaft is then translated into the larger concentric rotational movement of the flywheel, which transfers the rotation directly into the transmission. The transmission, through a series of gears, turns the drive shaft, which then turns the wheels to move the car. If the car is rear-wheel drive, the energy is transferred through the rear differential to the wheels.

Each part of an automobile engine and drive train connect to form a chain of linked movement—each part affecting and translating motion and energy into the next. This is the fundamental idea behind machine motion and is also a good way to define the concept of a linked hierarchy. Figure 6.34 shows the different motions that are translated through the various parts of the coolant pump in Sc-02.

The coolant pump animation also illustrates the idea that a single part of a machine assembly can be animated to control the rest of the machine. In this case, the only part of the pump that is animated is the flywheel—the rest of the parts are just along for the ride. Animating one part of a linked hierarchy to animate all the rest of the linked parts is the single most important concept to understand about Forward Kinematics (FK) and Inverse Kinematics (IK).

Understanding Forward and Inverse Kinematics: Coolant Pump Test Model

The coolant pump animation was patterned after the oil pumps that dot the landscape throughout the western United States and Canada. As a kid, I thought they looked like giant mosquitoes and the antennae that oil companies put on them emphasized the image of a bug sucking oil from the ground. Using this imagery as a basis for the coolant pump is the perfect visual meme connecting the weirdness of Area 51, the western desert, and a familiar mechanical icon.

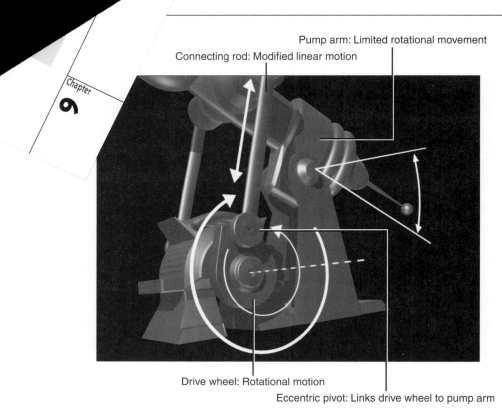

Connecting rod: Modified linear motion

Pump arm: Limited rotational movement

Drive wheel: Rotational motion

Eccentric pivot: Links drive wheel to pump arm

Figure 6.34 By attaching to the eccentric pivot on the drive wheel, the connecting rod uses linear motion to transfer the rotational motion of the flywheel into seesaw motion of the pump arm.

Tip

All machine motion must be patterned after real-world machines to animate them in a believable fashion. The more you understand mechanical linkage, sliding and rotational joints, power transmission, and so forth, the more realistic your machines will be. And the best place to look for inspiration and information is sitting in your garage. If you are going to animate believable machinery, you're going to have to get some grease under your fingernails by working on your car. You should buy two indispensable engineering compendiums for your animation library: *Ingenious Mechanisms for Designers and Inventors* by Franklin Day Jones and *Mechanisms and Mechanical Devices Sourcebook* by Nicholas P. Chironis and Neil Sclater.

The important factors to consider when using Forward and Inverse Kinematics are the placement of the machine parts, the pivot points for each part, the way the parts are linked together to form a hierarchy, the type of IK solver applied to the hierarchy, and the kind of animation controls used to bring the machine to life. You'll explore all these factors and learn how FK differs from IK as you create and animate the coolant pump test model.

> **Tip**
>
> 🎩 If you need help, the completed test model for this section can be found in
> `MAXWorkshop\Help_Files\Chapter_6\EXIK_Pump.max`.

Creating the Coolant Pump Test Model

Creating simplified test models to experiment with machine animation before final models are created is always a good idea. The intention is to quickly work out the bugs in the machine part interrelationships and to efficiently explore multiple approaches to the machine motion you want to achieve.

The basic IK_Pump is made from two cylinders, a tube, two boxes, and two helper objects. Create the cylinders, tube, and boxes first by following these steps:

1. Change to Perspective view, open the Create command panel , click Cylinder, and drag in the viewport to create a cylinder. Use the Modify command panel to rename this cylinder Flywheel and make the following changes to its parameters: Radius: 40; Height: 10; Height Segments: 1; Cap Segments: 2; Sides: 18.

2. Create a second cylinder named Eccentric Pivot with the following parameters: Radius: 6; Height: 20; Height Segments: 1; Cap Segments: 2; Sides: 18.

3. Create two boxes named Pump Arm and Connecting Rod with the following identical parameters: Length: 150; Width: 10; Height: 10; Length, Width, and Height Segments: 1.

4. Create a tube named Connecting Arm Lower Pivot with the following parameters: Radius 1: 10; Radius 2: 6; Height: 10; Height Segments: 1; Cap Segments: 1; Sides: 18 (see Figure 6.35).

> **Tip**
>
> When you create test models, it's not necessary to think about the final aesthetic form and detail of the model that will appear in the scene. Focus on the intended function and animation method first, and then apply it to the final model after you have a kinematics solution that creates an acceptable motion.

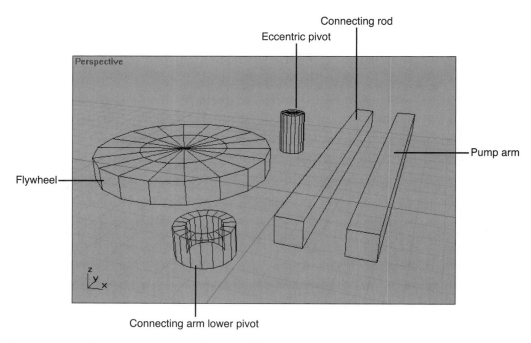

Connecting rod

Eccentric pivot

Perspective

Pump arm

Flywheel

z
y
x

Connecting arm lower pivot

Figure 6.35 The IK_Pump is a simple test bed for the animation you'll create for the Sc-02 cooling pump. The intent is not to match the final scene model's geometry size and placement, but to work out the FK/IK animation structure.

Using the Hierarchy Command Panel to Change Pivot Point Orientation

After all the parts are created, their orientation to each other and to the max world coordinate system needs to be adjusted. The Transform commands, the Transform Type-In fields, and the Hierarchy command panel will help you accomplish this task:

1. Click the Absolute Transform Mode toggle to change it to Offset Transform Mode and click Rotate in the Main Toolbar.

2. Select all the machine parts and type 90 in the X type-in field. This rotates the machine parts 90° around the X-axis, as shown in Figure 6.36.

3. Change to Front view and, with the machine parts still selected, click the Hierarchy command panel and click the Pivot rollout button, as shown in Figure 6.37.

4. Click Affect Pivot Only to activate the command selections in the Alignment section. Select Center to Object, as shown in Figure 6.38. When you activate the Affect Pivot Only selection, the pivot point gizmo appears showing the current orientation of the Local coordinate axes of the object.

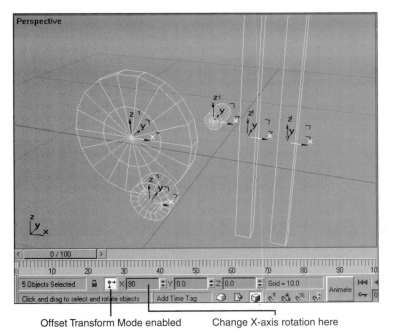

Offset Transform Mode enabled   Change X-axis rotation here

Figure 6.36   Creating the machine parts in the Perspective or Top viewport keeps their pivot points oriented correctly to the max world coordinate system. Rotating puts them into better orientation for animation and viewing but changes the orientation of the part relative to world-space and their original creation orientation.

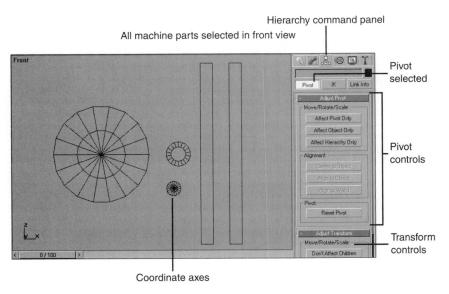

Hierarchy command panel

All machine parts selected in front view

Pivot selected

Pivot controls

Transform controls

Coordinate axes

Figure 6.37   When you rotated the machine parts, you changed the orientation of their pivot points in relation to max world-space. Notice the orientation of the coordinate system axes for the selected machine parts—it's important for this kinematics setup that the orientation of all the pivot points of the machine parts are identical.

3ds max 4

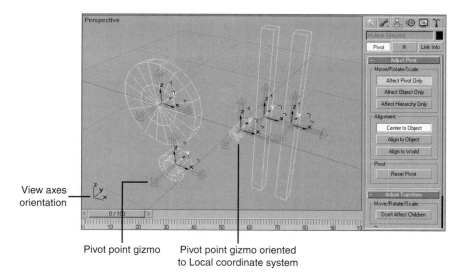

View axes
orientation

Pivot point gizmo   Pivot point gizmo oriented
to Local coordinate system

Figure 6.38   Notice that the orientation of the pivot point gizmo Z- and Y-axes is different
from the part's coordinate axes displayed in the viewport. This is a result of the
rotation transform in step 2.

5. After the pivot point is moved to the center of the object, it's very important to align the
pivot point gizmo orientation with the world coordinate system. Be sure all the parts are
still selected, and then scroll down to the Adjust Transform, Reset section of the rollout
and click Transform. This resets the pivot point and aligns it to the world coordinate system (see Figure 6.39).

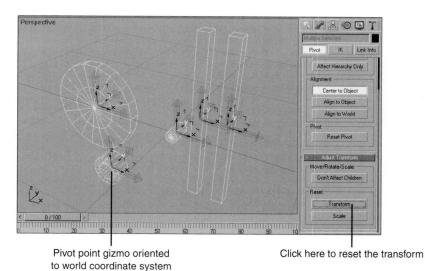

Pivot point gizmo oriented   Click here to reset the transform
to world coordinate system

Figure 6.39   Resetting the transform for the machine parts ensures that all of them use the
same coordinate system for transform commands. Mixed coordinate orienta-
tions can be useful for more complex animation; however, in this case, it would
cause problems when the parts are linked together in a hierarchy.

Placement of the Machine Parts: Using the Align Command

The next step is to place the machine parts into their proper orientation. Most of the time, eye-balling placement will be good enough, but it won't suffice for the machine precision needed for this model. Fortunately, max provides a way to precisely align objects with other objects in the workspace using the Align command.

Aligning one object with another is fairly simple: Select the object you want to move, activate the Align command, select the target object to which you want to align, and specify the alignment parameters in the Align Selection dialog box. When you activate the Align command, the cursor changes to the Align cursor, as shown in Figure 6.40.

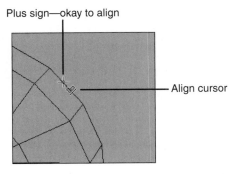

Plus sign—okay to align

Align cursor

Figure 6.40 When the cursor is placed over a valid object to which the selected object can be aligned, a plus sign appears.

The following steps will introduce you to the Align command in 3ds max 4:

1. Change to Perspective view and maximize your viewport. Select the eccentric pivot cylinder, click Align ![icon] in the Main Toolbar, and click the flywheel to select it as the Align target. When you select the flywheel, the Align Selection dialog box opens (see Figure 6.41).

2. Check the X Position, Y Position, and Z Position boxes in the Align Position (World) section of the dialog box. This aligns the eccentric pivot to the exact center of the flywheel. Click OK to exit the dialog box when you're done (see Figure 6.42).

3. Change to Front view and zoom in on the flywheel, which now has the still-selected eccentric pivot aligned to its center. Use the Y-axis and move the eccentric pivot up until it sits just inside the outer rim of the flywheel, as shown in Figure 6.43.

4. Change to Top view and zoom in on the flywheel. Click Align and once again select the flywheel as the target. When the Align Selection dialog box opens, click the Y Position check box to activate it.

5. Click Maximum in the Current Object section and click Minimum in the Target Object section. This aligns the base of the eccentric pivot with the front surface of the flywheel, as shown in Figure 6.44.

Align target name

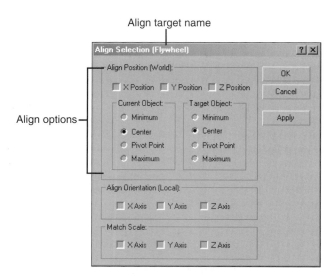

Figure 6.41   The target to which you are aligning your selection appears in parentheses next to Align Selection in the title bar of the dialog box. The align options allow you to precisely align the position, coordinate system orientation, and match the scale of a selected object to its align target.

Selected (current) object alignment options

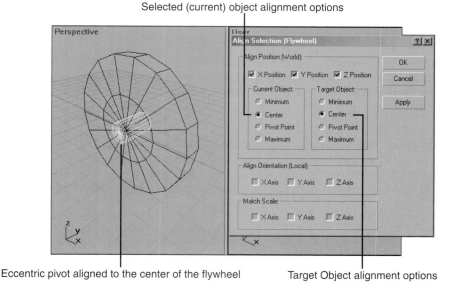

Eccentric pivot aligned to the center of the flywheel   Target Object alignment options

Figure 6.42   The selected object that you are aligning is called the Current object and the object to which it is being aligned is called the Target object. The check boxes in the Current Object and Target Object sections control how the objects are aligned to each other. The default selection in both sections is Center, which aligns the center of the eccentric pivot to the center of the flywheel.

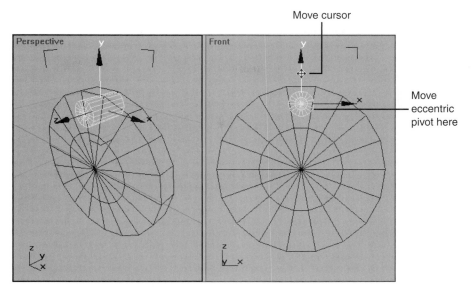

Figure 6.43   Aligning the eccentric pivot to the outer perimeter of the flywheel moves it off center—it's no longer concentric. This part orbits around the flywheel center and not around its own center, which is why it's referred to as an eccentric pivot.

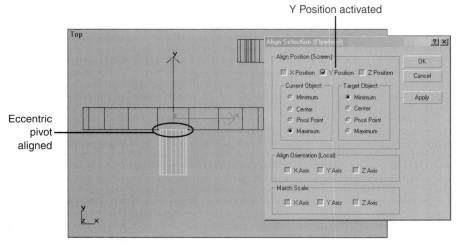

Figure 6.44   The eccentric pivot sticks out from the surface of the flywheel and will be the lower attachment point for the arm that transfers the flywheel rotational motion to the pump arm.

6. Select the connecting rod lower pivot tube, click Align ![icon], and select the eccentric pivot as the Target object.

7. When the Align Selection dialog box opens, you'll see that the alignment options are still set to the Maximum/Minimum settings used in the last step. Change the selection in the Current Object and Target Object sections back to Center and click the X Position, Y Position, and Z Position boxes to align the connecting rod lower pivot to the center of the eccentric pivot. Then click Apply to align the objects without leaving the Align Selection dialog box—don't click OK yet!

> **Note**
>
> Clicking Apply instead of OK in the Align Selection dialog box applies the specified alignment and resets the dialog box to its default state. And the dialog box stays open, ready for another round of alignment for the selected objects.

8. Check the Y Position box and click Minimum in the Current Object section. This aligns the base of the connecting rod lower pivot with the base of the eccentric pivot, as shown in Figure 6.45. Click OK to exit the dialog box when you are finished.

Connecting rod lower pivot aligned to eccentric pivot

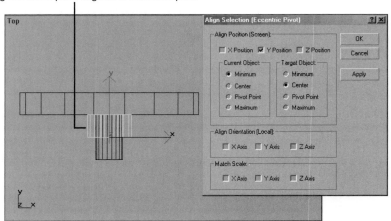

Figure 6.45   The connecting rod lower pivot will be used to attach the connecting rod to the eccentric pivot. Settings in the IK command panel will make this part follow the eccentric pivot as it rotates with the flywheel.

9. Change to Front view, select the connecting rod box, and click Align. Press H on the keyboard to open the Pick Object dialog box and double-click Connecting Rod Lower Pivot to select it as the Target object (see Figure 6.46).

10. When the Align Selection dialog box opens, change the selection in the Current Object and Target Object sections back to Center; click the X Position, Y Position, and Z Position boxes; and click Apply to align the connecting rod to the center of the connecting rod lower pivot.

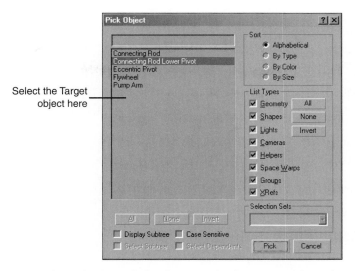

Select the Target object here

Figure 6.46 The Pick Object dialog box can also be accessed from the Main Toolbar by clicking the Select by Name icon.

11. The next step is to align the base of the connecting rod with the perimeter of the connecting rod lower pivot. Click the Y Position box, change the alignment to Minimum for the Current Object and Maximum for the Target Object, and click OK to exit the Align Selection and the Pick Object dialog boxes. The connecting rod should be aligned as shown in Figure 6.47.

The final steps in this process are to rotate the pump arm and then align it to the connecting rod. Be sure the Transform Type-In mode at the bottom of the interface is set to Offset Mode:

1. Change to Front view and select the pump arm box, and then right-click it, and select Rotate from the Quad Menu. Type 90 in the Z Transform Type-In box to rotate the pump arm 90° counter-clockwise about the Z-axis (see Figure 6.48).

2. Click Align and select the connecting arm as the Target object. When the Align Selection dialog box opens, change the selection in the Current and Target Object sections back to Center; click the X Position, Y Position, and Z Position boxes; and click Apply to align the pump arm to the center of the connecting rod.

3. Activate the X Position check box, change the Current and Target Object options to Minimum, and click Apply. This aligns the left end of the pump arm to the body of the connecting rod.

4. Activate the Y Position check box, change the Current and Target Object options to Maximum, and click Apply. This aligns the top surface of the pump arm to the top of the connecting rod.

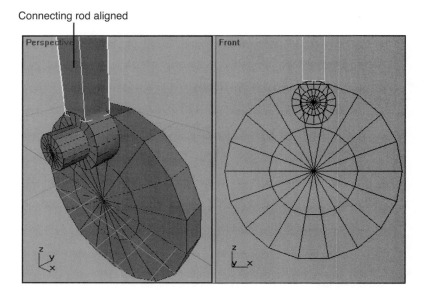

Figure 6.47 The connecting rod lower pivot is built into the final model of the connecting rod used in the coolant pump, and the eccentric pivot is likewise built into the flywheel. They're separate in the test model to simplify the modeling process. It's important to resist the temptation to make this model look pretty and to focus just on the mechanical aspects of the test apparatus.

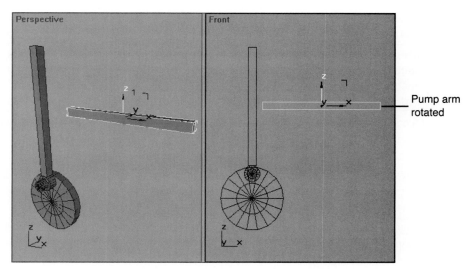

Figure 6.48 The final alignment step takes four separate rounds of alignment.

5. Activate the Z Position check box, change the Current Object option to Maximum and Target Object to Minimum, and click OK to complete the alignment and exit the dialog box. This aligns the front surface of the pump arm to the back surface of the connecting rod. Your pump arm should now be aligned as shown in Figure 6.49.

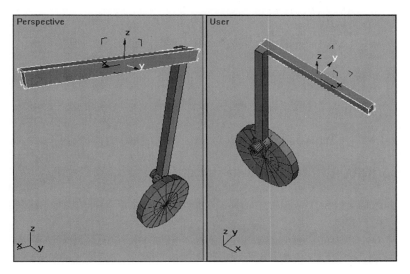

Figure 6.49   The front surface of the pump arm doesn't have to be aligned to the back surface of the connecting rod to create an accurate animation. However, it's important that this test model reflect the actual configuration of the pump arm and connecting rod shown in the pre-production sketches and the final model.

The Align command is a useful tool that will help you with precision alignment tasks. Over the course of time and experience, I've come to use it for all alignment processes in which precision is absolutely necessary—especially test models like this.

Adjusting the Pivot Points

Now that the parts of the pump are correctly aligned, it's necessary to change the pivot points of the connecting rod and the pump arm:

1. Select the connecting rod, open the Hierarchy 🔣 command panel, and click Affect Pivot Only in the Adjust Pivot section of the Pivot rollout.

2. Move the pivot point gizmo up in the Y-axis to the center of its intersection with the pump arm, as shown in Figure 6.50. This creates the axial joint pivot between the connecting rod and the pump arm.

3. Select the pump arm and click Transform in the Reset section of the Adjust Transform rollout. When you rotated this part in step 1 of the previous section, you consequently changed the orientation of its coordinate system. Resetting the transform returns the coordinate system back to its proper orientation.

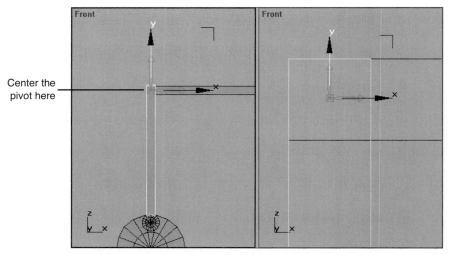

Center the
pivot here

Figure 6.50 For IK to work properly, all the parts of a machine must connect in a realistic way. Adjusting pivot points to create correct joints between connecting objects is a critical step—without it, your IK setup won't animate correctly.

4. Select Move from the Quad Menu and type -30 in the Y Transform Type-In box. This moves the pivot point off the center of the pump arm, as shown in Figure 6.51.

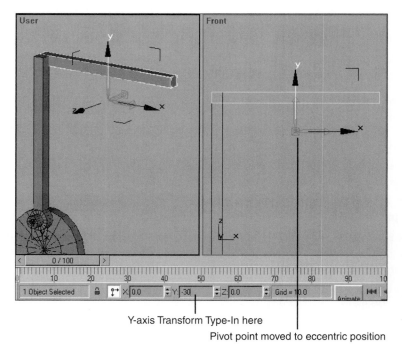

Y-axis Transform Type-In here

Pivot point moved to eccentric position

Figure 6.51 For the pump arm to rock correctly, the pivot point is moved to an eccentric position directly below the absolute center of the part. This exaggerates the rocking motion and creates more interesting and realistic animation.

Understanding Hierarchies

You can think of hierarchies using a genealogy paradigm to describe the relationship of ancestors and descendants in a family tree–type structure. Hierarchies are families of objects, which are linked together in a chain.

At the top of the chain is a Parent object, which is connected to the Child objects that sit below it in the chain. Child objects can have their own children, which can be thought of as the grandchildren of the Parent object. The last grandchildren in a hierarchy are also referred to as Leaf objects because they are the last part of the family tree at the end of all the branches connected to the limbs that extend from the trunk.

Using the example of the automobile engine, the pistons are the Parent object, which drives the camshaft that's connected to the flywheel and so on, out to the Leaves in the hierarchy: the wheels.

Animation hierarchies can be fiercely complex with dozens of interrelated hierarchies existing within the same model. Figure 6.52 shows a section of a massive hierarchy created by our Technical Director Dave Otte, for a character model in the animated TV series *Sitting Ducks*. This is just a small part of a hierarchy that consists of more than 200 separate objects.

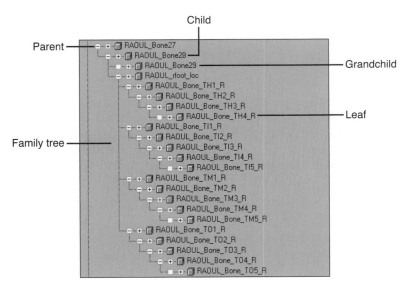

Figure 6.52   When you realize that this level of complexity is awaiting you as a professional animator, you might feel a little daunted by the prospect of building and using hierarchies in max 4. Mastering the ins and outs of hierarchical design is the reason good technical directors such as Dave Otte are worth their weight in gold.

Broken Hierarchies—Using Forward and Inverse Kinematics Together

The best way to understand hierarchies is to build one, and the IK_Pump model is a perfect place to start. The first question to ask yourself when you create a hierarchy is, "Which object is the parent in control of the family?" In this case, the IK_Pump flywheel can be considered to be the big boss of the entire family—it's rotating around its own axis taking the eccentric pivot along for the ride and driving the rest of the machine.

However, the kinematics problem in this machine is how to transfer the rotational movement of the flywheel into the rocking motion of the pump arm. With this in mind, it's best to split the machine into two parts and use both Forward and Inverse Kinematics to animate the separate halves.

The flywheel and the eccentric pivot comprise one half of the machine animation. The eccentric pivot cylinder will be linked as a child to the parent flywheel. When the flywheel rotates, the child will also rotate. This is the fundamental concept behind Forward Kinematics—child objects follow the movement of the parent.

Inverse Kinematics is so named because it is the conceptual inverse of Forward Kinematics—parent objects are controlled by the motion of the child objects linked to them in the hierarchical chain. The connecting rod lower pivot, the connecting rod, and the pump arm are linked in an IK chain, which allows movement of the pump arm to be controlled by the connecting rod, which is attached to the rotation of the flywheel by the connecting rod lower pivot.

As you gain experience, you'll learn how to use FK and IK together in mixed or broken hierarchies. In our studio, broken and mixed hierarchies are used with both Forward and Inverse Kinematics applied within the same model. This gives the animators the control they need to easily and effectively create the illusion of life.

Building Hierarchies Using the Link Command

Breaking the IK_Pump into two separate hierarchies simplifies the animation process and allows you to animate the parts using both Forward Kinematics and Inverse Kinematics. The first step is to create the two hierarchies for the machine. You'll use the Link command found in the Main Toolbar to create the hierarchical links between the parts. Hierarchical links are always made from the child up to the parent, regardless of whether you are going to use FK or IK for the animation.

When you click the Link command and drag your cursor in the viewport, it changes into the Link cursor shown in Figure 6.53.

As you drag the cursor, a dotted line appears, extending from the pivot point center of the selected object. When the cursor is over an object that can be linked to, it changes to the link cursor. If the cursor is over an object that cannot be used as a link, it changes to the cursor shown in Figure 6.54.

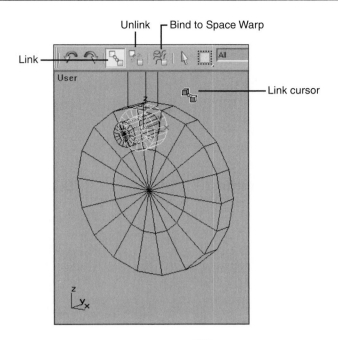

Unlink — Bind to Space Warp

Link

User

Link cursor

Figure 6.53 Next to the Link command are the Unlink and the Bind to Space Warp command icons. Select an object and click the Unlink command to break an unwanted link. You'll learn about Bind to Space Warp in Chapter 8.

1. Zoom in on the top of the flywheel, and then select the eccentric pivot cylinder, which will be linked as a child of the flywheel.

2. Click the Link command in the Main Toolbar and drag the link cursor to the outside edge of the flywheel, as shown previously in Figure 6.54, and release the mouse button. The flywheel wireframe will flash briefly, indicating that a link has been made.

You can check to see whether the proper link has been made by selecting the flywheel and clicking the Display command panel . Scroll down to the Link Display rollout and click Display Links, as shown in Figure 6.55. This will display the link you just created between the eccentric pivot and the flywheel.

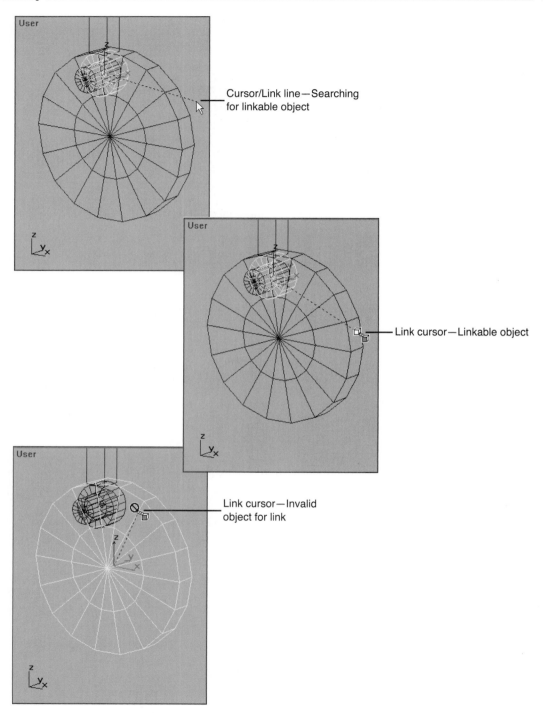

Cursor/Link line—Searching
for linkable object

Link cursor—Linkable object

Link cursor—Invalid
object for link

Figure 6.54   Understanding the visual meaning of each of the link cursors will help you
avoid mistakes while linking objects together.

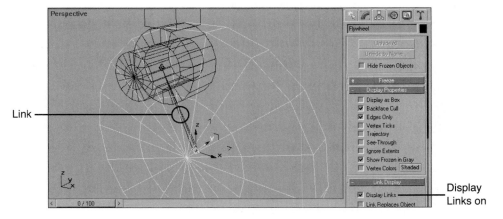

Link

Display
Links on

Figure 6.55 Links are displayed only for objects that have been selected and have had their link
display turned on in this rollout. If you want all your objects to show their links,
select them all in the viewport and click Display Links.

> **Caution**
>
> When you are in Link mode, it's easy to link to objects by mistake because the
> Link command remains active until you click Select Object 🔳 or select Move,
> Rotate, or Scale from the Quad Menu or Main Toolbar. This continues to be a
> major pain and, unless you are careful, you will mistakenly make links that you
> don't want. If this happens, select the child object that you want to unlink from
> the parent, and click the Unlink Selection button 🔳.

3. Stay in Link mode, change to Front view, select the connecting rod lower pivot, and link
   it to the connecting rod. Click the connecting rod to select it and link it to the pump arm.

4. Exit from Link mode, select all the IK_Pump parts, and click Display Links in the Link
   Display rollout of the Display command panel.

5. Check the links by pressing H to open the Select Objects dialog box. Click Display
   Subtree to see the two hierarchies you have created (see Figure 6.56).

If you select and rotate the pump arm, you'll see that the child objects—the connecting rod and
connecting rod lower pivot—rotate with it. If you select and rotate the flywheel, you'll see that
the eccentric pivot now follows its rotation as well.

Animating the IK_Pump

Animating the IK_Pump starts with creating the animation for the flywheel, which involves
using helper objects to control animation. To prepare for this process, select and hide the connecting rod, connecting rod lower pivot, and the pump arm and change to Front view.

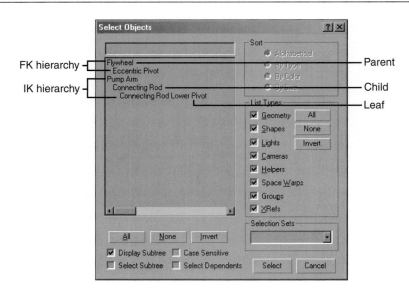

Figure 6.56   The Display Subtree command in the Select Objects dialog box is another way to verify that the hierarchies you create are correctly structured.

Helper Objects

Helper objects are the animation stunt doubles of the max world. They are nonrendering entities that can be linked to your scene geometry and then animated to make the linked geometry follow the same animation you created for the helper. In this way, helper objects can simplify the animation of complex objects. Open the Create command panel and click Helpers (see Figure 6.57).

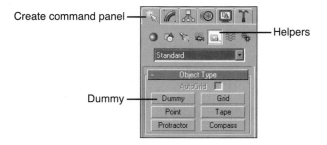

Figure 6.57   There are six standard helper objects to aid you in your work in max. Each one serves a different purpose and it's worth taking some time to experiment and understand how they work. You'll use a dummy object to animate the IK_Pump flywheel.

You could choose to animate the flywheel directly instead of using a dummy object to control the animation of the hierarchy. Over time, you'll find that using helper objects to control hierarchical animation is faster, simpler, and easier.

Using a Dummy Object to Animate the Flywheel

The following steps show you how to create a dummy object and link the flywheel to it to control the FK animation:

1. Click Dummy in the Object Type rollout and drag in the viewport to create a dummy helper next to the flywheel. Rename this dummy object as Flywheel Rotation Control.

2. Open the Hierarchy command panel and click Transform in the Adjust Transform, Reset rollout. Resetting the transform is important because it aligns the Local transform coordinate system of the dummy with the flywheel.

3. Use the Align command to align the flywheel rotation control dummy to the X, Y, and Z axial center of the flywheel (see Figure 6.58).

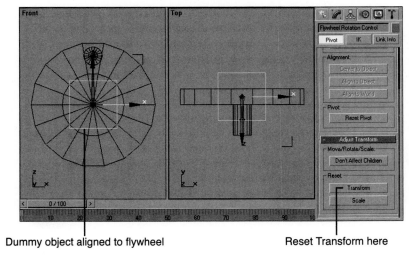

Dummy object aligned to flywheel   Reset Transform here

Figure 6.58   The flywheel will be linked to the dummy object, which will make the dummy the Parent object in the hierarchy.

4. Click Link, link the flywheel to the flywheel rotation control dummy, and exit Link mode. Press H to open the Select Objects dialog box and check the box next to Display Subtree to verify the addition of the dummy as the Parent object in the hierarchy (see Figure 6.59).

Figure 6.59 The next step is to select and animate the dummy object, which in turn will animate all the child objects in the hierarchy.

5. Change to Perspective view, select the dummy object, and then click the Animate mode toggle button [Animate]. Drag the Time Slider to frame 12, as shown in Figure 6.60.

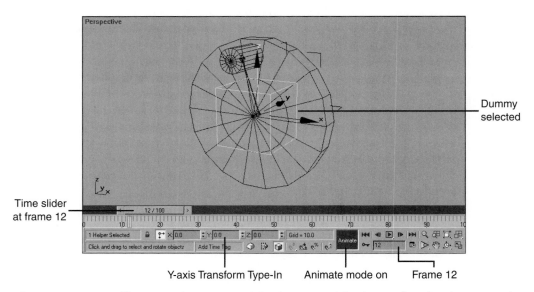

Figure 6.60 You'll animate the rotation of the dummy with keyframes (keys) at frame 0 and frame 12. You'll use these keys to create a repeating cycle.

6. Type 45 in the Y-axis Transform Type-In box. This rotates the hierarchy 45° and creates a rotation keyframe at frame 0 and at frame 12, as shown in Figure 6.61. Click the Animate button to exit Animate mode.

7. Right-click the selected dummy object and choose Track View Selected from the Transform Quad Menu, as shown in Figure 6.62.

8. When the Track view opens, click Rotation, as shown in Figure 6.63. This selects the Rotation animation track and is the first step to use its keyframes to create a repeating animation cycle.

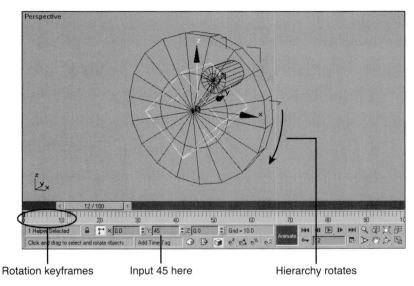

Rotation keyframes   Input 45 here   Hierarchy rotates

Figure 6.61   Keyframes for animated objects appear in the Track Bar when the object is selected. When you drag the Time Slider between frame 0 and frame 12, you'll see the 45° rotation you just created. However, the animation stops dead at frame 12. The next step shows you how to turn this into a continuous repeating cycle.

Figure 6.62   Track View Selected opens a Track view window, which only shows the selected objects and their animation parameters.

Parameter Curve Out-of-Range Types icon

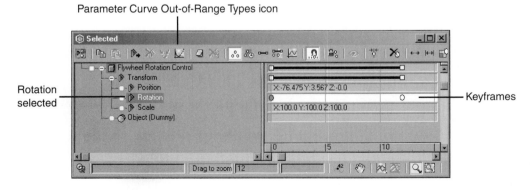

Rotation selected

Keyframes

Figure 6.63   The little white dots in the selected Rotation track are the keyframes you created in step 6. When you selected the Rotation track, the Parameter Curve Out-of-Range Types button activated.

9. Click the Parameter Curve Out-of-Range Types button ⬚. When its dialog box opens, choose Linear from the options, as shown in Figure 6.64.

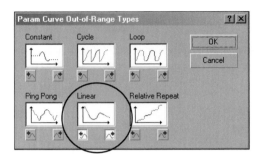

Figure 6.64   Parameter Curve Out-of-Range Types are used to define how an object's animation behaves outside the range of keys you've defined.

You've created the first two keyframes of the flywheel rotation animation. When you select Linear as the option in the Parameter Curve Out-of-Range Types dialog box, you told max to repeat those first two frames throughout the rest of the length of the animation. If you play your animation now, you'll see that the flywheel rotates in a repeating cycle of those frames. Using Parameter Curve Out-of-Range Types enables you to turn short segments of animation into the following different patterns:

- **Constant** ⬚—The default Out-of-Range type max assigns to your animation. It holds the value of the end key for all the keys in the track. Use this type when you don't want any type of repeating cycle before or after the range of keyframes.

- **Cycle** ⬚—The type to choose for simple repeating animation when the beginning key and the end key are in the same spatial location. Be sure the animated position of the object at the beginning and end frames is the same. If they aren't, you will see a jump or hiccup in your animation.

- **Loop** ⬚—Repeats the animation in your keyframe range and smoothes the transition or interpolation between the last keyframe and the first keyframe of the next cycle, creating an ongoing loop. In the case of the flywheel you are animating, because the rotation position of the first and last keyframes is not same, using Loop will create the same effect as Cycle.

- **Ping Pong** ⬚—Repeats your animation by alternating between a forward and reverse repeat of the keyframes; just like a ping-pong ball traveling back and forth on a table. This is a great option for machine motion.

- **Linear** —Use Linear when you want an animation to flow through a range of keys at a constant velocity.

- **Relative Repeat** —Repeats the animation defined by the keys. It also offsets each repetition by the value of the end key, which builds animation that grows more extreme as the cycle repeats over time.

Take a moment now and try out each range type to see the effect they have on your flywheel animation. Learning how to use these range types effectively can save you a lot of time by allowing max to help you create your repeating cycles. Close the Track view when you are finished.

Creating an IK Chain

The animation you just completed is a simple example of Forward Kinematics animation—a Parent object controls the movement of all the Child objects in the hierarchical tree. The upper arms of the IK_Pump mechanism will be controlled by this FK animation, but first the parts need to have an Inverse Kinematics solver applied to their hierarchy. This creates an IK chain and makes the hierarchy follow the movement of the connecting rod lower pivot.

> **Note**
>
> Inverse Kinematics in max uses different vocabulary when referring to objects and their position within an IK chain and to the technology used to control the animation. The Parent object of the IK Chain is also referred to as the *Root* and the last object in the IK chain is called the *Goal.* Solver refers to the mathematical algorithm used to calculate the kinematics solution.

Move the Time Slider back to frame 0 and click Unhide All in the Display command panel to unhide the rest of the IK_Pump. Now would be a good time to save your work.

> **Tip**
>
> The simple Kinematics examples in this chapter introduce you to the basic concepts behind this powerful set of tools, but it barely scratches the surface. If you want to master FK and IK in max, there is no substitute for the knowledge contained in your max User Reference. Feed your imagination; read your manuals and complete the tutorials.

To apply a solver, follow these steps:

1. Change to Front view and select the pump arm; it will be the Root object of the IK chain. When the pump arm is selected, click Animation, IK Solvers in the Menu Bar (see Figure 6.65).

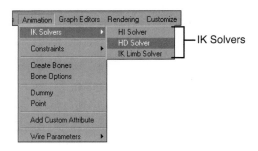

Figure 6.65   Three kinds of IK solvers are available in max 4, and each one is designed for a specific application and animation control. You'll use the History Dependant (HD) IK solver—it's especially good for machines.

2. Select HD Solver from the list to close the menu. A dotted line now extends from the pivot point center of the root object (the pump arm) following your cursor. This means that the HD Solver linking tool is active and the next object you click or select from the Pick Object dialog box will become the Goal object in the IK chain (see Figure 6.66).

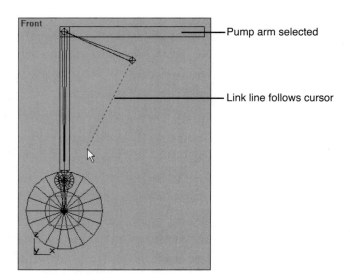

Figure 6.66   Creating an IK chain is a three-step process: Select the Root object first, select the IK solver you want to use, and then select the Goal object.

3. The connecting rod lower pivot and the flywheel hierarchy are a little close. To avoid choosing the wrong Goal object, press H to open the Pick Object dialog box and double-click Connecting Rod Lower Pivot in the list. This will create the IK chain.

4. Verify that the chain has been created correctly by selecting the connecting rod lower pivot and moving it around. The rest of the objects should follow it, as shown in Figure 6.67.

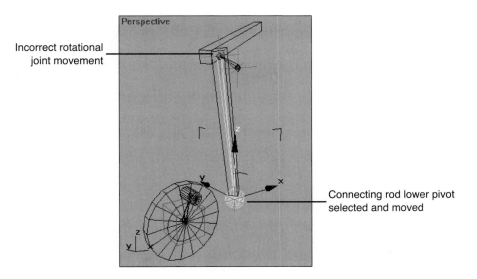

Incorrect rotational joint movement

Connecting rod lower pivot selected and moved

Figure 6.67   When you move the Goal of this IK chain, the parts are linked correctly but rotate incorrectly around their joints trying to follow the Goal as you move it around the viewport. You'll fix that in a moment by constraining their rotational movement to the Y-axis.

FK and IK Working Together—Using the Bind Command

Now that the Forward and Inverse Kinematics are set up, it's time to make them work together. You'll do this by binding the root of the IK chain to the eccentric pivot linked to the flywheel:

1. Select the connecting rod lower pivot, open the Hierarchy command panel, and click IK, as shown in Figure 6.68.

2. Click Bind in the Bind to Follow Object section of the Object Parameters rollout. Press H to open the Select Pin dialog box. Select Eccentric Pivot from the list and click Pin to bind the connecting rod lower pivot to the eccentric pivot (see Figure 6.69).

When you complete the binding process, the connecting rod lower pivot follows the eccentric pivot and the flywheel animation is now also animating the IK chain. If you play the animation now, you'll see two problems: The connecting rod lower pivot is having a hard time following the eccentric pivot and the IK chain rotational joint movement is still incorrect.

Restricting Rotational Joints

The Hierarchy IK command panel allows you to specify and restrict the X-, Y-, and Z-axes of rotational joints. Start the process by selecting the object in the IK chain that you want to restrict and scroll down to the Rotational Joints rollout in the Hierarchy IK command panel (see Figure 6.70).

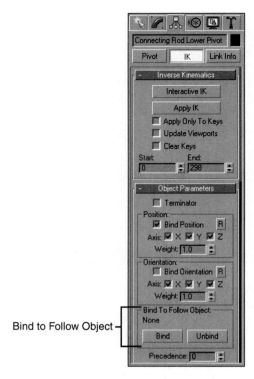

Bind to Follow Object —

Figure 6.68   The IK section of the Hierarchy command panel gives you access to the controls you'll need to adjust and refine your IK setup. You'll use the Bind command to link the flywheel FK hierarchy to the pump arm IK chain.

1. Select the pump arm and uncheck the Active boxes directly under X Axis and Z Axis in the Rotational Joints rollout. This leaves the Y-axis as the only active rotational axis (see Figure 6.71).

2. Follow the same procedure for the connecting arm and the connecting arm lower pivot and restrict their rotational movement to the Y-axis. When you play your animation, the joints will pivot correctly.

The last step in this process is to adjust the IK controller parameters to make the connecting arm lower pivot follow the eccentric pivot correctly.

Refining Movement—Adjusting IK Controller Parameters

Select the connecting arm lower pivot, click the Motion command panel 🔘, change the Thresholds Position amount to 4, and change the Solution Iterations amount to 50 (see Figure 6.72).

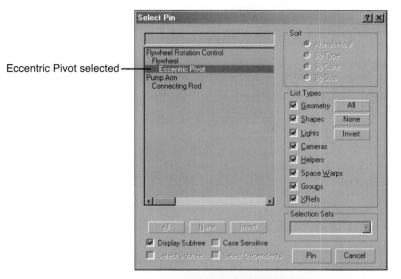

Eccentric Pivot selected —

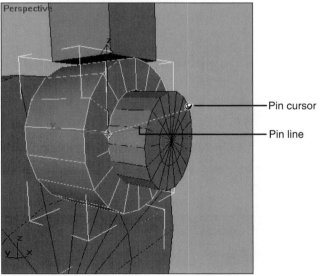

— Pin cursor

— Pin line

Figure 6.69 You can also pin to objects by dragging in the viewport from the selected model to the binding object. When you use this method, zoom in close enough to see the object you want to pin to and be careful—it's easy to pin to the wrong object.

Figure 6.70   The X-, Y-, and Z-axes are active by default for the rotational joints in the IK chain. To fix the joint rotation problem, all three of the IK chain objects will need to have their rotational joints restricted to the Y-axis.

Rotational Joints rollout

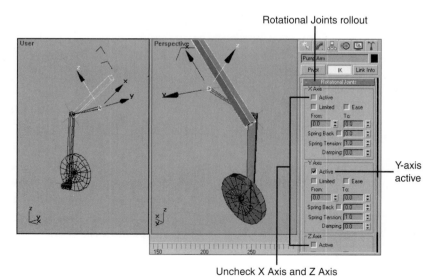

Y-axis active

Uncheck X Axis and Z Axis

Figure 6.71   The X Axis, Y Axis, and Z Axis sections in this rollout relate to the local coordinate system of the selected objects in the IK chain. This is another reason to be sure that all the objects in an IK chain like this have had their pivot point transforms reset to identical orientations.

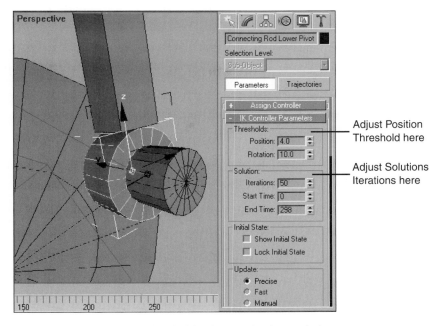

Adjust Position
Threshold here

Adjust Solutions
Iterations here

Figure 6.72 Lower Position and Rotation threshold values make the Goal objects in your IK chains follow the objects to which they are bound more closely. Adjust these parameters to make your machines animate smoothly.

Note

When you created the IK chain, an end effector was also created at the pivot point of the Goal object. The Position threshold value determines the limits of how far the goal can be moved from that end effector, which in turn affects how smoothly a goal will follow the object to which it's been bound.

The Solutions: Iterations value controls how many times an IK solver will try to find the best match between the end effector and the Goal positions. Higher numbers will smooth out jumpy animation. Changing the Iterations value to 50 is sufficient to smooth out the IK_Pump animation.

To see the effect that changing the Iterations value has, zoom in on the connecting arm lower pivot and use the spinners next to the Iterations amount to adjust the value. You'll see the connecting arm lower pivot start top move away from the eccentric pivot when the Iterations value drops below 10 and subtle alignment taking place when the Iterations value reaches 30.

3ds max 4

Next Steps

The next steps for this chapter are to create your own models for Sc-02 and use the animation techniques that you learned here to animate your own version of the coolant pump and the induction ring for the VandeGraaff generator. Use a dummy object for that process and create an animating cycle just as you did for the flywheel. Although the coolant pump model that was created for the scene looks complex, the FK and IK setup follows the principle and process of the steps you just used to create the test model.

Another next step is to understand how to quickly adjust the speed of the animation cycles that you create using the Parameter Curve Out-of-Range Types. This is easily accomplished by selecting the dummy object, controlling the animation, and right-clicking its end key in the Track Bar. Do that now by selecting flywheel rotation control and right-clicking the keyframe at frame 12. This opens the keyframe right-click menu shown in Figure 6.73.

Figure 6.73   The keyframe right-click menu enables you to access and adjust several animation parameters, including the frame number at which the specified animation takes place.

Click Flywheel Rotation Control: Rotation at the top of the dialog box. This will open the Flywheel Rotation Control: Rotation dialog box shown in Figure 6.74.

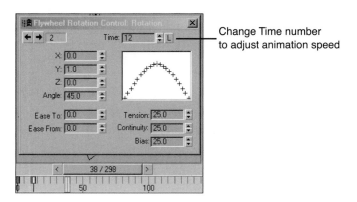

Change Time number to adjust animation speed

Figure 6.74   You can use this dialog box to adjust animation parameters without going into the Track view. To change the speed of the animation, change the frame number and leave this dialog box open while you play the animation. You can also drag the keyframe to a new position in the Track Bar to accomplish the same effect.

Animation speed is based on two factors: motion and time. The flywheel rotation control dummy rotates 45° every 12 frames. If you change the end frame number to 6, it will consequently rotate 45° in just 6 frames, resulting in a rotation twice the original speed. Changing the end frame number to 24 slows the animation to half its original rate, and so forth.

Nothing is more satisfying to a digital artist than having the right tools for the right job. And nothing can be more frustrating than not knowing how to use a tool or not having the right tool in the first place. 3ds max 4 is filled with the right tools, and your journey into mastering them is just beginning. The trip along the way is more than half the fun.

Chapter 7, "Character Design and Animation Principles and Process Overview," is next, where you'll learn the basics of character design and animation known as the Frankenstein Principles.

CREATING EFFECTIVE

CHARACTERS

0-7857-2546-0

Character Design and Animation Principles and Process Overview

"Unhappy man! Do you share my madness? Have you drunk also of the intoxicating draught? Hear me; let me reveal my tale, and you will dash the cup from your lips!" - Excerpt from *Frankenstein*, or *The Modern Prometheus*, by Mary Wollstonecraft Shelley, 1797–1851

As digital artists, we drink the draught of creation and are often intoxicated with the power of the tools we use. Unfortunately, there are no designated drivers to keep us from the wreckage of our own unprincipled application of the digital lightning that gives our max creations life. The madness we share as max artists is a fire in our bellies—we are obsessed with the creation of living, breathing digital creatures; human and otherwise. Indeed, we are the Doctor Frankensteins of our time.

Creating Effective Characters—The Frankenstein Principles at Work

The complex art of animating the characters seen in today's movies and games has evolved into its own specific discipline known as *performance animation*; and performance animators are among the most skilled of all animation professionals. They have to be; the results of their work are open to the critique of the most demanding and sophisticated audiences of all time— they know bad animation when they see it. You can avoid disappointing your audience if you build your work on the foundation of traditional skills and principles.

The bible of character animation is *The Illusion of Life—Disney Animation,* by Frank Thomas and Ollie Johnston. Traditional and digital animators who are intent on mastering their craft adhere to the basic principles of animation articulated so clearly by these two pioneers of animated feature films.

Appendix F, "Animation Principles in Practice," (on the CD in MAXWorkshop\Help_Files\ Appendix_F) contains an overview of the basic principles Frank and Ollie wrote about. I encourage you to read it, complete the tutorial that it contains, and use the principles in your work as a max artist.

Character design and animation in 3ds max 4 are comprised of a complex system of tools and techniques. Although each tool has been designed for a specific purpose, there is a lot of flexibility in how you use them in your process. It's important to understand what the specific tools are and their primary application in a professional process. To that end, the intentions of this chapter are

- To introduce you to the Frankenstein Principles—concepts that are used every day in the character design and animation work at Creative Capers

- To give you an overview of the basic process used for character animation setup

- To provide an overview of how Sc-02 was assembled using the tools and techniques discussed in this Workshop

The digital animators in our studio were traditionally trained 2D animators before their introduction to digital content creation, and this is not an uncommon practice in our industry. Indeed, it is the preferred way to enter into digital performance animation. If you want to be an effective character animator, learn traditional 2D animation as a foundation to your 3D work.

Before the Frankenstein Principles are discussed, there are two important pieces of the foundation of effective character design to look at: caricature and the concept of the Full Character Franchise.

Pixar Rules

This is an excerpt from the *Frequently Asked Questions* section of Pixar's Web site: `www.pixar.com`.

"We do not judge potential candidates on the basis of the school they attended (or didn't). We look at your work first, typically in the form of a videotaped reel... In choosing an animation related school, look for one that focuses on traditional skills, drawing, painting, sculpture, cinematography.

Learn enough about computer graphics to know how they work in general. Look for a school that has not substituted electronic arts for traditional (or vice versa). Ask them about how they balance the two. Avoid just learning packages of software... Learn enough to know you can learn it, but concentrate on the more expressive traditional skills."

Caricature—The Visual Rolodex

My college roommate, T. Daniel Hofstedt, learned the art of caricature from his father and honed it to a razor edge before becoming an animator for Walt Disney feature animation. T. Dan, like other master animators, is a keen observer of the way people look and never passes up an opportunity to doodle the caricature of an unsuspecting victim.

Dan taught me that the fundamental intent of the art of caricature is to exaggerate physical features to capture the visual essence of human form and expression. Through constant daily practice and thousands of drawings, character artists learn to see and interpret the body types and human features they observe into a caricature. The world around them becomes a visual Rolodex full of body parts, expressions, and attitudes waiting to be captured in a few strokes of the pen.

Drawing caricatures is the cornerstone of the foundation of effective character design. The basic technique can be broken down into four simplified steps and one prime directive that you must follow if you want to master the craft.

Caricature: The Prime Directive

If you want to be a master character designer, you must first master the art of caricature. To master the art of caricature, you must do three simple things: draw, draw, draw. When you aren't drawing, you must be observing. When you aren't observing, you must be thinking about drawing. In the words of Earl Nightingale, the strangest secret is "What you think about most of the time is what you'll become." Couple that idea with a sketchpad, a sharp pencil, and an addiction to drawing, and you are on your way to mastery. That is the prime directive.

Step One—Identify the Basic Shapes

The ability to recognize the basic head shape of the person you are drawing is the first skill required in the art of caricature. All head shapes can be derived from primitive shapes—squares, rectangles, triangles, circles, and so on (see Figure 7.1).

Figure 7.1   The steps to create a caricature will be familiar to you—they follow the same process of form development you've been exploring in this Workshop. The first step is to identify and use primitive shapes to develop the rough shape of the caricature. Image © 2001 CCE, Inc.

Step Two—Feature Spacing

Feature spacing is the division of the primitive shape into the proportional relationships of the face and features. Focus on how the head breaks into three basic sections—the forehead, the nose and eyes, and the mouth and chin areas (see Figure 7.2).

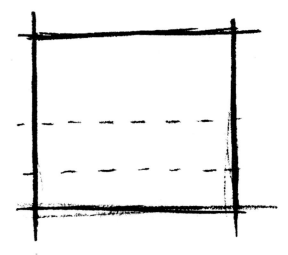

Figure 7.2   The ability to see how primitive shapes are divided into proportional areas is the next step to master. Image © 2001 CCE, Inc.

Step Three—Exaggerate Prominent Features

When the basic shape is divided, the most prominent features are added to the drawing. Exaggeration is the most important tool to use in this step—look for the most prominent features and exaggerate them to the extreme (see Figure 7.3).

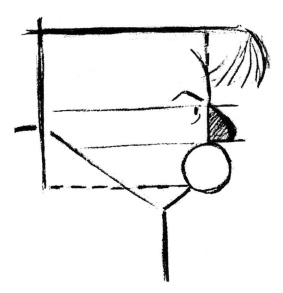

Figure 7.3   Exaggeration is not as easy as it might seem. It takes a kind of perverse enjoyment of visual truth to see and then exploit the opportunity people give us just by being themselves. This is a caricature of me drawn by David Molina. Image © 2001 CCE, Inc.

Step Four—Final Details: Hair, Teeth, and So On

The final details, such as hair, teeth, glasses, clothes, and so on, help complete the picture. But without the first three steps, the final details won't be visually effective. Pay attention to the basic structure and the rest will follow (see Figure 7.4).

Learning how to draw caricatures is an embodiment of the daily practice of learning how to see. When you learn to capture the essence of the living caricatures in everyday life, you will be able to create effective and interesting characters in 3ds max 4.

Figure 7.4   The intent of caricature is to use exaggeration to capture the visual essence of the person. The intention of the process is to train your eye to see shape, proportion, and detail. The final test of the caricature is the reaction it creates in the subject of the drawing. I never like the ones of me, which must mean they are good! Image © 2001 CCE, Inc.

The Full Character Franchise

"Full Character Franchise is more than just the *Back Story*. It is the visual language of the world the character lives in and the visual explanation of who, what, why, and how."
- Sue Shakespeare, President, Creative Capers Entertainment, Inc.

Designing and creating effective characters in our studio is always done in the context of the Full Character Franchise (FCF). This means that the character cannot be created separate from the world to which it belongs. Next to the character itself, the character's world is the most important actor in the script, and both of them must be conceived and created within the realm of four guiding concepts:

- **Physical Logic**—This is the set of rules that governs the physical world within which the character exists, such as gravity, energy, physics, and so forth. These rules must be exposed, explained, and followed. Then the rules must be exploited and sometimes broken for emphasis and to create danger, conflict, and resolution.

- **Memes and Visual Language**—You've read a lot about memes in this Workshop and here they are again. The visual language of the Full Character Franchise uses memes to establish the atmosphere of the world. Powerful examples of effective visual memes used to create a Full Character Franchise are *Bladerunner*, *Star Wars*, *Alien*, *Rambo*, *Spawn*, the *007* films, "Wild, Wild West" television show (not the movie), *Indiana Jones*, and so on.

- **Reality Exposure**—This is the visual exposition of the reality of the character's inner feelings and condition as it is manifested in the character's outer circumstance. The character might be afraid, happy, stupid, or evil, and that inner state must be reinforced by the character's outer world and vice versa. A good example of reality exposure in a character design is Willow Ufgood played by Warwick Davis in the film *Willow* by Ron Howard. Willow is an ordinary man called on his own hero's journey where his true inner nature is exposed and magnified.

- **Motivation Foundation**—This is the visual explanation of why the character is the way he is. You must create a foundation to evaluate the character's possible actions in any given situation.

The Frankenstein Principles—You Are What You Create!

Creating an effective character is the art of putting collected body parts and pieces together—like Dr. Frankenstein's monster. Add a brain and a heart and voilà! A star is born. The fundamental concept to understand is that there is a whole lot of you in the characters you create.

There are five principle elements to keep in mind when you create characters: the brain, the face, the body archetype, the heart and soul, and the infamous wrench. These elements and the principles of action and reaction, contrast and paradox, core motivation, and so forth are interrelated and powerful components of effective character design (see Figure 7.5).

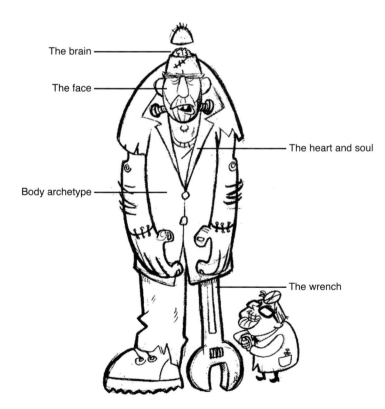

The brain
The face
The heart and soul
Body archetype
The wrench

Figure 7.5   Effective characters will have all five of these elements in their design. That's me as the Doctor and David Molina as the Monster. Image © 2001 CCE, Inc.

Cranium Command

"I could while away the hours, conversing with the flowers, if I only had a brain!" - the Scarecrow, played by Ray Bolger, singing "If I Only Had a Brain," by Harold Arlen, from *The Wizard of OZ*, Warner Brothers, 1939

The brain is the place where character design really starts. Creating the personality and the rules of how a character acts and reacts creates its brain: the control center of everything it does, says, and thinks.

Action/Reaction—Rocket Science

Your character's actions and reactions to external stimulus should follow a well-thought-out set of rules. The good news is that you get to make up the rules and also break them when it serves the story. However, if you try to make up the rules as you go, your characters will be ineffective and your audience will sense the lack of logic and integrity (see Figure 7.6).

Figure 7.6 Actions and reactions reveal the character's inner life and state of being and help the audience to relate to your creation. In this drawing, Koo-Koo Cow and Bacon Boy react to something that threatens them. Their demeanor changes from scared/goofy into ferocity. Koo-Koo Cow and Bacon Boy © 2001 CCE, Inc.

Characters, like children, must have rules for their behavior, if only for the sole purpose of breaking the rules to create humor and drama. That brings you to personality, which is all about contrast and paradox.

The Paradox of Personality

Personality is derived from paradoxical combinations of attributes and characteristics, which describe your character: innocent, sweet, vulnerable, curious, egotistical, angry, mean, happy, depressed, heroic, reluctant, and so on. An infinite number of combinations are possible. Making a cow and a pig into a superhero team provides the kind of contrast needed with character development.

The principles of paradox and contrast are very important and can be used to create unexpected combinations of emotion in your character's personality. Consider the reluctant heroics of characters, such as Neo in *The Matrix*, or the dim brilliance of Winston Groom's Forrest Gump. And don't forget the paradox of personality of the Cowardly Lion or the bumbling accidental success of Peter Sellers as Inspector Clouseau in Blake Edwards's *Pink Panther* movies.

The Face

The face is the window to the soul of the character. Also referred to as the countenance, the design of your character's face should be based on the following elements and concepts.

The Eyes

The character's eyes are the first facial feature with which the audience identifies. The design of the eyes is the foundation for the rest of the facial expression and can be considered the most important feature of the character's face (see Figure 7.7).

Figure 7.7 Eyes express self-importance, fear, anger, and in this case a kind of wide-eyed goofiness. Koo-Koo Cow is looking at Bacon Boy, her eyes are wide and eyebrows raised as if to say "Oops!"

The Expression

The combination of mouth shape and movement; brow, eyebrow, and eye position; facial shape; and design all add up to the expression. Be clear on what inner thought you are trying to convey, and exaggerate the expression for effect (see Figure 7.8).

Showing Emotion—The Mind-Body Connection

Two of the most important questions to answer when you are creating a character and its expression are "What emotional inner state are you trying to express? And what combination of facial and body elements will most effectively show that emotion?" The physical and facial expressions of emotion tell the story without words (see Figure 7.9).

Figure 7.8 Caricature, impersonation, and simple facial movement will yield a clearly understood visual language for the face. To create a believable and effective character, the face must have the ability to express the full range of emotions—even if it has a snout instead of a nose and a mouth!

Figure 7.9 Attitude is the physical expression of an emotional state. Whether it's cocky, sassy, or arrogant, all emotions are revealed in body posture and physical movement. This is the mind-body connection. Bacon Boy is happy until he drops the ham dinner he has made for Koo-Koo Cow. His eyes are sad and his little ears droop in disappointment.

3ds max 4

Archetypal Body Shapes

Archetypes are powerful generalizations that communicate massive amounts of subliminal information—they are memes of the first degree. There are four fundamental body archetypes to use as a place to start your character development. But remember, effective characters are interesting and paradoxical combinations of two or more of the archetypes—it's the interesting combinations that make them believable and memorable.

The Hero

From Xena to Buzz Lightyear, muscles, brawn, brains, and grit conspire to fashion the mighty and bold. The V-shaped torso, bulging biceps, exaggerated proportions, and statuesque poses all add up to the body heroic.

The Villain

Angular, skeletal, slug-like, spidery, and so forth are words used to describe the perfect opposite of the hero. Villains are meant to frighten, horrify, and even disgust us. Their body types must do the same. From Jabba the Hut to Cruella DeVil, villains are the parts of ourselves that we hide, repress, and deny. And they are the characters we love to hate.

The Fool

C3PO, Goofy, and Jar Jar Binks represent the lazy, accident-prone, nerdy, geeky, oblivious side of all of us. Every universe needs comic relief and a contrasting antithesis of the hero. Without the contrast, the hero would be less heroic and the villain less evil.

J. Average

This is the everyday boy or girl next door who embody the heroic in you and me. The body is of normal proportion and the intent of the design is to convey the idea that anyone can and is an everyday hero. *Toy Story*'s Woody, Mickey Mouse, and Stuart Little all populate the world of Joe Average.

Heart and Soul

Characters must have a heart and a soul—or lack of it, in the case of villains. Heart and soul is about the unseen inner life of the character. It's the character's personal mythology and the core motivation for everything the character does in the context of its world. Lily is a good example of what we call *Heart Mythology*! We defined her compassion, sweetness, and curiosity first and then developed a design to fit her heart and soul (see Figure 7.10).

Figure 7.10 Some of the elements of heart and soul include courage, persistence, irreverence, and so on. What grows in the garden of your character's soul shows up in the logic of its actions/reactions, facial expressions, body posture, walk, and so forth. This is the inner story or heart mythology by which your character lives. Lily Travels © 2001 CCE, Inc.

The Wrench

The wrench is the funny bone of a character's design. It appears when the audience thinks it has the character all figured out—such as a superhero cow that eats ham dinners served by her porcine assistant.

Wrenches are visual paradoxes that are designed to redirect the emotional energy of the audience—to turn laughter to tears, humor into disgust, and so on. They are subtle manipulations of reality that are absolutely necessary to simulate the contradictions of the human and inhuman condition. Exaggeration, shocking, anti-social, unexpected, and over-the-top abnormal behaviors are some important wrench terms to keep in mind as you design your characters. The Wrench is powerful; use it sparingly.

Caution

The Wrench is a dastardly and dangerous tool. Although it creates contrast, impact, and paradox, it must still fit into the logic and illogic of the universe within which it resides. When misused, it can have negative consequences, especially if the audience doesn't get the joke!

Myths, Legends, and the Inner Worlds

The basic principles and elements of effective character design give you a lot of freedom to explore the world inside your own mind. Great animators are students of the human condition, and great storytellers know how to reach into the depths of the human psyche. If you are interested in reading more about inner mythology, read the books by Robert A. Johnson. Start with *The Fisher King* and *The Handless Maiden*, which, like most of his books, are based on archetypal mythology.

The basics of character design and the principles of animation converge when you begin to explore the art of character modeling and animation in 3ds max 4. The Workshop section of this chapter is next and it introduces you to the process and some of the basic tools you'll need. This chapter contains a small drop in the very large ocean of this important part of max 4. Mastery of character design and animation will take years of experience and dedication, and more than this book can provide. Welcome to the first step in your own max character animation hero's journey!

Sharpen the Saw—Process, Tutorials, and Customizing the Quad Menus

At the beginning of this book, a time-honored maxim was used to set the tone for this Workshop: "Give a man a fish and you feed him for a day. Teach a man to fish and you feed him for a lifetime." The principles at the core of this saying are self-reliance, independence, and education, and those principles and the fishing analogy are perfect for much of what you'll do as a digital artist. Like fishing, learning to animate takes patience, timing, mastery of the basics, and consistent daily effort, and, most importantly, you have to know where to go to find what you are seeking. Knowledge is caught and wrestled into the boat of your mind—and sometimes an idea is thrown back into the river to mature a little more. And sometimes you catch the big one, the main concept, which makes all the daily effort worthwhile.

Dozens of books and hundreds of tutorials fill the shelves and tables in my office, and all of them hold gems of insight that have added to my independence and self-reliance as a max artist. So, as I began writing this chapter, I asked myself what I could say or show you about animation that would be of the most worth to you as an artist. The answer is "Process!"

The Power of Process

In *3D Studio MAX 3.0 Workshop* I said, "True creativity is creation within some structural constraint, whether self imposed or as the result of the time and budget limitations of a (digital) production. When these constraints are present, your individual creative process becomes the savior of your brilliant vision."

Our process at Creative Capers is a major part of the foundation of our reputation. Without exception, one of the first requests we get from production executives is "Tell me about your process!" This is a very common question. It shines a big spotlight of reality on our ability to get the job done, on time and on budget. Be ready, you will also be asked this question.

The process we use to get our vision onto the screen is the most important thing we create. Productions come and go and films arrive and disappear, but process endures and it is a key component of getting and keeping the clients we work with.

The technical directors on our staff are responsible for the production process and their day-to-day activities are focused on building the *pipeline*. Building the production pipeline includes everything from customized tools and asset management to texturing, animation, and lighting processes and the intricate tasks needed to set up character models for performance animation and lip synch dialogue. TV and film production is a monstrously complex undertaking, which will fail unless it's driven by an effective and powerful process.

So, the thing of most worth that I can give you regarding character design and animation is an overview of our process here at Creative Capers Entertainment. Although our process differs from other studios in some practical details, the principles are universal and use the great tools provided in max 4.

3ds Max 4 Animation Tools and Process Tutorials

Before you begin the overview of the character animation processes and tools in 3ds max 4, there is a homework assignment to complete. To help you fully understand the concepts in this chapter, go through the following excellent tutorials that came with your software:

- **Tutorial 11: Setting Up Bones**—Shows you how to set up a skeleton using max 4's new Bones system.

- **Tutorial 12: Setting up IK**—Takes you through the basic process of setting up and using max 4's revamped inverse kinematics to create and control character animation. It also shows you how to use the new Slider manipulator and the new Parameter Wiring dialog box.

- **Tutorial 13: Using Skin and Flex**—Skin and Flex are two key character animation modifiers in the max 4 toolbox. Skin allows you to attach the Bones and IK systems that you set up to the mesh surface of the characters you create. This makes the mesh into a skin controlled by the bones to which it is attached—hence the name of the modifier. The Flex modifier is used to add realistic secondary or overlapping motion to your models. It has a limited soft-body dynamic capability that enables you to simulate cloth and other materials that you want to drape over the objects in your scene.

- **Tutorial 14: Animating a Character**—Shows you how to create the most basic movement of all character animation: the walk cycle. It also takes you through the tool we use to animate facial expression and lip synch to dialogue: morph targets.

The tutorials are also available within the max workspace by clicking Help, Tutorials and opening the files. All the basic tools and processes in these tutorials were used to create the Alien animation you see in Sc-02. After you complete these tutorials, return to this chapter for an overview of how these tools and techniques fit into the step-by-step process of a production pipeline.

Sharpen the Saw—Customizing the Quad Menus

The max 4 interface can be customized to meet your animation and modeling processes. This is one of the greatest parts of the ergonomic design of max 4 and anticipates your long-term need to turn max into a personalized toolbox. Customizing the user interface, specifically the Quad Menus, is something that you should do now while you are first learning to use the software. You'll learn the basic process here, but you should study your User Reference to gain a complete understanding of the Quad Menu system.

 Tip

The Quad Menu system is new to 3ds max 4. Consequently, your User Reference goes into great detail about how to customize and use this great new interface tool. Use the keyword *Quad Menu* to access the information.

Take Care of Yourself

There are many compelling reasons to learn to use the Quad Menus in your max work, including increased productivity, physical health, and comfort. Touting comfort and health as a reason to learn a specific way of using max might seem odd until you read the medical reports of the many artists suffering from carpal tunnel syndrome or other repetitive motion ailments. When you consider the miles of mouse movement you will incur by roaming all over the interface looking for the tool you want, and the subsequent wear and tear on your hand and fingers used to manipulate the mouse, comfort becomes a huge factor in the long-term ease of use of the max software. Take care of yourself and your hands by learning to use max's interface shortcuts and by customizing your Quad Menus. You'll be glad you did.

So far in this Workshop, you have been using the default Quad Menus that appear when you right-click in the viewport or over a selected object. It won't be long before you get tired of using the Command Panels and toolbars, roaming from one to the other and back again. Since max 4 was released, I have been steadily customizing and refining my default Quad Menus to fit how I work on a day-to-day basis. It has made a big difference in my productivity and is a lot of fun to use. Figure 7.11 shows my customized version of a Quad Menu.

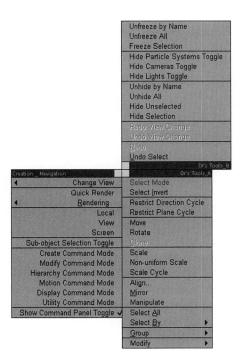

Figure 7.11   You might have to force yourself to give up using the rest of the interface to learn how to use the Quad Menus effectively. The first step is to add the Customize User Interface command to your default Quad Menu.

327

3ds max 4

To customize the Quad Menus, follow these steps:

1. Choose Customize, Customize User Interface in the main Menu Bar. When the Customize User Interface dialog box opens, click the Quads tab.

2. In the middle of the dialog box, you'll see an iconic version of the Quad Menu boxes. The lower-right quadrant is yellow, which indicates that it is currently selected and can be edited (see Figure 7.12). Click the upper-left quadrant to select it—the contents of this quad will appear in the list below it.

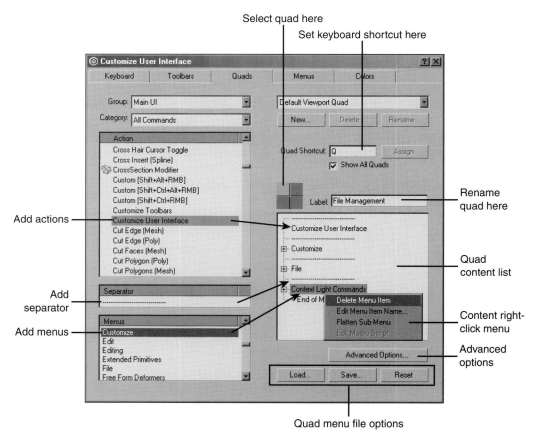

Figure 7.12 The Quad Menu options enable you to save and load your Quad Menus and reset them to the version that was active when you opened max for this work session. Advanced Options lets you change the color and font style of the selected quad and specify how it appears in the viewport.

3. Right-click the items in the list and select Delete Menu Item from the pop-up menu. Delete the entire list—each item in turn—to make room for your version of this quad.

Character Design and Animation
Principles and Process Overview

4. Rename this Quad File Management in the Label text box, and change the keyboard shortcut to a key of your choice in the Quad Shortcut text box. When you press this shortcut key, the entire default Quad Menu will open, not just the quad you are currently editing.

5. Drag and drop the Customize User Interface command from the Action List and the Customize, File menu from the Menus list on the left side of the dialog box into the content list on the right side, and then drag separator lines over to organize the content list. The Quads tab should look like Figure 7.12, shown previously.

6. Close the Customize User Interface dialog box when you are finished.

Caution

If you choose to save a specific version of the Quad Menu setup you just created, click Save and specify a new name. Don't save over any of the default or existing files in the 3ds max 4 UI folder; you might want to get back to the default settings. Saving under a different name will keep those settings intact for future use and also allow you to set up, save, and load specialized Quad Menus for repetitive processes.

Right-click in any viewport to access the new Quad Menu. You'll see that your changes are now embedded into the quad, as shown in Figure 7.13.

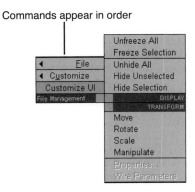

Figure 7.13 The added commands appear in the order they were added to the content list and in relation to the orientation of the quad in which they reside. In this case, Customize User Interface was first in the content list and appears at the bottom of this quad.

Whenever you select a command from the Quad Menu, the text turns blue, indicating that it was the command that was last selected and specifying it as the quick pick for that specific quad. When this is the case, you don't need to click the actual command in the Quad Menu again to invoke it, all you need to do is open the quad and click its title bar (see Figure 7.14).

Tip

At times, max's depth can seem a little overwhelming. But the depth is also what is most satisfying about max—there is always something to learn and discover about this great set of tools. There are several other recommended productivity tools that I use every day, which aren't covered in this Workshop. Open your User Reference and take some time to study the following subjects: Isolate Tool, Draft Render and Production Render rendering modes, ActiveShade, Auto Window/Crossing Direction, and the Array dialog box.

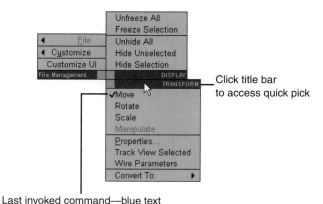

Figure 7.14   The quick pick feature of the Quad Menu system makes repetitive commands easy. Two right-clicks and the command previously selected in the quad is invoked. The quick pick command changes whenever a new command is chosen from the quad, which in turn makes the newly selected command the active quick pick.

Character Animation Setup Overview

Becoming a character animator is not something that can be learned in a few days or from an animation book or a tutorial—there's more to it than just knowledge of the tools involved. Two key factors will affect your progress toward mastering the illusion of life: your study and understanding of anatomy—the musculoskeletal system, the central nervous system, physiology, and kinesiology—and your dedication to learning max's character-animation tools. Along the path, you'll realize that the body is the most complex machine ever created, and it becomes easier to understand and simulate when it's simplified into its component systems.

Mirror, Mirror

Using the body and its systems as a paradigm for your character animation is similar in principle to using an automobile as the paradigm for all the machine animation you'll ever create. Both are machines of the highest order, and every kind of motion, restriction, cause, and effect imaginable can be observed within the context of their function. Of course, it's a lot easier, but still not recommended, to take your car apart to see how pistons work. Books will provide some of what you need and anatomy classes a little more. But the greatest animation reference you have is the bag of bones you sit in: your body. Master animators are unusually good physical actors that often use mirrors to look at their own facial expressions and body movement to create their animation.

The character creation, animation setup, and animation process can be equally mysterious and complex until each part of the system is defined and placed in the context of the holistic process. Knowing *when* to do something is as important as knowing what to do.

Tip

In addition to Angie Jones and Sean Bonney's excellent book, *3D Studio MAX 3 Professional Animation*, there is another book you should read: Isaac Victor Kerlow's *The Art of 3-D: Computer Animation and Imaging, Second Edition*, published by John Wiley & Sons. I met Isaac while he was VP of Design at Disney Interactive, and his book is an excellent resource for your journey.

A Nine-Step Program

In a production studio, the artists charged with creating a character work together through the common bond of a shared process. Each artist knows exactly what her fellow animators need to do their jobs and is guided by their shared vision of the end result and the process needed to get there. In smaller studios such as Creative Capers, the steps are just as clearly defined as in larger production studios. But the difference is that the same artist who creates the character model in our studio might very well be the one to set it up for animation and sometimes animate it as well. The same individual tasks tend to be more compartmentalized in larger production houses such as ILM or Pixar to meet production schedules.

The following sections outline nine basic steps in the character creation and animation process we use in our productions. It's important to note that many of these steps are iterative, interrelated, and often take place concurrently. Putting them in order gives you an idea of their order in a perfect world.

Tip

You can find completed models of the Alien head for Sc-02 and a complete Alien body to use for your own IK setup experiments in MAXWorkshop\Help_Files\ Chapter_7\ EXSc-03_Alien_Head.max and EXSC-02_Alien_Complete.max.

Step 1: Pre-Production Design

Character designs are finalized through sketches and 3D sculpted *figurines* before they are created in the computer. This is a sometimes painful and always iterative process because it is the birth of the character. Combining the often divergent and ever-changing input from the director, writer, and producer into an approved character design can take months of dedicated work (see Figure 7.15).

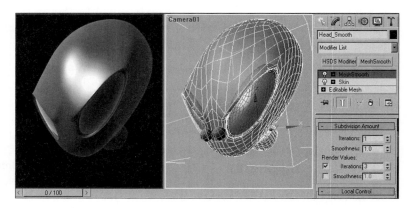

Figure 7.15 Artists that specialize in character design create the character concepts for Creative Capers. Effective character design embodies the ideas outlined in the Frankenstein Principles in this chapter. Of course, it's a lot easier when you are creating a character for your own productions; you only have to please yourself.

Step 2: Setting Up the World Scale

Characters are designed with their context and story in mind, which includes the world within which they reside and the other characters that will populate the world. While the character design is in process, the technical and art directors work together in the pre-production design of the character's world. This process includes 2D sketches and preliminary digital work to establish the relative size and scale of the world and the analogous size of the characters that will populate the world.

In recent work, we have been using real-world measurements for our worlds and the characters that populate them. In other words, feet and inches are used as units of measurement and the characters are created in that setup—an average adult male being 5'10" to 6'1", and so forth.

Establishing scale at the beginning of the process is critical. If it's set up later, after characters are skinned onto their IK systems for example, the character IK systems will have to be rebuilt. There are three dialog boxes that we use to set up the real-world scale we use in max 4: Units Setup, Preference Settings (System Unit Scale section), and Grid and Snap Settings (Home Grid page):

- **Units Setup**—The settings in the Units Setup dialog box define the measurement system used in the max 4 workspace. Click Customize, Units Setup to open this dialog box. We use US Standard, Decimal Feet for our work. The important thing is to use the same system throughout a production so that the characters, props, machines, and characters will work together correctly.

- **System Unit Scale**—Click Customize, Preferences to open the Preference Settings dialog box shown in Figure 7.16. In the top-left corner of the General tab, you'll see the System Unit Scale section. We set our system unit scale to 1 unit equals 0.05 inches. The System Unit Scale defines the scale of the basic 3ds max 4 unit, which is the standard measurement in the max workspace.

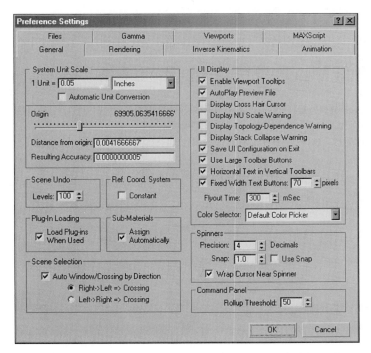

Figure 7.16   If you check the Automatic Unit Conversion box, merged objects that were created with a different measurement system will be scaled up or down to maintain their correct size. However, be advised that scaling merged objects will affect the scalable aspects of your environment settings, geometry, materials, and so forth.

- **Home Grid**—The settings in the Home Grid tab of the Grid and Snap Settings dialog box control the size and division settings of the world space grid that is displayed in your viewport. Press G to toggle it on and off. Right-click 3d Snap Toggle ⟨ icon ⟩ to display the Grid and Snap Settings dialog box, and then click the Home Grid tab to access and adjust the grid options (see Figure 7.17).

Figure 7.17 The home grid that we use is set to show a grid divided into .05 feet/units with the dark major division lines every 10 units. That means that the distance between each major division line is .5 feet.

Step 3: Creating the Mesh Model—One-Box Modeling

Although many studios use other methods, such as NURBS, to create their character models, we use the MeshSmooth technique you learned about in Chapter 6, "Machines in Motion: Modeling and Kinematics," and Appendix E, "How MeshSmooth Works" (on the CD).

 3D Studio MAX 3 Magic, published by New Riders, is a cool book that has some great tutorials from masters of 3D Studio MAX: Jeffrey Abouaf, Neil Blevins, Sean Bonney, Brandon Davis, Sanford Kennedy, Doug King, Michael Todd Peterson, Sung-wook Su, and one of my favorite max artists, the amazing Eni Oken. Check out her Web site at www.oken3d.com. Also watch for Sean's new book *3ds max 4 Magic*.

Tip

Using Turn-Around Drawings

After the sketches for a character are approved, the character designer will create a *turn-around* drawing. The turn-around creates front, right, rear, left, and sometimes top views of the character to be used as a guide for the digital artist in his modeling work. The sketch is scanned in and then used in the Diffuse color component map of a material applied to Plane objects. The materials I use are 100% self-illuminating, which allows me to see the sketch regardless of the light settings in the scene.

A front and side view plane will usually be sufficient for the process. The model is then created by starting with a primitive object, usually a box, in a method known as *Box Modeling* (see Figure 7.18).

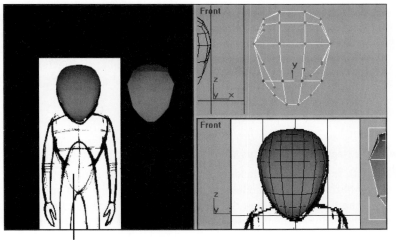

Turn-around drawing

ActiveShade Viewport mode   See-Through mode

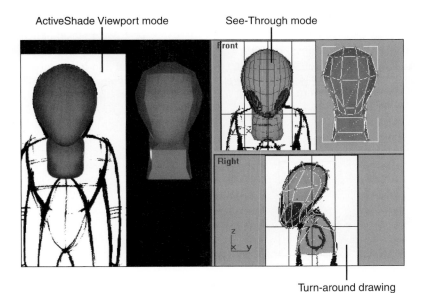

Turn-around drawing

Figure 7.18 The purpose of the one-box modeling method is to create a single contiguous mesh skin. This single skin and the bones attached to it create the realistic look of muscles and skin stretching as your character animates.

3ds max 4

I use the See-Through mode for selected objects to see the turn-around drawing behind them while the viewport is set to Shaded mode. You can activate the See-Through mode in the Display command panel, Display Properties rollout. I also use the ActiveShade mode to see the rendered version of the model as I am creating it. This helps me to evaluate it in terms of its shadows and highlights without having to stop my modeling process to test render the model.

Starting with the Head—Halves Versus Wholes

I like starting with the head in my models, but where you start is up to you. Other artists prefer to create half of the character model first and then mirror-copy it to create the other side and attach it to the first half, welding the centerline vertices together. I prefer to model the whole forms of the head and main torso at the same time—it takes a little more concentration and care in the process to keep vertices lined up, but it helps me to see the entire form without having to wait for the second-half copy (see Figure 7.19).

Modeling Extremities

The most difficult parts of a character model are the expressive parts—face, hands, and feet. These are the parts that express, gesture, and dance the life into the character you are animating. Your knowledge of anatomy, specifically facial muscles, hand and foot bones, and structure is an invaluable asset in this part of the modeling process (see Figure 7.20).

Model one arm/hand

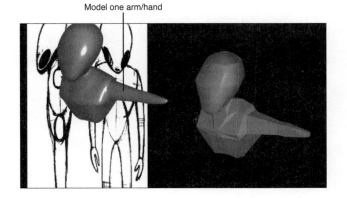

Mirror copy and attach

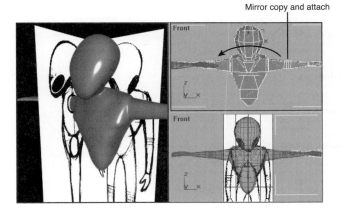

Extruded faces

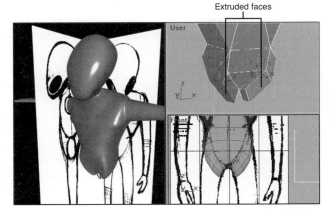

Figure 7.19 I always model extremities such as arms, hands, and fingers on one side first and then mirror copy the entire arm-hand mesh to the other side. Creating hands and fingers is one of the most challenging and interesting parts of the process, and getting it right will draw upon your knowledge of anatomy.

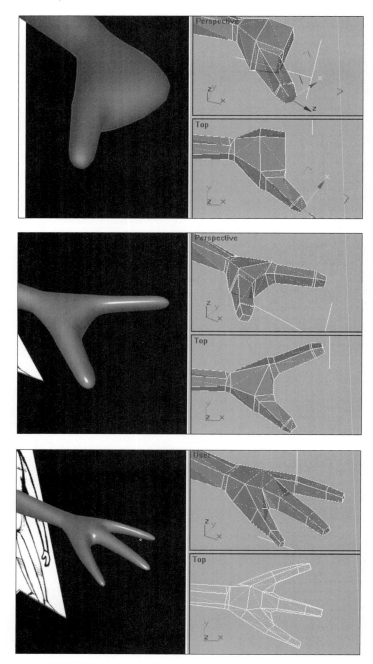

Figure 7.20 Getting the proportion of the hands and feet is critical and they can be exaggerated for the sake of caricature. However, any exaggeration should be dictated by the approved character design sketches you are using to guide your process—don't try to invent the details as you model; use drawings to guide you.

The da Vinci Pose

All character models are modeled with their arms outstretched, hands and palms facing the ground, feet in normal relaxed standing posture. Known as the da Vinci pose, this position facilitates the modeling process and the addition of the bones and other animation controls, and helps the mesh deform correctly when the model is animated pose to pose (see Figure 7.21).

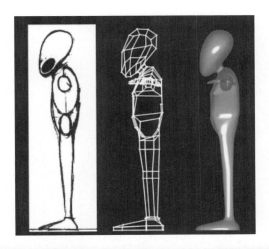

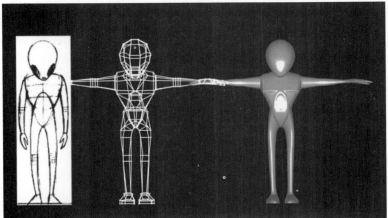

Figure 7.21   If the arms were hanging down from the shoulder, it would be difficult if not impossible to model the underside of the arm. Creating a spread-eagle pose alleviates that problem and keeps the mesh from being pre-bent at any of the joints.

Step 4: Adding the Skeleton—Max Bones

The first subsystems of the body, which correspond to animation tools in max, are the skin, muscles, and bones. The skin is created using the MeshSmooth modeling process and the bones are created using the max Bones system, helper objects, and other max geometry. Adding bones to the model creates the skeleton that will be animated to run, walk, jump, and so forth—whatever the scene action requires. Figure 7.22 shows the Alien with the bone skeleton in place before the Skin modifier is applied.

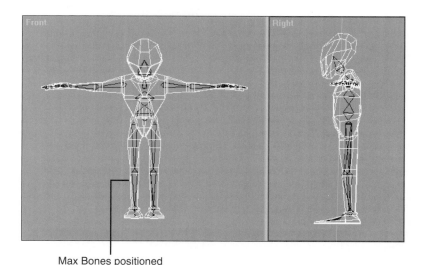

Max Bones positioned

Figure 7.22   In max 4, as in our bodies, muscles and bones control the movement of the skin. Any object can be used as a bone or a muscle control object—in this model some max helper objects were created to help define and orient the bones correctly.

Step 5: The Muscles and Nervous System—IK Setup and Wiring the Skeleton

Max's IK solvers and the way you apply them to the bones correspond to the muscle and nervous systems of the body, which is the next major subsystem you'll add to the skeleton before using the Skin modifier. Other helper objects, such as dummy and point helpers, nonrendering splines, and so on, are linked and wired to the basic IK setup using the Link command and the Wire Parameters tool. This is the nervous system that controls the IK muscles attached to the bones.

Slider manipulators are set up and wired to the dummy and control objects to make the animation process easier. Customized scripts are written to control finger and hand movement, and eyes are controlled by Look At constraints or wired to follow other helper objects (see Figure 7.23).

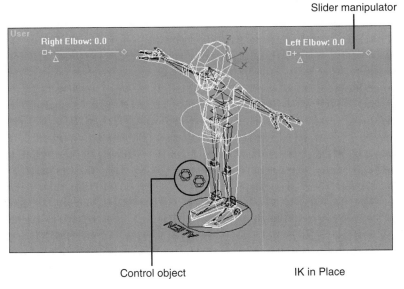

Slider manipulator

Right Elbow: 0.0   Left Elbow: 0.0

Control object   IK in Place

Figure 7.23   After the entire IK system is wired and in place, the model is ready to be skinned. After it's skinned, the performance animators can begin working on their part of the project using low-rez versions of the model.

Step 6: Low Rez, High Rez, and the Tootsie Roll

Typically, three versions of the model are used to develop the animation for a character in our process. Performance animators and technical animators at this point in the process have divergent needs. The performance animators need to work quickly and don't want the high-rez models to slow their system or their animation process. The tech animators need to refine the skeletal system and bone envelopes to make the mesh skin deform correctly. Using low-rez versions of the model can accommodate both needs.

There are two basic ways to create low-rez models. Placing the Skin modifier below the final MeshSmooth modifier in the modifier stack allows an animator to animate using a low-rez version of the model while still having access to the high-rez version further up the stack (see Figure 7.24).

The process, at this point, usually has some conflict. The technical animators charged with setting up the Bones systems might still be refining the bone envelopes to get the final mesh to deform correctly—and the performance animators need to move ahead with their work. The solution is to give the performance animators a different kind of low-rez model that doesn't need to include the finished bone envelopes. This creates what is known as a *tootsie roll model* and allows the animator to begin his work while the tech director works to complete the bone envelopes. To create a tootsie roll model, split up the mesh by selecting and detaching the polygon mesh for the fingers from the hands, the hand mesh from the forearms, the forearm surfaces from the upper arms, and so forth. This creates a puppet-like model, which can be used by the performance animators while the tech animators finish their work.

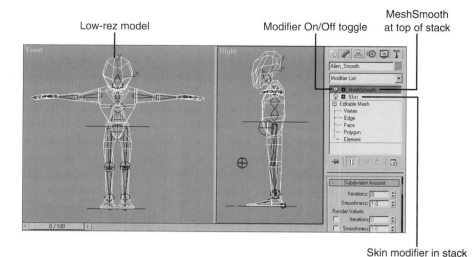

Low-rez model — Modifier On/Off toggle — MeshSmooth at top of stack — Skin modifier in stack

Figure 7.24 By turning the top-level MeshSmooth modifier off, you can animate using the low-rez version of the model.

Step 7: Adding the Skin Modifier—Adjusting the Envelopes

The Skin modifier enables you to attach bones to the mesh skin of the character model. It's applied to the mesh model of the character first, and then the bones are added and their envelopes adjusted to deform the mesh correctly during animation to complete the skin process. The tutorials in your 3ds max 4 documentation will show you how to adjust the envelopes to create realistic deformation and animation.

Step 8: Adding the Top-Level MeshSmooth Modifier

The next step after the bone envelopes are adjusted is to add the top-level MeshSmooth modifier to the modifier stack. There are several ways to do this and some tech animators don't do it at all, preferring to adjust the density of the mesh using the existing MeshSmooth modifier that sits in the stack before the Skin modifier. The intent of this part of the process is to refine the IK and control setup without being slowed down by high-rez meshes.

Step 9: Animating the Alien Head—Morph Targets

The tool of choice in 3ds max 4 for facial expression and dialogue lip synch animation is the Morpher modifier. The steps to animate the Alien head for Sc-02 are to make several copies of the original Alien head and then deform the mesh copies into discreet facial expressions. Adding a Morpher modifier to the original head then allows you to use the modified copies as morph targets animating from expression to expression. The procedure is outlined in detail in Tutorial 14: Animating a Character in your max User Reference. Figure 7.25 shows the morph targets for the Alien head animation in Sc-02 and the slider manipulators that have been wired to drive the morph targets.

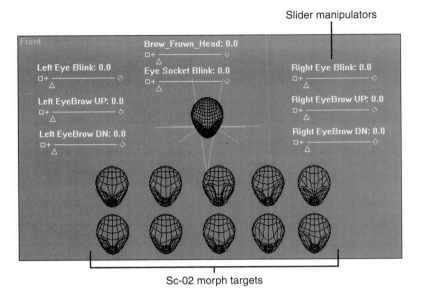

Slider manipulators

Sc-02 morph targets

Figure 7.25 Selecting and transforming the vertices of the head mesh can create expressions such as happy, curious, scared, and so on. Morph-target animation isn't just for facial expressions; it can be used to create weird organic transformations in any object.

Max Workshop—Assembling Sc-03

This section of the chapter gives you an overview of some of the other types of animation techniques in max and how they were used to create Sc-02. But, first things first—there are always some important things to put in place before you start a new scene. And the story at this point needs to be discussed as well.

Sc-03 Scene Setup

Sc-03 is a new scene and shares only one asset with the other scenes in Area51.avi—a still image from Sc-02 used as the background layer. The completed files for Sc-02 can be found in MAXWorkshop\Help_Files\Chapter_7. In addition to the Alien head and body models referenced in the previous chapter, the completed scene, EXSc-03.max, is also in the Help Files directory. If you want to make your own Alien head using the MeshSmooth/one-box technique, use EXSc-03_Alien_Head as a reference for you work. EXSc-03.max will help you as you set up your own version of the scene.

The frame rate for Sc-03 is set to Film (24 FPS), frame count of 192, and the same 640×346 output size as the rest of the Area51.avi scenes.

The Story

Sc-03 takes place inside the cooling tower, adjacent to the massive generators and coolant pumps in Sc-02. The disembodied Alien heads are wired into the control circuits of the power plant. When the scene opens, a klaxon warning is sounding and wakes the Alien in the foreground—sleeping on the job again. It wakes up, blinks, and looks around for the source of the problem. Then the Alien looks into the camera and frowns just as the scene cuts to Sc-04_05 and the explosion that destroys the cooling tower.

Sc-03 Background Image—Animating Material Editor Components

Sc-03 uses a still image of the interior of the cooling tower borrowed from one of the final frames of Sc-02 and added as the background Environment map in the Environment dialog box. The problem is that the BG image is blue, which is fine for half of the shot when the red alert lights aren't pulsing. But it needs to be red for the other half of the shot, alternating between red and blue in synch with the warning klaxon.

At this point, there are two alternatives. I could take the blue BG into Photoshop, change its color to red, and save it as another image file. I could then add both the red image and the blue image into Video Post in separate Image Input Event layers and adjust their VP Start and End Times to alternate between red and blue background images. This would create the basic look I want but not the abrupt change and the brief fade from one color to the next. The second alternative is to animate the color of the background image using the Color Map settings in the Material Editor.

Animating Material Output Parameters

The following steps show how to animate the Color Map settings in the Output rollout of the background image in the Material Editor:

1. Open the Material Editor, select the background material, and open its Output rollout, as shown in Figure 7.26.

2. Change to Animation mode and animate the Output Amount to the following: at frame 0: 1.0; frame 36: 3.0; and frame 48: 1.0.

3. At frame 36, drag the right control point of the control curve for the G and B channels down to zero. This leaves only the Red channel active and creates the red image needed for the background at this point in time.

4. At frame 48, return the control point for the G and B channels to their full values by dragging it back to its original position. This returns the BG image to its original blue color.

5. Open Track view and select in turn the Output track, the Curve 2 (Green) and Curve 3 (Blue) tracks, and change their Parameter Curve Out of Range Types ⬚ to Cycle ⬚, as shown in Figure 7.27.

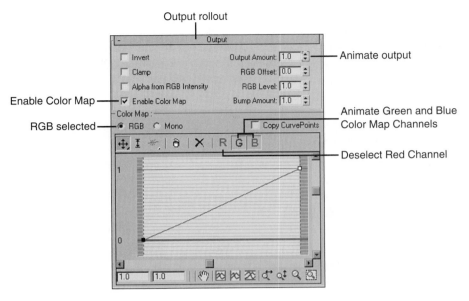

Figure 7.26 Animating the Output Amount brightens the background map when it's in red mode. Animating the Green and Blue channels of the Color Map changes the BG color from its original blue to red.

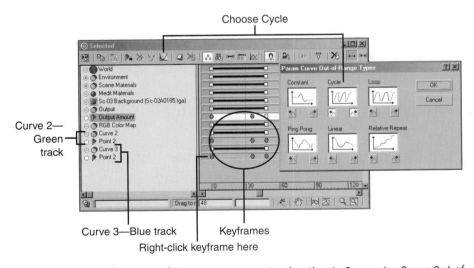

Figure 7.27 Changing the Material Output component animation to Parameter Curve Out of Range Cycle type makes the specified animation repeat for the entire length of the scene.

6. The last step in this basic process is to right-click all the keyframes and change their Bezier Tangents to make the Red BG pop on abruptly and then ease back to blue starting at frame 36 and ending at frame 48. At frame 49, the cycle begins again as the Red BG pops on. Figure 7.28 shows the Bezier Tangent controllers for the Output Amount at the three frames of the cycle. Curve 2 and Curve 3 are also set up with the same sequence of Bezier Tangent controllers.

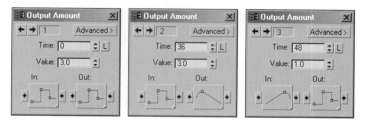

Figure 7.28 The Bezier Tangent controllers are explained in full detail in Appendix F (on the CD). Animating material components is a powerful and enjoyable facet of material development in 3ds max 4.

The same process was applied to the diffuse color of the containment vessels, animating their color from red to blue and back again using the same three-frame animation cycle. In addition to the animating BG map and containment vessel diffuse color, the color of the light offscreen to the left was also animated in the same 0,36,48 three-frame cycle (see Figure CP.12 in the color section).

Sc-03FG—Creating Bubbles

Chapter 8, "Trompe L'oeil: The Art of Visual Effects," takes you through the process to add a PArray particle system to your scene and show you how to use scene geometry as a particle emitter. You'll use the process to blow up the cooling tower in Sc-04_05. A variation on that process uses the optional presets in the PArray's Modify command panel and a Gravity Space Warp to pull the bubbles up correctly. Figure 7.29 shows the Alien's head emitting bubbles and the Load/Save Presets rollout.

Creating Depth Using Render Effects Blur

The last major effect to talk about is an important component of all scene development: depth of field. Cameras in max have an infinite depth of field, which means that everything in the scene is in crystal clear, sharp focus regardless of how far it is from the camera POV. This is interesting but not the way we see our world, nor is it the way real cinematographers would shoot a scene such as Sc-02.

The star of this scene is the Alien and, with all that's going on around it, there is a real possibility that it will get lost in the visual noise of the warning lights, the gravitron animation, and so forth. Blurring the background slightly while leaving the Alien and his containment vessel in clear focus in the foreground creates a more interesting image and enhances the 3D feel of the scene.

Figure 7.29 The Load/Save Presets rollout contains some pretty cool premade particle effects to add to your max scenes.

Max has several ways to blur your backgrounds, including some very sophisticated multi-pass rendering technology available in the camera parameters. I chose to keep it simple and render the scene in two layers. The foreground Alien is rendered in focus and the background layer—consisting of the rest of the vessels, the fluidics gravitron, and the BG environment map—is blurred to create the depth needed for this shot.

Appendix G, "Adding Rendering Effects to Your Max 4 Imagery," can be found on the CD in MAXWorkshop\Help_Files\Appendix _G.pdf. This appendix takes you through the process of adding special lighting and image effects to your rendered imagery. Figure 7.30 shows the

Rendering Effects dialog box used to create the imagery shown in Figure CP.12 in the color section of this book. Look for opportunities to use this technique in your max scenes. It will show that you understand a basic cinematic principle, which brings me to my final book recommendations for this chapter.

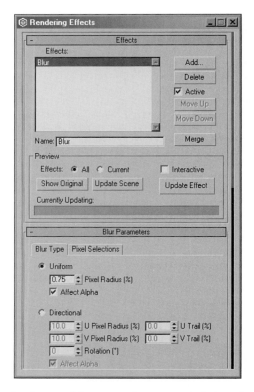

Figure 7.30 Blurring the background imagery of your scenes brings the foreground images in to sharp relief and enhances the feeling of depth and atmosphere in your close-up and medium-range shots.

Cinematography

If I were to create a curriculum for aspiring digital artists, a major component would be structured around the principles and elements of cinematography. Several books can help you understand the basics of this important subject, but like everything else about max and digital-content creation, the learning process is a journey that never ends—one or two books won't do it. Here they are anyway. Dr. D's recommendations for books on digital and traditional filmmaking:

- *The Five C's of Cinematography: Motion Picture Filming Techniques* by Joseph V. Mascelli; published by Silman James Press.

- *Film Directing Shot by Shot: Visualizing from Concept to Screen* by Steven D. Katz; published by Focal Press.

- *The Filmmaker's Handbook: A Comprehensive Guide for the Digital Age* by Steven Ascher, Edward Pincus, Carol Keller (Illustrator), Robert Brun, and Ted Spagna (Photographer); published by Plume.

- *Special Effects* by Richard Rickitt; published by Watson-Guptill.

- *The IFILM Digital Video Filmmaker's Handbook 2001* by Maxie D. Collier; published by Lone Eagle Publishing Company.

Next Steps

The next step for Sc-02 is to create your own version of the scene, including the animated Alien head and control area. If you're feeling adventurous, use the complete Alien body model and animate it in the scene. It could be walking through or holding a clipboard, checking up on the slackers in the containment vessels.

One lighting effect that you could add to the scene is the Tesla light you'll learn about in Chapter 8. Use the effect to create some offscreen light on the right side of the scene models.

Another particle system added to the Alien and animated to correspond to an inhale-exhale cycle would make the Alien look like it was breathing the fluid in the containment vessel. A snoring sound effect synched up to the animation would complete the effect.

The final next step for this chapter is to render out the blurred background and the foreground layers and use Video Post to composite them. Render out the 192-frame sequence in 640×346 output and update your animatic.

Chapter 8, "Trompe L'oeil: The Art of Visual Effects," is next and will introduce you to the fundamental concepts to keep in mind as you create special visual effects in max. And you'll learn how to blow things up—personally my favorite thing to do.

SPECIAL EFFECTS

PRINCIPLES / PROCESS

0-7857-2545-0

Trompe L'oeil: The Art of Visual Effects

Trompe L'oeil literally means the *trick of the eye* and is defined as "visual deception, especially in paintings, in which objects are rendered in extremely fine detail emphasizing the illusion of tactile and spatial qualities." When the eye is fooled, it triumphs over the cognitive rational brain—*trompe l'oeil*.

The purpose of visual effects is to fool the mind by tricking the eyes of the audience members into seeing what you want them to see; for example, optical illusions. Whether it's the digital re-creation of a 3,000-year-old mummy or the use of Q-tips to create a crowd of people watching a race in a far-away galaxy, visual effects shots have become the modern expression of magic and illusion in TV shows, commercials, and feature films.

Scientists have proven that our minds don't know the difference between reality and what they are seeing on the screen—subconsciously we want to believe it's all real. The power and challenge of trompe l'oeil, as it's applied to digital visual effects, is to create illusion without breaking the audience's suspension of disbelief.

TV, movies, and other intense visual media bypass our imagination by feeding imagery directly to the visual cortex. The danger to the audience members is that when nothing is left to the imagination, their ability to imagine can be impaired or even destroyed. For trompe l'oeil to be effective, you must engage the audience members' minds by not showing every possible minute detail in a shot. Alfred Hitchcock and Ridley Scott are masters of engaging the brain and eye in a more imaginative and cognitive process by always leaving something to the imagination.

Today's special effects and digital animation studios produce thousands of minutes of animation and effects for virtually every film made in the industry. And now this visual effects revolution is changing the face of television. The bottom line is that there has never been a better time to become a digital visual effects artist.

On the Shoulders of Giants

Ray Harryhausen and George Pal built the foundation of modern visual effects. VFX pioneers, such as John Dykstra, Joe Johnston, Dennis Muren, Ridley Scott, and Phil Tippet, have continued the expansion of this amazing field of imagination and magic. They are a few of the visual effects giants upon whose shoulders we all stand. To learn more about visual effects, I recommend the following six books: *Industrial Light and Magic: The Art of Special Effects* by Thomas G. Smith (George Lucas, Introduction); *Industrial Light & Magic: Into the Digital Realm* by Mark Cotta Vaz and Patricia Rose Duignan; *Future Noir: The Making of Blade Runner* by Paul M. Sammon; *Ridley Scott: The Making of His Movies* by Paul M. Sammon; *The Adventure and Discovery of a Film: The Story of the Fifth Element* by Luc Besson; *CG 101, A Computer Graphics Industry Reference* by Terrence Masson.

Special Effects Guiding Concepts

Several basic visual effects need to be created for `Area51.avi` to give a finishing touch to the scene imagery. Before moving on to making explosions, glowing lights, and high-voltage electrical arcs, there are some important concepts to keep in mind.

Keep It Simple

Creating visual effects is centered on your ability to find simple answers to sometimes complex questions concerning the creation of physical phenomena. Your ability to look at a visual effect for a shot and approximate its reality using the simplest method possible is absolutely critical.

Remember the quote from Alberto Giacometti in Chapter 5, "Photon Paint: The Art of Lighting": "...the object of art is not to reproduce reality, but to create a reality of the same intensity." To create a reality of the same intensity, you must understand the reality in the first place. Considering some of the effects you are about to create in this chapter's Workshop, you might ask yourself, "What is an arc of electricity or a glowing light, really?" or "What are the simplest visual elements of an explosion?" Glowing light, hot color, flying debris—all these are acceptable elements of the reality you are trying to synthesize using the effects tools in max.

> **Industrial Strength Illusion**
>
> Academy award–winner Dennis Muren, VFX Supervisor, led the creation of more than 2,000 special effects shots for *Star Wars Episode 1: The Phantom Menace*. When some of the shots in the Pod Race scene required a large crowd of people filling the stands, Dennis and his crew used cotton-tipped swabs painted in different "crowd people" colors. Digitally multiplied and combined, they are a convincing example of a simple, elegant effect that embodies the concept of tricking the eye into seeing what the artist wants.

Don't Rely on Plug-In Solutions

There are a lot of wonderful plug-ins, some quite expensive, for max that will help create the visual effects you see in the eyes of your imagination. In the hands of master animators, plug-ins are useful and powerful tools, but if an artist doesn't really understand explosions, for example, he can't create the appearance of the phenomenon effectively, no matter how sophisticated the plug-in. If you rely solely on the fancy tool, you run the risk that all your images will look like those created by everyone else who also uses the same plug-in.

The same independent stance applies to any ready-made tool or tutorial. First, you must understand the fundamental science behind the effect by gathering knowledge of real-world phenomena. Second, you must create the simplest process possible to create a reality of the same intensity.

Inspiration for the solutions to your max visual effects can come from many sources. However, the nonlinear, paradoxical solutions that you create, more or less by common sense, are the most interesting, entertaining, and rewarding. The greatest compliment for you as a visual effects artist and the highest honor you can receive from your peers is the question, "How'd you do that?" Imagine the pride in being able to just smile and reply, "Q-tips!"

Curiosity and Observation: Question Everything

The first step in forming an approach to a specific special effect is asking the question: How could I do that in max? The answer lies in keen observation of the world around you, which will give you clues as to how to re-create the effect you are trying to achieve. Develop the ability to think outside the box—nonlinear thinking is essential. A good example of this is found in how Richard Feynman explains the relative size of an atom, which is about 1 or 2×10^{-8} centimeters in diameter. Feynman illustrates the meaning of this incredibly small number by saying, "If an apple is magnified to the size of the earth, then the atoms in the apple are approximately the size of the original apple."

Illustrating the size of an atom by using an analogy creates a vivid, easily remembered description because it relates the size to familiar memes. Creating by analogy was a key component of Dennis Muren's use of colored Q-tips for the crowd scene in *The Phantom Menace*. Not only did he step back from the problem for a fresh perspective, he allowed common sense to dictate the solution.

Standard linear thinking would have restricted the description of the size of atoms to mathematical terms understandable only by another physicist. Or Dennis could have spun his wheels trying to digitize and duplicate real actors to fill the seats of the stadium at the pod race. The nonlinear thinking seen in the Feynman and Muren examples resulted in paradoxical solutions—apples the size of the earth and a cast of thousands of Q-tip extras appearing in a 150-million-dollar movie.

Your work in max 4 needs this kind of nonlinear paradoxical thinking. Try to find the simplest method possible to explain the effect you are trying to achieve, and build on that foundation.

Experiment with Reality

Another concept that is critical in your visual effects work is to be fearless in your experimentation—all success is built on a foundation of failed experiments.

In his book *Genius, The Life and Science of Richard Feynman*, author James Gleick quotes Feynman, who was proposing that children in the first grade be taught algebra:

> "We must remove rigidity of thought... We must leave freedom for the mind to wander about in trying to solve the problems... The successful user of mathematics is practically an inventor of new ways of obtaining answers in given situations. Even if the ways are well known, it is usually easier for him to invent his own way—a new way or an old way—than it is to try to find it by looking it up."

Feynman was decrying the death of improvisation and invention, which is caused by slavish reliance on precise formulas. The parallel for your visual-effects work in max is to learn the effects tools, and then experiment, invent, and don't rely too much on formulas or tutorials.

Keep the End in Mind: Support the Story

The movies of the last 25 years have certainly been entertaining, and some have even been great. The audience, your audience, is now the most visually spoiled and sophisticated audience of all time. They are special-effects junkies with very discriminating standards. Unfortunately, not all artists and producers are so discriminating.

The main visual effects problem to solve today is how to create believable effects for an audience that has been desensitized by visual overload. The solution is to first figure out *why* you want the audience to see the visuals you are creating, *what* the story is you want them to know, and *how* to tell the story; consequently, how to create the visual effects will flow naturally from that understanding. When visual effects cease to be the most important thing in a production, true artistic genius emerges by putting the visual effects back in service to the story.

Don't Follow the Crowd

The goal of visual effects is to help you tell a story worthy of your audience's devotion. When you are tempted to use the awesome power of max to show off some great new effect, just remember that the audience has already seen it in some previous iteration. For example, how many times have they seen the starship Enterprise jump to light speed? Do the math: 40 years × 365 days × 500 syndicated reruns per day × 3 jumps per episode. 21,900,000 jumps later, the effect has lost something of its original impact.

The question then becomes, "Okay, so what's left if they've seen it all, what do I have to do to create the next greatest visual effect?" The answer is to not try to create the next visual effect! The effect should blend within the context of the entire shot and sometimes it should be unobvious that you've created an effect at all. Let the imagination of your audience go to work for you and don't be a visual-effects slave!

Taking a Step Back

The first step forward in creating simple visual effects is to take a step back. Visually, mentally, step back from the image you are trying to create and ask the question, "What am I actually seeing here?"

In the case of *The Phantom Menace* crowd scene, you see a bunch of fuzzy-colored blobs that, when viewed from a distance, look like people. When looked at this way, the challenge becomes, "How do I create a bunch of fuzzy-colored blobs?" not "How do I create a crowd scene?" Practicing the ability to take a step back is important to your development as a max visual-effects artist. It's a Zen thing!

In This Chapter

This chapter introduces you to the fundamental visual effects that I use every day in my work as a max artist. Also, be sure to read Appendix G, "Adding Rendering Effects to Your Max 4 Imagery," on the CD. It's a brief tutorial on how to use rendering effects and can be found in `MAXWorkshop\Help_Files\Appendix_G.pdf`.

At the end of this chapter, you'll have all the information you'll need to complete Sc-04 and Sc-05. Along the way, you'll learn how to create glow effects and animated electrical arcs, and how to use max particles to blow up the cooling tower.

Tip

 An AVI format movie of the electrical arc created in the next section can be found in `MAXWorkshop\Help_Files\Chapter_8\Arc_Light_Test.avi`.

Trompe L'oeil: The Art of Visual Effects

Introduction to High Voltage: Creating Electrical Arcs

Creating the high-voltage arc effects shown in Figure 8.1 requires four basic steps: Create the correct geometry for the arc, add the proper animation controllers and constraints, create the material, and add the appropriate rendering effects.

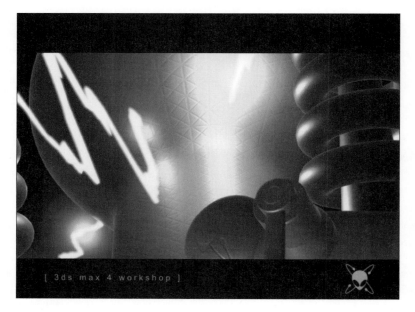

Figure 8.1   The electrical arc effect in this image was created with a cylinder primitive, a Noise modifier, an Attachment controller, two Omni Lights, and a Glow rendering effect added to the arc material.

Start max and open the file on the CD: MAXWorkshop\Help_Files\Chapter_8\EXSC-02_Arc_Test.max. You'll use this model to create a test version of the electrical arc effect and then apply the results of your test to the rest of Sc-02A and Sc-02B. When the scene opens, save it as Sc-02_Arc_Test in your MAXWorkshop\Scene Models\Sc-02 directory.

> **Tip** The completed scene with the arc effect can be found in MAXWorkshop\Help_Files\Chapter_8\EXSC-02_Arc_Test_Final.max.

This scene also includes hidden models of the VandeGraaff generator, the Tesla coil tower, an Omni Light, and a camera.

Electric Arc—Cylinder Primitive

The results of the Arc_Test model will be used to create the electrical arcs erupting between the VandeGraaff generator and the Tesla coil towers. Start by changing to Top view, and then follow these steps to create the arc:

1. Create a cylinder with the following parameters: Radius: .5; Height: 65; Height Segments: 100; Cap Segments: 1; Sides: 4; Smooth: On. Rename the cylinder Arc.

2. Use the Align command to move the arc cylinder to the center of the test induction globe, as shown in Figure 8.2. Check the Top view as well to be sure it's aligned correctly with the base of the arc as close to the center as possible.

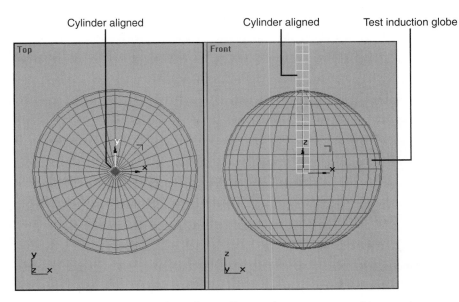

Figure 8.2 The test induction globe and VandeGraaff test sphere were created to speed up the test process. Remember, test models should be focused on creating and testing a visual effect process—you can make it look pretty later.

The VandeGraaff test sphere and the test induction globe were created as stand-ins, and they reside at the same location as their more complex counterparts, which are currently hidden. If you use the complete models of the generator and Tesla coil towers during this test process instead of the stand-ins, it will take too long to render the test AVIs you'll need to evaluate your work along the way. When you have created an arc effect that you like, hide the stand-in objects, unhide the full versions of the models, and then render out your final test images to evaluate the result.

Tip

Trompe L'oeil: The Art of Visual Effects

3ds max 4

3. Change to Front view and rotate the arc about 40 degrees in the Z-axis (see Figure 8.3).

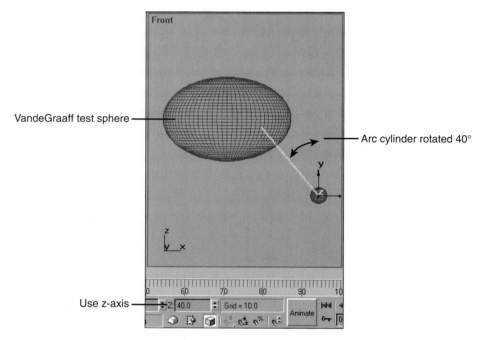

VandeGraaff test sphere

Arc cylinder rotated 40°

Use z-axis

Figure 8.3 You'll use a Noise modifier to animate the vertices of the arc mesh surface. Converting the arc to an editable mesh will prepare for that step.

4. Convert the arc cylinder to an editable mesh or add an Edit Mesh modifier to it. This will enable you to select a section of the mesh vertices for the addition of the Noise modifier in the next section.

5. Open the Material Editor and click an empty material preview slot. Name this material ARC, make it 100% self-illuminating, and apply it to the arc cylinder. You'll adjust the rest of its parameters later.

Adding Noise to Create the Arc Animation

The ends of the arc must be restricted so that the effect looks like the electricity is zapping out from the test induction globe and scintillating over the surface of the VandeGraaff test sphere. The first step is to select the vertices to which the Noise modifier will be added, leaving the vertices inside the test induction globe and the VandeGraaff test sphere unselected to anchor them in place:

1. Select Arc Rotate ⬒ from the Viewport Navigation Controls and rotate the Front view until the arc cylinder is horizontal, as shown in Figure 8.4. This will enable you to accurately select the vertices to which the Noise modifier will be applied.

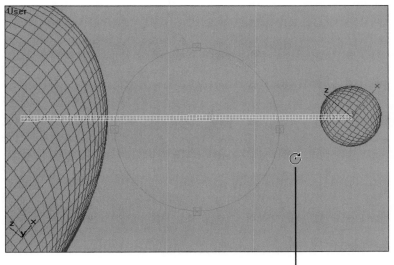

Viewport Arc Rotate cursor

Figure 8.4   All the vertices between the VandeGraaff test sphere and the test induction globe and some vertices inside of them will be selected using the Soft Selection option in the Edit Mesh rollout. The remaining unselected vertices will hold the ends in place.

2. Open the Modify command panel and select Vertex as your active subobject. Drag a selection rectangle around the vertices in the middle between the two test spheres, as shown in Figure 8.5.

3. Open the Soft Selection rollout, click Use Soft Selection, and be sure Affect Backfacing is also checked. Adjust the Falloff amount to 23, as shown in Figure 8.6.

Note

Soft Selection Falloff controls where and how quickly soft selection ends in relation to the initial subobject selection. It subsequently controls the effect on the modifiers added to soft-selected subobjects. In this case, the Noise effect will be very powerful in the immediate vicinity of the dark vertices in the middle of the arc and diminish rapidly as the selection nears the ends of the cylinder, leaving the unselected vertices to anchor the arc's position.

4. Click the Lock Selection 🔒 toggle at the bottom of your screen. This will keep the vertices selected while you add the Noise modifier.

5. Hold down the Ctrl key and right-click the selected vertices. Select Modifiers from the Quad Menu, and click Noise in the list of Parametric modifiers.

Selected vertices

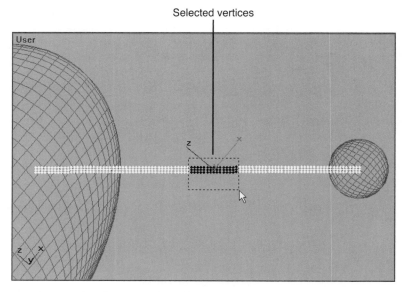

Figure 8.5   Applying Soft Selection to the selected vertices will help modulate the Noise modifier effect, creating a better arc animation.

Soft Selection parameters

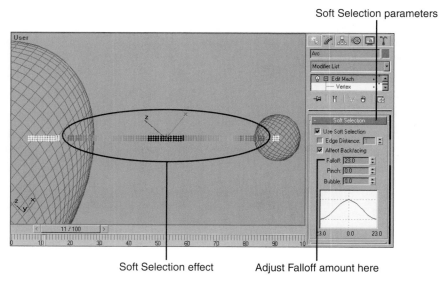

Soft Selection effect   Adjust Falloff amount here

Figure 8.6   Soft Selection enables you to specify the range of selected subobjects that will be affected by transform commands and modifiers. The colors of the vertices indicate the range of the effect by using red-orange for the vertices closest to the original selected set of vertices and changing to dark blue for those farthest away.

The Noise modifier is used to create a random spatial displacement of the subobjects to which it's applied. Because you are using Soft Selection, the Noise effect is partly controlled by the Soft Selection Falloff amount.

6. The Modify command panel now shows the parameters for the Noise modifier, and it also shows that the Noise modifier has been added to vertices. Make the following adjustments to the Noise section—Scale: 33; Fractal: On; Roughness: 0.1; Iterations: 8. Change the X Strength amount to 100, check the box next to Animate Noise, and change the Frequency amount to 1.0 (see Figure 8.7).

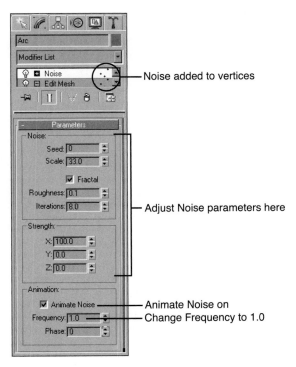

Figure 8.7 By checking the Animate Noise box, the Noise effect will automatically animate—there's no need to turn on Animate mode or create keyframes. Frequency controls the speed of the noise animation. You can adjust the effect of the noise by adjusting the Noise rollout parameters or by changing the Falloff amount in the Edit Mesh Soft Selection rollout.

You can tell which subobject level a modifier has been added to by looking to the right of the modifier in the stack. The Noise modifier was added to vertices; consequently, the vertex icon appears beside the Noise modifier in the stack, as shown previously in Figure 8.7.

7. Click Edit Mesh in the Modifier stack. This drops you down one level below the Noise modifier back to the vertices subobject level. The Noise effect disappears and the vertices return to their original position, as shown in Figure 8.8.

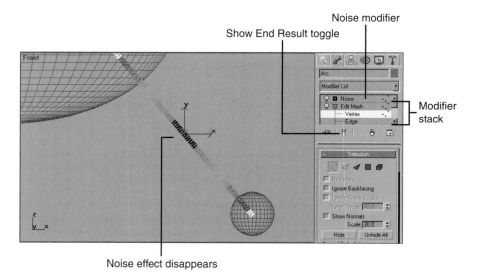

Figure 8.8 When you select the Edit Mesh level below the Noise modifier in the Modifier stack, the modifier is still there but its effect is not visible.

8. You can adjust the vertices and soft selection to fine-tune the Noise effect, but it would help to see the end result as you make the changes. Click the Show End Result toggle and adjust the Falloff to see the resultant change in the vertex selection and the Noise effect, as shown in Figure 8.9.

When you're finished with your adjustments, click Noise at the top of the stack. The next step is to add the Omni Lights that will simulate the light emitting from the arc as it strikes the surface of the VandeGraaff sphere.

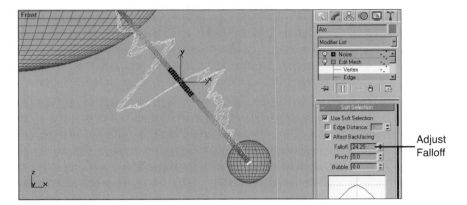

Adjust Falloff

Figure 8.9   The Falloff amount has been adjusted to 24.25, which leaves one row of vertices unselected in the end of the arc inside the test induction globe. Your results might be different depending on the location and number of the vertices you selected in step 2.

Attaching Lights to the Arc Using the Attachment Controller

The Attachment controller enables you to attach an object to the surface of another animating object. This is similar to the Link command you used in Chapter 6, "Machines in Motion: Modeling and Kinematics," except Attachment allows you to specify and even animate the precise location of the attachment point. Follow these steps to create and attach a light at both ends of the animating arc:

1. Create two Omni Lights named VandeGraaff_Light and Tesla_Light in the Top view of your max workspace. Select VandeGraaff_Light, open the Motion command panel ⊚, and open the Assign Controller rollout. When you click Position: Bezier Position, the Assign Controller arrow activates (see Figure 8.10).

2. Click Assign Controller ▶⁺ to open the list of controllers, and click Attachment (see Figure 8.11).

Motion command panel

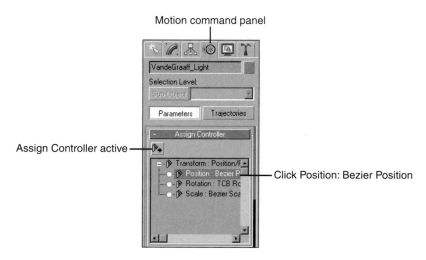

Assign Controller active —

Click Position: Bezier Position

Figure 8.10 Animation controllers are tools that allow you to use a variety of different parameters to control the animation of your objects in max. The default controllers under Transform give you basic position, rotation, and scale control.

Select Attachment —

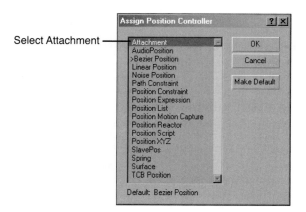

Figure 8.11 If you select a controller and then click Make Default, it will make that controller the default type for the selected transform in the Assign Controller rollout. This is useful if you find that you prefer to use Position XYZ instead of the current default Bezier Position controller, for example.

3. After you've selected the Attachment controller, click OK. Then scroll down in the Modify command panel to the Attachment Parameters rollout and click Pick Object in the Attach To section. Be sure that Align to Surface is checked and click the arc cylinder (see Figure 8.12).

Arc name appears here

Align to Surface: On

Figure 8.12 The only indication that you've successfully attached the Omni Light to the arc is that the arc's name appears in the rollout and you can no longer move the light in the viewport.

4. Right-click in the viewport to get out of Pick Object mode and change to Front view. Zoom in on the intersection of the arc and the VandeGraaff sphere. Scroll down to the Key Info, Position section and click the Set Position button. Click the arc near the point where it touches the outside surface of the VandeGraaff sphere—the Omni Light attaches itself to the surface of the arc, as shown in Figure 8.13. When you're done setting the position, click the Set Position button to exit the mode.

Omni Light attached to arc

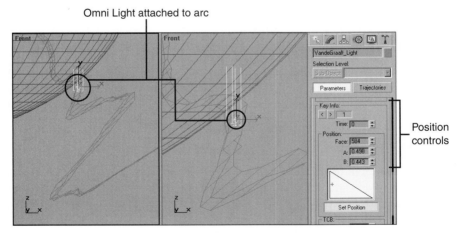

Position controls

Figure 8.13 The Position controls enable you to adjust which face you're attached to and fine-tune the attachment location within the boundaries of the face. Use the spinners next to the Face, A, and B text boxes to adjust their values and note the resultant change in the viewport.

Caution

If your light is attached too close to the surface of the VandeGraaff sphere, it might not illuminate the sphere correctly. Adjust the light's attachment location at any time by selecting the light and using the Set Position controls in the Motion command panel to correct this problem.

3ds max 4

5. Select Tesla_Light and repeat the attachment process—this time attaching the selected light to the other end of the arc just outside the surface of the Tesla sphere. Both lights should be in position, as shown in Figure 8.14.

VandeGraaff_Light attached   Tesla_Light attached

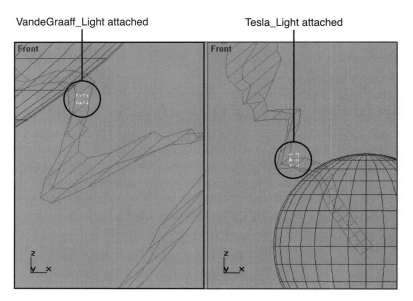

Figure 8.14   After the lights are correctly attached, click Play Animation ▶ in the animation controls at the bottom of your screen. The lights follow the surface to which they are attached as it moves around the scene. The next step is to adjust the light parameters.

Adjusting the Omni Light Parameters

At this point, the Omni Lights are not attenuated and are lighting up the entire scene. Adjusting their parameters will change that and create the effect of the hot end of the arc illuminating the surface just around the point of impact with the surface of the test induction globe and the VandeGraaff test sphere.

> All the parameters given for the creation of the arc test are placeholders. Make your final adjustments to the lights and animation when you re-create the effect in the final scene and can see how it looks in the context of the shot.

Tip

Adjust the Omni Lights in the following steps:

1. Select Tesla_Light and adjust its parameters in the Modify command panel to the following settings—HSV color: 138,113,216; Shadows: Off; Far Attenuation Use and Show: On; Far Attenuation Start and End values: 6, 10.

2. Select VandeGraaff_Light and adjust its parameters in the Modify command panel to the following settings—HSV color: 138,113,216; Shadows: Off; Far Attenuation Use and Show: On; Far Attenuation Start and End values: 20, 40.

Render out as test AVI to see how the lights and the arc are animating. Adjust your lights and the Noise parameters to create the effect you are trying to achieve. Your progress so far should look like Figure 8.15.

Figure 8.15   The next step in this process will add a Glow effect to the lights to enhance the visual heat of the electrical arc.

Adding Render Effects Glow to the Omni Lights

There are several ways to add a Glow effect to the objects and lights in your max scenes. For lights, you can use the Atmospheres & Effects rollout at the bottom of the light's Modify command panel.

> **Note**
>
> If you haven't already done so, now would be a good time to go through the tutorial in MAXWorkshop\Help_Files\Appendix_G.pdf, which goes into detail about many of the aspects of render effects that won't be covered in this section.

To add a Glow effect to the lights, follow these steps:

1. Select Tesla_Light and open the Modify command panel. Scroll down to the Atmospheres & Effects rollout.

> **Note**
>
> Use the commands in the Atmospheres & Effects rollout to add, delete, and set up a Volume Light or Lens Effects component for the lights in your scene.

2. Click the Add button and double-click Lens Effects in the list. This adds Lens Effects to the list window, as shown in Figure 8.16. Click Lens Effects to select it, and then click Setup.

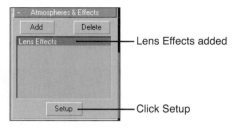

Figure 8.16 Effects added to this list must be selected before their parameters can be modified using the Setup dialog box.

3. When the Rendering Effects window shown in Figure 8.17 opens, rename this effect Tesla_Light, select Glow from the list, and click the top arrow to add it to the list of active effects on the right side. After you have added Glow, check the Interactive box.

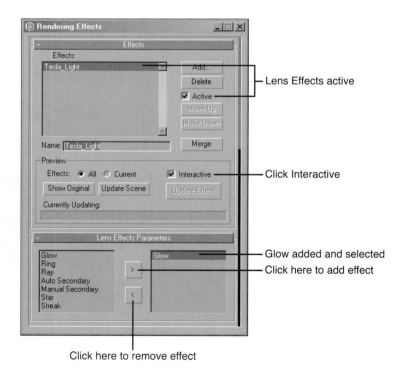

Figure 8.17 To modify the Glow parameters, it must be selected in the right-hand list. When you click Interactive, the virtual frame buffer opens and max renders the scene. When you make changes to the Glow effect, the VFB will update, enabling you to interactively adjust the Glow parameters.

4. Scroll down to the Glow Element rollout and make the following changes—rename the Glow effect: Tesla_Light_Glow; Size: 45; Intensity: 200; Use Source Color: 100. Your VFB image and the Glow Element rollout should look like Figure 8.18.

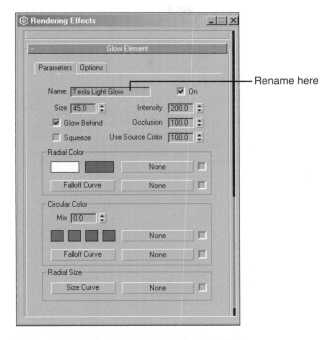

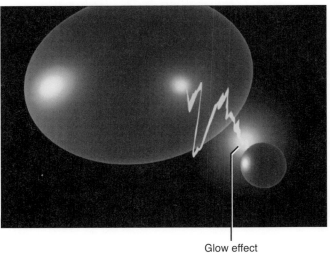

Glow effect

Figure 8.18 Try adding other effects to Tesla_Light, such as ray, streak, or star, to emphasize the intensity of the light coming from the arc as it emits from the induction globe.

5. Minimize the Rendering Effects and VFB windows and select VandeGraaff_Light. Follow the same procedure that you just completed for Tesla_Light and add a lens effect in the Atmosphere & Effects rollout of the Modify command panel.

6. Add a Glow effect to the active list, rename it VandeGraaff_Light_Glow, and make the following parameter adjustments in the Glow Element rollout—Size: 65; Intensity: 230; Use Source Color: 100. Your VFB image and the Glow Element rollout should look like Figure 8.19.

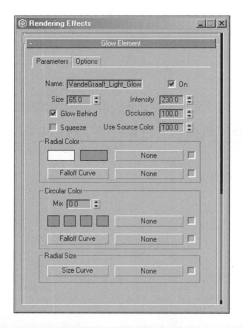

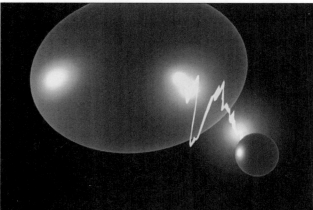

Figure 8.19   If you scroll up to the top of the Rendering Effects window to the Effects rollout, you'll see that you now have two lens effects added to the list. The sequence that effects are added to this list does matter, and adjusting the order of effects by using the Move Up and Move Down buttons can yield different results in your imagery.

Figure 8.20 shows some examples of other effects added to the Omni Lights for this test. Some of these will show up in the final imagery for Sc-02. Take some time to experiment before you move on.

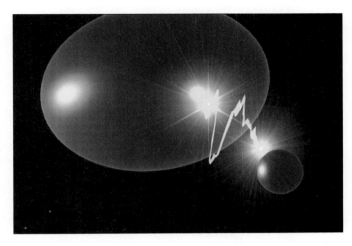

Figure 8.20   In addition to the Glow effect, Ray and Star lens effects were added to VandeGraaff_Light and a Ray effect was added to Tesla_Light. Adding multiple effects can enhance your imagery, but be careful; they will impact your rendering time.

Creating the Arc Material

Now that the ends of the arc are glowing properly, it's time to add a Glow effect to the arc. Press M to open the Material Editor, and click the preview window for the arc material you created earlier:

1. Adjust the color to match the color of the Omni Lights attached to the arc by changing the Diffuse and Ambient color to HSV values 134, 181, 255.

2. Assign a Material Effects channel to the material by clicking the Material Effects channel icon 0, which is currently set to 0, and choosing channel 1 from the matrix shown in Figure 8.21.

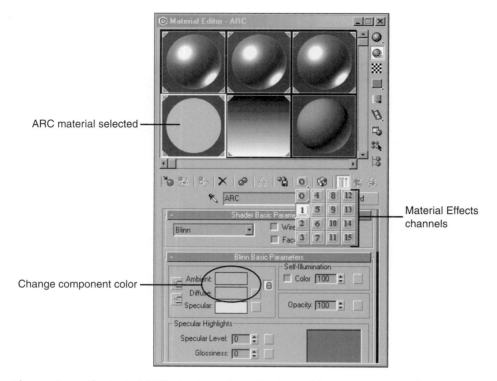

ARC material selected

Material Effects channels

Change component color

Figure 8.21 The Material Effects channel number is used by max to control the assignment of rendering effects to the materials you create. Regardless of their parameters, color, material type, and so forth, all materials with the same Material Effects channel will be affected by the rendering effect that uses the shared effects channel number.

Adding Render Effects Glow to the Arc

Click Rendering, Effects in the main Menu Bar. This will open the now-familiar Rendering Effects interface where you'll see the two effects you previously added in the list. The next steps will show you how the Material Effects Channel numbers are used:

1. Click the Add button and select Lens Effects from the list of options. Rename this effect Arc_Glow, and then add a Glow effect as shown in Figure 8.22. So far, so good—this is the same process you've been using.

2. Scroll down to the Glow Element rollout, click the Options tab, and then check the Effects ID box. Leave the number set to 1—it matches the Material Effects number you specified for the arc material in the Material Editor (see Figure 8.23).

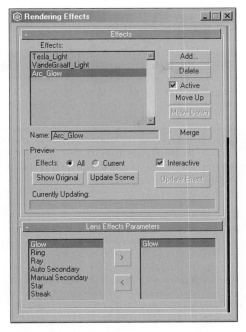

Figure 8.22 Giving your lens effects unique names will help you access and adjust them more quickly.

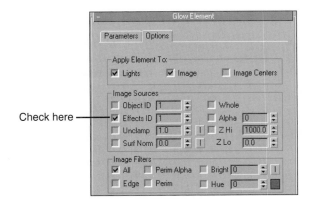

Check here ————

Figure 8.23 The Options tab contains the controls that determine how the effect is applied to the selected light, object, material, or image.

3. Click the Parameters tab and make the following changes—rename the Glow effect: Arc_Glow_Element; Size: .05; Intensity: 110; Use Source Color: 100. Your VFB image and the Glow Element rollout should look like Figure 8.24.

Trompe L'oeil: The Art of Visual Effects

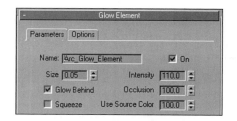

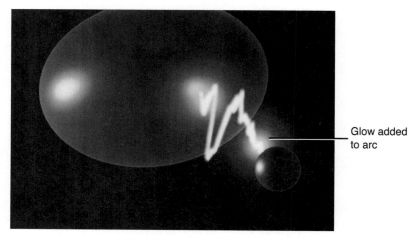

Glow added
to arc

Figure 8.24 *The glows for this test are good examples of the fun and power of the render effects process.*

When you added the lens effect this time, you probably noticed that there were several other options to choose from in the list. This test scene is probably not a good scene to use to explore these other effects—try them out on Sc-01. Save your work and render out an AVI of the arc test to see the results. You'll be able to add these arcs to Sc-02 using the process and tools that you've just explored. Enough high voltage—it's time to blow up the cooling tower.

Max Workshop—Completing Sc-04 and Sc-05

Creating explosive effects in max has always been a fun and interesting challenge. The challenge is not in the tools max gives you to use; it's in discovering and understanding what an explosion is, exactly. Translating the knowledge of that discovery into digital content requires an application of some fundamental animation concepts, such as the speed and the timing of the explosion. After you understand the basics, you can add as many effects layers as you want to the composite to create your own unique explosion.

Tip

The completed scene for Sc-04 and Sc-05 can be found in MAXWorkshop\Help_Files\Chapter_8\EXSC_04_05.max.

Setting the Stage

Open your `Sc-01.max` file, and then save it as `Sc-04_05.max` in a new folder titled `Sc-04_05` in your `MAXWorkshop\Scene Models` directory. Although these two scenes are only half the length of Sc-01, you don't have to adjust the time configuration; you'll specify the proper frame numbers when you render the images.

Re-Using Sc-01

Sc-04 is 48 frames (2 seconds) long and Sc-05 is 96 frames (4 seconds) long, which yields a frame count of 144 frames total. Although you'll be adding another layer to the imagery for Sc-04, you won't be actually making a new scene in the strictest sense of modeling, lighting, and so forth. Instead, you will reuse the first 2 seconds of Sc-01 to make Sc-04, and you'll learn how to transition seamlessly into the explosion for Sc-05. Because Sc-04 is already set up, the rest of this section focuses on how to create the explosion for Sc-05.

Deleting Cooling_Tower_Lattice

Select and delete the Cooling_Tower_Lattice model. Its mesh is too complex to use in the explosion and, with some visual effects trickery, it won't be missed in the final layer imagery.

Modifying Cooling_Tower_Master

Select the Cooling_Tower_Master model and use the Quad Menu to convert it to an editable mesh. Change to the Right view and modify the mesh surface by selecting and deleting the polygons on the top surface of the model and the bottom two or three rows. This will simplify the model geometry by removing polygons that aren't seen in the camera field of view (see Figure 8.25).

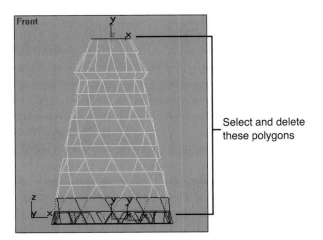

Figure 8.25   Be sure you don't delete any polygons that can be seen in the Camera view. The explosion you'll create will operate on all the surface geometry of the cooling tower, and deleting geometry that won't be visible in the scene will optimize the processing of the explosion effect.

Trompe L'oeil: The Art of Visual Effects

After you've deleted the polygons indicated, select all the polygons in the mesh, scroll down to the Surface Properties rollout, and click Unify. Unifying the normals ensures that all the polygon normals in the remaining mesh surface are pointing in the same direction.

The last modification you'll make to the model might seem a little counterintuitive, but you'll understand why you are doing this when you create the explosion. Right-click the cooling tower and select Properties from the Quad Menu. When Object Properties opens, uncheck the Renderable box in the Rendering Control section (see Figure 8.26).

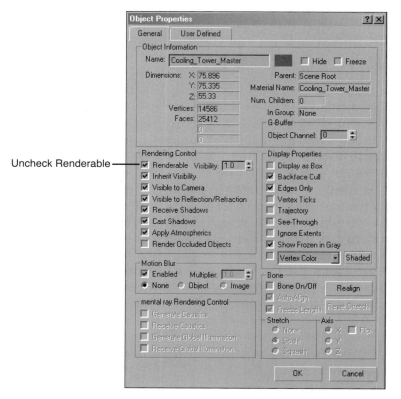

Figure 8.26   The explosion effect will use Cooling_Tower_Master as a source for the explosion—you won't be blowing up the actual model. Consequently, you'll need to use the model but not see it in the layer images. Deselecting Renderable makes an object invisible in the rendered imagery but allows it to remain visible in the viewport.

Adding the Particle Spheres

Explosions aren't just one single ka-boom. Several layers of debris are blown out from the center of the explosion, and the shockwave can and will cause secondary explosions. In addition to the cooling tower, two spheres will be used to create the layers of debris and the secondary detonations.

Shockwaves: Bada Boom

The shockwave of a high explosive, such as TNT, moves out from the epicenter of an explosion at about 10,000 feet per second—just under 7,000 miles per hour—and detonates any explosive material in its path. Secondary explosions caused by the shockwave happen after the initial event. The timing is important—I call it the Bada-Boom-Bada-Bing effect.

The following steps will show you how to set up the geometry used for the secondary explosions:

1. Create a sphere named Little Sphere with these settings—Radius: 10; Segments: 48. Create a sphere named Big Sphere with these settings—Radius 20; Segments 56.

2. Align the spheres with the center of the cooling tower model and adjust their vertical location with the little sphere lower than big sphere. Your Front view and Camera view should look like Figure 8.27.

3. Right-click both spheres in turn and select Properties from the Quad Menu. When the Properties dialog box opens, make them invisible by deselecting Renderable in Rendering Control just as you did to the cooling tower.

Creating the Explosion Materials

The materials assigned to the models used in this effect will determine the material of the particles seen in the explosion. The cooling tower should be textured with the Cooling Tower Master material, which was assigned to it when you created Sc-01.

The spheres will use a bright blue, self-illuminated material that will help create the appearance of hot particles and debris emanating from the explosion epicenter. The blue color was chosen to relate to the interior color scheme and atmosphere of Sc-02. If you've been using a different color for your version of Area51.avi, match this particle material to your own scheme:

1. Press M to open the Material Editor, and click an empty preview slot. Rename this material Particle Glow.

2. The Ambient and Diffuse color components in this standard material are locked by default. Leave them locked and change the color of one of them to HSV values 136, 185, 255. Because they're locked together, changing one color will change both of them.

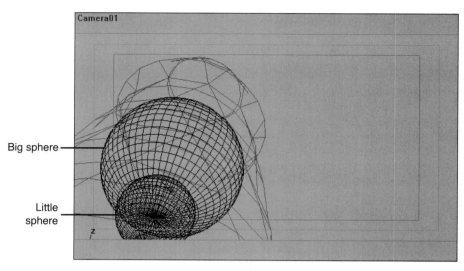

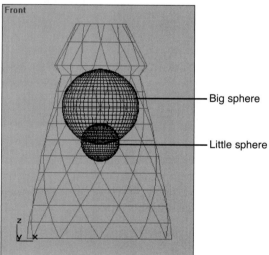

Figure 8.27 The size and segment values are used to determine the secondary explosion effects, and the position of the spheres creates a spatial offset for a more interesting spread pattern for the flying debris.

3. Change the Self-Illumination value to 100, and then change the Material Effects channel to 1. When you are finished, don't forget to assign this material to Little Sphere and Big Sphere (see Figure 8.28).

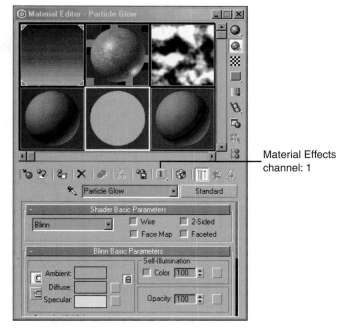

Material Effects
channel: 1

Figure 8.28 You'll add a Lens Effects Glow to the particles using Material Effects channel number 1.

Sc-05—Using Particle Array to Create an Explosion

There are several ways to create an explosion in 3ds max 4. The simplest way is to use a Bomb Space Warp or a Fire effect, which was formerly known as Combustion. However, these tools don't yield the kind of effect needed for this shot. The tool needed for this scene is a particle system known as PArray, which was chosen after some experimentation with the other options available.

> ☝ If you want to learn how to create explosions using the Bomb Space Warp or the Fire effect, consult your User Reference for full details—keywords *Bomb*, *Explosion*, or *Fire*!

Tip

Creating the Tower PArray

Follow these steps to create the first particle array (PArray), which will be used to blow up the cooling tower master:

1. Open the Create command panel and click the arrow next to Standard Primitives, which will open the list of other types of objects that can be created. Select Particle Systems from the list, as shown in Figure 8.29.

Figure 8.29   Particle Systems is one of seven major types of objects that can be created using the Create command panel. The Tab Panels contain the same list and their respective objects in graphic icon form.

2. After you select Particle Systems, the Create command panel changes to show you the six basic particle systems provided in 3ds max 4. Click PArray and drag in the Top view to create the first particle system next to the cooling tower (see Figure 8.30).

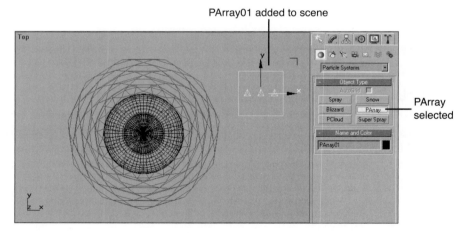

Figure 8.30   PArray was chosen as the basis for this effect because it allowed complete control over the visual and animation parameters of the explosion.

3. With PArray selected, open the Modify command panel and change the name of this system to Tower PArray. Click Pick Object in the Object-Based Emitter section of the Basic Parameters rollout. Then pick the Cooling_Tower_Master model to be the emitter, as shown in Figure 8.31.

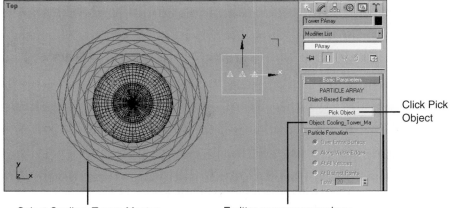

Click Pick
Object

Select Cooling_Tower_Master   Emitter name appears here

Figure 8.31   The PArray system will use the cooling tower as the emitter source for the particles
in the explosion. The cooling tower properties have been modified to make it
invisible in rendered imagery. However, the particles generated by the PArray will
be visible in the rendered scene. The PArray object itself is a nonrendering
entity—you can see it in the viewport but it doesn't appear in rendered imagery.

Adjusting the Tower PArray Parameters

Open the Particle Generation rollout and make the following changes in the indicated sections.
When you are done with the changes, your Particle Generation rollout should look like
Figure 8.32:

- **Particle Motion**—Controls the animation speed, speed variation, and divergence of the
  particles. Change the Speed value to 1.5, leave Divergence set at the default value of 10,
  and leave Variation set at 0.

- **Particle Timing**—Make the following changes—Emit Start: 47; Display Until: 143; Life:
  143; Variation: 15.

Open the Particle Type rollout and make the following changes in the indicated sections:

- **Particle Type**—Select Object Fragments from the list. This makes the array use fragments of the Cooling_Tower_Master model as the emitted particles.

- **Object Fragment Controls**—Make the following changes—Thickness: .5; All Faces: On.
  This tells the PArray to add a thickness to the object fragments, which is something you
  can't get with the Bomb Space Warp and a main reason to use this method.

- **Mat'l Mapping and Source**—Change the selection to Picked Emitter and click Get
  Material From. This tells the PArray to use the material assigned to the model specified
  as the emitter source.

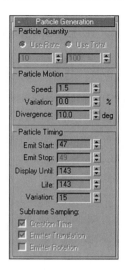

Figure 8.32   The Emit Start value specifies the frame number at which the particles begin emission. The Display Until value tells max to display the particles in the viewport for the specified number of frames. The Life value makes the particles live for the specified number of frames and the Variation parameter value specifies how many frames that any given particle can deviate from the specified Life value.

Caution

The particle material won't change if you don't click the Get Material From button after you have made a new material mapping and source selection.

Open the Rotation and Collision rollout and make the following changes in the indicated sections. When you are done with the changes, your Particle Generation rollout should look like Figure 8.33:

- **Spin Speed Controls**—Change Spin Time to 96. This tells the emitted particles to spin about their local axis once every 96 frames. Lower values create faster spin animation.

- **Spin Axis Controls**—Click User Defined and change the X Axis value to 1.0. This tells the particles to spin around their local X-axis. The numeric value in these boxes creates a vector or direction for the spin around the specified axis.

Figure 8.33 The depth of control in the PArray system can be used to create everything from asteroids moving in space to a field full of flowers waving in the wind. The possibilities are limited only by your imagination and willingness to think in a nonlinear, paradoxical fashion.

Creating the Little Sphere and Big Sphere PArrays

Follow the same process you just completed by creating two more PArrays in the scene and naming them Little Sphere PArray and Big Sphere PArray. Make the changes indicated in the following list. If a parameter isn't listed, leave it at the default value. When you're finished, you'll have all the models and particle systems needed for the basic explosion effect for Sc-05 (see Figure 8.34).

For the Little Sphere PArray, set the parameter options to the following:

- **Particle Generation Rollout**—Picked emitter: Little Sphere; Particle Motion—Speed value: 2.75; Particle Timing—Emit Start: 60; Display Until/Life: 143, 143.

- **Particle Type Rollout**—Particle Types: Object Fragments; Object Fragment Controls—Thickness: 1.0, All Faces selected; Mat'l Mapping and Source: Picked Emitter, click the Get Material From button.

- **Rotation and Collision Rollout**—Spin Speed Controls—Spin Time: 12; Variation: 25.0%.

For the Big Sphere PArray, set the parameter options to the following:

- **Particle Generation Rollout**—Picked emitter: Big Sphere; Particle Motion—Speed value: 2.75; Particle Timing—Emit Start: 46; Display Until/Life: 143, 143.

- **Particle Type Rollout**—Particle Types: Object Fragments; Object Fragment Controls—Thickness: .25, All Faces selected; Mat'l Mapping and Source: Picked Emitter, remember to click the Get Material From button.

- **Rotation and Collision Rollout**—Spin Speed Controls—Spin Time: 18; Variation: 50.0%.

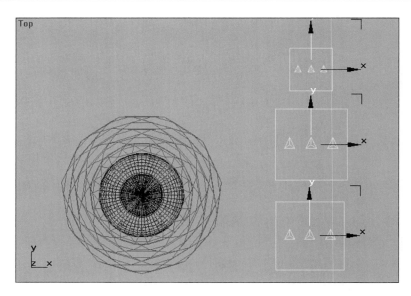

Figure 8.34 The particle arrays will be used to create a basic three-layer explosion. You can create more sophisticated effects by adding more layers of glowing debris or an animating fire effect to the composite.

Adding a Glow Effect to Material Effects Channel ɪ

When you created the material assigned to the particles, you specified the Material Effects channel number 1 to be used for the Lens Effects Glow. Click Rendering, Effects and use the process you learned earlier in this chapter to add a Glow effect with the following parameters to the Particle Glow material: Options Tab—Effects ID: 1; Image Filters: All. Parameters Tab—Glow Size: .05; Intensity: 110; Use Source Color: 100.

Pre-Roll and Motion Blur

Now is a good time to try a test render and see how cool the PArray method is for creating explosions. Press C to change to Camera view, move the time slider to frame 47, and render the scene (see Figure 8.35).

Understanding Pre-Roll

Frame 47 is the frame number you specified for the start of the particle effect, but Sc-04 ends at frame 48. This means that Sc-05 is set up to start one frame before the end of Sc-04. Starting animation or effects before they actually appear in an image is known as *pre-roll*—it allows you to give your animation a running start in advance of the actual start frame and provides extra frames to use as you work with your image composites.

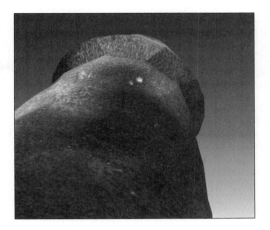

Figure 8.35   Before the particles begin to move, they conform to the surface geometry of the emitter object. This looks like and is textured like the cooling tower, but it isn't the cooling tower—it's a procedural replica of the model created from the original object by the PArray.

Tip

Pre-roll is a cinematography term used to describe the action that takes place before the camera begins filming the real action. Max doesn't use the term pre-roll, but changing the Particle Timing Emit Start value to a number before the start frame creates pre-roll. This enables particles and other animation to be in full motion before a scene begins.

Now move the time slider to frame 49 and render the scene. You'll see the faces of the tower beginning to fly apart and the first glimpse of the big sphere particles piercing through the outside surface of the tower. The Glow effect is working as well, but the imagery is lacking one essential element: motion blur (see Figure 8.36).

Adding Motion Blur

Motion blur is used to achieve a more realistic visual approximation of objects moving at speed. In this case, it can be used to stretch the particles of the exploding cooling tower into streaks of white hot metal. Adding motion blur to this scene is a simple process but determining how much motion blur to use is a matter of trial and error. Too much blur, and you'll lose the structure of the image; too little, and the imagery looks too perfect—too digital!

Right-click the tower PArray particle system and select Properties from the Quad Menu. Down near the bottom of the dialog box are the Motion Blur settings. Click Enabled to activate the effect, choose Image, and change the Multiplier to 3.0, as shown in Figure 8.37.

Figure 8.36 Motion blur is a telltale sign of animation experience—knowing when to use it and how much to use creates a subtle level of realism in your max imagery.

Figure 8.37 There are two basic types of motion blur provided in 3ds max 4: Image and Object motion blur.

> **Note**
>
> Motion blur can be applied to an object as well as an image, but object motion blur takes significantly more time to render. Using image motion blur usually will be sufficient for most of your needs. The default multiplier setting is 1.0, and specifying a higher value than 1.0 will create the required streaks of debris and realistic motion of the exploding tower.

Select the Big Sphere PArray system, enable its image motion blur, and set the multiplier to 8.0. Then select the Little Sphere PArray system and set its multiplier to 10. Re-render frame 49 to see the Motion Blur effect (see Figure 8.38).

> **Note**
>
> To see the objects in the images illustrating the effect of motion blur, the Environment Map BG Sky (Gradient) background was enabled. If you choose to do this, be sure you turn it off before you render the Sc-04 explosion Targa images.

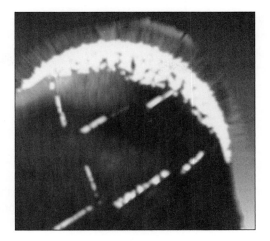

Figure 8.38   The still image of frame 49 looks very blurred but the only real way to evaluate the effect is to render out the scene. The Preview mode doesn't render out Glow or Motion Blur effects, so the only useful evaluation tool is a reduced-size AVI.

Rendering the Sc-05 Explosion Layer

When you are ready to render the scene, save your work and press Shift+R to open the Render Scene dialog box. Be sure the environment background is off and the three PArrays aren't hidden. Your Camera view should be the active view for this process.

Adjust the settings in the Render Scene dialog box to the following: Time Output—Range 47 to 143; Output Size—Width: 640, Height: 346. Click Files and save the explosion images as 32-bit, premultiplied alpha Targa image files titled Explosion.tga in a new folder titled Sc-05_Final Targas in your MAXWorkshop\Area51_Final Targas directory.

Video Post—Putting It All Together

After the sequential Targa images are created, click Rendering, Video Post to open the Video Post dialog box. The Video Post Queue that you'll create to complete Sc-04 and Sc-05 will introduce you to a new image filter event and one final essential component of a good explosion: *flash frames.*

Creating the Sc-04_05 Queue

Start by adding the four Image Input Events indicated in the following steps to the queue in the order they are listed. When you're finished, your queue should look like Figure 8.39:

1. Add the still frame for the BG Sky: MAXWorkshop\Area51_Final Targas\Sc-01\Sc-01Targas\ Sc-01_BG_Sky.tga.

2. Add the entire sequence of cloud images from MAXWorkshop\Area51_Final Targas\Sc-01\ Sc-01Clouds\Clouds.tga.

3. Add the explosion Targa sequence you just created from MAXWorkshop\Area51_Final Targas\Sc-05_Final Targas\Explosion.tga.

4. Add the Sc-01 cooling tower image layer sequence from MAXWorkshop\Area51_Final Targas\Sc-01\Sc-01FGTower\FGTower.tga.

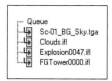

Figure 8.39   Be sure the layers are added in their proper order and that you've selected the correct and complete sequences of images or the corresponding Image File List (IFL) from the specified directories.

Adjusting the Image Input Layers

You'll change the respective VP Start and End Times for each layer in the queue and also adjust their image input options so that you maintain the established Area51.avi format:

1. Double-click the Sc-01_BG_Sky.tga image input event in the queue. When the Edit Image Input Event dialog box opens, click Options in the Image Input section at the top of the dialog box. This will open the Image Input Options dialog box.

2. Click Do Not Resize, and then click the center box in the Alignment presets matrix, as shown in Figure 8.40. This will keep the 640×346 format intact and center the image on the 640×480 screen format used for Area51.avi.

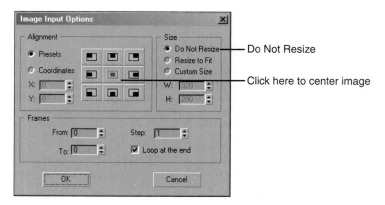

Figure 8.40   Because this is a new queue with newly added image input events, you must make these initial adjustments to the image alignment before rendering the final composites.

3. Repeat the process for each of the remaining three layers. When you are done, save your work and double-click the Sc-01_BG_Sky.tga image input event in the queue. When the Edit Image Input Event dialog box opens, change the VP End Time to frame 143; leave the VP Start Time set to 0 (see Figure 8.41).

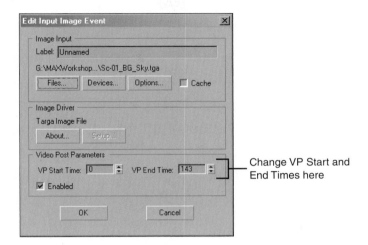

Change VP Start and End Times here

Figure 8.41 The BG Sky image will be visible for the entire 144-frame scene. The next time adjustments set up the trompe l'oeil of the scene: transforming the fully rendered cooling tower from Sc-01 into the PArray version, which you just created.

4. Change the remaining layers' VP Start and End Times to the values shown in Table 8.1. The VP Queue will look like Figure 8.42 when you're finished.

Table 8.1   Sc-04_05 Video Post Layer Start and End Times

Layer Name	VP Start Time	VP End Time
Sc-01_BG_Sky.tga	0	143
Clouds.ifl	0	143
Explosion0047.ifl	49	143
FGTower0000.ifl	0	48

Adding Flash Frames

Creating flash frames is a technique used to emphasize the bright and very fast flash of light that appears when an object detonates. The flash frames for this sequence are created using three Contrast Image Filter Events:

1. Be sure no image layers are selected in the queue, and then click Add Image Filter Event ▨. When the Add Image Filter Event dialog box opens, select Contrast from the list, rename the event Black Frame A, and change both the VP Start and End Times to frame 48. Don't click OK yet (see Figure 8.43).

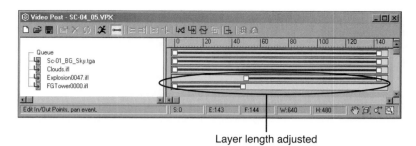

Layer length adjusted

Figure 8.42 You might have noticed that the Explosion Targas will be behind FGTower Targas, that they're set to begin at frame 49, and that the FGTower Targas end at frame 48. This creates a pre-roll for the explosion sequence, which will be covered by the flash frames.

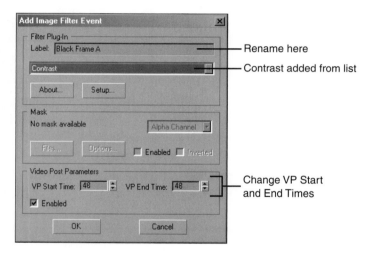

Rename here

Contrast added from list

Change VP Start and End Times

Figure 8.43 The first black flash frame turns the scene completely black for a single frame. This intensifies the effect of the white flash frame that follows it. Flash frames work because of a phenomenon called persistence of vision, which is also why we see bright spots in our field of vision after looking at a glaring lamp or glancing at the summer sun.

2. Click Setup to open the Image Contrast Control dialog box. Change the Brightness value to -1 and click the Absolute option button (see Figure 8.44).

3. When you have made the contrast adjustments, click OK to exit the dialog box and click OK again in the Edit Filter Event dialog box to add the Contrast filter to the queue.

4. Add a second Contrast Image Filter event to the queue. Name this event White Frame and change its brightness value to 1.0 and its VP Start and End Times to 49.

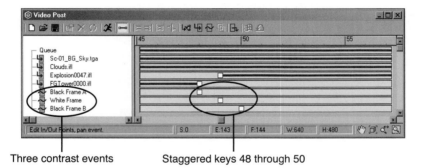

Figure 8.44 Flash frames usually follow a three-frame black, white, black sequence, but you can also create and use colored frames to emphasize the atmosphere of the shot. In this case, a blue flash frame instead of white would be an acceptable alternative.

5. Repeat this process a third time to add another contrast filter named Black Frame B to the queue. Change its VP Start and End Times to frame 50, and adjust its brightness down to -1.0. Your VP Queue should look like Figure 8.45.

Figure 8.45 The next step to complete the queue is to create the Alpha Compositor pairs to composite the layers together. The Alpha Compositor will be added to the layers in a little different way this time.

Adding the Alpha Compositor

When working on this scene, I discovered that you can't always just divide the scene layers into neat pairs and use the Alpha Compositor to create a tidy hierarchy structure.

When you composite layers that use Glow or other atmospheric effects, don't pair them up with another image layer—the layers with the glow will change the appearance of the other layers in the queue composite hierarchy. It's best to combine these orphan layers directly with an existing Alpha Compositor image layer event. Follow these steps to create the Alpha Compositors for the Sc-04_05 queue and illustrate this orphan compositing process:

1. Hold down the Shift key and select Sc-01_BG_Sky.tga and Clouds.ifl in the VP Queue. Click Add Image Layer Event and select Alpha Compositor from the list. Rename this event Alpha Compositor 1 and click OK. This creates the kind of composited layer structure you've seen before in this Workshop.

2. Now select Alpha Compositor 1 and `Explosion0047.ifl` and combine them with a new Alpha Compositor image layer event named Alpha Compositor 2.

3. The last step in this process is to select the Alpha Compositor 2 event and the `FGTower0000.ifl` and combine them with a third Alpha Compositor event titled Alpha Compositor 3. Your Video Post Queue now looks like Figure 8.46.

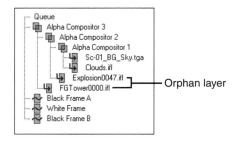

Figure 8.46 If you run into problems with layers that have Glow effects rendered into their imagery, try using this orphan Alpha Compositor technique.

Adding the Image Output Event

The last step in creating the Sc-04_05 VP Queue is to add the Image Output Event by clicking its icon . When the Add Image Output Event dialog box opens, click File and browse to your `MAXWorkshop\Area51_Final Targas` directory. Create a new folder within this directory named `Sc-04_05_Final_Targas` and save the images as 32-bit, uncompressed, premultiplied alpha Targa images named `Sc-4_05_Final.tga`. Change the VP End Time to 143. Your VP Queue is now complete (see Figure 8.47).

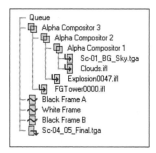

Figure 8.47 The last step in the process to complete Sc-04 and Sc-05 is to render their composited imagery.

Execute the Sequence

Begin the rendering process by clicking Execute Sequence [image]. Select Range as the desired Time Output mode and change the range to render frames 0 to 143; the size should be set to 640×480. Then click Render to launch the rendering process.

Sharpen the Saw—Using the RAM Player

3ds max 4 provides a great way to view test AVIs and sequential Targas like the ones you just rendered without having to wait until you complete the compositing to create Area51.avi. It's called the RAM Player, and I use it every day to evaluate my work in progress. Access the tool by clicking Rendering, Ram Player—which opens the RAM Player interface shown in Figure 8.48.

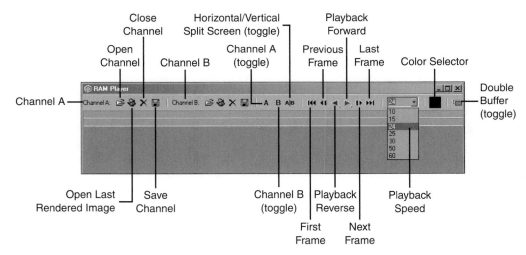

Figure 8.48 Your max 4 User Reference has a complete section on the RAM Player, including a list of keyboard shortcuts available while working within its interface. Keyword search: RAM Player.

Click Open Channel A [image], browse to MAXWorkshop\Area51_Final Targas\Sc-04_05_Final_Targas, and open the sequence of images that start with Sc-4_05_Final0000.tga, as shown in Figure 8.49.

When you click Open, the Image File List Control dialog box opens, as shown in Figure 8.50. This dialog box enables you to specify how many frames of the file you want to load in the RAM Player. Click OK to move on to the process of finishing loading the sequence.

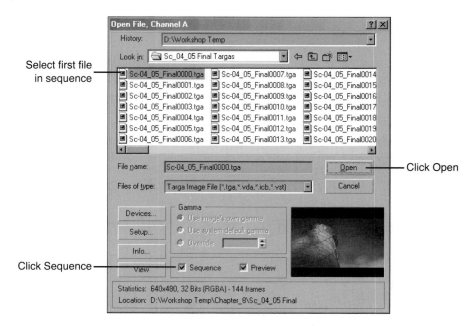

Select first file
in sequence

Click Open

Click Sequence

Figure 8.49 You can load any still or animating image file into the RAM Player for evaluation. It has quickly become an indispensable tool for quickly creating and evaluating daily work in our studio.

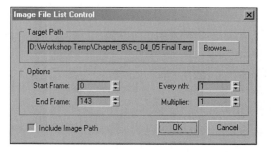

Figure 8.50 The RAM Player uses your computer system's random access memory (RAM) to load and process sequential images into real-time virtual AVIs. The more memory your system has, the better the performance and the larger the file sequences that can be viewed.

The RAM Player Configuration dialog box opens and enables you to configure the RAM Player for optimum performance. You can specify how much system RAM the RAM Player will use, the aspect ratio/size, and the number of the frames you want to load (see Figure 8.51).

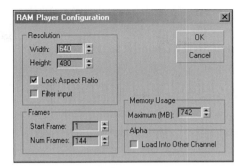

Figure 8.51 When you click OK, the RAM Player will begin to load the sequence frame by frame into your system RAM.

While the player loads your file, you can see the progress in the Loading File dialog box; the images being loaded appear in the frame buffer in the player (see Figure 8.52).

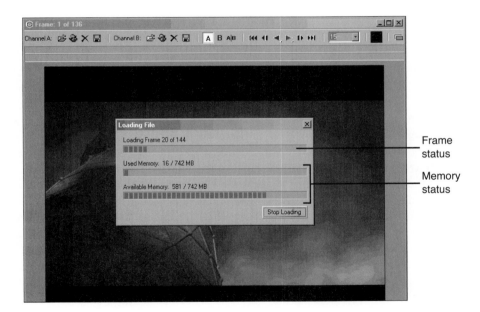

Frame status

Memory status

Figure 8.52 You can also save sequential images, which have been loaded into the RAM Player, out into AVI files and most other image formats, such as tiff, bitmaps, and so on.

Use the playback controls ◄◄ ◄◄ ◄ ► ►► ►►◄ to play the sequence. You can adjust the playback speed by selecting preset speeds from the list [24 ▼] or by typing in a frame rate number. You can also open multiple RAM Player windows; be careful, it takes up memory space to have one, let alone three or four, RAM Players open at the same time.

Next Steps

The next steps for this section of the Workshop include additional image layers for Sc-01, Sc-04, and Sc-05. A nice finishing touch would be the addition of red blinking lights on top of the cooling tower in Sc-04 and Sc-05. That can be accomplished by creating a sphere with a self-illuminating material applied to it. The material color can be animated to turn black and then back to red at one- or two-second intervals (see Figure CP.17 in the color section).

Another very cool effect would be to delve into the Fire (formerly Combustion) effect to create one or two superheated plasma layers for the explosion.

Finally, intermediate-level animators could animate a two-part camera shake in sync with the bada-boom of the explosion. The first shake should be subtle—just a little jump caused by sub-sonic waves in the ground movement. The big shake should be timed to feel like it happens at the same time the shockwave hits the camera location and then slowly diminishes as the wave moves through the camera POV. Some sort of visual representation of a shockwave would be interesting as well, perhaps an animating ring wave.

Learning to create and animate visual effects in max is always fun and often incredibly tedious. The level of organization can be overwhelming, especially as you begin to create ultra-sophisticated shots combining many image layers to achieve the effect. My personal record for visual effects layers so far is 17! I was able to keep track by using my max journal to record the various effects settings, layer sequencing information, and my failed experiments. Otherwise, I would get lost in the minutiae.

Coming up next, Chapter 9, "The Creative Sword: The Art of Post-Production in 3ds Max 4," is the last chapter in this Workshop. The process used to complete Sc-02 will be outlined and you'll work to create the title and credit sequences for Sc-00 and Sc-06. The final `Area51.avi` composite will use a soundtrack provided on the CD, but feel free to adapt your own music if you have the tools available. When I look at the Alien in Sc-03, I can imagine it on a coffee break, listening to an old tube-type radio he's cobbled together using extraterrestrial spare parts from the power plant. I think it probably likes to listen to Tony Bennett crooning "Fly Me to the Moon" or Elton John singing "Rocketman." Now it's on to Chapter 9 and the finish line of *3ds max 4 Workshop*.

Chapter 6

The Creative Sword: The Art of Post-Production in 3ds Max 4

"In an atmosphere of liberty, artists... are free to think the unthinkable and create the audacious; they are free to make both horrendous mistakes and glorious celebrations." - Ronald Reagan, 40th President of the United States of America

Creative freedom is a two-edged sword that artists wield to create brilliant work and horrendous mistakes. It's true that we are "free to think the unthinkable" as Reagan said. But when digital artists create without the end in mind, they will vanquish their creative intent.

The art of post-production begins with the start of the pre-production process. At the same time you are creating the sketches, storyboards, character designs, visual effects concepts, and so on, to guide the production process, you must be planning for the post-production elements that will be used to produce your final product—begin with the end in mind.

The elements added during post-production create the final visual and auditory experience of the audience. Music, voice-over dialogue, sound effects, and special visual effects are combined with the composited image layers. The completed scenes, sequences, and shots are then edited together using cinematic transitions specified by the storyboards to create the shot sequences in their proper order and timing to produce the finished film.

In many ways, what happens in post-production is the ultimate creative process. Post-production tools provide the freedom to creatively augment and modify the production imagery to achieve your artistic vision. Digital tools have made the entire production process even more flexible and provide a unique level of artistic freedom. Similar to other complex and synergistic processes, the end result of digital-content creation takes on a life of its own—the sum of the parts is always greater than the individual pieces.

When Worlds Collide— Technology Versus Tradition

Filmmakers that embrace digital-content creation are finding that it gives them a level of creative freedom and artistic expression that traditional film production and post-production techniques can't offer. This is a controversial subject and often the source of heated debate between traditional-minded cinematographers and visionary technologists, such as George Lucas. It isn't surprising that Lucasfilm and ILM under his direction are revolutionizing filmmaking and film watching. Now the potential of satellite downloads of digital movies to theatres that project the images using Texas Instruments DLP technology is rocking the entertainment world. The writing is on the wall, and digital-content creation and exposition will eventually dominate the entertainment industry. It's a good time to be a digital artist!

Your career as a digital artist not only depends on your ability to show your proficiency with max, but also you must reveal the unique and interesting way you use the entire suite of production and post-production tools to create the vision in your mind.

Post-Production Tools and 3ds Max 4

"A poor mechanic blames his tools" - Warren Studman, Greatest Mechanic on Earth

You've been using max 4's built-in post-production tools to create rendering effects and motion blur, and to composite your scene layers. However, as you progress as a max artist, you'll soon outgrow the limitations of Video Post and max rendering effects and need to buy an effects and editing package. There are three software packages I recommend for post-production of your max imagery. They are, in order of my recommended choice, combustion, Adobe After Effects, and Adobe Premiere.

Adobe After Effects is to animation and moving imagery what Adobe Photoshop is to still images, and it costs between $600 and $1400, depending on the version you buy. It's the best inexpensive, professional-quality effects tool beyond max Video Post to create and composite your visual effects.

Nonlinear editing software enables you to take your final image layers and put them together with a soundtrack and cinematic transitions to create a complete movie. Adobe Premiere is a high-quality, low-cost nonlinear editing solution and costs less than $600. It's an inexpensive and ideal tool that is well suited to the job of adding multiple soundtracks, creating sophisticated transitions between shots, and rendering out your final scenes.

The combined cost of After Effects and Premiere is around $1700. If you buy these two packages, you will be well served but you will be dealing with three distinctly separate software packages, and your production process can get a little convoluted. Because you will eventually outgrow these tools as well, I recommend another path to post-production excellence.

Make the leap financially and buy discreet's combustion. For $3495, it will give you the feature-film and digital broadcast–quality visual effects and compositing capability superior to comparable packages costing tens of thousands of dollars. The cost is more than twice that of After Effects and Premiere combined, but combustion gives you distinct speed, power, and process advantages, including its capability to work seamlessly inside the max workspace. With combustion, you won't have to switch back and forth between three programs, as you will with Premiere and After Effects. Because of combustion's power, ease of use, and increased productivity, the time required to recoup the higher cost of the product can be as short as a few weeks of production time—or a couple of freelance assignments. It's well worth the extra money and I know you'll be glad you made the investment.

Area51.avi Post-Production—Preparation and Principle

Now is a good time to take a moment to step back and evaluate what remains to be done to finish the Workshop. It's also an appropriate time for a brief discussion of some of the principles that are important to keep in mind during the post-production process.

At this point in the Workshop, you've completed the sequential images for Sc-01, Sc-03, Sc-04, and Sc-05. However, three components of Area51.avi have yet to be created or remain incomplete: Sc-00 and Sc-06—the opening title sequence and the end credits—and Sc-02, which must be assembled before its image layers can be rendered and composited.

Completing Sc-02 is an important step needed to finish Area51.avi. It includes the visual effects you learned in Chapter 8, "Trompe L'oeil: The Art of Visual Effects," and the coolant pump from Chapter 6, "Machines in Motion: Modeling and Kinematics." Appendix H, "Completing Sc-02," on the CD, contains the steps I went through to complete this scene. You can find it in

`MAXWorkshop\Help_Files\` `Appendix H`. If you don't want to work through the completion process for Sc-02, the completed scene can be found on the CD in `MAXWorkshop\Help_Files\Chapter_9\` `EXSc-02.max`.

Take the time to read Appendix H and use it to create your own version of Sc-02. The appendix also outlines the basic tools and methods I use every day in my work as a max artist. These tools include using XRef objects for scene assembly, using Exclude/Include in max 4 lighting, creating an interdependent series of individual layer files, adjusting seed parameters for procedural animation, using the Matte/Shadow material to create matte shots, and creating offset animation for cloned objects.

Preparation—Sharpen the Saw

When you've completed Sc-02 as outlined in Appendix H, you'll go through a three-step process to prepare for the final cut of `Area51.avi` at the end of this chapter.

The first step is to insert all the final scene images, except for Sc-00 and Sc-06, into the Area 51 animatic and render out a test AVI. This is the point at which you can evaluate the timing and length of the scene transitions and the length and visual content of the scenes. This AVI will also be used to create the soundtrack.

The second step, if you so choose, is to revise or add image layers to implement the content suggestions from the Next Step sections at the end of each chapter. You can adjust the length of your scenes or modify the scene-to-scene transitions. You can accomplish these modifications by returning to your original scene or individual layer file, adjusting the scene length, creating the image or effect layer you desire, adding it to the video post queue for that scene, and re-rendering the sequential images. Then adjust the Area 51 animatic to reflect the changes you want.

The third step has two tasks to complete. The first task is to render a combined series of composited images for Sc-01 through Sc-05 titled `Area51-A.tga`. Again, this won't include Sc-00 and Sc-06; you'll add those two scenes separately during the final cut process in the Workshop section at the end of this chapter.

The next task is to add the combined series of composited images into a new video post queue in preparation for the final post-production process. After that queue is created, Sc-00 and Sc-06, your personalized screen format information, and the soundtrack will be added and `Area51.avi` can be rendered out into an AVI format movie or sequential Targas.

Principle—Measure Twice, Cut Once

Two important teachings rolled into one time-honored saying guide the post-production process: "Measure twice, cut once!" The wisdom of these words is powerfully applicable to our work as digital artists. We pre-visualize our work and use pre-production design to guide the digital creation process. That's the principle of *measure twice* at work, and it guides the process of putting the final production images together into the *final cut* of the project.

The ultimate result of the post-production process is the movie that is presented to the audience. Driven by the constraints of budget, schedule, and artistic intent, sequences and shots are often cut from the film during the editing process. The deleted material, known as *outtakes*, is usually never seen by the audience—that is, until the director releases his version of the film "The Director's Cut," which is always longer but not always better than the original film. Outtakes are a normal and healthy part of the filmmaking process.

Although directors shoot more material than they will actually use in the final product, during the editing process they often discover that they need an additional shot or sequence to achieve the impact they are trying to create. These shots are called *pickups* and are a part of every production process, which are scheduled after the shots created during the regular production schedule have been filmed. You can view this not as a mistake, but as a re-measure of the project before the final cut is made.

JAWS

Verna Fields was the film editor for Steven Spielberg's movie *JAWS*. Spielberg loved working with her, and her editing is a great part of the success of this benchmark film. After the movie had been edited and test screened, the producers came back to Spielberg and asked for some changes. They knew that they potentially had a blockbuster thriller on their hands and wanted to amplify the intensity of the film by taking advantage of every possible opportunity to create fear and terror in the audience. They requested that one shot in particular be re-done to produce a few more screams. Out of budget and out of time, Spielberg shot the pickup at his own expense in Verna's swimming pool. It cost him a few thousand dollars, which for him at the time was a small fortune. Judging by the continued popularity of the film and the effect of this pickup in particular, it was a wise investment. The pickup is considered to be the single most shocking and frightening shot of the movie—the mangled remains of fisherman Ben Gardner bumping out of a hole in the bottom of his derelict boat, terrifying Hooper and shocking the audience.

Master craftsmen and artists are known primarily for the results they achieve with their tools and not necessarily for the tools they use. They bend their tools to serve their artistic will by mastering the basic principles of their craft and innovating within the constraints of their projects. Your artistic reputation will be built on what you can accomplish with max on a day-to-day basis and not solely on the fact that you use max. Indeed, the goal should be to create visuals that defy identification of the software by which they were created.

Step One—Completing `Area_51_Animatic.max`

Completing the animatic serves two purposes: It provides the evaluation tool needed to make final adjustments to the scene length and layer imagery and it's used to sync up the soundtrack to the scene action. The following steps show how to make your final adjustments to the animatic:

1. Open your `Area_51_Animatic.max` file and click Rendering, Video Post to open the Video Post window. Make sure that the queue has all the composited final layer images for Sc-01 through Sc-04_05 (see Figure 9.1).

Image file lists in place

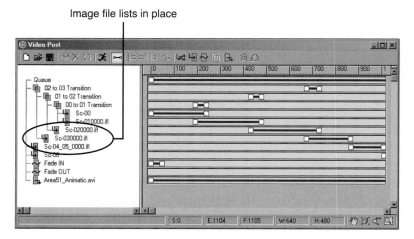

Figure 9.1   The final layer composites have been created in their own compositor files and the final images are ready to be combined for one last evaluation. The purpose of the animatic is to provide you with a tool to evaluate your work in progress—to measure twice—before you make the final cut!

2. Double-click the Output Image Event currently titled Area51_Animatic.avi and click Files in the Image File section of the Edit Image Output Event dialog box. Browse to your MAXWorkshop\Avi's\ directory, create a new folder titled Final_Animatic_Targas, and change the file format for the Output Image Event to Targa files—you can leave the name as it is. Then click OK and return to the VP queue (see Figure 9.2).

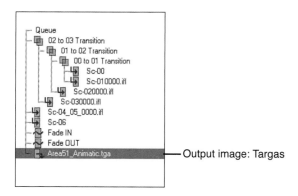

Output image: Targas

Figure 9.2   Changing the output image format to Targa prepares for the next steps and a different and effective way to make Targa images into AVIs using the RAM Player.

3. Click Execute sequence ![icon] and make sure the Time Output is set to Range 0 to 1104 and the output size is 640×480, and then click Render to create the sequential images.

4. After the rendering is complete, close Video Post and click Rendering, RAM Player. When the RAM Player opens, click Open Channel A 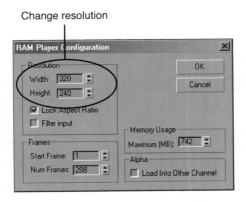 and browse to the directory where you saved the sequential Targas you just created.

5. Click the first Targa image in the sequence and check the Sequence box to the left of the image preview window. When the IFL dialog box opens, click OK to accept the settings, which opens the RAM Player Configuration dialog box. Change the aspect ratio in the Resolution section to 320×240, as shown in Figure 9.3, and click OK.

Figure 9.3 The RAM Player can be used to save the images loaded into its channels out into other formats, including AVI. It can also be used to save your AVIs out into sequential images.

6. After the images are loaded, click Playback Forward ▶ to view the animatic Targas. When you are finished viewing your work, click Save Channel A 🖫 to open the Save File, Channel A dialog box, change the format to .avi, and save this sequence as Area51_Animatic_320x240.avi (see Figure 9.4).

Using the RAM Player to convert sequential Targas is becoming my preferred way to make AVIs for three reasons:

- You can't render out reduced imagery automatically from Video Post when you have specified Do Not Resize in the Image Input options; you must go through the hassle of resizing every Image Input Event added to the queue!

- The RAM Player allows you to load sequential images for evaluation and then save them into a standard movie format such as .avi, .mov, .flc, and so on.

- You can easily create sequential images from an AVI by saving the AVI into a still image format of your choice. This enables you to extract still images from existing AVIs for asset re-use in post-production and for use in discreet's combustion, SGI's RBG format, or Kodak's Cineon process.

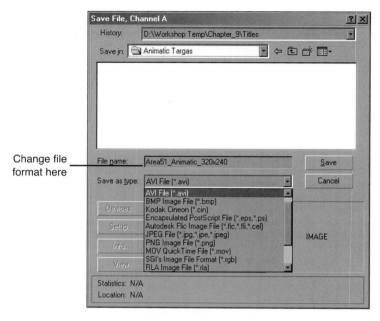

Change file
format here

Figure 9.4   The RAM Player's power becomes evident when you load two sequences of animation into Channels A and B. This allows you to evaluate differences between new versions of an animation in side-by-side comparison to its predecessor, to experiment with frame rate and so forth.

Step Two—Layer Image Revisions

The power of the layer-compositing process is that it gives you the freedom to easily modify your work. The side benefit is that it also facilitates the creation of your own version of Area51.avi by making it easy to add layers of your own.

After completing the basic image layers, two additional layers were added to the scenes in my version of the project using the techniques and tools you've learned in this book. You can see the composited results in the color section of this book or in the final AVI—MAXWorkshop\ Help_Files\Chapter_9\EXArea51.avi.

Additional Image Layers

The additional image layers added in my version of the composites for Sc-00 and Sc-04_05 are UFOs streaking by in the sky background and blinking green and red warning lights on top of the cooling tower.

UFOs

The UFOs were created from spheres with Lens Effects Glow and Ray elements added to the spheres. A dummy object was animated streaking through the field of view and the UFOs were linked to follow it. After the sequential Targas were rendered, the sequence was added into the Video Post queue. Then the sequence was added again in a second layer and their VP Start and End Times were offset to produce two flights of UFOs. See Figure CP.1 in the color section of this book.

 Tip ☛ The max file including the Video Post queue for the UFO layer can be found on the CD in `MAXWorkshop\Help_Files\Chapter_9\EXSc_01_UFO.max`.

Warning Lights

The warning lights for Sc-01 are made from modified spheres to which a black material with a bright green self-illumination component was assigned. The lights in the Sc-04_05 version used the same black material with a bright red self-illumination component.

Lens Effects was used to add a glow element to the lights and the self-illumination color of the material was animated alternating between RGB values of 0,255,0 and 0,0,0 for the on/off blinking effect. This is the same technique used for Sc-00, which you'll learn about in this chapter.

The lights were then added to new individual layer files created from Sc-00 and Sc-04. A Matte/Shadow material was assigned to the cooling tower to make the lights appear behind the model correctly.

 Tip ☛ The max file with the model used to create the lights for these image layers appears on the CD in `MAXWorkshop\Help_Files\Chapter_9\EXSc_01_Warning_Lights.max`.

Step Three—Preparing `Area51_Compositor.max`

The last preparation step before creating Sc-00 and Sc-06 is to make the compositor file and the combined images that you'll use for the final cut of `Area51.avi` in this chapter's Workshop. Save your work, open Video Post, and make the following adjustments:

1. Click File, Save As, and save your max file with the new name `Area51_Compositor.max`. This file is also on the CD in `MAXWorkshop\Help_Files\Chapter_9\EXArea51_Compositor.max`.

2. Double-click the `00-01 Transition` Cross Fade transition event and turn it off by unchecking its Enabled box in the Video Post Parameters section of the Edit Layer Event dialog box (see Figure 9.5).

3. Using the same process, select and disable the following additional layers and events in the queue: Sc-00, Sc-06, Fade In, and Fade Out. Your VP queue should now look like Figure 9.6.

Selected event

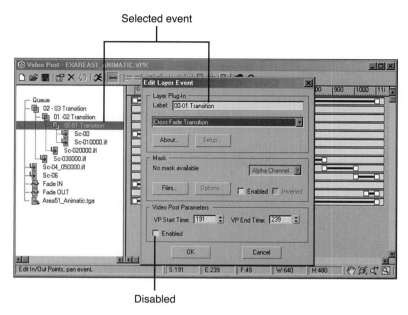

Disabled

Figure 9.5 Some of the transition events aren't needed in the final rendered images that combine Sc-01 through Sc-05. They can be disabled temporarily while those images are rendered.

Disabled events turn gray

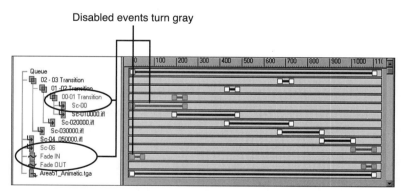

Figure 9.6 When an event is disabled in the VP queue, it won't affect the final imagery.

> **Note**
> These events must be turned off so that the combined images for Sc-01 through Sc-05 can be rendered without the effects of the Cross Fade transitions and Sc-00 and Sc-06, which are still in the queue.

4. Double-click the Area51_Animatic.tga Output Image Event, and then click Files in the Image File section of the Edit Image Output Event dialog box. Browse to your MAXWorkshop\ Area51_Final_Targas directory, create a new folder titled Sc-01-05_Final, and name these combined images Area51_A.tga. Then click OK and return to the VP queue.

5. You are going to composite Sc-01 through Sc-04_05 only. Sc-01 starts at frame 193 in the VP queue and Sc-04_05 ends at frame 1056. Click Execute Sequence and change the Time Output Range to 193 To 1056, and change the aspect ratio back to 640×346, and then click Render (see Figure 9.7).

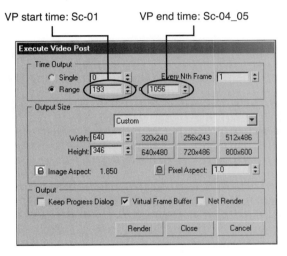

Figure 9.7   The combined images will be added back into the VP queue, taking the place of the multiple separate layer files that are there now. Sc-00, Sc-06, and your personalized information will be composited with the combined images and a soundtrack to create Area51.avi.

6. Save this VP sequence by clicking Save Sequence 🖫 and save it as Area51_Animatic.vpx in your MAXWorkshop\Video Post\Sequences directory. VPX is the file format max uses to save and load your Video Post sequences.

You'll be returning to this max file later in the Workshop, but first you must create the titles and the graphics you'll need to customize your work. Save this file and reset max to a new workspace.

Introduction to Onscreen Graphics—Completing Sc-00 and Sc-06

There are several companies in Hollywood specializing specifically in title and credit sequences and they produce some of the best digital content seen on the screen today. Sometimes the titles are better than the movies they introduce.

Effective onscreen graphics, such as titles, work best when they set up and support the story that follows them—kind of like a visual hors d'oeuvre! The titles for *Independence Day*, *The Matrix*, and *Fight Club* are great examples of innovative digitally animated graphics that you should study and emulate.

Onscreen graphics is a specialized field of endeavor, and some artists have devoted their careers to creating the titles and onscreen graphics that you see every day. If you choose this path, you are heading into one of the most creative and comprehensive uses of max possible. Onscreen graphics span the spectrum of max modeling, effects, and animation—it's the ideal field of play for the artist who wants to do everything. Unfortunately, this chapter, like this book, can only introduce you to the minimum of what is possible in 3ds max 4—the rest is up to you.

> **Tip**
>
> ☙ If you want to learn how to create professional-quality animated title sequences and onscreen graphics, check out *3D Studio Max 3 Media Animation* by John P. Chismar, published by New Riders. This beautifully written and illustrated manual is written by a master devoted specifically to the subject of onscreen graphics and animation. Buy it, read it, and use it—you'll be glad you did!

In this section of the Workshop, you'll learn how to make simple onscreen graphics for Sc-00 and Sc-06, and how to put personalized information into the black borders above and below the active image area of Area51.avi. All the processes you've learned so far in this Workshop can be put to good use to create your titles. But, as always, please experiment freely to create your own unique graphics.

First Things First—File Setup

You'll create two separate max files titled Sc-00.max and Sc-06.max to make the titles and credit crawl sequences. It's important that they be set up correctly, and a brief review of the specifics will help. To anticipate the possibility that you might need longer scene lengths than specified in the storyboards, create both files with the following parameters:

1. Click Time Configuration and change the Frame Count to 600 and the Frame Rate to Film (24 FPS).

> **Note**
>
> Adjusting the Frame Count to more than you need provides some flexibility in the creative process. When you render out the final images, you'll specify the Start and End Frames you want in the Render Scene dialog box.

2. Click Render Scene 🖳 and change the Output Size to 640×346, as shown in Figure 9.8.

Figure 9.8   Adjusting the output size will keep the format for titles and credits consistent with the rest of the scenes. Making this adjustment now will avoid a misrender later.

Creating Sc-00.max

One of my favorite and well-used onscreen graphics is the blinking cursor typing out military computer messages seen in *The Hunt for Red October*. The animatic specifies that the length of Sc-00 will be 10 seconds (240 frames). However, to create a blinking cursor and computer-like text, the title will be much longer than originally planned.

> **Note**
>
> Sc-00 is not a title sequence in the strictest sense of the term, and Area51.avi is more of a trailer than a short movie if accurate terms were applied. The term *title sequence* as it applies to this Workshop refers to the onscreen graphics placed at the front of the movie.

Understanding Safe Frames

Although it's become a visual cliché, the blinking cursor and computer text technique is worthy of exploration. It's also a lot of fun to make, using the tools that you have learned in this book:

1. Open your Sc-00.max file and change to Front view, maximize the view, and press G to turn off the grid.

2. Right-click the viewport name and click Show Safe Frame to display three safe frame rectangles, as shown in Figure 9.9. Safe frames help you in your image development by showing where it's safe to place objects, animation, and text in your shot. The three safe frame rectangles are defined as follows:

   - **Safe Frame: Live Area**—This is the outermost yellow rectangle and indicates the maximum area of your viewport that will be rendered in the final imagery of the shot.
   - **Safe Frame: Action Safe**—This is the middle green rectangle and outlines the safe area where your action and animation can take place.
   - **Safe Frame: Title Safe**—This can also be referred to as Video or TV Title Safe. This is the innermost orange rectangle enclosing an area where the titles and credits of your imagery can be placed safely for viewing on a TV monitor.

Put title within Title Safe limits

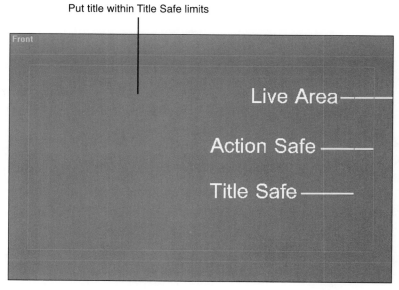

Figure 9.9 Keeping your imagery within the different video safe frames ensures that specific elements and animation you want included in the shot will show up in the imagery when it's displayed on TV monitors.

 Tip The keyboard shortcut toggle to display and hide the safe frames is Shift+F. The aspect ratio of the safe frame rectangles is linked to the aspect ratio specified in the Render Scene dialog—in this case it's 640×346. You can access the completed scene for Sc-00 by opening `MAXWorkshop\Help_Files\Chapter_9\EXSc_00.max`.

Creating the Title Text

Creating the titles for your version of `Area51.avi` is an opportunity to explore your own version of the title. In addition to some creative writing, selecting a font and text color of your choice, you can experiment with the Lens Effects settings to achieve a variation on the glow created in this section:

1. Open the Create tab panel and select Shapes ⬚. Click the Text button. Scroll down to the Parameters rollout and type over the default text, changing it to `Groom Lake: Western Nevada Badlands`, and click in the front viewport to create the text. Move the text string to the center of the viewport inside the Title Safe rectangle, as shown in Figure 9.10. Give it a little room on the sides; you're going to adjust its kerning to make it wider and more readable.

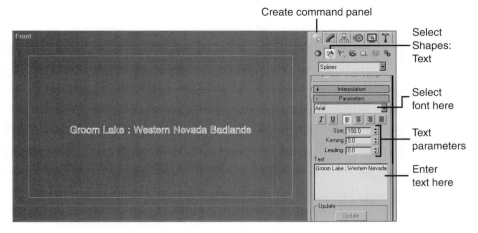

Create command panel

Select Shapes: Text

Select font here

Text parameters

Enter text here

Figure 9.10 To achieve the illusion that a computer is creating the text, a Mask object will be placed in front of the title and animated to reveal the text one letter at a time.

2. Select the text, open the Modify command panel, and scroll down to the Parameters. Change the font by clicking the arrow next to the text style list and select a font you want to use for the title.

3. Change the Kerning so that the text fills the title safe area, and leave some space—about the width of one character—at both ends. Zoom out in the Front view until the text just fits inside the Title Safe rectangle and center the text in the viewport, as shown in Figure 9.11.

Text inside Title Safe frame   Change font type here

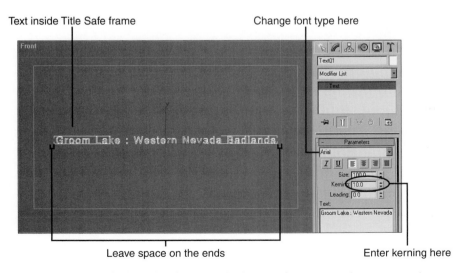

Leave space on the ends   Enter kerning here

Figure 9.11 Kerning controls the space between the letters of your text. The space on the ends of the text string makes some room for the blinking cursor.

The Creative Sword: The Art of Post-Production in 3ds Max 4

4. Click Views, Save Active Front View. This saves the Front view as it is currently config-ured with your text in its proper location. If you use the zoom in or out navigation con-trols and change your Front view, you can get back to this saved POV by clicking Views, Restore Active Front View.

> **Note**
>
> Saving active views helps create custom views that can be restored and used as an aid to your modeling process when you need to see specific parts of a shot or when you don't want to use a camera.

Adding the Text Material

Text is a line shape, and if you rendered it now you wouldn't see anything—there are no sur-faces to catch and reflect light. Converting the text to an editable mesh will create the surfaces needed to make the text visible:

1. Right-click the text and select Convert, Convert to Editable Mesh from the Quad Menu to change the text from a line shape into an editable mesh.

2. Open the Material Editor and create a material named Text with a black Diffuse and Ambient color component. Check the box next to Color in the Self-Illumination section of the Blinn Basic Parameters rollout and change the self-illumination color to bright green— RGB: 0,255,0. Assign the material to the text and render the Front view (see Figure 9.12).

Figure 9.12   The text for Sc-oo is simple and designed with the intent to contrast with the complexity of the subsequent scenes. This is one way to apply the principle of contrast to create more interesting and sophisticated imagery.

Creating the Blinking Cursor

The blinking cursor is a Box primitive that was created with the following parameters: Length: 15; Width: 70; Height: 10. It was then positioned just below and in front of the first letter of the title text, as shown in Figure 9.13.

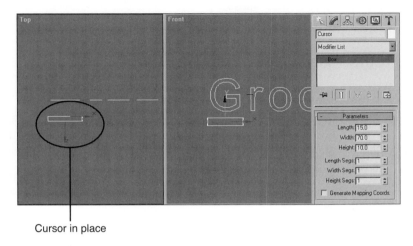

Cursor in place

Figure 9.13   The cursor will blink in place for a few seconds and then move quickly to the right end of the text string.

To create the blinking cursor, follow these steps:

1. Open the Material Editor, copy the Text material you created, and rename it Cursor. Then click the Material Effects Channel icon and change the channel number to 1.

2. Click Rendering, Effects to open the effects dialog box and add Lens Effects to the stack and a Glow element to the active list. Open the Options Tab in the Glow Element rollout. Check Image in the Apply Element To section, check the Effects ID box in Image Sources, and change its number to 1. Leave the Image Filters box set to All and click the Parameters tab.

3. In the Parameters tab, set the size, intensity, and color to achieve the look you want and render a test of the image (see Figure 9.14).

The next step in this process is to create the masking object, which will be used to reveal the letters. To create the reveal animation, it will be linked to the cursor object after the cursor is animated.

Creating the Mask Object

The Mask object is a Box primitive that was created with the following parameters: Length: 135; Width: 2050; Height: 10; Name: Mask. Position it to cover the title text, lie between the text and the cursor box, and align with the end of the cursor, as shown in Figure 9.15.

Figure 9.14 The glow for the cursor in this image used a glow size of 1, an intensity of 200, and a Use Source Color value of 100%.

Figure 9.15 Your box might be a different size, depending on the size of your text and the layout of the title you are creating.

Make a Mask object that covers the type completely and align it with the left side of the cursor. Don't allow the elements to touch each other. If elements intersect, the rendered images will be incorrect.

Open the Material Editor and create a Matte/Shadow material named Mask, uncheck Opaque Alpha, and assign the material to the Mask object. Press Shift+Q to render the Front view—the text is now hidden behind the mask and the cursor remains in the foreground. The next step is to animate the cursor's blink cycle and its move across the screen.

Animating the Blinking Cursor

To animate the blink and the text reveal, you will use the tools and techniques that you have used in the other chapters and appendixes of this book. You'll create the blink first and then animate the movement across the scene. The blink animation uses the Material Editor, the Track Bar, the Track View Editor, and a Parameter Curve Out-of-Range Types Relative Repeat controller. After the animation of the blink is complete, you will link the Mask object to the cursor to create the text reveal.

When you create the blink animation, you are not animating the object; instead, you are animating the material that has been assigned to the object. Make sure that you keep the cursor object selected for each stage of the blink-animation process. The animation keyframes for the material will only show in the Track Bar if the object to which the material is assigned is selected.

Follow these steps to animate the blink and the text reveal:

1. Make sure the Time Slider is at frame 0, select the cursor, and hide the mask and text elements. Open the Material Editor and click the Cursor material preview window to select it. Click the green color swatch next to Self-Illumination and change it to pure black—RGB: 0,0,0.

2. Click Animate, move the Time Slider to frame 20, and change the Self-Illumination color back to RGB: 0,255,0. When you make the change, two keyframes appear in the Track Bar, one at frame 0 and one at frame 20, as shown in Figure 9.16.

3. Create the third and final keyframe of the blink by moving the time slider to frame 40 and change the Self-Illumination color back to black—RGB: 0,0,0. Click Animate to exit Animate mode and close the Material Editor.

If you rendered out the cursor animation at this time, you would see the Cursor material fade smoothly from black to bright green and back to black. The glow element, which uses the self-illumination color of the Cursor material to control the glow color, will fade in and out as well. This is perfect for a pulsating glow effect, but not useful for the abrupt on/off blink needed for the cursor.

Cursor material

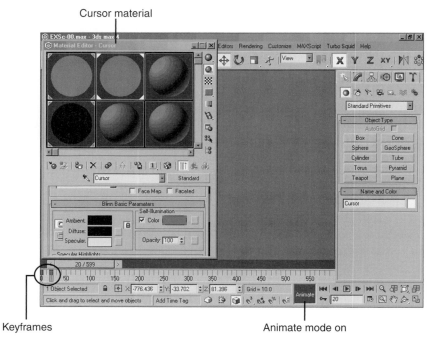

Keyframes

Animate mode on

Figure 9.16 The cursor starts out black and changes to bright green at frame 20. After the next keyframe is created, you'll use each keyframe's Bezier Tangent controllers to make the cursor blink correctly.

In max animation, Bezier Tangent controllers are used to create different types of keyframe interpolation. You'll use the Step Tangent controller to create the blink and then change the Parameter Curve Out-of Range Type to Relative Repeat:

1. Right-click frame 0 in the Track Bar to open the right-click menu, and then click Cursor: Self-Illum Color.

Tip

🥄 Bezier Tangent controllers are described in detail in Appendix F, "Animation Principles in Practice," in MAXWorkshop\Help_Files\ on the CD.

Note

The keyframe right-click menu enables you to access and modify the keyframe parameters. Clicking Cursor: Self-Illum Color enables you to access the animation parameters for the Self-Illumination component of the Cursor material without having to use the Track View Editor.

2. Change the In and Out Bezier Tangent controllers to Step, as shown in Figure 9.17, and then click the right-facing arrow next to the keyframe number to advance to the second keyframe at frame 20. Changing all three keyframe Bezier Tangent controllers to Step In and Step Out will create the appropriate blinking cursor effect for this title.

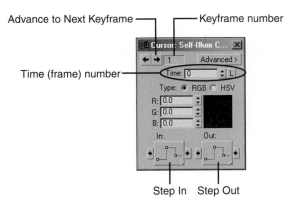

Figure 9.17 Step Tangent controllers are used to create the effect of something turning on or off abruptly—a light bulb, an explosion, and so forth.

3. The Out controller of the previous frame automatically becomes the In controller of the next frame and vice versa. Change the Out Tangent controller for frame 20 to Step, use the arrow to advance to the third keyframe at frame 40, and change its Out Tangent controller to Step as well.

4. Close the Cursor: Self-Illum Color dialog box, right-click the cursor object in your viewport, and click Track View Selected in the Quad Menu.

5. When the Track View Editor for the animating cursor opens, click Filters [icon] in the upper-left corner of the dialog box and change the Show Only selection to Animated Tracks, as shown in Figure 9.18.

6. Open the hierarchy, select Self-Illum Color in the list, click Parameter Curve Out-of-Range Types, and select Relative Repeat (see Figure 9.19).

The animation for the blink cycle is complete. To see the effect, render out a test AVI—the cursor turns on for 20 frames and off for 20 frames, repeating in a cycle of approximately one second per blink.

Animating the Text Reveal

The last animation task in Sc-00 is to create the illusion that the text is appearing letter by letter, as it would on a computer screen. Finding the correct speed for the text reveal will allow you to fool the eye—trompe l'oeil once again! To determine the correct text reveal speed, follow these steps:

1. Unhide the text and mask elements and if you changed your Front view, click Views, Restore Active Front View to return to the view you previously saved.

Select Animated Tracks

Figure 9.18   Large scenes can have hundreds of objects, each with their own animation track. Changing the Track View Filter setting to show only what you need for your immediate work will make it easier to select and modify your max animation.

Select Self-Illum Color

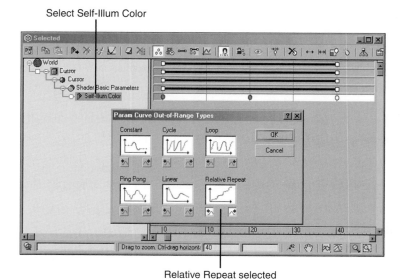

Relative Repeat selected

Figure 9.19   The max User Reference says that "Relative Repeat will cause the three-frame animation you created for the self-illumination value of the Cursor material to repeat by offsetting each repetition by the value at the end frame." Although the definition is somewhat obtuse, I found that this was the type of controller that created the 20-frame on/off blink cycle I wanted to achieve.

2. Select the cursor and right-click the Track Bar to open the menu shown in Figure 9.20. Select Filter, Current Transform as indicated. This will hide the material keyframes that you created in the last process. You'll be animating the lateral motion of the cursor using the Move transform, which is why Current Transform is selected as the filter.

Figure 9.20   Using the Track Bar filter options helps to simplify the animation process for selected objects by displaying only those types of frames needed for your current work. It also protects the keyframes you created for the material animation from accidental movement.

3. Click Animate and move the time slider to frame 10. Move the cursor to the right until it sits in the empty space just past the s in Badlands and exit out of Animate mode (see Figure 9.21).

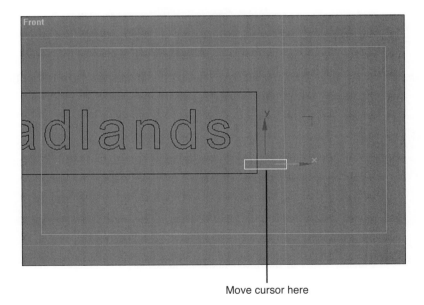

Move cursor here

Figure 9.21   You can adjust the speed of the text reveal by changing the number of frames between the start and end frames. If it's too fast, the eye won't register the movement; too slow and the computer typing effect will be lost. Ten frames looked right in the test AVIs created during the animation process.

The speed of the reveal animation is good but it starts moving at frame 0—the goal was to have the cursor blink a few times before it moves to reveal the text. The cursor should also be on for a moment at the end of the reveal to establish its new location. The blink cycle turns the cursor off at frames 0, 40, 80, 120, and so on. Moving the reveal animation forward to a position just before the beginning of an Off cycle will give the blink time desired before the text reveal and allow the cursor to be on for a short time after the text reveal is finished. Follow these steps to create the correct cursor blink animation:

1. Right-click the keyframe at frame 10 and select Cursor: Position to open the Cursor: Position keyframe dialog box. Change the Time value to 190 and change the Out Tangent to Step, as shown in Figure 9.22.

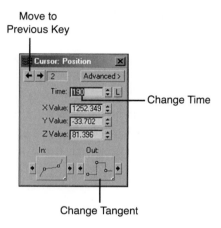

Figure 9.22   The keyframe dialog boxes can also be accessed in the Track View Editor. The same keyframe information is also available in the Motion Control command panel.

> **Note**
>
> Animation is all about mathematics—addition, subtraction, trigonometric elements such as tangent and cosign, logarithmic curves, and so on. Basic keyframe animation is just the start; the real fun begins when you explore expression-controlled animation and max scripts. A script could be written that would animate Sc-00 without using a control panel, Quad Menu, keyframe, or the Track view.

2. Click the left-facing arrow to move to the previous key, which changes to keyframe number 1. Adjust the Time value to 180 and change the In Tangent to Step, as shown in Figure 9.23.

3. Return the time slider to frame 0 and select the Mask object. Click Link 🔗 and link it to the cursor. This makes the mask follow the cursor and completes the reveal animation.

Change Time

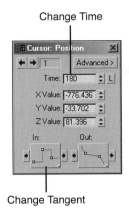

Change Tangent

Figure 9.23   The Step Tangent locks the cursor animation in place until frame 180 when it starts its move to the end of the text.

Render a test AVI of the Front view to evaluate the title animation. The cursor blinks on and off for a few cycles, reveals the title text, and continues to blink as the scene transitions into Sc-01—it's simple and basic, and sets the stage for the weirdness to come.

The final step in the process is to render and save the sequential Targas. Name the images Sc-00.tga and render frames 0 through 480 using the 640×346 format. This will give you 20 seconds of title animation to use. At this point, you could choose to use the images just as they are and add them into the VP queue for the final Area51.avi composite. However, another part of the composite process is an important part of the basic tools you'll use every day: the Image File List (IFL).

Sharpen the Saw—Smart Compositing Using IFLs

In the original animatic VP queue you created at the beginning of the Workshop, you added a Fade In event at the beginning of Sc-00, which created a fade-from-black transition at the beginning of the movie. As you completed the scenes for the project, you added their sequential images into the queue to update the animatic, working toward the end result. The VP queue you created in Area51_Compositor.max now has all the completed sequential images for Sc-01 through Sc-04_05 (see Figure 9.24).

The VP queue for the SC-00 composites is structured with three events: the sequential images, the Fade In event from the original animatic, and a rendered output of the final images with the Fade In transition. You could render the entire 480 frames—again! But that's a waste of valuable time just to *bake* the Fade In transition into the first 48 frames. It would be better to work smarter and use the Image File List to control the process.

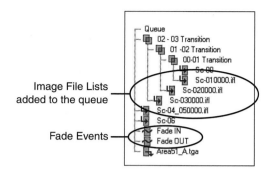

Image File Lists added to the queue

Fade Events

Figure 9.24 When sequential Targa images are added into the VP queue, an Image File List (IFL) is created by max to control the sequences' parameters.

> Just like the ingredients that are baked into a pie, the term *bake* is slang for the end result of a max process that inseparably and permanently combines elements together. To simplify the final compositing process, the effect of the Fade In event will be baked into the first 48 frames of Sc-00. This enables you to eliminate the Fade In event from the Area51.avi Video Post Queue. A completed version of Sc-00_Compositor.max can be found in MAXWorkshop\Help_Files\Chapter_9.

Tip

Using the Image File List is a little tricky the first time around, so here's the step-by-step process:

1. Open a new max file and save it as Sc-00_ Compositor.max. Click Rendering, Video Post. When VP opens, delete ☒ any existing events to clear the queue for this process.

2. Add an Image Input Event 🔲 into the queue, and then double-click it to open the Edit Image Input Event dialog box. Click Files in the Image Input section. When the Select Image File for Video Post Input dialog box opens, browse to the directory where you saved the Sc-00.tga sequential images.

3. Select the first image, click Sequence, and then click Open. This opens the Image File List Control dialog box (see Figure 9.25). Click OK to accept the settings, which will create the IFL and return you to the Edit Image Input Event dialog box.

4. Click Options to access the Image Input Options dialog box for these images. Specify Do Not Resize, and align the images to the center of the screen.

The Video Post Queue now has the Sc-00000.ifl event loaded. Understanding the Image File List Control dialog box is the first step to understanding and using Image File Lists effectively in your work.

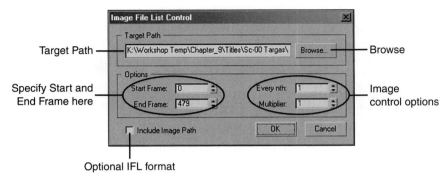

Target Path — Browse

Specify Start and End Frame here

Image control options

Optional IFL format

Figure 9.25 The settings in this dialog box determine the contents, the name, and the location of the Image File List, a text file, which is used to control the sequence and frame count of the images added to the VP queue.

Note

Each time you added a new sequence of images to the VP queue, the Image File List Control dialog box shown in Figure 9.25 opened. The parameters you specified in this dialog box were used to automatically generate a text document known as the Image File List, which contains an ordered list of all the images in the sequence. The IFL can be edited to control which images are loaded into the Image Input Event and the order in which they will appear in the final imagery.

Understanding: Image File List Control

The Image File List Control is a deceptively important little dialog box. The following definitions will help you understand the purpose of the individual sections before you get the practical experience of using the IFL to modify Sc-00:

- **Target Path**—When you add an Image Input Event in the Video Post Queue, you are not adding the physical images you specified; instead, you're making an IFL in a location to which the Target Path points. The default location is the folder containing the images in the IFL, and the default IFL name is the name of the first image in the selected sequence. If you want to create the IFL with a different name and location, click Browse, navigate to the new directory, and save the IFL with a name of your choice.

- **Start Frame/End Frame**—Normally used when you want to specify a specific section of your sequence and load just that part onto Video Post—frames 35 through 194 in a 600-frame sequence, for example. But what if you want a sequence of images to run in reverse, like smoke being sucked back into a chimney or a genie being pulled back into its bottle, while surrounding animation continues in forward motion? Your sequences can run in reverse by putting the end frame number into the Start Frame slot and the start frame number into the End Frame slot (see Figure 9.26).

Tip

The default location for the IFL is in the folders that contain the images they reference. If you so desire, you can use the Target Path option to save your IFLs to a different location than the images. This would be helpful in large projects that have a centralized asset library on a network server or if your images reside in different drive locations. If this is the case, you might want to make one folder containing all the IFLs for a specific scene instead of having them spread among the individual folders. If you specify a different location, you must click Include Image Path in the Image File List Control dialog box. If you don't, the IFL won't know where to look for images and it will fail to load when you try to access it in Video Post or the RAM Player.

Swap Start and End
Frame numbers to —
reverse sequence

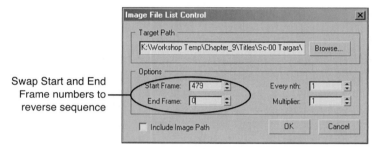

Figure 9.26   Reverse sequences were a mystery until I discovered this aspect of the Image File List Control dialog box. The real power of the list is the fact that it can be edited like any other text document using standard word-processing tools.

- **Every nth**—When set to 1, which is the default value, the IFL will be generated with all the images specified by the Start and End Frame settings. You can load every other frame by changing this value to 2; every 10th frame: 10; and so forth. This setting can be used to create a fast-forward effect in your imagery or to load only a fraction of the images in a sequence for quick evaluation.

- **Multiplier**—Used to stretch out the length of your sequences by multiplying the number of frames specified by the multiplier value. If your image sequence has 50 frames and you specify a multiplier value of 3, each frame in the sequence will be loaded three times for a total length of 150 frames.

- **Include Image Path**—When selected, the IFL will include the complete target path of the directory where the images are stored. For example, an IFL line item for Sc-00, created without the Include Image Path selection active, would appear like this: `Sc-000000.tga`. When Include Image Path is selected, the IFL text string looks like this: `\\Dloose\Dr_Zeus\Workshop Temp\Chapter_9\Titles\Sc-00 Targas\Sc-000000.tga`. You must select this option if you are saving the IFL to a location that's different than the folder containing the images that it controls.

Max stores (writes) the Image File Lists inside the folder that contains the images that you select and load. If you try to add sequential images from a drive that is write protected or from a CD-ROM, the IFL process will fail because the file can't be written back to the drive. To get around this problem, copy the image files to your hard drive first and then create the IFL.

Completing the Sc-oo Video Post Queue

Now that you understand some of the theory behind IFLs, the following steps will take you through a practical example of the process involved to edit the IFL for Sc-00. The intention of this process is to achieve the following goals:

- To eliminate the Fade In event from the final compositing process for Area51.avi.

- To bake the Fade In event into the first 48 frames of Sc-00 and edit its IFL to use the baked images instead of the 48 original frames.

- To help you understand the basics of how to create, edit, and use IFLs in your max compositing work.

The following steps finish the VP Queue you started in the previous section by adding an Image Filter Event and an Image Output Event to the VP Queue, which already contains the Sc-000000.IFL:

1. Click Add Image Filter Event ⊞ in the VP toolbar and select Fade from the list. The overall length of the Video Post Queue determines the initial VP Start and End Times for the Fade event. In this case, it's the length of the Sc-00 IFL.

2. After you've selected Fade from the list, rename the event Fade In, change the VP End Time to 47, and click Setup. When the Fade Image Control dialog box opens, click In, and click OK to exit the dialog box. Click OK again to add the Fade event to the queue (see Figure 9.27).

3. Add an Image Output Event ⊞ to the queue, and edit it to save these images directly into the folder where the other images for Sc-00 are stored. When the Targa Image Control dialog box opens, add your comments and be sure to check the boxes next to 32 Bits-per-Pixel and Pre-Multiplied Alpha. It's very important to give these files a different name. If you call them Sc-00.tga, you'll overwrite the original image files and the asset will be lost. Name the baked images Sc-00_Baked_In.tga. Return to the Edit Output Image Event dialog box, change the VP End Time to 47, and click OK. The VP Queue for this process is now complete (see Figure 9.28).

4. Click Execute Sequence ⊠ and change the Time Output to Range: 0 to 47; change the Output Size to 640×346; and then click Render. When rendering is complete, close Video Post.

Click Setup   Select In

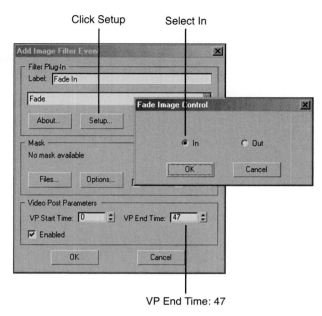

VP End Time: 47

Figure 9.27 The first 48 frames of the scene are black until the cursor first blinks on at frame 20. You'll see the Fade In effect as the cursor slowly brightens until frame 40, when it blinks off.

All events added
to the queue

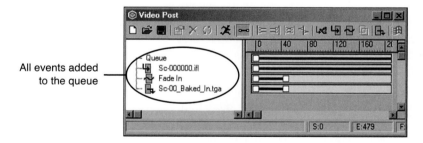

Figure 9.28 The final VP Queue for this process contains Sc-000000.ifl: 480 Frames; Fade In Event: 47 Frames; and SC-00_Baked_In.tga Output Event: 47 Frames. The next step is to execute the sequence and then edit the IFL to include the new images.

Using the IFL Manager

The next part of your introduction to IFLs and their use in max 4's compositing process brings you to the IFL Manager utility found in the Utilities command panel. The intent of this process is to modify the existing Sc-00 IFL to make it use the new baked images instead of the original images created when you made the title sequence. Creating a new IFL for the baked images first will help you understand the basic controls of the IFL Manager:

1. Click the Utilities command panel 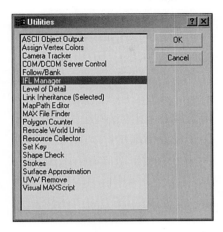 and click More to open the Utilities dialog box shown in Figure 9.29. Select IFL Manager from the list and click OK.

Figure 9.29   Creating, editing, and using IFLs was a difficult and sometimes arcane process before the IFL Manager utility existed. Utilities, like the IFL Manager, are tools that are intended to make your max work easier. Almost 30 standard utilities come with max 4 and many more are available on the Internet.

2. The first step to creating a new IFL using the IFL Manager is to click Select (see Figure 9.30).

Figure 9.30   The controls in the IFL Manager allow you to create and edit Image File Lists. Creative use of IFLs and this Command Panel can simplify and accelerate your compositing process and your use of Video Post.

3. When the Browse Images for Input dialog box opens, browse to the folder containing the Sc-00 sequential images and select the first baked image file, `Sc-00_Baked_In0000.tga`, but don't click Sequence as you have previously (see Figure 9.31).

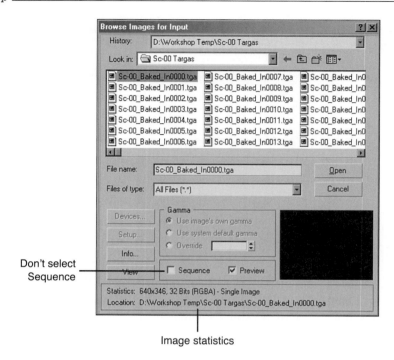

Don't select
Sequence

Image statistics

Figure 9.31 Make it a habit to scan the information at the bottom of this dialog box. It's a quick and easy way to confirm the statistics and location information of the still image you've selected for use in the IFL Manager.

4. Click Open to load the image into the IFL Manager, which will show all 48 images of the baked sequence loaded into its rollout, as shown in Figure 9.32.

File prefix

Frame numbers

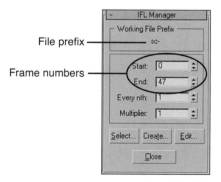

Figure 9.32 Selecting a single image instead of a sequence as you have previously bypasses the familiar Image File List Control dialog box and returns you to the IFL Manager. The prefix shown in this figure is the first three letters of the image name.

If you inadvertently select Sequence in the previous step, the Image File List Control dialog box opens and prompts you through the process of creating and storing an IFL. Then when you exit the Image File List Control dialog box, the alert dialog box shown in Figure 9.33 appears. When this happens, just click OK to return to the IFL Manager. In spite of the dire warning in the alert dialog box, the IFL for the images has been created successfully and is in the folder with the images; it just isn't loaded into the IFL Manager as desired. To recover from this misstep, click Edit in the IFL Manager command panel to open the Select IFL for Editing browser. Browse to the folder that contains the Sc-00 sequential images and click `Sc-00_Baked_In0000.ifl` to open the file.

Figure 9.33   This warning box appears when Sequence has been inadvertently selected in the previous step in the process.

5. The IFL Manager provides essentially the same controls as the Image File List Control dialog box, except there are no Target Path or Include Image Path options in the basic controls—those are accessed by using the Create command. Leave the settings as they are currently configured and click Create to open the Create IFL File dialog box. Browse to the Sc-00 images folder and save this IFL as `Sc-00 Baked Title`—max automatically adds the `.ifl` suffix. The `Sc-000000.ifl` you created in Video Post is already in the list. The task now is to put them together using the same cut-and-paste process used in all word-processing programs.

When you click Save, the Create IFL File dialog box closes and you return to the IFL Manager. The next step is to access and edit the IFL that you just created.

Editing the IFL

Click Edit in the IFL Manager and open `Sc-00 Baked Title.ifl`. This is your first look at an actual IFL (see Figure 9.34).

The following steps will show you how to edit the IFL for Sc-00 to combine the original Targas with the baked images for this scene:

1. Leave `Sc-00_Baked_Title.ifl` open and click Edit again in the IFL Manager. This time open `Sc-000000.ifl` and place both IFLs side-by-side in your viewport. You are going to copy the text from `Sc-000000.ifl` into `Sc-00_Baked_Title.ifl`. This is important, because if you modify `Sc-000000.ifl`, any Video Post Queue that references it will also be modified.

2. Select all the images from `Sc000000.tga` and copy them into `Sc-00_Baked_Title.ifl` after the last image file `Sc-00_Baked_In0047.tga` (see Figure 9.35).

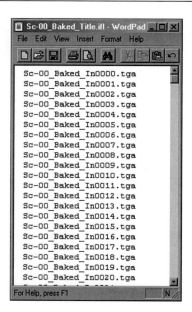

Figure 9.34 Any editing changes you make to this list will affect the sequence and end result of any Video Post event that currently uses this list in the compositing process.

IFL—ASCII Editing

WordPad is the default editor that max uses to view and edit your IFLs, but any text editor can be used for this purpose. IFLs are written using standard ASCII (American Standard Code for Information Interchange) text formatting and conventions. For example, any text following a semicolon (;) is called a remark and is ignored by Video Post. Remarking out an image file (like this: ;Sc-00_Baked_In0000.tga) would be the same as if you deleted the text string for the image from the IFL altogether.

Remarks are a convenient way to add notes to your IFLs with instructions to fellow artists or revision dates and so forth. Editing the IFL follows the command protocols for selecting, cutting, and pasting all other text documents in the PC world. Ctrl+A selects all text, Ctrl+C copies text, and so forth.

3. Close Sc-00000.ifl without saving it. The first 48 frames of the original Sc-000000.tga images that you just pasted into Sc-00_Baked_Title.ifl must be deleted or remarked out so that the baked sequence will load the correct images in their proper order. Select and delete Sc-000000.tga through Sc-000047.tga. The Image File List should look like Figure 9.36. When you are finished with your editing, press Ctrl+S to save the IFL and close the file.

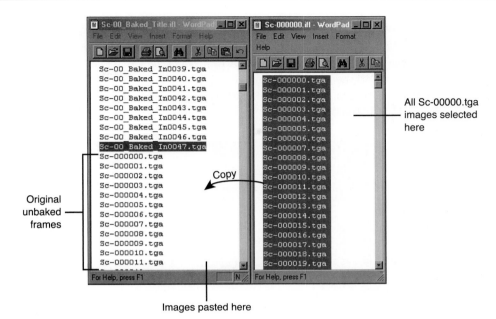

All Sc-00000.tga images selected here

Original unbaked frames

Copy

Images pasted here

Figure 9.35 Be sure that the images are pasted after the baked Targas in the list. The image list you copied from Sc-000000.ifl still contains the original Targas that don't have the baked-in Fade event. The next step removes the original Targas from the list.

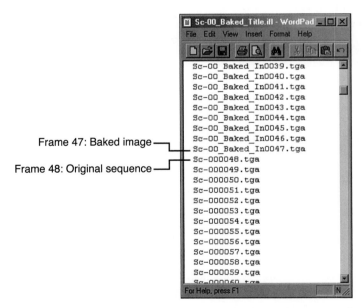

Frame 47: Baked image

Frame 48: Original sequence

Figure 9.36 You've now created and edited your first IFL. You've created the script for an entirely new sequence, without modifying, deleting, or re-rendering any of the actual image files—and you have preserved the original Sc-oo IFL for future use. IFLs can be edited in this way to achieve your artistic vision.

Viewing the Results of the Edited IFL

You can get immediate visual confirmation of whether the IFL you created is working by opening the RAM Player and clicking Open Channel A ⬚. When the Open File, Channel A browser window opens, browse to the folder containing the images and IFLs for Sc-00. Find and select the Sc-00_Baked_Title.ifl file, as shown in Figure 9.37. Don't select Sequence, which will divert you to the IFL Control dialog box to create a new IFL!

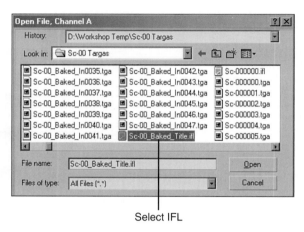

Select IFL

Figure 9.37   Loading an IFL directly into the RAM Player is different than loading sequential images or AVIs as you have done previously. The RAM Player is the best viewing tool to load and evaluate the IFLs you create in max 4.

This completes your introduction to Image File Lists in 3ds max 4. This same process was used to bake the Fade Out event into 96 frames near the end of Sc-06. This process could be used to bake the other transition events into your Area51.avi sequences, but it's not recommended. Baking imagery is an important technique to understand and use when it's appropriate. It's also very important to retain the flexibility to modify intra-scene transition events during the final cut compositing.

This process is unique to the limitations of Video Post; you won't have the same restrictions in other compositing and effects programs such as discreet's combustion or After Effects. Knowing when to bake transitional imagery and when to retain flexibility will come with time and experience, driven by the specific need of the project. To prepare for the final cut process, you need to complete the final scene for Area51.avi: Sc-06.

Creating Sc-06.max

The credit sequence for Area51.avi was created from two composited image layers. The first layer uses an animating plane to create the spinning Alien logo and the credit crawl moving upward in the foreground. The second layer is a single Targa image named Sc-06BG.tga that fades in at the end of the scene. Creating and animating the credit crawl is basically the same process you used to create the text for Sc-00, and the spinning logo is the animated cycle technique you've used before.

Creating the Spinning Logo

To create the spinning logo, follow these steps:

1. Create a plane in the Front view and rename it Logo_Plane. Adjust the following parameters: Length: 100; Width: 100. Display the safe frames and zoom in on the plane until it is centered in the viewport, as shown in Figure 9.38.

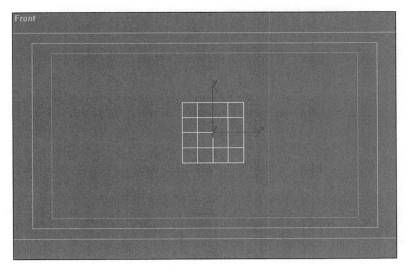

Figure 9.38   You'll animate this plane by spinning it around its Y-axis and creating a cycle animation using Parameter Curve Out-of-Range Types.

2. Create a standard material and add the Alien_Logo.tga into the Diffuse color component map slot. Name the material Logo, change its Material Effects Channel to 1, and drag the map from the Diffuse component onto the Opacity component map slot. Select Instance as the clone mode. Click the 2-Sided box in the Shader Basic Parameters rollout to make this a two-sided material and assign the material to the plane (see Figure 9.39).

The Creative Sword: The Art of Post-Production in 3ds Max 4

Alien logo

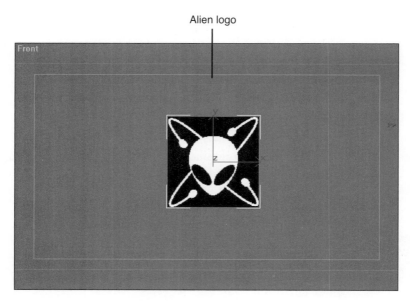

Figure 9.39 Plane objects are single-sided surfaces—they have no backside. If you don't assign a two-sided material to the Logo_Plane, you won't see anything on its other side when the plane spins around. Two-sided materials put their imagery on both sides of the surface, even if there is only one mathematically defined surface to begin with.

3. Select the plane, click Animate, and move the time slider to frame 12. Rotate the plane 45 degrees around its Y-axis and exit Animate mode. Right-click the plane and click Track View Selected in the Quad Menu. When the Track View Editor opens, add a Parameter Curve Out-of-Range Linear controller to the Rotation track.

4. Add a Lens Effects Glow element to the Logo material using Material Effects Channel 1 as specified in step 2. Then change the parameters in the Options tab of the Glow Element rollout as follows: under Image Sources, Effects ID: 1; under Image Filters, select Bright and change its value to 30.

5. Adjust the settings in the Parameters tab of the Glow Element rollout to the following: Size: .5; Intensity: 105; Use Source Color: 0. Click the left color swatch in the Radial Color section and change the color to HSV: 133,255,255—bright blue.

When you're finished, render a test AVI to evaluate your animation. Make any necessary adjustments and save your work (see Figure 9.40).

How to Make the Credit Crawl

I enjoy watching movie credits and am usually glued to my seat until the film runs out of the projector. And I am amazed at how many people it takes to make a movie now compared to films from the 1930s and 1940s when the entire credit list could be shown in one screen.

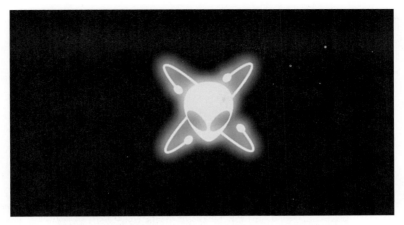

Figure 9.40   The completed background layer is typical of a quick first pass created as a test layer for final imagery. After a layer of this type has been created and inserted into the composite, final imagery can be designed and created to meet the changing needs of the production.

On the Journey

The first time I saw my own name credited on the screen was surreal and outrageously fun. My kids jumped up and down, embarrassing me in public. But screen credits, regardless of how well deserved, can't match the thrill of the journey to the end result. Learn to love the terrible daily-ness of artistic endeavor and let your passion be for the journey! The credits will come as a result of the natural consequence of walking the artist's path.

The intent of a credit sequence is to acknowledge the contributions of the entire production team. Your credit list for Area51.avi is up to you and you should have some fun with this step. But remember, you might be showing this as a part of your reel and the credit crawl will be the last thing that your audience will see on the screen—make it count.

The same text-creation process used in Sc-00 was employed in Sc-06 to create a tall paragraph of text. This was then linked to a dummy object to control the crawl animation. Multiple text groups were created and assigned two different materials to visually organize and segment the credit headings and the names in the credits. Organizing the elements in this way allows you to create more sophisticated graphic layouts (see Figure 9.41).

After the basic materials were created and assigned to the credit crawl, a completely black material and a Lens Effects Glow element were assigned to the Area 51 text element that cross fades in over the logo at the end of the scene (see Figure 9.42).

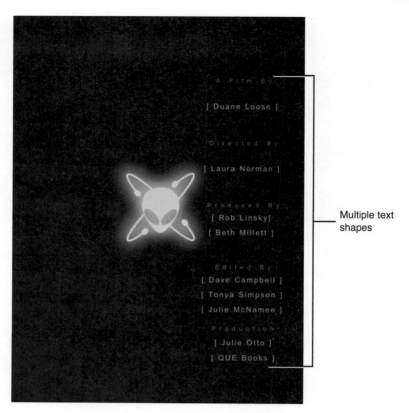

Multiple text shapes

Figure 9.41   Text layout for titles and credits is fundamentally a graphic design problem. The same design principles used throughout this book, such as balance, rhythm, proportion, contrast, and so on, also apply to your onscreen graphics.

Figure 9.42   The Area 51 text, `Sc-06BG.tga`, is the last image on the screen at the end of `Area51.avi` as the movie fades to black. A Lens Effects Glow element was added to black text with a colored Self-illumination component using the Material Effects Channel. The image was rendered at 640×346 and saved as `Sc-06BG.tga`. It can be found on the CD in `MAXWorkshop\Help_Files\Chapter_9`.

The credit crawl was animated by first linking the text elements to a dummy object and animating the dummy to move slowly up through the field of view, which is why this type of credit sequence is known as a *crawl*. When the animation was completed, the sequential Sc-06.tga images were rendered and Sc-060000.ifl was created using the IFL Manager.

Sc-06 Final Composites

For the final imagery for this sequence, I wanted the Sc-06_BG to fade in beginning at frame number 409 and be the only image onscreen at frame 504, remaining visible until the end of the scene at frame 599. While Sc-06BG.tga is fading in, I wanted Sc-06 to fade out starting at frame 409 and disappearing completely by frame 504.

This transition was too complex to set up in the same Video Post Queue as the final cut of Area51.avi, so I baked a Cross Fade transition and Sc-06BG.tga into frames 409 through 599 and created a new Image File List to use in the final cut compositing. The following steps outline the process:

1. Add Sc-060000.ifl ⊞ to the queue at the top of the list. In the Image Input Options dialog box, select Do Not Resize. Choose the centered alignment and enter 0 in the From box and 599 in the To box under Frames. Uncheck the Loop at the End check box. When you exit the Image Input Options dialog box and return to the Edit Input Image Event dialog box, leave the VP Start and End Times set to 0, 599 (see Figure 9.43).

IFL control options —

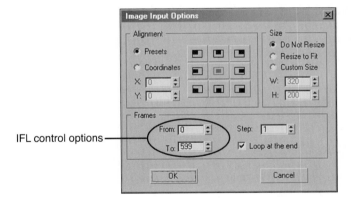

Figure 9.43   The Image Input Options dialog box also contains some options that control the Image File List. Changing the Frames settings loads the specified range from the IFL into the queue.

2. Next, add the Sc-06BG.tga ⊞ still image to the queue and choose Do Not Resize and centered alignment. Then change its VP Start and End Times to 409 and 599. This will make the image last to the end of the credit sequence, providing several seconds of imagery to use in the final cut.

3. Hold down the Ctrl key, and select the Sc-060000.ifl and the Sc-06BG.tga layers. Add a Cross Fade Transition ⊞ Image Layer event to these two images, and adjust the Cross Fade VP Start and End Times to 409 and 504.

4. The last step to complete the queue is to add an Image Output Event 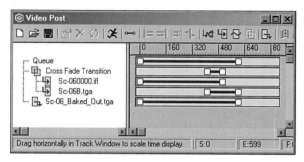, change its VP Start and End Times to 409 and 599, and save these images as `Sc-06_Baked_Out.tga` in the same folder as the images for `Sc-060000.ifl`. The queue can be seen in Figure 9.44.

Figure 9.44   The baking process adds a pre-rendered Fade Out transition into the Sc-06 sequence. The edited IFL created to control the imagery will be added into the Video Post Queue for the final cut.

5. Execute the sequence rendering frames 409 through 599 in 640×346 format. After the images are rendered, use the IFL Manager to create a new Image File List named `Sc-06_Baked_Out.ifl`, and add `Sc-060000.tga` through `Sc-060408.tga` from `Sc-060000.ifl` to the baked frames you just created, as shown in Figure 9.45.

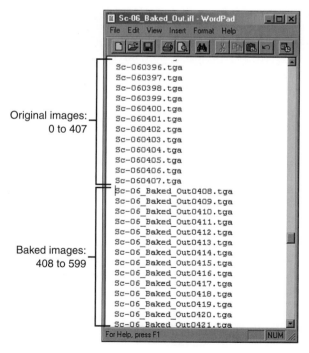

Figure 9.45   Using Video Post as a compositing tool is a brute-force approach to editing and compositing. Mastering the IFL process will bend it to your will. The alternative is to bite the bullet and buy discreet's combustion or After Effects.

Creating Customized Screen Formats

You can use several methods and different software tools to create onscreen graphics and text for your titles, credits, and customized screen formats. Any 2D-imaging package, such as Adobe Photoshop, can be used for this purpose. Photoshop is a basic tool in every digital artist's toolbox. Another great tool I use every day is Bryce 3d; it's an awesome sky and texture tool.

The concepts you have been learning in the previous sections of this Workshop provide the basis for creating the customized format shown in Figure 9.46.

[3ds max 4 workshop]

Figure 9.46   Your version of a customized screen format can be composited in the final Area 51 Video Post sequence. It will be the last Image Input event in the queue and is used to customize your version of the end result of this Workshop.

The first step is to save Sc-06.max as Area51_Format.max. The image aspect ratio for the customized screen layer was changed to 640×480, so text and graphics could be placed into the blank area created above and below the 640×346 format of the scenes. The spinning logo created for Sc-06 has been moved into the lower-right corner of the screen. Text was added in the format desired and 96 sequential images were rendered out and titled Area51_Format.tga.

The spinning logo makes a complete 360-degree revolution once every 96 frames. It's a repeating cycle that can be used in Video Post instead of rendering 1,700 sequential images. To make this happen, the image input options were used to make Video Post loop or repeat the sequence of the small spinning logo (see Figure 9.47).

The Creative Sword: The Art of Post-Production in 3ds Max 4

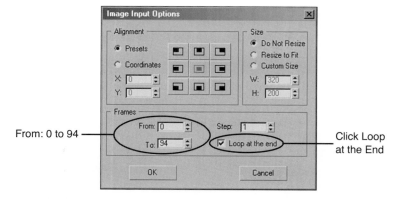

From: 0 to 94

Click Loop
at the End

Figure 9.47   The animation cycle for the spinning logo begins at frame 0 and completes its rotation at frame 95—96 frames in all. You'll add this sequence into the Video Post Queue for the final cut of Area51.avi.

Max Workshop—Area51.avi Final Cut

"This is the end, Beautiful friend, This is the end, My only friend, the end..."
- The Doors, 1967

When images are combined with music and sound, a power is unleashed that transcends their individual and separate powers to move and entertain us. Ask yourself why Steven Spielberg and George Lucas prefer to work with composer John Williams and vice versa. Among all the reasons that could be listed, the fundamental reason is that they understand the combined power of the art—they get it!

When artists of this caliber combine their efforts, they create experiences that tap into the memes that exist in our shared experiences as human beings. Music and images *are* the experience we create as digital artists, and one without the other is no experience at all. The lesson is to design and create your content with the music and sound in mind.

Aural Memes

One of the movies that has had the most cinematic influence on me is *Apocalypse Now*, directed by Francis Ford Coppola and starring Martin Sheen, which I first saw in 1979—it was as disturbing then as it is now in its portrayal of the war in Viet Nam. Other than the explicit and often surreal visuals, I remember the way the music and the soundtrack worked with the imagery. It was the first time I understood the power music and sound have in a film, and I had an epiphany about its importance. I went home with the music and the images roiling around in my awareness.

One scene in particular, and one song specifically, stand out in my memories of the movie. The song is "The End," by the Doors from their self-titled debut album *The Doors*, released in 1967. And every time I come to the end of some intense project, like this book, that song plays in my head—it's a powerful aural meme at work.

Sound and 3ds Max 4

Although max 4 is primarily a content-creation tool, some artists love to create all aspects of their projects, including sound. Professional studios usually have in-house or contract sound engineers who are charged with the creation of dialogue, sound effects, music tracks, and so on. As a beginning max 4 user or if you are working in a small studio, you might not have access to that capability, so it's up to you. There are several basic tools you can use to add sound to your projects. Foley Studio MAX (FSM) is the best product I've found and it works seamlessly within the max 4 environment.

FSM was developed by Boomer Labs and published by Digimation in December 1999. A demo of the latest version of this plug-in for 3ds max 4 is included on the companion CD for this Workshop. The other program is Sound Forge by Sonic Foundry, which can be used to create and edit sound effects and music tracks and then add them into max using FSM. Sound Forge is inexpensive and is the standard for low-cost, high-quality two-track stereo editing and sound creation.

These are the basic beginning tools I use to create sound for my max work, which is not very often. I leave it to the amazing talents of the musicians and sound engineers who work with our studio. However, for this Workshop, I've provided a completed soundtrack for you to add to `Area51.avi`. It's on the CD in `MAXWorkshop\Help_Files\Chapter_9\Area51.wav`.

`Area51.avi`: Final Cut

You have been using Video Post to create test composites of the images you've been creating and the animatic for this Workshop. The final process to create `Area51.avi` and finish this Workshop returns you to Video Post to create the final cut for the project. The following sections outline the process to complete the final Video Post Queue and show you how to add the `Area51.wav` file to the movie.

At this point in the Workshop, you know how to use the different tools and commands in Video Post to create the final queue. If you've followed all the steps up to this point, the VP Queue for the final cut will be the easiest one you've created so far.

> **Tip**
>
> The final queue for `EXArea51_Compositor.max` is named `EXArea51_Final Cut.vpx` and is on the CD. You can load it into a new VP Queue by opening Video Post, clicking Open Sequence, and browsing to `MAXWorkshop\Help_Files\Chapter_9`.

First, take a look at the last queue you created:

1. Open your `Area51_Compositor.max` file and then open Video Post to return to the VP Queue shown in Figure 9.48.

2. If you didn't already do it, click Save Sequence and save this queue as `Area51_Animatic.vpx` in your `MAXWorkshop\Video Post\Sequences` directory. Click Queue at the top to highlight the entire queue and click Delete to clear the queue.

3. Using the information in Table 9.1, add the specified Image Input Events, in the order indicated from top to bottom, into the queue and adjust their VP Start and End Times as indicated. When you are finished, the final cut VP Queue should look like Figure 9.49.

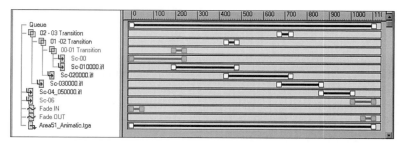

Figure 9.48 This is the queue you created to composite the combined sequences for Sc-01 through Sc-04_05. Take one last look at it—it has served you well, but it's time to say goodbye.

Table 9.1 Area 51 Final Cut Video Post Queue Image Input Events

Order in Queue	IFL Filename	Frame Count	VP Start/End Times
1	Sc-00_Baked_Title.ifl	328	0, 327
2	Area51_A0191.ifl	817	279, 1095
3	Sc-06_Baked_Out.ifl	600	1024, 1623
4	Area51_Format0000.ifl	96	0, 1623

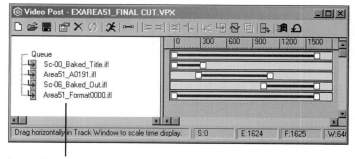

Image File Lists in place

Figure 9.49 The hardest part of creating this queue is doing the math to create the correct scene transitions—just remember to include frame 0 in the overall frame length of the scene. The next step is to adjust the Image Input settings for each of the IFLs.

4. Double-click each IFL to open the Edit Image Input Event dialog box and click Options to open the Image Input Options dialog box. Use Table 9.2 to make the indicated adjustments to all four of the IFLs in the VP queue.

Table 9.2 Area51 Final Cut IFL Image Input Options

IFL Filename	Size/Alignment	Frames: From—To	Loop
Sc-00_Baked_Title.ifl	Don't Resize/Center	0, 327	Don't Loop
Area51_A0191.ifl	Don't Resize/Center	0, 816	Don't Loop
Sc-06_Baked_Out.ifl	Don't Resize/Center	0, 599	Don't Loop
Area51_Format0000.ifl	Don't Resize/Center	0, 95	Loop

Don't confuse the Frames: From and To settings in the Image Input Options dialog box with the VP Start and End Times in the Edit Input Image Event dialog box. The Frames settings specify which segment of the IFL to use in the queue, and the VP Start and End Times specify the location of the segment as it relates to time.

5. There are two Cross Fade transitions to add to the queue. Create the first transition by selecting Sc-00_Baked_Title.ifl and Area51_A0191.ifl and then click Add Image Layer Event ⬚. Select Cross Fade Transition from the list and change the name of this event to Cross Fade One. Change its VP Start and End Times to 279 and 327 and click OK to add the transition to the queue.

6. Select Cross Fade One and Sc-06_Baked_Out.ifl and add the second Cross Fade Transition event. Name it Cross Fade Two and change its VP Start Time to 1024 and the VP End Time to 1096. Your final cut VP Queue is almost finished (see Figure 9.50).

Cross Fade transitions added

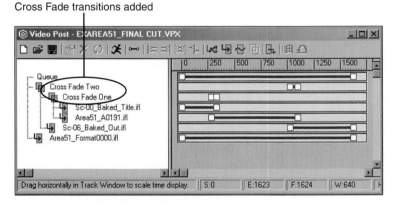

Figure 9.50   The next step is to make the customized format visible in the final images by using an Alpha Compositor.

The VP Start and End Times of the Cross Fade transitions are determined by the VP Start and End Times of the two image layers between which the transition is taking place. These are the only cross fades needed in the final cut; the others have been baked into the individual IFLs.

7. Select Cross Fade Two and Area51_Format0000.ifl and click Add Image Layer Event ⬚. Select Alpha Compositor from the list and click OK to return to the VP Queue (see Figure 9.51).

Alpha Compositor in place

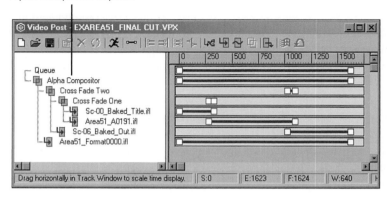

Figure 9.51　The Alpha Compositor enables the customize screen format to overlay all the images in the queue by combining Area51_Format0000.ifl with the other Cross Fade transitions in the queue. All that's needed in the queue now is the Image Output Event.

8. The last step to finish the queue is to add the Image Output Event to the queue. Click Add Image Output Event [ ]. Browse your MAXWorkshop\Area51_Final_Targas directory, and create a new folder titled Area51_Final Composites. Save these final cut images as Area51_Final.tga. Render the 1,625 final images out at 640×480 format and save your file. The final cut Video Post Queue is completed and should look like Figure 9.52.

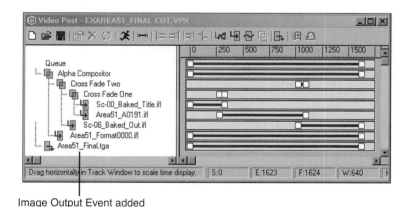

Image Output Event added

Figure 9.52　The completed Video Post Queue for the final cut of Area51.avi should be kept pretty simple. Make any changes and adjustments in the scene individual layer files and use the power of the IFL to replace re-rendered imagery in the composites.

Video Post might not be the most elegant compositor around but I have grown to enjoy it even more now that I understand how to create and modify Image File Lists. While the final cut images render, read the next section on how to add a .wav sound file to the Track view.

Adding Sound—The Max Way

The intent of the sound capability in max 4 is to give you a simple tool to load and use sound files to guide your animation. But the process can also be adapted to add preliminary sound to your digital content. To prepare `Area51_Compositor.max` to add the soundtrack, click Time Configuration and change the frame count to 1624. This will play the sound file for the entire duration of the compositing process. The following steps show you how to add a soundtrack to your 3ds max 4 scenes:

1. Click the Main Toolbar tab panel and click Open Track View ![icon]. The first item in the hierarchy list under the World icon is Sound. Click it to select it, and then right-click it to open its right-click menu. Select Properties from the list to open the Sound Options dialog box shown in Figure 9.53.

Click here to select
and load sound file

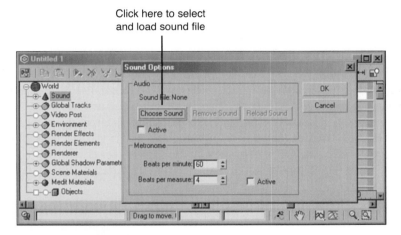

Figure 9.53 A sound file added to the Soundtrack in the Track view can be used for dialogue lip sync or, in this case, to add the `Area51.wav` file to Video Post as you render `Area51.avi`.

2. Click Choose Sound and select `MAXWorkshop\Help Files\Chapter_9\Area51.wav`. Click OK to add the track to the Sound Options dialog box and click OK again to return to Track view. Click the plus sign next to Sound to expand the Soundtrack and see the waveform, as shown in Figure 9.54. Click Play Animation ![icon] to hear the soundtrack, and then close Track view and save your file.

A new feature in max 4 is the capability to show the sound file in the Track Bar. Right-click the Track Bar and select Configure, Show Soundtrack to see the `Area51.wav`.

> **Tip**
>
> The capability to show the soundtrack in the Track Bar will help you lip sync dialogue, match sound effects to visual effects, and so on.

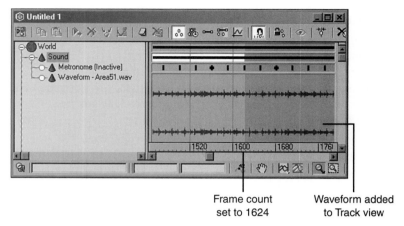

Frame count   Waveform added
set to 1624   to Track view

Figure 9.54   The Area51.avi soundtrack was created with a length of 1624 frames to last the entire length of the movie.

Rendering the Area51.avi

After the Area51_Final.tga images are rendered and saved, you can use them to create an AVI with the soundtrack you've loaded into the Track view. Open a new Video Post Queue and add the Area51_Final0000.ifl into the queue. Then create an Image Output Event named Area51.avi and render it out. This will add the soundtrack to the AVI, which you will hear when you play the movie.

Creating AVIs

I prefer to create AVIs from pre-rendered sequential files rather than rendering them out directly from the final cut VP Queues. Lately I've been experimenting with using the RAM Player to make AVIs by loading in sequential images and saving them out from there, rather than going through Video Post. It helps to have a lot of RAM, at least 500MB (megabytes), if you are going to try this with Area51.avi. Otherwise, use Video Post. Better yet, use Premiere to combine the sequential images and the soundtrack. If your system RAM is less than 256MB and you want to try using the RAM Player to make an AVI, you might want to specify that the sequential images be reduced to 320×240 when you load them in the player.

This chapter has taken you through some of the more esoteric tools used in the Video Post compositing process, creating credits and titles, and customizing your screen format. Even though Video Post is somewhat limiting, these basic techniques can be applied in principle to the other editing and effects software you might use to create your reel.

Next Steps

It's early morning, February 24, 2001, and *3ds max 4 Workshop* is now finished. I can hear the Doors singing...*This is the End!* This has been a much bigger project than its predecessor and hopefully it has empowered and enriched your growth towards max mastery.

The next step for me is to reacquaint myself with my family and learn what it's like to have one job for a few weeks. After a little time off, I'll be starting on a new book full of ideas, concepts, and techniques from my work as a game artist. The book will be on the principles and practice of using 3ds max 4 to develop art for video games and will be published in Fall 2001.

I've learned many new and important things about the tools and techniques in max during this process, and that new knowledge has sparked some ideas for future projects and experimentation. I have enjoyed introducing you to 3ds max 4 and hope that you have found this part of your journey worthwhile. And I'm very excited for you to see the two main projects we have been working on here at Creative Capers Entertainment. Both projects are being created in max—one in MAX 3.0 and one in 3ds max 4. Watch for our animated TV show, *Sitting Ducks*, which will be coming to your TV in Fall 2001. I hope you like it—it's "Seinfeld" for kids! Also watch for the first episode of our third-person action adventure game: *Intergalactic Bounty Hunter* published by Pan Interactive.

My wish for you is that you are successful in your desire to bring the stories in your imagination out to show the world. You have the brains, the talent, and the drive and now you have the tool! Until next time...the journey continues.

Duane Loose

Duane Loose
Writer/Creative Director
Creative Capers Entertainment, Inc.

The Author as a child, somewhere in Illinois. Photograph by Gordon Loose, 1962.

3ds Max 4 Installation and Setup

Congratulations! You are about to install the premiere tool for digital content creation: 3ds max 4. This could be your first step into a transition from the traditional artistic disciplines you have previously mastered. Be assured that everything you already know will be put to good use in this amazing software. And the things you don't know will be easily learned along the way as you master this latest revision of max from discreet. The information in the next few pages will walk you through the installation, authorization, and setup of 3ds max 4. First, look at what max 4 needs to run effectively on your computer.

Your Computer and 3ds Max 4

Discreet has defined the minimum hardware and operating system requirements that your system will need to run the software. However, as you progress as a max artist, a computer configured with the minimum requirements will not provide adequate performance. Given that you just paid about $3,500 to purchase this software, you probably won't be able to go out and buy a new system just to run max. But don't despair, the cost of hardware components, such as RAM and hard disk drives, can fluctuate dramatically and you should always be on the lookout for system upgrades to bring your hardware up to recommended specifications.

Professional Systems

The new professional-grade systems that we buy at our studio cost between $2,500 and $5,000 per system. That includes the monitor, dual processors, at least 512MB of RAM, and a high-end video card with a minimum 32MB of onboard memory. Four years ago, the first Pentium Pro 200MHz system we purchased cost $25,000. Gulp! Those were the days.

The bottom line is that the more powerful your system, the better max 4 will perform—and you are more likely to enjoy your work and the learning process. So, at some point in your development as a digital artist, you will need to purchase a professional-quality system. It's an investment in your future, and the difference it will make can't be overstated.

Upgrading Your System: Quality and Balance

The first step to upgrading your existing system is to understand what you've already got under the hood. Your motherboard might already be able to handle an additional processor or RAM. But beware! 3ds max 4 is multithreaded, which means it can use the power of dual processors; however, Windows 98 is not capable of multithread processing—for that you'll need Windows 2000 or Windows NT. However, keep in mind that 3ds max 4 is intended for use under Windows 2000, which is the only OS officially supported by discreet.

Experience has shown that a smart approach to component upgrades is to always buy name brands and to carefully match the components with existing system hardware. You might need to seek out some professional advice to get the match-ups just right. Adding more RAM will certainly increase performance, but might not be enough by itself. Adding a hardware-accelerated video card with a minimum 32MB of onboard memory is one of the best investments you can make in rendering and creation speed. A fast, big hard drive in the 18–30GB range spinning at 10,000rpm or faster is also an important upgrade. You'll need that kind of size and speed to be able to effectively store and view the animated scenes you'll be creating.

The other factor to consider is the quality of the upgrade components you purchase. There are well-known name brand motherboards and hard disks that we won't buy because of quality, reliability, and performance issues. We learned this by experience and through the max user grapevine. So, you can't always judge a component by its brand. But research the name brands first, do your homework, and find out what other max artists use and like—they're your best resource for system performance information.

Follow these important steps to upgrade your system:

- Know how your system is currently configured.
- Seek out professional advice to determine what you need to purchase.
- Purchase name brands, but do your homework first.
- Find out what other max artists use and recommend.
- Be patient—watch for sales and prowl the computer shows.

3ds Max 4 System Requirements

Table A.1 shows the minimum requirements as established by discreet.

Table A.1   3ds Max 4 System Requirements

Hardware/Software	Minimum	Recommended
Processor Speed	Intel-compatible 300MHz processor	Dual Intel PIII 600MHz or more or Single Intel P4 1.4GHz

Table A.1 Continued

Hardware/Software	Minimum	Recommended
Operating System	Windows 2000 Professional only recommended OS; Windows NT or Windows 98 not officially supported	Windows 2000 Service Pack 1
RAM	128MB	512MB
Free Disk Space	400MB of space to install max	4GB to complete this book's Workshops
Swap File Disk Space	300MB	1.5GB (three times your RAM is recommended)
Display	Graphics card supporting a minimum resolution of 1,024×768 High color	1,024×768 True color, Open GL, Direct 3D, 3D graphics hardware accelerated
Mouse/Keyboard	Windows-compliant mouse and keyboard	Microsoft Intellimouse or Logitech Cordless iTouch Keyboard and Mouse

Note

Be sure you have installed the appropriate video drivers from your video card manufacturer and that your card is approved for use with your operating system and with 3ds max 4. These drivers are always available from the board manufacturer's Web site. Keeping current with the latest versions of your drivers will ensure maximum efficiency from your system, so it is well worth while keeping abreast of new driver releases.

3ds Max 4 Installation

Compared to its previous releases, 3ds max 4 is a delight to install for one simple reason: no dongle. The *dongle* was the hardware lock used to protect the software from being illegally used by software pirates. Discreet finally worked the bugs out of a software lock system and it came as good news to those who currently have eight inches of 3ds max dongles connected to our parallel ports. Thank you, discreet.

Installation: Simple and Easy

Max 4 installation follows the standard Windows format for installer screens and protocols. To begin the installation process, insert the 3ds max 4 CD into your CD drive and follow these instructions:

1. The 3ds max 4 installer should automatically open when your CD is inserted into the CD drive. The first screen you see is the discreet install window (see Figure A.1).

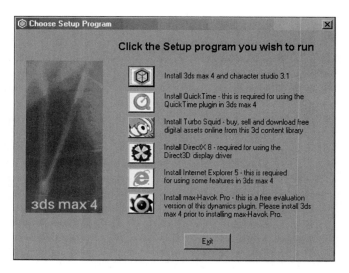

Figure A.1   The discreet install window appears each time you install software from this CD.

If 3ds max 4 does not automatically begin installing when you insert the CD, it might mean that Autorun has been disabled on your system. If this is the case, you can get to the installer by double-clicking My Computer, and then double-clicking the CD. This should start the Install process.

2. Click the Install 3ds max 4 button, as shown in Figure A.2.

3. After initialization, the 3ds max 4 Installation Wizard appears. Take a moment and read the text, follow the advice to exit all Windows programs before running this setup program, and click Next.

4. When the license agreement appears, review the text of the agreement, click I Accept, and then click Next to continue the installation (see Figure A.3).

Figure A.2   You can install five programs from the discreet install window, including Microsoft Internet Explorer, which is required for the User Reference and help features in 3ds max 4. To optimize your use of max 4, install all the programs listed.

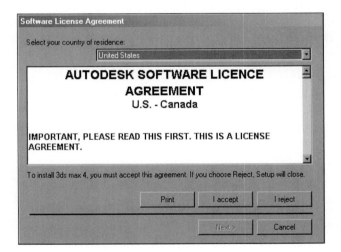

Figure A.3   Read the software license agreement for information about upgrades, additional users, backup copies, and so forth.

5. The Serial Number Dialog screen appears next and is where you will enter the serial number and the CD Key for this copy of max 4. On the bottom of the back of the 3ds max 4 CD jewel case or envelope, there is a yellow label containing the serial number and CD Key. Enter these numbers in the fields as shown in Figure A.4, and then click Next.

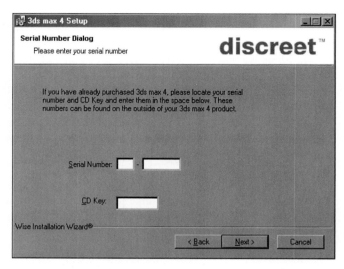

Figure A.4   The serial number is an 11-digit number and the CD Key is composed of 6 numbers and letters. You will need both to install, register, and authorize the software.

Software Licensing and Ownership

An important thing to remember is that the software on this CD does not belong to you; it is the property of Autodesk and its subsidiary, discreet. You can't legally sell it or even give it away to someone when the next rev of max is released. Unlike this book, what you have purchased from discreet is a nontransferable license to use its software.

6. In the next window, you can review the Readme Information file, which contains additional notes about this version of 3ds max 4. When you are finished, click Next to continue with the installation.

7. The next screen you see is the User Information window, as shown in Figure A.5. Fill out the information requested. If you are the only user of this software, select the Only for Me option. If other artists will be using this seat of max, choose the Anyone Who Uses This Computer option. Click Next when you are finished.

Create a 3ds max 4 Journal

For the past three years, I have kept a 3ds max journal and the notes in it have become the basis for many of the techniques in this book and its prequel. I use Bienfang NoteSketch books, which have lines for written notes on one side and a blank area for sketching on the other half of the page. When you receive your max authorization code, put it in this book along with the software serial number and CD Key. Use the journal to make notes on the technique settings and processes in this Workshop, keep track of any error messages you might get, and write down those flashes of inspiration that will come as you use the program. You'll find that keeping a working journal empowers your learning process.

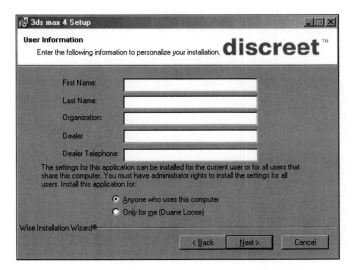

Figure A.5 It's in your best interest to provide discreet with all the information requested. It will be used to verify and validate your qualification for ongoing technical support, product revision information, and so forth.

8. The Destination Folder screen is next. Here you can specify the hard disk location where 3ds max 4 will be installed. If the destination that the installer chooses is okay, click Next to continue with the installation. Use the Browse button to specify a different location. Click Next after you have specified the Destination Folder (see Figure A.6).

9. 3ds max 4 gives you the choice of three types of installation: Typical, Compact, and Complete. When the Select Installation Type window opens, choose Typical and click Next to continue the installation (see Figure A.7).

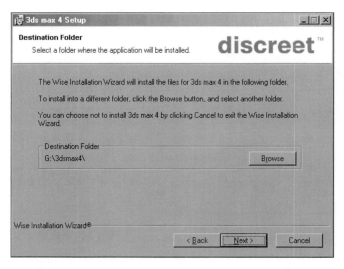

Figure A.6 The default drive max chooses for installation is your system's main hard drive. If this drive doesn't have enough available disk space for installation, you'll be prompted to choose a different install location.

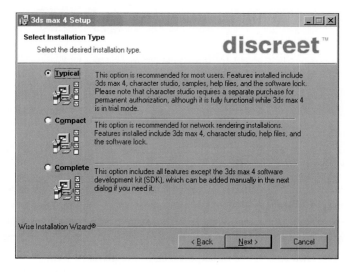

Figure A.7 Typical installation is appropriate for the majority of max users, especially beginners. This type of installation gives you the full suite of max tools you'll need for this Workshop and beyond.

Note

Besides Typical, the other two installation options for max are as follows:

- **Compact installation**—Minimum option install of max, which is recommended for when you are setting up a max rendering server on your network.

- **Complete installation**—For users who want to install the max SDK, all the sample files on the CD, or Character Studio 3.1.

10. When the Ready to Install the Application window appears, the installer is ready to copy the 3ds max 4 software files to your hard disk (see Figure A.8). Click Next to proceed with installation.

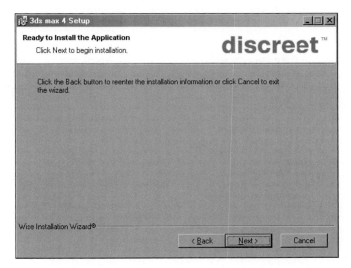

Figure A.8 If you have any doubt about the installation information you've provided, click the Back button to review and revise it.

11. The Updating System window shows you the installation progress. This should take just a few minutes, depending on the speed of your system (see Figure A.9).

12. Click Finish when the window proclaiming that the software has been successfully installed appears. The installer then prompts you to restart your computer. If you plan to install additional software from the CD, click No; otherwise, click Yes and reboot your system (see Figure A.10).

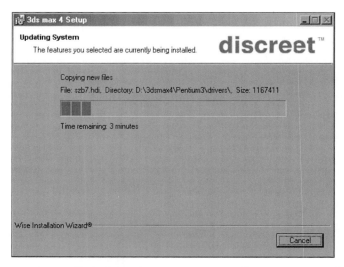

Figure A.9   After max is installed, the authorization process allows you to complete your product registration electronically. Do it! Discreet is a great company to deal with and it provides a lot of informative news about 3ds max and its related products to the registered users of the software.

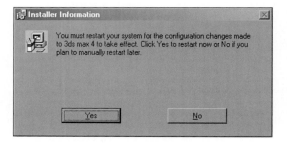

Figure A.10   3ds max 4 is not immune to the chronic Windows restart requirement. While you are waiting, peel off the yellow 3ds max 4 serial number and CD Key code sticker from the label that came with the software and stick it into your max journal. When you reboot, the installation process adds a 3ds max 4 icon to your desktop.

Registering and Authorizing 3ds Max 4

Before you officially use 3ds max 4 for the first time, it must be registered and authorized to protect the software from piracy.

When you installed the software, you also installed the C-Dilla License Management System—the software replacement for the dongle. When an authorization code is put into the system, C-Dilla creates a lock that links the software to your specific workstation. This protects max from being illegally used by multiple artists on multiple workstations.

Authorizing Max

The following steps take you through the authorization process that retrieves an authorization code over the Internet. This is the easiest and quickest method to authorize the software and one of the innovative additions discreet has made to this process.

> **Note**
>
> If you already have an authorization code, start 3ds max 4 and follow the prompts to enter the code and authorize your software.

1. After restarting your computer, click the 3ds max 4 icon 🔲 on your desktop to begin the authorization process. When the program starts, you will see the splash screen shown in Figure A.11.

Figure A.11 The 3ds max 4 splash screen always appears when you launch the program. The first time you launch max 4, there will be two interruptions. The first interruption takes you through the authorization process described in the next step.

2. The Authorization Code window interrupts the max load process and asks what you would like to do. Select the first option—Authorize 3ds max 4—and click Next (see Figure A.12).

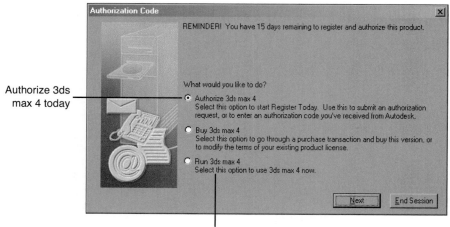

Authorize 3ds max 4 today

Run max without authorization code

Figure A.12 You can use the software temporarily without authorization by selecting the third option: Run 3ds max 4.

3. At the top of your Register Today screen, you'll see a Serial Number and a Request Code generated by the installer. Both are used to identify your specific workstation and this one-time request for an authorization code. Copy these numbers down in your journal. Then select Register and Authorize (Get an Authorization Code) and click Next (see Figure A.13).

4. You will now be asked to provide the preliminary information needed to register your software. Choose Company or Individual, select the country of your residence from the list, and click Yes if you are upgrading to 3ds max 4 from a previous version of 3D Studio 3.0 or 3.1 (see Figure A.14).

Write these numbers down

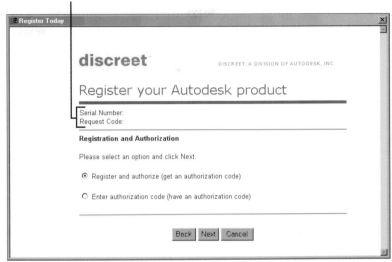

Figure A.13 Max automatically generates the Serial Number and the Request Code. Write down these numbers exactly as shown in this window.

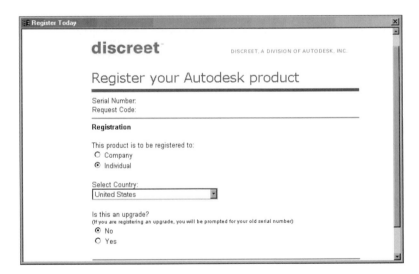

Figure A.14 Other than buying max 4 with an educational discount, upgrading to 3ds max 4 from an authorized version of a previous release of 3D Studio MAX is the cheapest way to buy this software. If you are a student, you might qualify for a discount.

5. The registration information gathering process continues with the screen shown in Figure A.15. Fill out all the contact information. You can't skip the fields marked with a red asterisk. If you do, you'll be kicked back to this screen to complete the missing required fields. When you are finished, click Next at the bottom of this form.

Figure A.15 Using electronic registration saves a lot of paperwork and time. Later, if you choose to mail or fax your request for authorization, you can print this form out for that purpose.

6. The next screen asks you to verify the registration information that you've provided. Review the info and click Next if it's correct. Otherwise, scroll down to the bottom of the dialog and click Back to return to the previous screen and make the necessary revisions.

7. You have four options to obtain your authorization code: via the Internet, fax, email, and mail. If you choose Fax Request or Mail Request, you can print the registration information and send it to discreet for your code. Using Fax Request or Mail Request to obtain your authorization code will take the longest time. Using the Email Request option will take approximately four days. In all three cases, you can use the software until the code is received. The fastest way is to register over the Internet. If you have an Internet connection, select Connect Directly via the Web, and click Next (see Figure A.16).

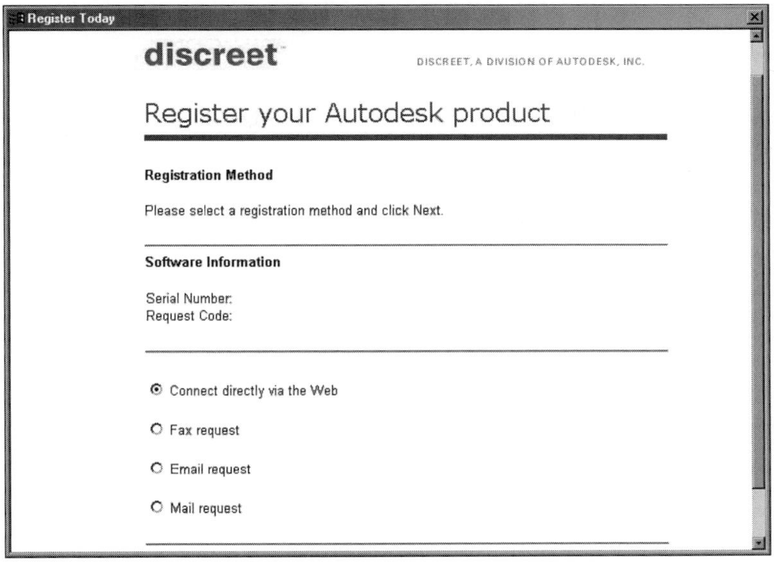

Figure A.16 Obtaining your authorization code via the Web is simple and fast. When your code is received, the installer software automatically authorizes 3ds max 4.

> ☟ You can also phone in your authorization request. Listed here is all of discreet's contact information used for registration purposes:
>
> - **Web**—http://register.autodesk.com
> - **Email**—authcodes@autodesk.com
> - **Fax**—(800) 225-6490 or (415) 507-4690
> - **Telephone**—(800) 551-1490 or (415) 507-4690
> - **Mail**—Product Registrations, Autodesk Inc, 111 McInnis Parkway, San Rafael, CA 94903
>
> If you use the phone to obtain your authorization code, ask the discreet service representative to wait while you enter the code and complete the authorization. This way, you can be sure the code was correct and it will save you a second phone call.

Tip

3ds max 4

8. The next screen prompts you to connect to the Internet. When you are connected, click Next and complete the registration and authorization process (see Figure A.17).

Figure A.17   Depending on the speed of your Internet connection, the installer will take a few moments to transmit your registration data, receive the authorization code, and authorize the software.

9. The Authorization Confirmation and Software Information window appears as shown in Figure A.18. Click Print to print the registration information and keep the printout in your journal. Then click Finish to continue loading max 4.

Cryptonomicon

Neil Stephenson is the author of the most innovative and interesting science fiction stories you will ever read. Unlike other authors in this genre, his books *Snow Crash* and *Diamond Age* contain real science behind the fiction. The books are edgy, creative, funny, and substantial. His latest book, *Cryptonomicon*, is a fascinating journey into the real and fictionalized past and present development of cryptography and encryption machines and software. This spooky spy stuff is also the basis for the max 4 encrypted software lock protection.

Max Video Driver Setup and Troubleshooting

As max continues to load, the 3ds max Driver Setup window interrupts the load process a second time, as shown in Figure A.19.

Figure A.18   Your software information will look different than the data in this image. This information is a unique, randomly generated set of numbers created by sophisticated encryption software.

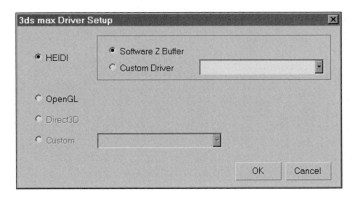

Figure A.19   3ds max 4 performance is enhanced by your video card's hardware acceleration. Be sure you select the driver for your card in this screen to boost max 4's performance. If you are unsure about your card's video driver compatibility with max 4, leave the driver set to the default HEIDI settings.

Plug-In Architecture

3ds max 4 is made up of a core engine surrounded by many pieces of custom-designed software called *plug-ins*. This is one of the reasons it's such a powerful, popular, and versatile tool. Hundreds of plug-ins are available to create anything you can imagine.

The text flashing by at the bottom-left side of the splash screen is max 4 loading the plug-ins and other software components needed to operate the program. If a problem occurs with any of these components, the program opens an error message window.

Caution

Video cards can use drivers that might not work with 3ds max 4. Check with the board manufacturer and ask specifically about 3ds max 4 drivers. Drivers are usually available on the manufacturer's Web site. If you try to load an incompatible driver, max 4 won't open until you either change your driver selection or load the proper driver from the board manufacturer.

If you aren't sure which drivers your video card is using, leave the window selections set to their default HEIDI and Z-buffer settings and click Next. Otherwise, select the appropriate button for your specific card and driver configuration.

If you receive a fatal error message, as seen in Figure A.20, you have selected a video driver that is incompatible with max 4 and you'll need to follow the next set of instructions. If your driver selections are correct, your installation and configuration process is complete and max 4 opens ready for work.

Figure A.20   If you see this screen, your video driver settings are not compatible with 3ds max 4. Until this is remedied, the program won't open.

If your driver selections were incorrect, follow the next set of instructions carefully to manually configure your drivers:

1. Click OK to exit the Fatal Error window.

2. Right-click the 3ds max 4 shortcut on your desktop and click Properties to open the dialog box shown in Figure A.21.

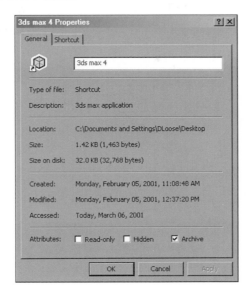

Figure A.21   The 3ds max 4 Properties window provides some useful information about the program that enables you to troubleshoot the video driver problem.

   3. Click the Shortcut tab to open the shortcut page as shown in Figure A.22.

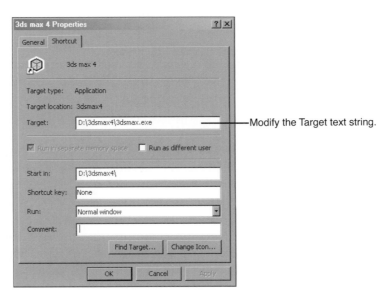

—Modify the Target text string.

Figure A.22   To set up a different video driver in max and troubleshoot the fatal error, modify the text in the Target text box on the Shortcut page. You can also specify a Shortcut Key and how you want max 4 to open on your screen when the program is started.

4. In the Target text box, you will see the path to where 3ds max 4 is installed on your system. Click your cursor in the text window at the end of that text line. Be sure the cursor is right up against the end of the `3dsmax.exe` text string, insert one space, and type `-h` (see Figure A.23).

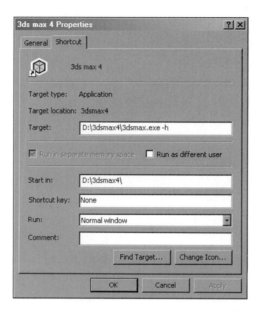

Figure A.23 By adding `-h` to the end of the shortcut path, max 4 will open the video setup window each time you launch the program. To disable this feature, return to the 3ds max 4 Properties Shortcut tab and delete the `-h` from the text string.

5. After you have added the `-h` to the text string, click Apply, and then click Close. Now you are ready to restart max 4 and bypass the driver failure problem.

Adding the `-h` command tells the software to open the Driver Setup window each time you launch max 4—sort of a safe mode for launching the program. When max 4 opens this time, select HEIDI driver and SoftwareZ Buffer modes and click OK. This will get you into max without the fatal error you had before.

You will want to take full advantage of the hardware acceleration capabilities of your video card. Obtain the appropriate drivers from your card manufacturer's Web site and install the drivers according to the instructions in the `read me` file that comes with the drivers. When you start max 4 again, the new drivers will be in the Video Driver Setup screen menus, available for your selection.

You can also change and configure drivers while you are using max 4 by clicking Customize, Preferences and clicking the Viewports tab, as shown in Figure A.24.

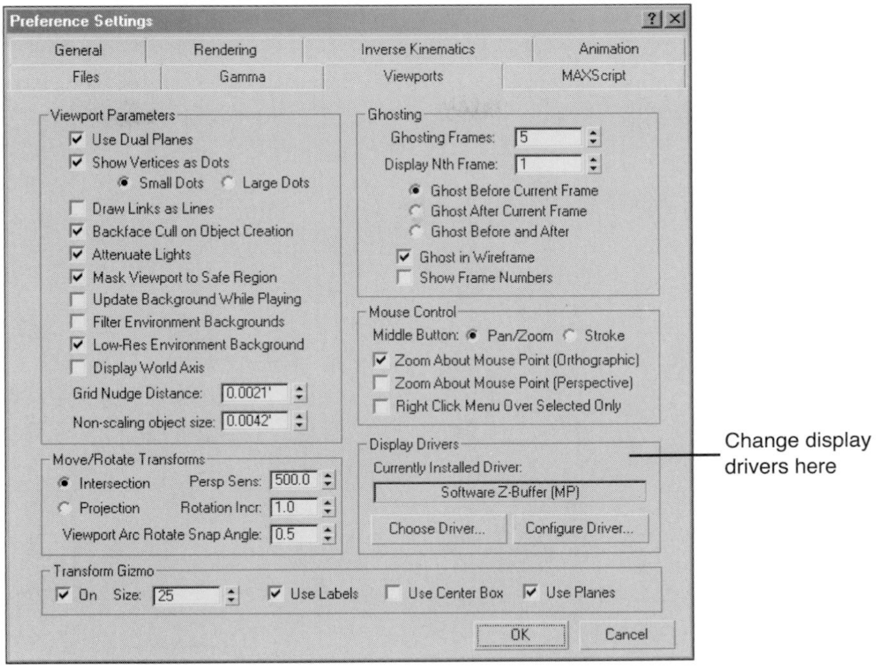

Change display drivers here

Figure A.24 Configure or change your drivers by clicking the appropriate button in the Display Drivers section of this window.

After you have used the outlined process to correct the video driver problem, remove the `-h` from the command line. This will allow 3ds max 4 to load without a detour into the video driver setup. The program is now set up and ready for use.

Dr. D's Essential Guide to Standard Material Component Maps

"Where principle is put to work, not as a recipe or as a formula, there will always be style." - Le Corbusier

I'm always impressed with the creativity of the artists in the 3ds max community. They are constantly experimenting and inventing new processes within the max toolset to achieve their vision—creating unique visual styles in the process. Your style is built on a foundation of knowledge of the basic principles behind your use of the digital tools and techniques in max. It is a visual language all your own and you'll create it by putting those principles into practice.

Chameleon Style

The ability to adopt and use the visual language created by an art direction team is essential to your success as a max artist. At the beginning of your career, most of the production work you do will be guided by a visual style created by some-one else. As you gain experience, there will be ample opportunity to create and express your own visual language. Knowing when to be a chameleon, blending your work with the rest of the production team, and when to be an individual, freely expressing your own style, will help you gain the trust and confidence of your producer and art direction team.

One of the major creative tools in max 4 is the Material Editor. Learning how the Material Editor is organized and about its basic functions is relatively easy. But after you get beyond the basics, the incredible depth of this tool and the variety of ways that it can be used to create materials can be somewhat daunting. Understanding more about the material component maps—how they are used and what they are capable of creating—will accelerate your learning of max 4 and help you in your quest for a style of your own.

Material Component Map Basics

Every material in max has a basic set of common components, which determines its color, reflectivity, opacity, and so on. Each of the material components can be controlled by numeric values, by color changes, and by using one of max's 35 map types as a component map. In other words, you can use bitmap images, procedural noise, and falloff, among others, to affect ambient and diffuse color, opacity, specular, reflection, and so on. Figure B.1 shows the Material Editor and the associated Maps rollout for a default standard material using a Blinn shader.

> For information that defines the material component maps discussed in this appendix, search for the name of the material component in the Search or Index portion of your max 4 User Reference.
>
> Tip

The examples in the remaining sections of this appendix will show you the effect that material component maps can have on material appearance.

Ambient Color Component Maps

Ambient light affects every surface of an object via indirect illumination—the light reflected off the other objects and surfaces in an environment. The Ambient material component is locked to the Diffuse material component by default. Leaving them locked will work for the majority of your material needs but sometimes you'll want the subtle effect that a map in the Ambient component can achieve.

To add a map to the Ambient color component, you must first unlock it from the Diffuse component. Then click its adjacent Map slot and choose a map from the material map browser. After the map is added, there is a parameter setting that must be adjusted so you can actually see the map in the Material Editor and in your scene.

The Hidden Knowledge

In previous versions of max, the Global Ambient Lighting found in the Rendering/Environment dialog box was on by default. Discreet found out that a majority of max artists didn't use the global ambient light and just turned it off when they started lighting a scene. Discreet listened to its users and the result is that in 3ds max 4, global ambient lighting is now off by default.

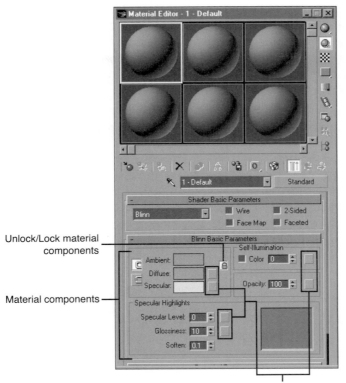

Unlock/Lock material components

Material components

Material component Map slots

Unlock/Lock material components

Material components

Material component Map slots

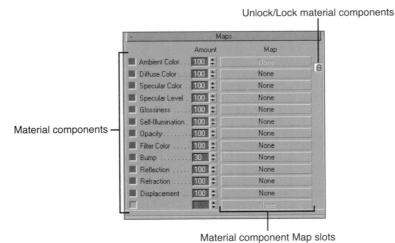

Figure B.1 The small box next to each material component is a Map slot, which is linked to its counterpart in the Maps rollout. Each of max 4's 10 material types and 7 shaders have similar and unique material components.

3ds max 4

That's good! However, the hidden knowledge that isn't found in the max User Reference is that global ambient light must be on to be able to see a map in the Ambient color component of a material in the Material Editor.

The Global Ambient Light settings can be changed in the Rendering/Environment dialog box. They can also be adjusted in the Material Editor. Right-click any material preview window and choose Options from the menu. When the Material Editor Options window shown in Figure B.2 opens, click the color swatch next to Ambient Light and change the HSV settings to 0,0,25; then click Apply. This gives just enough ambient light to see the map in the Material Editor and in your rendered imagery.

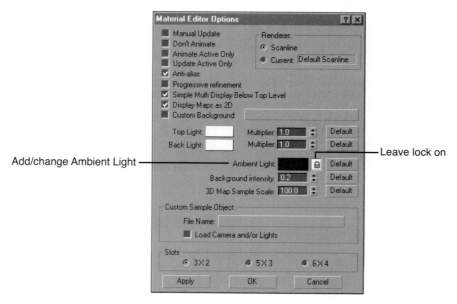

Figure B.2 When the lock next to Ambient Light is on, the changes you make here will also be made in the Environment dialog box. Leave this lock on to see the Ambient component map in both the Material Editor and in the rendered scene.

Decals and Tattoos

A map in the Ambient component can be used to create a decal on the side of an object or a tattoo. The bitmap image used in the material for the alien head in Figure B.3 is a simple black-and-white targa image. The effect of the Ambient component is that the high contrast image blends in with the rest of the surface, allowing the skin texture underneath to show through.

When the surface to which the image is applied is illuminated by direct light, the bitmap appears washed out. When seen in surfaces facing away from the light, the bitmap darkens to become its true color: black.

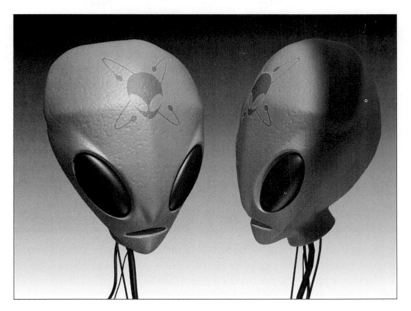

Figure B.3   A bitmap in the Ambient color component creates a subtle painted-on look like a stencil applied to the surface of a piece of metal or a tattoo on skin.

Diffuse Color Component Maps

Diffuse color is the color of a material seen in the surfaces that are illuminated directly by a light source. Maps added to this component are used to create variegated colors and surfaces texture. Figure B.4 shows the effect of a Zebra skin image added as a Diffuse component map.

Adjusting the Diffuse amount as shown in Figure B.5 mixes the diffuse color with the map in the Diffuse component slot. The amounts in these spinner boxes are percentages—a setting of 100 means that 100% of the map will be used as the surface color; a setting of 0 uses 100% of the component color and none of the map; and a setting of 50 creates an equal mix of the map and the diffuse color.

Figure B.4   Diffuse component maps can be used to simulate everything from aircraft aluminum to zebra pelts. In this image, the zebra bitmap was also added to the Reflection map on the eye material and a Cellular procedural map was added as a Bump map. Creepy!

Specular Color Component Maps

Specular color determines the color of the highlight seen in the material surface. It's determined by three factors: the color of the light source, the diffuse color of the material, and the type of material, such as painted, metal, plastic, wood, and so forth.

Specular color is not necessarily the same hue as the diffuse and ambient color. The highlights seen in surface materials take on the color of the light source and are also affected by the ambient light in the environment. You can change the specular highlight color by clicking the Specular color swatch in the Basic Parameters rollout. You can also change the specular color by adding a map.

When a map is added to the Specular color component, its image will appear wherever a specular highlight is created. Notice how the diffuse texture and color blends with the specular texture in the highlight area in the image in Figure B.6.

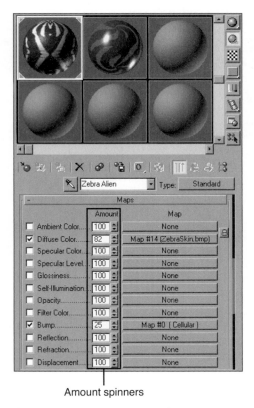

Amount spinners

Figure B.5 You can use the Amount spinners next to the component maps to adjust the visual blend between the component settings and an image or procedural map in the component map slot. These spinners can also be used to adjust the intensity or effect of a procedural map such as Raytrace or Falloff.

Specular Level Component Maps

Specular level defines the intensity (relative brightness) of the specular highlight and is determined by the same three factors as specular color. A bitmap added to this component affects the intensity of the highlight by using the image's grayscale values. White portions of the map allow the specular level to be at full intensity. Black or darker portions of the bitmap drop the intensity to zero. The Amount spinner on this component can be adjusted higher than 100, which creates more intensity in the highlight.

Figure B.7 shows the Alien's eye before and after a Cellular procedural map has been added to the Specular Level component.

3ds max 4

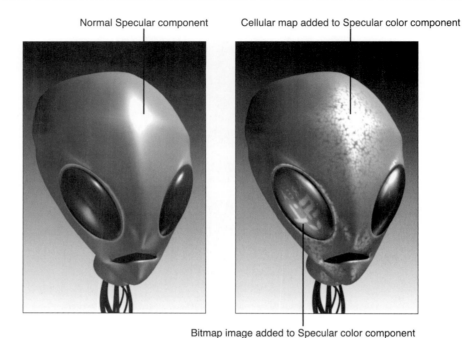

Normal Specular component

Cellular map added to Specular color component

Bitmap image added to Specular color component

Figure B.6 A map in the Specular color component creates texture and images that will be seen in the highlight portions of the surface. A mirror image "Area51" bitmap was added to the specular component of the Alien's eye to simulate a reflection.

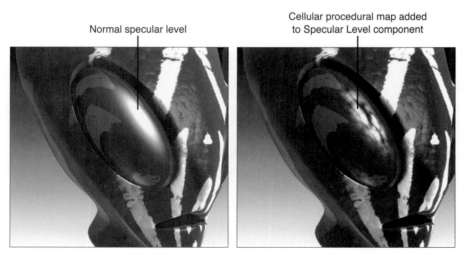

Normal specular level

Cellular procedural map added to Specular Level component

Figure B.7 The procedural map breaks up the highlight, creating a more complex reflection in the image. Specular Level maps can also be animated to simulate reflections of moving water seen in an eye—much faster than raytracing actual reflections.

Glossiness Component Maps

Glossiness is also affected by the factors that determine specular color and specular level. The Glossiness value controls the size of the specular highlight. Larger values focus the highlight into a smaller diameter area and smaller values make a larger-diameter, less-focused high-lighted area.

Copying the map used in the Specular Level component into the Glossiness component slot and increasing the Specular level amount to 250 produced the effect shown in Figure B.8.

Cellular procedural map added
to Glossiness component

Figure B.8   Using the map from the Specular Level component in the Glossiness component increases the apparent depth and detail of the highlight intensity.

Self-Illumination Component Maps

Self-illumination creates the appearance of a light-emitting material, such as a light bulb, a fire-fly, lightning, or other glowing substance. The highest value, 100, means that the material is a 100% self-illuminating, intrinsic light source and will not be affected by other lights in the scene.

The maps added to this component use their grayscale to determine which parts of the surface will be self-illuminated. Figure B.9 shows the effect that a Gradient map has when added to the Self-Illumination component.

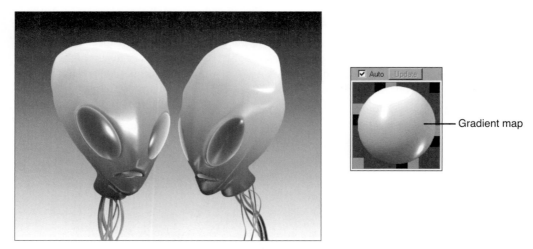

Figure B.9   The Gradient map starts out white at the top and gradually changes to black at the bottom. The effect in the material is that the top of the Alien's head is totally self-illuminated, corresponding to the white of the Gradient map. As the map gradates to black, the Alien's head becomes less self-illuminated.

A Falloff map added to the Self-Illumination component creates a kind of electron microscope effect, illuminating the outer edge of the Alien's head (see Figure B.10).

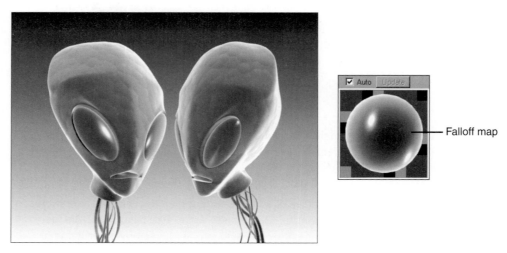

Figure B.10   By using the grayscale of the Falloff map to determine which parts of the material will be self-illuminated, several different effects can be achieved, including the radiosity effect discussed in Chapter 5, "Photon Paint: The Art of Lighting."

Opacity Component Maps

The *Opacity component* determines the transparency of a material. When a map is added to the Opacity component, the map's grayscale is used to determine which parts of the surface will be transparent and which will be opaque. White areas of the bitmap create opaque surfaces, black areas create complete transparency, and gray areas create different levels of transparency depending on the relative value of the grayscale. Figure B.11 shows this effect of copying the Falloff map from the Self-Illumination component from Figure B.10 into the Opacity component.

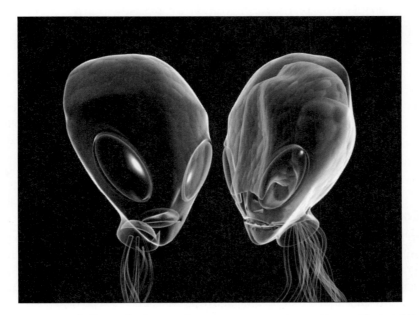

Figure B.11   Using a Falloff map in the Opacity component creates an X-ray effect. Adding a skull and sensory organs inside the Alien's head will help emphasize the X-ray imagery.

Figure B.12 shows the effect of a Checker procedural map added to the Opacity component. Making the material two-sided allows you to see the inside surfaces of the head.

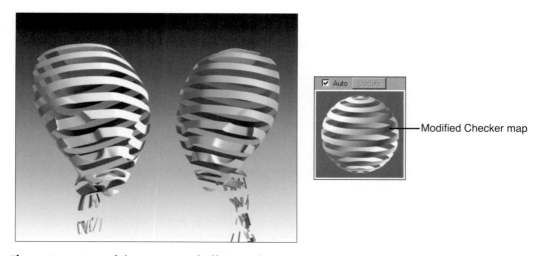

Modified Checker map

Figure B.12   One of the unexpected effects in this image can be seen in the veins coming out of the Alien's neck. These were created procedurally, using renderable splines, which means that the tube geometry that appears in the image doesn't exist as actual mesh surfaces in the max workspace. However, when the Checker map is added to the Opacity component, it creates tube sections that appear to have a wall thickness.

Filter Color Component Maps

When light strikes a transparent material, some of it is absorbed and not allowed to pass through. A blue glass, for example, is blue because all the other colors of the light illuminating it are absorbed; only the blue is reflected and subsequently transmitted through the material. The ambient light bouncing around an environment also passes through and takes on the color of the glass. This transmitted color is defined by the Filter Color component.

The decal applied to the Alien's forehead has been added to the Filter Color component. This allows the decal image to be projected onto the ground plane and determines the color and value of the light passing through the decal (see Figure B.13).

Note

When light passes through a piece of glass, it changes direction—bent by the refractive quality of the material. The Thin Wall Refraction map is used to simulate the refractive effect of light passing through glass, plastic, or any other thin transparent surface material.

Figure B.13   When used with transparent or semitransparent materials, the Filter Color component creates the effect of light passing through an object, such as a piece of
glassware with an etched image on its surface. The Alien's head in this image also
has a Thin Wall Refraction map added to the Refraction component.

Bump Maps

Bump maps are used to simulate the appearance of surface detail and texture. A bitmap image
or procedural map used in this component will appear in the surface texture of the object. This
is similar in effect to the Displacement map except that the Bump map doesn't modify the 3D
surface mesh of the object. Many of the images in this appendix use maps in the Bump component to create surface texture.

In a manner similar to many of the other component maps, the grayscale of the Bump component map combined with the Amount value produces the bump effect. The Amount value can
be positive or negative—positive values create a texture that appears to push out from the surface; negative values push the texture into the surface. Figure B.14 shows this effect.

Positive bump amount   Negative bump amount

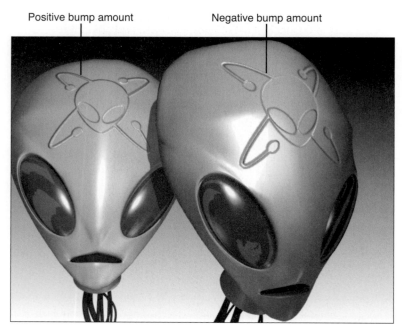

Figure B.14   You can use an instance of the Diffuse color component map in the Bump component to create realistic natural textures such as craters, rock fissures, wood grain,
and skin textures.

Reflection Component Maps

Maps used in the Reflection component slot affect the reflectivity and reflections seen in the
surfaces to which the material is applied. Reflections are created by three factors: the object's
form, the texture (smooth versus rough), and the environment surrounding the object.

The Raytrace material produces the most accurate reflections for organic forms. Other
Reflection maps that can be used in the Reflection component are the Flat Mirror and the
Reflect/Refract maps. Figure B.15 shows the Alien's head with a Raytrace map applied to its
material. It's sitting on a reflective surface that uses the Flat Mirror map in its Reflection component.

Figure B.15   Reflections add an important touch of realism to your max scenes. They can also increase rendering times dramatically, especially if you're using the Raytrace material or a Raytrace map in a material's Reflection component. Make wise choices about the kind of Reflection map/material to use and the objects in the scene to which the materials are applied.

Refraction Component Maps

The *Refraction component* creates the appearance of the light-bending phenomenon known as refraction seen in glass lenses, water, marbles, crystal balls, and so forth. The *IOR*, or *Index of Refraction*, is a numerical value that determines the level of a material's refractivity. When light is transmitted through glass or other transparent materials, it's refracted into concentrated areas of light referred to as *caustics*. The refracted light caustics also change the appearance of the shadows cast by transparent objects.

Figure B.16 shows the effect of a Reflect/Refract map added to the Refraction material component.

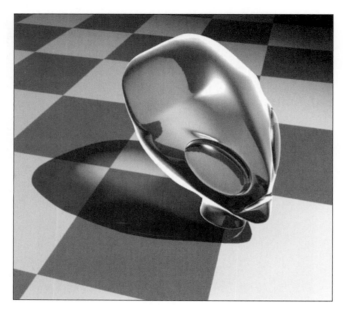

Figure B.16   Three maps can be used to achieve realistic refraction effects; Reflect/Refract, Thin Wall Refraction, and Raytrace.

Displacement Component Maps

Displacement maps are used to create complex surface details using bitmap images and procedural maps to create a 3D surface derived from the grayscale of the map. Lighter values in the image create more severe detail protrusion and darker values create indentations in the surface.

Displacement maps can be used to create the details seen in a sculpted column, the craters on the moon, or, in this example, an elderly Alien. The model for these two Alien heads is exactly the same; the difference is the bitmap added to the displacement component of the elderly Alien's material (see Figure B.17).

An important factor in creating and using displacement maps is the density of the mesh surfaces to which the map is assigned. In general, you'll need a high-density mesh to be able to use a Displacement map effectively. The art of Displacement mapping lies in the creative map images you'll create to affect the mesh surfaces.

Elderly alien

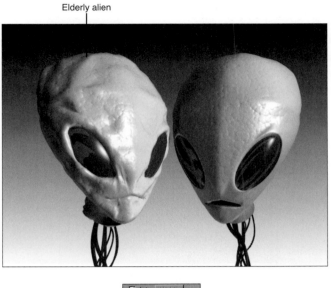

Displacement bitmap

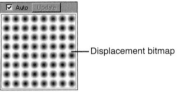

Identical mesh models

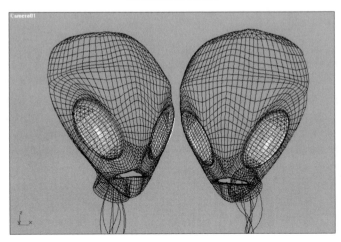

Figure B.17   With some intense and time-consuming effort, you can create the wrinkly skin of the elderly Alien with max's mesh-modeling tools. Using Displacement maps is a smart and viable alternative.

Next Steps

3ds max 4 comes with 10 material types and 7 shaders. Understanding the components of each of the materials and how maps and shaders can be used to achieve the material effect you are looking for will take a lot of study and experimentation. Figure B.18 shows the Maps rollout for the Raytrace material—a total of 19 component maps as compared to 12 for the Standard material.

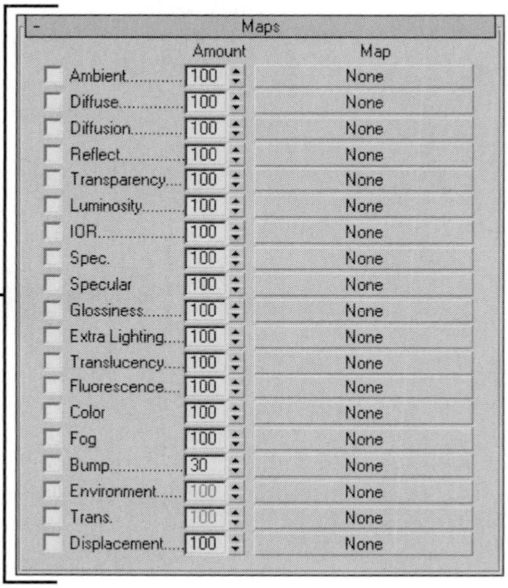

Figure B.18 Understanding the Raytrace material is a good next step. After you have studied it thoroughly, experiment with the remaining seven max 4 material types.

To master the Material Editor, all 10 max 4 materials and their components need to be explored in depth. Employ the same approach used in this appendix and experiment with each component separately to understand its effect. Also consult the User Reference for the basic application information on the specific component-mapping process, and then let your imagination run wild.

The sustaining food of the imagination is knowledge. Feed your imagination and creative process by understanding the capability of every material component and shader in max. This will empower your artistic vision and help you achieve a style all your own.

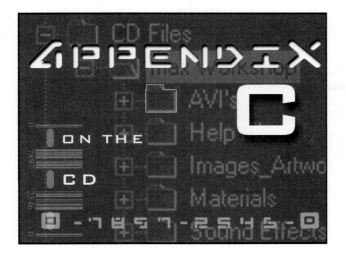
What's on the CD-ROM

Max Workshop File Structure

The files created for this Workshop follow a simplified production structure for file management in a production environment. With the exception of the Help files for the chapters in this Workshop, your work as a 3ds max artist can be organized in a similar manner. Keeping track of your work is absolutely imperative—there is no such thing as being over meticulous when it comes to digital content file organization.

Each chapter of this book has been created to show the production process and techniques you'll need to create the short movie Area51.avi. The CD contains all the 3ds 4 max files, image references, sound files, and sample files that you'll need to finish the Workshop. Figure C.1 shows how the files are organized on the CD.

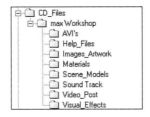

Figure C.1   The files on the CD are organized into functional easy-to-remember categories.

The Workshop files are located on the CD-ROM under the `max Workshop` directory, inside the following folders:

- **`AVI's`**—Includes 2 versions of `Area51.avi`. This is the short movie that you will be creating during the Workshop. The two versions are identical in content but they are compressed using different video compression codecs. `Area51_A.avi` was compressed with the Indeo Video 5.10 compression codec, available on the Web at `http://www.ligos.com/indeo`. `Area51_B.avi` is compressed using the Radius Cinepak codec. Other `.avi` format movies included on the CD relate to examples created or shown in each chapter.

- **`Help_Files`**—You'll find a folder for each Workshop chapter containing the 3ds max 4 files used to create the scenes necessary for each step along the way to the completion of `Area51.avi`.

- **`Images_Artwork`**—Contains the still images used to create the animatic of the Workshop—the color plates from each chapter and the color section of the Workshop—and the concept sketches and storyboards used to create the project.

- **`Materials`**—Includes the max material library created for the Workshop and the bitmap images used as textures in the material development.

- **`Scene_Models`**—This folder contains zipped files of all the finished max scenes used in `Area51.avi`. WinZip is included on the companion CD and can be used to unzip these files.

- **`Sound Track`**—Contains the final sound track used to create the movie.

- **`Video_Post`**—Includes the compositor files, sequences, and video post filters used for the Workshop.

- **`Visual_Effects`**—Contains folders for video post effects and render effects settings required to re-create the visual effects for the scenes in `Area51.avi`.

Third-Party Software

- **Adobe**—Provides Adobe Acrobat Reader, free software that lets you view and print Adobe Portable Document Format (PDF) files on all major computer platforms.

- **Applied Ideas**—Provides *The Ultimate MAX Internet Guide*, a searchable database of more than 450 sites.

- **Digimation**—Several trial versions, including Clay Studio Pro, Particle Studio, and Illustrate 5.1.

- **MainConcept**—Video editing software that's easy enough for beginners, yet powerful enough for demanding professionals.

- **Sonic Foundry**—Provides Sound Forge, a great introduction to software media content creation.

- **WinZip**—WinZip brings the convenience of Windows to the use of Zip files and other compression formats.

Supplemental Help Files

Also included in the Help Files section of the CD are six supplemental appendixes. These files, some of which are taken from *3D Studio MAX 3.0 Workshop*, are provided to help you learn some of the basics needed to complete and enhance your version of `Area51.avi`. These appendixes are titled `Appendix_D.pdf`, `Appendix_E.pdf`, and so on.

- **Appendix D**—Takes you through the process of changing the Sc-01 cooling tower model into the interior set for Sc-02.

- **Appendix E**—Shows you how MeshSmooth works on the surfaces you create and how its effect can be controlled using subobject manipulation, the vertex and edge weights tool, and the crease tool.

- **Appendix F**—This is an excerpt from *3D Studio MAX 3.0 Workshop* that shows you how to use basic animation tools. The tutorial leads you through a fundamental animation exercise: creating a bouncing ball.

- **Appendix G**—This appendix is also an excerpt from *3D Studio MAX 3.0 Workshop*. It shows you the basic concepts behind adding special rendering effects to your max imagery.

- **Appendix H**—This file shows the basic process and tasks required to finish Sc-02 for `Area51.avi`.

- **Appendix I**—The last excerpt from *3D Studio MAX 3.0 Workshop* shows you the principles and concepts behind how to create the firefly effect for `TheEnd.avi` and how these concepts were adapted for the end title sequence of `Area51.avi`.

- **Appendix J**—A PDF file containing the tear card from *3D Studio MAX 3.0 Workshop*. It includes MAX 3.0 main interface tab panels, keyboard shortcuts, and Viewport Navigation tools.

C

C-Dilla License Management System, 459

C3PO, 322

cable guide, 271

calculating scene lengths, 77

camera move instructions, 57-58

camera point of view (POV) instructions, 57-58

Camera view shortcut, 111

Camera Viewport Navigation Controls, 145-146

Camera views, 24

cameras

    adding to scenes, 143-147

    animating, 229

    field of view, animating, 227-228

    master scene cameras, CD-98–CD-99

    movement of, 58-60

Cameras command, 18

Campbell, Dave, 116

Campbell, Joseph, 47-49

camshafts, automobile engines, 275, 289

caricature, animating characters, 311-313

carpal tunnel syndrome, 327

cars, engines, 275, 289

Cast Shadows check box (lighting parameters), 209

caustics, 485

CCE, Inc., 312

CD, installing 3ds max 4 from, 452-457

Center subobject, 120

CG 101, A Computer Graphics Industry Reference, 352

chains, Inverse Kinematics (IK), 299-300

chambers, 252

changing. *See also* adjusting

    3ds max 4 user interface, 32-33, 35-38

    animatics, 147-149

    animations, Track View Editor, 298

    background sky (Sc-01), 139-141

    bone envelopes, 342

    Cooling_Tower_Master model, 375-376

    display modes, viewports, 26

    extrusions, 127-129

    Frame Count, 408

    IFL Manager, 429-430

    Image Input Event tracks, 72-77

    image input layers, 388-390

    Inverse Kinematics (IK) controller parameters, 302, 305

    merged objects, 250

    parameters

        Omni Lights, 366-367

        particle array (PArray), 381-382

        Taper modifiers, 121

    pivot points, 287-288

    Quad Menus, 326, 329-330

    Sc-00 Image File List (IFL) to use baked images, 426-429

    segments, topologies, 102

    sizes, rendered images, 136

    speed, text reveal, 419-421

    storyboards, 147-149

    VandeGraaff Proxy_Source model, 259-261

    vertices, 104-107, 112-113

character animation

    caricature, 311-313

    Frankenstein Principles, 310-311, 315-320, 324

    Full Character Franchise (FCF), 314-315

    production steps, 330-336, 339-343

Character Bible (back-story), 52-54

character layers, *Area 51* workshop, 40

check boxes, Animate Noise, 361

Child objects, 289-290, 299

Chironis, Nicholas P., 276

Chismar, John P., 408

choosing

    formats, animatics, 69-70

    primitives, 101

    subobjects, Select mode, 125

cinema. *See* cinematography

cinematography

    books about, 348-349

    compressing, Indeo, 83

    imagination in, 352

    The Matrix, 198-199

    Saving Private Ryan, 198

    structure of, 47

Circle setting (directional lighting parameters), 211

Circular Selection Region command, 13

circum-diameter, 134

erasing

    Cooling_Tower_Lattice model and polygons, 375

    mistakes, CD-27

ergonomics (Human Factors), 91

errors, video compression, 83

events

    Alpha Compositor Layer, 239-240

    Contrast Image Filter, creating flash frames, 389-391

    Cross Fade Transition Layer, adding in Video Post Queue, 77, 82-83

    Fade Image Filter, adding in Video Post Queue, 80-82

    Image Input

        adding to animatics, 71-72

        changing tracks, animatics, 72-77

    Image Output, 240-241

        adding in Video Post Queue, 82-83

        adding to flash frames, 392

Every nth section, Image File List Control, 424

exaggerating prominent character features, 313

Exclude/Include list (lighting parameters), 208

excluding objects, CD-103

Execute scene dialog box, 86

executing

    rendering, flash frames, 393

    scenes, Video Post, 86-87

experiments with reality, designing visual effects from, 354-355

Expert mode, 10

explosions, creating, 374-395

exposure, reality, 314

expressions

    characters, 318

    observing in mirrors, 331

EXSc-02A.max file, CD-100–CD-101

EXSc-02B.max file, CD-102–CD-103

EXSc-02C.max file, CD-104–CD-105

EXSc-02D.max file, CD-108–CD-110

extremities, modeling, 336

Extrude tool, 127

extrusions

    adjusting, 127-129

    grouped, 266

    local, 266

eyeball icon, 7

eyes, characters, 317

F

faces

    characters, 317-318

    described, 103

    observing expressions in mirrors, 331

    polyhedrons, 134

    returning to starting position, 127

Fade Image Filter events, adding in Video Post Queue, 80-82

faking ambient radiosity, 223-226

Falloff maps, 224-226

Falloff setting (directional lighting parameters), 211

FCF (Full Character Franchise), animating characters, 314-315

feature spacing, 312

features, exaggerating in characters, 313

Fence Selection Region command, 13

Feynman, Richard, 353-354

FG Tower layer, rendering, 232-234

FG (foregrounds), 62, CD-104–CD-105, CD-108–CD-110

field of view (camera), animating, 227-228

Field of View control, 146

Fight Club, 58, 408

figurines, 332

File menu commands, 9

    Merge, CD-1

    Save As, CD-3

    XRef Objects, CD-96

File Overwrite Warning, 86

files

    3ds max Workshop, 489-490

    automatic backups, 84

    image, viewing, 40-42

    map, moving with drag and drop, 138

    merging, CD-1–CD-2

    overwriting, 86

    Portable Document Format (PDF), 490

    Readme Information, 454

    saving, CD-3

    Sc-00.max

        creating, 409-421

        setting up, 408

    Sc-02.max, setting up, 246-247

G

M

Index

World Space Modifiers (WSMs), 113-114

World War II, survival of England during, 48

wrenches, characters, 323-324

Write Keyboard Chart button, 111

The Writer's Journey: Mythic Structure for Writers, 49

writing titles, Area51.avi, 410-412

WSM (World Space Modifiers), 113-114

Wu, John, 58

X-Z

Xena, 320

XRef dialog box, CD-96

XRef Merge dialog box, CD-96

XRef objects, CD-96–CD-98

XRef Objects command (File menu), CD-96

XYZ coordinate system, 19-21

yellow icon, 28

Zip files, 490

Zoom command, 28

Zoom Extents All command, 28

Zoom Extents All control, 146

Zoom Extents tool, 75

Zoom Region tool, 75

zooming in
 images, 143
 representing on storyboards, 58
 tracks, 75

zooming out
 images, 143
 representing on storyboards, 58
 tracks, 75

Index

Read This Before Opening the Software

By opening this package, you are agreeing to be bound by the following agreement:

You may not copy or redistribute the entire CD-ROM as a whole. Copying and redistribution of individual software programs on the CD-ROM is governed by terms set by individual copyright holders.

The installer and code from the author are copyrighted by the publisher and the author. Individual programs and other items on the CD-ROM are copyrighted or are under GNU license by their various authors or other copyright holders.

This software is sold as-is without warranty of any kind, either expressed or implied, including but not limited to the implied warranties of merchantability and fitness for a particular purpose. Neither the publisher nor its dealers or distributors assume any liability for any alleged or actual damages arising from the use of this program. (Some states do not allow for the exclusion of implied warranties, so the exclusion may not apply to you.)

NOTE: This CD-ROM uses long and mixed-case filenames requiring the use of a protected-mode CD-ROM driver.

Installation Instructions

Windows 95/NT 4:

1. Insert the CD-ROM into your CD-ROM drive.
2. From the Windows desktop, double-click the My Computer icon.
3. Double-click the icon representing your CD-ROM drive.
4. Double-click the icon titled START.EXE to run the installation program.

NOTE: If Windows 95/NT 4 is installed on your computer and you have the AutoPlay feature enabled, the setup.exe program starts automatically whenever you insert the disc into your CD-ROM drive.